Strengthening Research Methodology

Strengthening Research Methodology

Psychological Measurement and Evaluation

EDITED BY

Richard R. Bootzin
Patrick E. McKnight

AMERICAN PSYCHOLOGICAL ASSOCIATION
WASHINGTON, DC

Published by
American Psychological Association
750 First Street, NE
Washington, DC 20002
www.apa.org

To order   Tel: (800) 374-2721; Direct: (202) 336-5510
APA Order Department   Fax: (202) 336-5502; TDD/TTY: (202) 336-6123
P.O. Box 92984   Online: www.apa.org/books/
Washington, DC 20090-2984   E-mail: order@apa.org

In the U.K., Europe, Africa, and the Middle East, copies may be ordered from
American Psychological Association
3 Henrietta Street
Covent Garden, London
WC2E 8LU England

Typeset in Century Schoolbook by World Composition Services, Inc., Sterling, VA

Printer: United Book Press, Inc., Baltimore, MD
Cover Designer: Berg Design, Albany, NY
Technical/Production Editor: Tiffany L. Klaff

The opinions and statements published are the responsibility of the authors, and such opinions and statements do not necessarily represent the policies of the American Psychological Association.

Library of Congress Cataloging-in-Publication Data

Strengthening research methodology : psychological measurement and evaluation / edited by Richard R. Bootzin and Patrick E. McKnight.—1st ed.
    p. cm.—(APA science volumes)
   Includes bibliographical references and index.
   ISBN 1-59147-324-1
   1. Clinical psychology—Research—Methodology. I. Bootzin, Richard R., 1940-
II. McKnight, Patrick E. III. Series: Decade of behavior.
  RC467.8.S8 2006
  616.89′0072—dc22   2005020255

British Library Cataloguing-in-Publication Data
A CIP record is available from the British Library.

Printed in the United States of America
First Edition

APA Science Volumes

Attribution and Social Interaction: The Legacy of Edward E. Jones

Best Methods for the Analysis of Change: Recent Advances, Unanswered Questions, Future Directions

Cardiovascular Reactivity to Psychological Stress and Disease

The Challenge in Mathematics and Science Education: Psychology's Response

Changing Employment Relations: Behavioral and Social Perspectives

Children Exposed to Marital Violence: Theory, Research, and Applied Issues

Cognition: Conceptual and Methodological Issues

Cognitive Bases of Musical Communication

Cognitive Dissonance: Progress on a Pivotal Theory in Social Psychology

Conceptualization and Measurement of Organism–Environment Interaction

Converging Operations in the Study of Visual Selective Attention

Creative Thought: An Investigation of Conceptual Structures and Processes

Developmental Psychoacoustics

Diversity in Work Teams: Research Paradigms for a Changing Workplace

Emotion and Culture: Empirical Studies of Mutual Influence

Emotion, Disclosure, and Health

Evolving Explanations of Development: Ecological Approaches to Organism–Environment Systems

Examining Lives in Context: Perspectives on the Ecology of Human Development

Global Prospects for Education: Development, Culture, and Schooling

Hostility, Coping, and Health

Measuring Patient Changes in Mood, Anxiety, and Personality Disorders: Toward a Core Battery

Occasion Setting: Associative Learning and Cognition in Animals

Organ Donation and Transplantation: Psychological and Behavioral Factors

Origins and Development of Schizophrenia: Advances in Experimental Psychopathology

The Perception of Structure

Perspectives on Socially Shared Cognition

Psychological Testing of Hispanics

Psychology of Women's Health: Progress and Challenges in Research and Application

Researching Community Psychology: Issues of Theory and Methods

The Rising Curve: Long-Term Gains in IQ and Related Measures

Sexism and Stereotypes in Modern Society: The Gender Science of Janet Taylor Spence

APA Decade of Behavior Volumes

Contents

Contributors

Richard R. Bootzin, PhD, Department of Psychology, University of
Arizona, Tucson

Robert F. Boruch, PhD, Graduate School of Education, Fels Institute of
Government and Statistics Department, The Wharton School,
University of Pennsylvania, Philadelphia

Andrew C. Butler, PhD, Beck Institute for Cognitive Therapy and
Research, Bala Cynwyd, PA

M. H. Clark, PhD, Department of Psychology, Southern Illinois University,
Carbondale

Lawrence H. Cohen, PhD, Department of Psychology, University of
Delaware, Newark

Thomas D. Cooke, PhD, Institute for Policy Research, Northwestern
University, Evanston, IL

David S. Cordray, PhD, Psychology and Human Development
Department, Vanderbilt University, Nashville, TN

Stephanie Fagin Jones, PhD, Department of Counseling and Clinical
Psychology, Teachers College, Columbia University, New York, NY

A. J. Figueredo, PhD, Department of Psychology, University of Arizona,
Tucson

Ronald Gallimore, PhD, Department of Psychology, University of
California, Los Angeles, and LessonLab, Santa Monica, CA

Kathleen C. Gunthert, PhD, Department of Psychology, American
University, Washington, DC

Alan E. Kazdin, PhD, Yale University School of Medicine, New Haven, CT

Petra L. Klumb, PhD, Technical University of Berlin, Germany

Jason K. Luellen, PhD, Department of Psychology, University of
Memphis, Memphis, TN

Katherine M. McKnight, PhD, Department of Psychology, University of
Arizona, Tucson

Patrick E. McKnight, **PhD,** Department of Psychology, George Mason
University, Fairfax, VA

Elizabeth Midlarsky, PhD, Department of Counseling and Clinical
Psychology, Teachers College, Columbia University, New York, NY

Rudolf H. Moos, PhD, Department of Veterans Affairs Health Care
System and Stanford University School of Medicine, Palo Alto, CA

Robin K. Nemeroff, PhD, Department of Psychology, William Paterson
University, Wayne, NJ

Georgine M. Pion, PhD, Psychology and Human Development
Department, Vanderbilt University, Nashville, TN

Rossella Santagata, PhD, Department of Psychology, University of
California, Los Angeles, and LessonLab, Santa Monica, CA

William R. Shadish, PhD, School of Social Sciences, Humanities, and Arts, University of California, Merced

Souraya Sidani, PhD, Faculty of Nursing, University of Toronto, Ontario, Canada

Bradley H. Smith, PhD, Department of Psychology, University of South Carolina, Columbia

Timothy R. Stickle, PhD, Department of Psychology, University of Vermont, Burlington

Carl F. Weems, PhD, Department of Psychology, University of New Orleans, New Orleans, LA

Stephen G. West, PhD, Department of Psychology, Arizona State University, Tempe

Werner W. Wittmann, PhD, Department of Psychology, University of Mannheim, Mannheim, Germany

Series Foreword

In early 1988, the American Psychological Association (APA) Science Directorate began its sponsorship of what would become an exceptionally successful activity in support of psychological science—the APA Scientific Conferences program. This program has showcased some of the most important topics in psychological science and has provided a forum for collaboration among many leading figures in the field.

The program has inspired a series of books that have presented cutting-edge work in all areas of psychology. At the turn of the millennium, the series was renamed the Decade of Behavior Series to help advance the goals of this important initiative. The Decade of Behavior is a major interdisciplinary campaign designed to promote the contributions of the behavioral and social sciences to our most important societal challenges in the decade leading up to 2010. Although a key goal has been to inform the public about these scientific contributions, other activities have been designed to encourage and further collaboration among scientists. Hence, the series that was the "APA Science Series" has continued as the "Decade of Behavior Series." This represents one element in APA's efforts to promote the Decade of Behavior initiative as one of its endorsing organizations. For additional information about the Decade of Behavior, please visit http://www.decadeofbehavior.org.

Over the course of the past years, the Science Conference and Decade of Behavior Series has allowed psychological scientists to share and explore cutting-edge findings in psychology. The APA Science Directorate looks forward to continuing this successful program and to sponsoring other conferences and books in the years ahead. This series has been so successful that we have chosen to extend it to include books that, although they do not arise from conferences, report with the same high quality of scholarship on the latest research.

We are pleased that this important contribution to the literature was supported in part by the Decade of Behavior program. Congratulations to the editors and contributors of this volume on their sterling effort.

Steven J. Breckler, PhD
Executive Director for Science

Virginia E. Holt
Assistant Executive Director for Science

Volume Foreword

Thomas D. Cook

Not surprisingly perhaps, the chapters in this Festschrift for Lee Sechrest mirror his own broad achievements and so cover a broad range of topics. I characterize them roughly as dealing with theory of method, measurement theory and practice, and experimental design and data analysis for evaluation purposes; issuing challenges to methodological orthodoxies; and studying individual behavior in social contexts.

As a bound volume, the Festschrift represents the ultimate form of scholarly respect. Scholars know how much effort it takes to write a chapter so well that the person being honored will appreciate it. They would not undertake such an onerous task for anyone but are more than willing do it for a teacher/colleague/mentor/friend. They also know that the Festschrift will end up in libraries where it joins the honoree's own books and papers to create what is essentially each scholar's intellectual immortality. A Festschrift attests to *others'* formal respect for the honoree and his work. Of course, it is not the only form of such respect. Libraries also contain others' citations to the honoree's writings. Yet these citations are to individual parts of the corpus, not to the corpus as a whole. The Festschrift is unique as a tribute to a scholar's entire life and work that is destined to survive as a mark of esteem so long as libraries or librarylike institutions exist.

"The red thread," as Goethe liked to call it, that links these particular Festschrift papers is a professional life. It is not a single idea, theory, or research style. These things often evolve over scholarly careers, sometimes radically so. Lee Sechrest is not one of Isaiah Berlin's hedgehogs who spent a professional lifetime exploring a single dominant idea, though his concepts of incremental validity and unobtrusive measures are weighty enough that they could have been the foundation of a lifetime's work. Instead, Lee has always been open to stimulation. He has followed his evolving interests, insights, and enthusiasms wherever they took him. In addition, he is a good collaborator, sometimes harnessing his own activities to ideas that others have initiated. All these stylistic features mean that he does not have a single way of framing issues or constructing knowledge.

Lee is a pragmatist to the core, always wanting to bring the best practical evidence to bear, whatever the topic and whatever the constraints to choice of method a particular setting forces on the researcher. Yet his pragmatism never prevents him from taking the evidence he and his colleagues have generated and appraising it from the perspective of the very best textbook methods, publicly noting the limitations to the knowledge claims he himself makes. His self-criticism is admirable, all the more so because it never becomes debilitating.

Lee is first and foremost an actor on the stage of social science research, not a ruminator in its wings.

Intellectually, his major contributions are on two fronts. The first is represented by his seminal research in the areas of measurement theory and evaluation, such as his work on unobtrusive measurement and incremental validity. The second touches on institution building, particularly at the American Psychological Association (APA) and with the Evaluation Group for the Analysis of Data (EGAD) at the University of Arizona. EGAD is a funny and striking name, very Lee-like. However, it understates what EGAD members actually do, because their activities betray a broad interest in theory of method writ large. Data analysis is a major focus, but not an exclusive one.

To understand better the person whose life holds this Festschrift together, one may find it worthwhile to begin by reading the chapter by McKnight, McKnight, and Figueredo (chap. 13). They give an account of Lee's major research contributions, especially emphasizing his leadership in creating and maintaining EGAD. Lee is obviously a much-loved person at the University of Arizona, where he is manifestly a highly effective organizer and motivator. He particularly understands the needs of younger scholars and can creatively balance support and tough feedback to them. He also goes out of his way to generate research opportunities for them and to get them to present their results to important audiences. To the extent that his phenomenal success in this effort rests on replicable skills, efforts aimed at stimulating collaborative and multidisciplinary research badly need to identify and disseminate the Lee Sechrest recipe for creating and maintaining EGAD! The group will long outlive him, so committed to its agenda are his former graduate and postgraduate students as well as those others from the United States and abroad who have attached themselves to the theory group.

Among sociologists of science (and obituary writers for scholars), the conventional wisdom seems to be that individual scientific lives should be evaluated in terms of the prizes and prestigious fellowships won, the terms they have coined that have become commonplace, the technologies they developed that have been widely adopted, their citation counts if they are very high, the number and size of grants they have received, the prize-winning students they have placed in prestigious institutions, the leadership roles they have played in scientific societies, and so on.

Lee has done just fine by these criteria. All one needs to do is draw attention to his neologisms, like the incremental validity and unobtrusive measures already mentioned, or note the many offices he has held and the awards he has received from the APA and the American Evaluation Association in particular.

However, Lee is a world-class evaluator as well as a wise head, and he surely knows that the traditional criteria outlined earlier are unduly narrow. For one thing, they leave out the importance of institution building. In addition to founding EGAD, Lee has contributed to improving various divisions of the APA, and it is no coincidence that APA is publishing this volume. He has made his contributions through straight talk that is always aimed at the topic on hand and never at individuals, and this straight talk always puts scientific criteria and the scientific quality of the evidence before the financial or political interests of some guild. He has been consistently critical of those in psychology who want to overclaim its benefits or who try to substitute clinical experience for science. In institutional contexts, he is forceful and controversial; but he is never dismissed as out of hand, because it is obvious to all that his main interest is in APA's welfare as a science-justified entity. Playfulness and shock value lie behind some of the stands he takes, but never ego, negative impulses, or irrelevance.

Another limitation of traditional evaluative criteria in science is that scholarly lives are also human lives. Thus, they should also be judged by human criteria. Lee's research life is predicated on the compatibility of having fun while doing quality research and on enjoying all the human relationships that are involved in collaborative research and in relating to students. Despite being busy, he sees his research colleagues of all ages, not just at work but also socially at home or at conventions. He asks about their lives and the relationships in them, out of both genuine interest and concern and also because he knows that a colleague's total life affects his or her work life. Lee enjoys the social interaction that research requires, and this shows up not only in his words of support and appreciation but also in his body language—the body turned fully to you, the eyes glued on you, and the hearty, full-throated laugh at his own and others' jokes. More than anyone else I know, Lee has incorporated science into his entire life. To paraphrase the title of a book on Jewish life in poor European villages a century ago, for Lee, "Science is with people."

So this book is about an intellectually restless person who is excited by many different ideas, possibilities, and people and who can make a research project out of any opportunity that offers entrée to a site or group of people. Moreover, he is quite pragmatic about his choice of methods, so long as the methods chosen are the best ones in context. He is fearless in attacking the pompous and self-serving. However, he is invariably supportive with younger scholars, despite giving them feedback that is often hard hitting—but always from within a context of warmth and appreciation that is universally acknowledged by all in the research communities he frequents.

These are some of the hard-to-grasp realities that form "the red thread" that holds this book together. Seen as a whole, these chapters are a fitting tribute to a very special person, artfully reflecting his open, tolerant style that never gives up on high standards or on having fun while also doing serious science.

Acknowledgments

There are many organizations and individuals whose efforts were critical in making this volume a success. The sponsors of the conference, which took place in Tucson April 25–27, 2003, were the following: The American Psychological Association (represented by Alan E. Kazdin for the Science Directorate and the Executive Director's Office) provided a grant for the meeting and the publishing of this book; the American Psychological Society (represented by Alan G. Kraut, executive director) supplemented the financial assistance for the Festschrift and awarded Lee the APS Lifetime Achievement Award; the Veterans Administration (VA) Health Services Research Branch (represented through videotape by John G. Demakis, director) provided financial support and presented a plaque honoring Lee for his many contributions to the VA; the Public Interest Research Services (represented by Katherine McKnight); and the University of Arizona (represented by Alfred W. Kaszniak, head of the Department of Psychology).

A steering committee composed of individuals from Lee Sechrest's local evaluation group, EGAD (the Evaluation Group for the Analysis of Data), made sure that every detail of the weekend was handled professionally. Our grateful appreciation goes to Judi Babcock-Parziale, Kathleen Insel, Vicki Cunningham, Mende Davis, Rebecca Hill, Gwen Johnson, Katherine McKnight, and Michele Walsh. Many other members of EGAD, too numerous to mention, also receive our heartfelt appreciation for their volunteered time and labor, for what at times seemed like an endless list of tasks.

And, of course, the guests and the speakers played an enormous role in making the Festschrift a success. We and Lee are appreciative of everyone's contribution to the success of the weekend and this volume.

Strengthening Research Methodology

Introduction

Richard R. Bootzin and Patrick E. McKnight

Lee Sechrest is a methodological pioneer, an astute critic, and a tireless teacher. Some may describe his scientific contributions by only one of these roles, but simple characterizations fail to capture his uniqueness. It is through these various roles that Lee is and continues to be a multifaceted scholar. The range of his contributions and influence is reflected in the chapters written in his honor for this collection.

As a pioneer, Lee contributed to work that shaped the way many researchers viewed measurement, evaluation, and data analysis. *Unobtrusive Measures* (Webb, Campbell, Schwartz, & Sechrest, 1966) is often viewed as Lee's initial pioneering effort. That work influenced countless others to view measurement as a means of measuring theoretical constructs in a way that was a contrast with the prevailing trend of operational definitions. In truth, however, it was his earlier work on incremental validity (Sechrest, 1963) that marked his first contribution to measurement.

Prior to his "recommendation," most measurement theorists failed to take into account the practical implications of incremental improvement over previous measures. Lee's measurement contributions continued later with his work on the measurement of effects. A collaborative effort with Bill Yeaton resulted in four articles dissecting the prominent measures of effect size (Sechrest & Yeaton, 1981a, 1981b, 1981c, 1981d). Still later, Lee's long-term goal of tackling how measures of the same construct interrelate was addressed in his 1996 article on calibration (Sechrest, McKnight, & McKnight, 1996). These contributions reflected Lee's effort to better understand scientific contributions through improved measurement.

Lee's work in measurement translated well into the areas of health services research, program evaluation, and general outcomes data analysis, improving the quality of the research in all of those areas. Nevertheless, he has frequently expressed the frustration that research practice remains entrenched in traditional, unexamined methods. For example, incremental validity—important in the eyes of measurement experts—has yet to take hold as an essential aspect of instrument evaluation. The dominance of more general, hard-to-define terms such as construct validity and reliability certainly outweighs the presence of incremental validity signs. Moreover, researchers and evaluators have failed to adopt unobtrusive measures as even supplemental methods of measurement.

Self-report surveys and other easily administered methods dominate social science. Finally, calibration has yet to catch on as an important method compared with the traditional reliance on significance testing and effect size estimation. Simply put, Lee's pioneering efforts have influenced the leading theorists in measurement and evaluation more than they have had a direct impact on the everyday behavior of researchers and evaluators.

Lee's substantial contributions to measurement and methodology, on the one hand, coupled with his failure to have influenced researchers more directly, on the other hand, might be attributable to three forces. The first and most relevant force to Lee's own work is the inertial force that keeps people from changing their behaviors. Lee understood and appreciated the difficulty of behavioral change and recognized that successful intervention was no simple matter. His collaborative research on psychotherapy (Goldstein, Heller, & Sechrest, 1966), criminal rehabilitation (e.g., Sechrest, White, & Brown, 1979), and cross-cultural psychology (e.g., Brown & Sechrest, 1980) bears out his recognition of the complexity of intervention. His work on policy issues, including peer review, health care policy, and professional education, also shaped his appreciation that widespread change was both difficult and rare but was made more likely if evaluations of one's own efforts were included. Lee has always been an unflinching evaluator of his own contributions as well as of unexamined assumptions underlying many traditional methods. It appears that he appreciated the difficulty in getting people to change and provided the initial force to overcome inertia but left the subsequent and essential forces to others.

A second force that may have decreased the influence that Lee's work had on the behavior of social science researchers may paradoxically come from his insatiable curiosity. Without question, Lee's curiosity has taken him down many content paths. Lee is one of the rare individuals in science for whom the process of how knowledge is advanced matters more than the specific content of the research area. He ventured into more content areas than most psychology departments cover in the same life span. A quick perusal of his vitae shows that each year he was working in a different content domain.

Lee's work covers the following areas (listed in chronological order): combat performance, group psychotherapy, measurement theory, unobtrusive measures, projective tests, construct evaluation, learning, psychotherapy, teaching, deviancy, personality assessment, personality theory, smoking traits, behavioral theory, mental competency, mental disorder, cross-cultural norms, cross-cultural effects, naturalistic assessment, clinical prediction, musical experience, astrology, graffiti, exercise, attitude assessment, humor, homosexuality, mannerisms, interpersonal behavior, behavioral assessment, health care quality, incarceration, program evaluation, clinical psychology education, professional psychology policy, experimental design, encounter groups, health insurance, evaluation research, peer review, translating research into policy, effect size estimation, hyperventilation, rehabilitation, remote data collection, memory, group decision making, no-difference findings, organ transplants, professional training, consensus conferences, research theory, graduate training, competency assessment, aptitude by treatment interactions, licensure, research dissemination, prevention research, rural health, survey research, health care reform, alexithymia, public policy, qualitative methods, calibration, therapeutic communities, organizational change, chronic stress, alternative medicine, research design, analysis of change, cultural predictors, prescription privileges, and clinical experience. There are over 75 unique areas covered in a span of approximately 50 years. Even if Lee thought that his ideas might change the behavior of researchers, his intellectual voyage did not permit him the luxury of the singular focus that is often required for successful dissemination.

Finally, Lee's contributions may not have had a dramatic, immediate effect on social science research methodology because of how his contributions related to his theory of "nudge effects." Lee subscribes to the idea that some forces simply "nudge" people to change. The theory postulates a probabilistic association between the nudge force and the eventual change. After all, one of Lee's favorite mantras is "I give advice freely and have no expectations that you'll use it." This apparently laissez-faire attitude might explain why he expended little additional energy to persuade others that he was correct.

Although direct, observable change in research methodology was not forthcoming from his scientific contributions, Lee's consultation and teaching responsibilities provided substantial immediate reward and long-term influence. His teaching offered him the opportunity to influence many and start people off in their careers well grounded in the scientific method. One of his most important influences was through teaching and individual mentoring. Lee is an educator at the heart of all his work. He presents ideas in a succinct manner and offers them without any expectations. Because of this presentation style, the bulk of his influence lies in the subtleties of mentorship and modeling. He worked extensively with students throughout his career, frequently publishing with them and promoting their joint efforts as if they were his students' original thoughts. He is more interested in nudging others along to examine ideas than to get credit for the idea. His dedication, selflessness, and constant intellectual engagement provided him with the ability to span so many content areas and influence so many people.

Lee's work as a consultant to the Department of Veterans Affairs, National Futures Board, National Academy of Sciences, American Board of Radiology, Institute of Medicine, and National Institutes of Health, among others, provided him with the opportunity to help shape policy decisions. During his extensive consultation career, he provided thoughtful, constructive criticism to every group he joined. Through his critiques, he frequently shaped policy in ways that are difficult to trace, let alone attribute solely to his efforts. His published criticism of measurement, cross-cultural psychology, program evaluation, health care policy, graduate education, professional certification, and peer review are all well documented and cited in the literature. Through these works, Lee was able to apply his vast experience from many different disciplines to the vexing problems of a single endeavor. Many of the listed organizations he consults with have honored him either directly with awards or indirectly by praise of his contributions.

This volume, prepared as part of a Festschrift for Lee, is an example. The American Psychological Association, the American Psychological Society, the Veterans Affairs Health Services Research Branch, and the University of

Arizona all contributed to make the Festschrift a success. The Festschrift brought together many of the best methodologists in the world to reflect on Lee's contributions to measurement, methodology, and evaluation.

Although we began the task of summarizing Lee's scientific contributions as they might be listed in his curriculum vita, we found it impossible to characterize him only in that way. Lee is more than just the sum of his vita entries. His colleagues, students, and friends are testaments to the broad, influential contributions he has made through their own work.

The Chapters in This Volume

Lee's contributions to measurement are seen vividly in the first four chapters. It is noteworthy that it is not the content areas of investigation that reflect Lee's influence. These four chapters are drawn from widely different domains. Nevertheless, Lee's emphasis on excellence and realism in measurement and methodology is seen in all.

Ronald Gallimore, a renowned educational researcher who worked with Lee as a graduate student at Northwestern University, and Rosella Santagata write about a creative, innovative, and state-of-the art methodology to use video surveys to measure change in educational settings. Their chapter is a model for how to use formative evaluation to improve educational interventions.

Elizabeth Midlarsky, a distinguished personality researcher who also was a graduate student of Lee's at Northwestern University, Stephanie Fagin Jones, and Robin K. Nemeroff have written a compelling account of their research on the personality correlates of heroic rescue during the Holocaust. As they show, much can be learned about the measurement of personality if unusual, but intense, responses are examined.

Rudolf H. Moos, a longtime professional colleague of Lee's through their work with the Department of Veterans Affairs, writes about his research on measuring social environments and coping. The problem of measuring social environments has been a critically important task for understanding the etiology and treatment of mental disorders. No one has tackled this measurement issue better than Moos. His chapter provides a wonderful overview of the research as related to understanding how social environments and coping interact.

Lawrence H. Cohen, who received his PhD at Florida State University with Lee, Kathleen C. Gunthert, and Andrew C. Butler examine the relationship between daily stress and coping in cognitive therapy outcomes. Cohen and his colleagues point out that their research on examining personality principles as mechanisms of change in psychotherapy is inspired by the classic text by Goldstein, Heller, and Sechrest (1966) titled *Psychotherapy and the Psychology of Behavior Change.*

The next five chapters are focused on issues of methodology in research and evaluation, and all are tied closely to Lee's methodological contributions. The chapter by Alan E. Kazdin, one of the former graduate students from Northwestern University, continues in the thread of mechanisms of action in psychotherapy, particularly psychotherapy for children, and is a call to arms for studies that pay attention to methodological issues emphasized by Lee, such as treatment integrity, the calibration of outcome measures, and understanding moderators of change. As Kazdin emphasizes, his chapter follows a constructive theme in Lee's writings to provide methodological solutions as well as clear-eyed critiques. Kazdin's chapter provides both.

Building on the theme of treatment integrity, David S. Cordray and Georgine M. Pion, colleagues during Lee's Northwestern University tenure, examine the importance of variations in treatment strength as a means of validating the links between hypothesized causes and outcomes. Their work is motivated by the desire to help change adverse social conditions, and they see that as an important theme in Lee's writings that has influenced them. Cordray and Pion give a compelling methodological analysis of treatment strength that provides a promising way to discover how to influence social change.

Souraya Sidani, who received her PhD in nursing at the University of Arizona and who continues to work collaboratively with Lee, has written a review of the advantages and disadvantages of random assignment, particularly within clinical trials. She points out that random assignment does not always ensure group equivalence in small-sample research. She recommends more attention on baseline measurement as well as the exploration of alternative designs that do not require random assignment.

William R. Shadish, who was a postdoctoral fellow at Northwestern during Lee's tenure there, Jason K. Luellen, and M. H. Clark continue the theme raised in Souraya Sidani's chapter about nonequivalent groups and quasi-experimental designs by exploring a particular statistical solution to nonequivalent groups called propensity scores. Shadish, Luellen, and Clark thoroughly evaluate the usefulness and limitations of propensity scores and provide recommendations for their use.

Stephen G. West, a colleague of Lee's from their Florida State University days, extends the focus on how to understand data and provides an exploration and tutorial on graphical exploratory data analysis. This chapter connects with Lee's continuous emphasis on examining data for the purpose of advancing our understanding of how and why interventions work and presenting our findings in ways that illuminate the data, not obscure them.

The next two chapters focus on aspects of validity and assessment within the evaluation domain. Werner W. Wittmann, a friend and colleague of Lee's from Germany, and Petra L. Klumb have written a chapter that puts the impact of the "Northwestern school" of methodology into historical context and traces the contributions of Don Campbell, Thomas D. Cook, Robert F. Boruch, William R. Shadish, and others, along with those of Lee's, in building a methodology for policy evaluation. Wittmann and Klumb move beyond the Northwestern school to integrate the Brunswik lens model to help conceptualize evaluations. They provide specific examples of how to avoid fooling ourselves with mindless evaluations.

Timothy R. Stickle, one of Lee's graduate students from the University of Arizona, and Carl F. Weems write about improving prediction from clinical assessment, another continuing thread in Lee's career. Stickle and Weems describe the problems with traditional methods of evaluating the validity of measures and propose the application of methods from areas other than clinical assessment that may have promise. Particularly intriguing is their discussion of the promise of using receiver operating characteristic (ROC) curves as a means of examining individual differences.

The final two chapters focus on the important interactions between Lee's style of mentoring and the advances that he and his students, friends, and colleagues have accomplished. Bradley H. Smith, one of Lee's former graduate students from the University of Arizona, catalogues Lee's famous "laws" and how they set the tone for advances that his students and colleagues have made. However, as Smith points out, being right about how to improve methodology is not always sufficient to change entrenched methodological practices.

In a similar vein, Patrick E. and Katherine M. McKnight, recent graduate students and current colleagues of Lee's, along with another colleague, A. J. Figueredo, all from the University of Arizona, have written an overview of Lee's methodological legacy. Their thesis is that Lee's style of enthusiastic curiosity and generosity is as important as the methodological contributions he has made.

Although this Festschrift is an impressive documentation of how measurement, methodology, and evaluation have been influenced by Lee Sechrest, there is still much to be done. Fortunately, Lee continues to work at the same pace he has throughout his career. We look forward to his continued insights and contributions. Even so, there is much for the rest of us to do so that the insights described throughout his writings and reflected in the following chapters are indeed implemented.

References

Brown, E., & Sechrest, L. B. (1980). Experiments in cross-cultural research. In H. Triandis (Ed.), *Handbook of cross-cultural psychology* (Vol. 2, pp. 297–318). Boston: Allyn & Bacon.

Goldstein, A. P., Heller, K., & Sechrest, L. B. (1966). *Psychotherapy and the psychology of behavior change*. New York: Wiley.

Sechrest, L. B. (1963). Incremental validity: A recommendation. *Educational and Psychological Measurement, 23*, 153–158.

Sechrest, L. B., McKnight, P., & McKnight, K. (1996). On calibrating measures for psychotherapy research. *American Psychologist, 51,* 1065–1071.

Sechrest, L. B., White, S., & Brown, E. (Eds.). (1979). *The rehabilitation of criminal offenders: Problems and prospects*. Washington, DC: National Academy of Sciences.

Sechrest, L. B., & Yeaton, W. (1981a). Assessing the effectiveness of social programs: Methodological and conceptual issues. In S. Ball (Ed.), *New directions in evaluation research* (Vol. 9, pp. 41–56). San Francisco: Jossey-Bass.

Sechrest, L. B., & Yeaton, W. (1981b). Critical dimensions in the choice and maintenance of successful treatments: Strength, integrity, and effectiveness. *Journal of Consulting and Clinical Psychology, 49*, 156–167.

Sechrest, L. B., & Yeaton, W. (1981c). Empirical bases for estimating effect size. In R. F. Boruch, P. M. Wortman, D. S. Cordray, & Associates (Eds.), *Reanalyzing program valuations: Policies and practices for secondary analysis of social and educational programs* (pp. 212–224). San Francisco: Jossey-Bass.

Sechrest, L. B., & Yeaton, W. (1981d). Estimating effect size. In P. M. Wortman (Ed.), *Methods for evaluating health services* (pp. 61–85). Beverly Hills, CA: Sage.

Webb, E., Campbell, D. T., Schwartz, R. D., & Sechrest, L. B. (1966). *Unobtrusive measures: A survey of nonreactive research in social science*. Chicago: Rand McNally.

Part I

Excellence and Realism in Measurement

1

Researching Teaching: The Problem of Studying a System Resistant to Change

Ronald Gallimore and Rossella Santagata

Consider the analogy of medicine. For thousands of years, folk remedies have been used to cure disease or relieve symptoms. But the successes of modern medicine have emerged in the last 75 years and derive from advances in the sciences of physiology and biochemistry that allowed us to understand the mechanisms of disease, and from the wide use of randomized clinical trials to determine which prevention and treatment approaches drawn from these sciences work as intended. . . . Or consider the analogy of agriculture. . . . The abundance of inexpensive and nutritious foods . . . today results from agricultural practice that has moved from reliance on folk wisdom to reliance on science.

When we come to education, the picture is different. The National Research Council has concluded that "the world of education . . . does not rest on a strong research base. In no other field are personal experience and ideology so frequently relied on to make policy choices, and in no other field is the research base so inadequate and little used." . . . There is every reason to believe that, if we invest in the education sciences and develop mechanisms to encourage evidence-based practice, we will see progress and transformation in education of the same order of magnitude as we have seen in medicine and agriculture. (Whitehurst, 2002b)

The goal of a strong research base for education is now the law of the land. It was incorporated into a major legislative initiative, the No Child Left Behind Act (NCLB) of 2001. NCLB includes 111 references to "scientifically based research" (Feuer, Towne, & Shavelson, 2002; National Research Council, 2002).

To help build a research base, in 2002 the U.S. Congress created the Institute for Educational Sciences (IES). In early 2003, the IES issued Requests for Applications, promising substantial funding for field-initiated investigations deploying rigorous methods and designs, including randomized trials. A

Many thanks to Jim Stigler for helpful suggestions on the manuscript.

new era in educational research had been launched. Feuer et al. (2002, p. 4) noted, "After years of envy for federal support received by their compatriots in medical, technological, agricultural, and physical research, educational researchers can now rejoice. Research is in."

To realize an evidence-based education, many barriers must be overcome. Although the chronic lack of funding is presumably going to be addressed by new sources, the existing research base is perceived by many to be so limited that it will take years to build an adequate one (Feuer et al., 2002). A National Research Council review noted that many critics, including educational researchers,

> lament weak or absent theory, accumulations of anecdote masquerading as evidence, studies with little obvious policy relevance, seemingly endless disputes over the desired outcomes of schooling, low levels of replicability, large error margins, opaqueness of data and sources, unwillingness or inability to agree on a common set of metrics, and the inevitable intrusion of ideology at the ground level. (Feuer et al., 2002, p. 5)

Not everyone agrees with this gloomy assessment. Some argue that the critics themselves are using inadequate scholarship or overstating the situation in other fields such as medicine. For instance, some have noted that the frequent use of clinical trials in medical research produces conflicting or contradictory results, and medicine is divided regarding the role of scientific evidence in clinical practice (Berliner, 2002; Feuer et al., 2002). Others question whether the emphasis in NCLB on scientific methods is a realistic or even an appropriate goal, as opposed to a more explicit mixed-methods strategy (Erickson & Gutierrez, 2002). However these disputes are resolved, if they are, in the meantime they surely slow the assembly of scientific and professional knowledge and consensus on which an evidence base must rest (Feuer et al., 2002; National Research Council, 2002; Whitehurst, 2002a).

Regarding the focus of this chapter—the difficulty of changing teaching—there is a fair degree of agreement that it is a formidable barrier to the goal of an evidence-based education. In one way or another, at least a temporary change in teachers' practices is necessary to address many critical research questions. Others require stable changes over extended periods, for example, any study that has as a dependent variable the high-stakes tests NCLB mandates to assess adequate yearly improvement in student achievement. The development of an evidence-based education will require the barrier to be repeatedly overcome, because it is hard to study what one cannot change.

We wish to be clear on this point: Many important questions can be addressed with rigorous designs that do not require changing teaching. Examples include, among many others, an increase in the ratio of content to method courses for teachers in training, broadening the recruitment pool to include nontraditional sources, single-gender schools, small versus large schools, traditional versus alternative calendars and schedules, and so on. However, teaching is the final common pathway of numerous intended reforms and innovations. For many research questions, teachers must reliably implement different instructional practices over an extended period to secure an adequate test of the experimental treatment.

In this chapter, we describe some of the reasons teaching is so difficult to change and some of the barriers this presents to rigorous designs and methods. We then offer a solution in the form of an alternative vision of educational research. The means to this different end is a reorganized research-and-development (R & D) system that supports teacher professional development and creates opportunities for ambitious educational research, including more frequent use of randomized experimental trials—a system that enlists the efforts of practitioners as well as researchers and takes advantage of emerging technologies. Such an R & D system might enable the nation to achieve the transformations of teaching that are required to achieve the NCLB goal of an evidence-based education.

Why Is Changing Teaching So Hard?

Implementation: The "I" Word

The "I" word, *implementation*, is probably more alarming to educational researchers than the "F" word is in everyday discourse. There is good reason. The failure to implement more than a fraction of intended changes in teaching haunts many efforts, from whole-school reform, to small-scale local efforts, to the most ambitious and well-funded research projects. After a while, everyone in educational research gets uncomfortable when the "I" word is used in polite company.

Of course, education is not the only field that struggles with implementation, as Sechrest and his colleagues have persuasively argued (Figueredo & Sechrest, 2001; Sechrest, West, Phillips, Redner, & Yeaton, 1979). There have been many spectacular failures, in which a conclusion of "no effects" was because an experimental treatment was never actually implemented as intended, or was in so weak a dose that no effects were possible or detectable.

Following several major disappointments—for example, the failure of "New Math" (Sarason, 1971) and change-agent studies (Berman & McLaughlin, 1978), faith waned in the power of new policies, programs, and books alone to improve achievement. There was growing recognition that the agents of implementation themselves—teachers—could not be taken for granted. Instead of training, which implied brief, episodic interventions, new ideas emerged about engaging teachers in the career-long development of the capacity to change, subject matter knowledge acquisition, and self-directed practical R & D. It took a while, but eventually districts, states, and the federal government began to fund more ambitious professional development (PD) programs. When Congress reauthorized the Elementary and Secondary Education Act, the bill allocated $3 billion annually for teacher education and professional development (Whitehurst, 2002c).

Substantial appropriations are one indication of how hard it is to change teaching. Another is implied in the following abbreviated list of consensus standards for the conduct of professional development (National Staff Development Council, 2001):

- Requires and fosters a norm of continuous improvement.
- Entails long-term sustained involvement rather than brief, one-shot sessions.
- Aligns with school and district content and performance standards.
- Requires adequate time during the workday for staff members to learn and work collaboratively.

Are these conditions necessary to secure sustainable changes in teaching? Probably. There is a lot of practical experience behind the standards and sufficient consensus, at least for the moment, to assume that they are necessary (Goldenberg, 2004), and they are what teachers report as most effective (Garet, Porter, Desimone, Birman, & Yoon, 2001). Time, continuity, and alignment are essential to implementing teaching changes at dosage levels necessary to detect effects, either in classroom practices or in student learning. Just as no one would want to experimentally compare short-term neurosurgery experiences with full residency training, few who have tried to change teaching doubt the need for long-term, site-based, and classroom-focused professional development.

This means that even before one starts changing teaching to field an experimental trial, one has to change the context in which the teaching change is to be launched. Why? Most schools and districts do not have a system in place that meets the standard of incorporating long-term, classroom-focused professional development into the weekly routine of their teaching staffs. Most rely on short-term workshop approaches.

One more point: A specific goal of NCLB is increased use of randomized experimental trials, which critics have quite rightly pointed out are too seldom used in educational investigations (Cook, 2002). Increasing their use, particularly for controversial, high-stakes questions, would be a good thing (e.g., Feuer et al., 2002). However, what it takes to change teaching is a formidable barrier to greater use of randomized trials, because they are most feasible when treatments are short and require little or no teacher training, patterns of coordination among school staff are not modified, and the units receiving different treatments cannot communicate with each other (Cook, 2002).

The best conditions for randomized experiments are, to put it mildly, at odds with consensus standards for professional development: long-term, sustained involvement aligned with school content carried out collaboratively during the workday. How many researchers are in position to request, demand, or provide these requirements? How many school districts are capable of creating such contexts? We agree that there are many important studies to be done that do not entail long-term teacher training and that can be best done by fielding true experiments. Yet many others require extensive, extended teacher professional development. Overcoming the perception and reality of educational research as underwhelming will take more than a commitment to rigorous designs. There is really no way to avoid getting engaged in PD implementation in the context in which an experimental or quasi-experimental trial is conducted. The distinction between educational research and PD practice is sometimes hard to maintain.

The Cultural Nature of Teaching

So, if the contextual factors favorable for changing teaching are available, is the implementation problem solved? No, because even under optimal conditions, changing teaching remains difficult because of its cultural nature, which by definition means that it has evolved to resist change. Even when the most rigorous PD standards are met, teaching changes can be hard to come by.

Despite many attempts to change it, in some ways teaching today differs little from instructional practices described about a century ago by Rice (1893) and Stevens (1912). Hoetker and Ahlbrand (1969, p. 163) found a "remarkable stability" in the patterns of instruction described in over a century of reporting, so much so that they have been described as the "default teaching script" (Cazden, 1988, p. 53).

This persistence and stability reflect the cultural nature of many aspects of teaching (Cuban, 1990; Feiman-Nemser & Floden, 1986; Fullan, 1991, 1993; Little & McLaughlin, 1993; Sarason, 1971; Tharp & Gallimore, 1989; Wagner, 1994). Over time, teaching, like all cultural activities and routines, has become relatively transparent, taken for granted, and embodied in beliefs about what is right and proper. Teaching is fitted to the structure, organization, and operation of schools, because all these features have coevolved over time. They are adapted to multiple conditions and represent a stable pattern that balances what is desirable (values) with what is possible (ecological realities). History, politics, economics, social factors, and other forces multiply and redundantly support current practices.

This redundancy is the basis of normative behaviors. If "everyone does the same things," the sources of alternatives are limited. Thus, the narrow range of instructional practices teachers observe as a student prior to entering the profession and afterward is one of the major barriers to changing teaching. This point was underscored by the TIMSS Video Study (Stigler & Hiebert, 1999). As part of the Third International Mathematics and Science Study, the TIMMS Video Study research team conducted a video survey of nationally representative samples in three countries (Germany, Japan, and the United States). The TIMSS team concluded that each nation had a distinctive teaching pattern (Stigler & Hiebert, 1999). No matter from where in the United States a video had been collected as part of the random sampling, the investigators began to have déjà vu experiences. After watching a few dozen U.S. videos, it became clear that the same pattern of instruction was in use. The ubiquity of a common pattern was confirmed in a follow-up study that collected a new random sample of U.S. mathematics lessons and that again found a common pattern in use (Hiebert et al., 2003).

The ubiquity of common patterns suggests another reason that it is so hard to change teaching: How can teachers ever envision and implement alternative practices if they seldom see any? When the teachers were students themselves, from kindergarten through preservice induction, the TIMSS Video Studies suggest that they are likely to have seen the common pattern enacted thousands of times. If most teachers teach the same way, and most teachers never to get to observe alternatives, it is not surprising that the common pattern persists despite the billions spent on professional development in recent years.

The TIMSS Video Study underscored a second reason changing teaching is hard. Discussions of teaching are linked mainly to words, not images of classroom practice. By using words to describe something as complex as teaching, definitional confusion is hard to avoid. This was also confirmed by the work of the TIMSS Video Study teams when they developed a system for coding the lesson videos. Although the literature on teaching provides operational definitions, for example, of "problem solving," it quickly became clear that expert teams using lesson videos to ground definitions discovered many problems. What one expert meant by "problem-solving approaches" referenced different instructional actions than what others meant. Likewise, in most PD programs, discussions of new instructional practices rest heavily on words and on brief demonstrations, rather than frequent, extended observation of alternatives.

You Can't Research What You and the Teachers Don't Know How to Do

The limited research base in education poses another barrier. Frequently, investigators must first develop and pilot the innovative teaching practices that must be implemented to field a randomized trial—meaning that not only will the teachers in the preliminary testing be asked to do something new, but so, too, will the researchers. The TIMSS Video Study provides an example of the barrier this presents investigators with a promising hypothesis to test.

Results from the TIMSS 1999 Video Study show that across countries, eighth-grade mathematics teachers devote the bulk of their classroom time to working on problems (Hiebert et al., 2003). The nature of these problems and how they are worked on determine, in large part, the learning opportunities available to their students. Because all of the countries outperform the United States in mathematics achievement, a special effort was made to code for problems that provide rich opportunities to learn mathematics. The question was whether countries with higher achievement were presenting a richer curriculum to their students than is done in the United States.

The answer appeared to be a clear "no." Six of the seven countries participating, including the United States, present about the same number of rich problems to students. However, looking beyond how a problem is presented to how it is worked on in the lesson revealed a very different picture.

What high-achieving nations had in common was not the number of rich problems they present. It is the way they were implemented that distinguished the high-achieving nations from the United States (and, to some degree, Australia, both of which are on the lower end of the achievement distribution). Instead of using these problems as opportunities to explore mathematical concepts, U.S. teachers typically broke them down into procedural elements and took students through the procedures step by step. Because the way a problem is presented represents its potential for engaging students in serious mathematical work (Stein & Lane, 1996), perhaps converting rich problems into procedural exercises is one reason for the relatively poor mathematics performance of U.S. students.

The reason for this pattern of results in the TIMSS Video Study is not clear, but here are some hypotheses. First, it is possible that U.S. teachers lack the content knowledge that would be necessary for them to facilitate rich discussions of mathematics (Ma, 1999). Another hypothesis is that U.S. teachers have little experience—either as teachers or back when they were students—engaging in conceptually rich discussions of mathematical problems. As we suggested earlier, if the latter is true, then it will be difficult for U.S. teachers to practice instructional strategies that are rare in their own culture, and difficult for them to observe examples of others doing so.

Consider the challenge to investigators who wish to follow up on this finding. Simply providing teachers with a curriculum that includes rich problems is not enough, because the TIMSS Video Study indicated that U.S. teachers already present enough challenging work. The problem is maintaining that richness as the students work on problems. To test whether actually implementing rich problems will make a difference, investigators will need to find either teachers who already know how or teachers who can learn to do it. Because zero percent of teachers in the randomly selected, nationally representative U.S. sample implemented a rich problem, what is the likelihood of finding American collaborators who already know how? Not good. So, to follow up on this promising finding means developing and testing a PD program to build teacher capacity to reliably implement rich problems. Even if the investigative goals are modest—for example, embedded assessments rather than standardized tests—figuring out how to get U.S. teachers to implement rich problems will be a challenge that could take an extended period to solve.

Sechrest and Figueredo (1993) suggested that such circumstances might require an iterative research process that deploys

> the full array of research methods, data collection techniques, and so on. [The process is iterative, so that] at each step data from the previous step [are] fed back into the system to direct changes and refinements. Although extensive use [can be] made of the qualitative procedures, such as interviews and observations, and of formative evaluation approaches, summative (outcome) evaluations [are] required on a regular basis to determine the effectiveness of each successive version of the program [under development]. It is well known that the highly successful Sesame Street television program was developed by a similar iterative model of testing, feedback, and revision. (Sechrest & Figueredo, 1993, pp. 661–662)

Sechrest and Figueredo (1993) cited another example of the iterative approach with which we are personally familiar (Tharp & Gallimore, 1979, 1989). It took more than 5 years to develop an effective reading program for Native Hawaiian children before the investigators concluded that the program was stable enough to warrant an investment in summative evaluation by randomized experimental trial (Tharp, 1982). During the 5 years of R & D, many components were tried, with some eliminated or greatly revised through an extended, trial-and-error iterative process. In some cases, some were tested by case study methods or small-scale experiments that did not rise to the standard of peer-referred journals but were useful for internal project purposes. This tinkering in realistic classroom conditions eventually led to an instructional problem that could be reliably instantiated and subjected to a randomized trial. Much of this iterative process could be described as evolving, through trial and error, a PD system that ensured that intended changes in instructional practices were reliably implemented into daily lessons.

The timing of clinical trials needs to be part of the debate about rigorous experimental designs in educational research. In the case of the Native Hawaiian project, full-scale summative evaluation by randomized trial came only after the investigators were sufficiently confident of the outcome to invest the substantial resources such an experiment required. To have launched a randomized trial without the years of iterative research would likely have been a costly mistake.

Unlike the well-funded laboratory school in which iterative research was successfully sustained for a long enough time to evolve a program stable enough to evaluate, most schools and districts are not well equipped to host such work. Even if they are willing to cooperate with investigators, the working conditions in most cases make it difficult to sustain a long-term investigation even with the best of intentions. Funding agencies are understandingly reluctant to pay so much so long for essentially pilot studies antecedent to an experimental or a quasi-experimental trial. The iterative test beds in which the levers for changing teaching can be developed are not easily or widely available. Opportunities to develop evidence on and for alternative practices are consequently limited.

How Can We Change Teaching?

We noted earlier that there is a growing consensus that a different kind of structure is needed to achieve sustainable changes in practice. It must be school based and long term, so that teachers have sufficient and dependable time on the job to learn new instructional practices that are aligned with what they are expected to teach.

But structural changes that provide teachers more time to work on improving practices are not enough. Even with time to work on improving teaching, teachers often lack the knowledge they need and want to make changes in practices (Goldenberg, 2004; Hiebert, Gallimore, & Stigler, 2002). Efforts to provide that knowledge have taken a variety of forms, including government-produced summaries of "what works," interpretations of research for educators, and prescriptions for effective teaching, among others (Anderson & Biddle, 1991; Berliner & Casanova, 1993; Joyce, Wolf, & Calhoun, 1993; National Research Council, 1999; Rosenshine, 1986; U.S. Department of Education, 1987; Willinsky, 2001).

To a large extent, none of these efforts have worked very well (National Education Research Policy and Priorities Board, 1999) because the knowledge teachers are typically given to implement changes in their practices may be the wrong kind (Cochran-Smith & Lytle, 1993; Doyle, 1997; Eisner, 1995; Hiebert et al., 2002; Huberman, 1985; Kennedy, 1999; Leinhardt, 1990; Stigler & Hiebert, 1999). The knowledge that teachers need to change their practice is not the kind researchers usually produce or trainers typically feature in PD programs. The kind of knowledge they need is often described as craft or practice knowledge, and it has at least three distinguishing features (Hiebert et al., 2002):

1. *Knowledge linked with practice.* Knowledge for teaching is useful when it is developed in response and linked to specific problems of practice. Such knowledge can be applied directly, without translation, but only to a restricted number of situations. It is linked with practice by being grounded in the context in which teachers work and being aligned to the content they are responsible for teaching.
2. *Knowledge that is detailed, concrete, and specific.* Although the knowledge might apply more generally, it is more directly related to particular lessons. This differs from the propositional knowledge researchers seek to build.
3. *Knowledge that is integrated.* Of most use to teachers is the integration of all types of knowledge, organized not according to domain but rather to the problem the knowledge is intended to address. This includes, for example, knowledge of students—what they know and how they learn—that accomplished teachers use to make content comprehensible to learners (Ma, 1999). Knowledge domains separated for purposes of research must, to be of use to teachers, be integrated and organized around problems of practice.

Although teachers produce this kind of knowledge every day to guide their own practice, it has no general utility because it is private and rarely validated. Even when the knowledge a teacher develops produces effective student learning, it is only haphazardly shared, and when that individual leaves the profession, the knowledge is lost. As a result, there is no accumulation of validated knowledge essential to changing teaching, and there never has been.

To become useful and support change, practitioner knowledge must be public, verified, and stored and shared. To this audience, these three qualities are immediately recognizable as hallmarks of research knowledge:

4. *Knowledge that is public.* For practice knowledge to become evidence-based knowledge, it must be public and represented in such a way that it can be communicated to others. It must be created with the intent of public examination, with the goal of making it shareable and open for discussion, verification, and refutation, modification, or improvement. Collaborations are essential because they force participants to make their knowledge public and understood by peers during its creation.
5. *Knowledge that is verified.* To be evidence based, knowledge must be accurate, verifiable, and continually improving. Teachers working together or a teacher working with his or her students might generate knowledge that undermines, rather than improves, learning. Local knowledge is immediate and concrete but almost always incomplete and sometimes blind and insular and even seriously wrong (Goldenberg & Gallimore, 1991).

6. *Knowledge that is storable and shareable.* Even public knowledge is gradually lost if there is no means of accumulating and sharing it across space and time. Practitioner knowledge exists in a particular time and place. Its life might be extended briefly if shared locally with a small number of colleagues. But this is not sufficient to create a professional knowledge base. There must be a means of storing knowledge in a form that can be accessed and used by others.

We believe that the only way to construct knowledge with all six features is to create a new R & D system in which both researchers and practitioners participate—a system that departs radically from the current system and an idea already explored by others (Clark, 2001; Gallimore & Stigler, 2003; Hargreaves, 1998; Hiebert et al., 2002; Munby, Russell, & Martin, 2001; National Research Council, 2003; Olson & Bruner, 1996; Richardson, 1994). It should be a system in which practitioners engage in long-term school-based professional development, develop practice knowledge to be validated and verified in collaboration with researchers, and cooperate in fielding researcher-initiated investigations. This might help solve the dual implementation problem: sustaining changes in teaching to conduct research and implementing validated findings into practice.

The multifaceted nature of the system we envision is reasonably viewed with skepticism, given the last 100 years of futile efforts to change teaching and move research findings into the classroom. One reason to be optimistic that such a complex, new national R & D system could develop in the United States is the example of one that has worked well in Japan for many years.

The Japanese System of Lesson Study

Throughout their careers, many Japanese elementary school teachers participate in a continuing in-service program described as *lesson study* (Fernandez, Chokshi, Cannon, & Yoshida, in press; Lewis & Tsuchida, 1997, 1998; Shimahara, 1998; Shimahara & Sakai, 1995; Takemura & Shimizu, 1993; Yoshida, 1999). To conduct lesson studies, groups of teachers meet once a week to collaboratively plan, implement, evaluate, and revise lessons. Many groups focus on only a few lessons over the year, with the aim of perfecting them. They begin by choosing a problem. In some cases, the problem is one identified from a local needs assessment, and in others, it is selected from a list provided by the central education authorities who have surveyed national concerns and issues. The "national" list of problems is distributed to a national network of educators who carry on practice-linked R & D through the method of lesson study.

Once a problem is identified, lesson study groups begin their investigation by reading published sources (by practitioners and researchers), examining student assessment data, and doing other preparatory work. Sometimes university or national agency researchers are invited to provide consultation and assistance. Next, a lesson group commences what is essentially an iterative research (Sechrest & Figueredo, 1993) or design experiment process (Kelly, 2003). Typically, a lesson study group begins by collaboratively designing one or more lessons, trying them out while the others observe, and evaluating what works and what does not. Using embedded assessment data—for example, student misunderstandings and learning progress—the group analyzes what works and does not, and then revises and reteaches the lessons. Then the lessons are revised and taught again. This method of repeated observations across multiple trials may continue for months.

When lessons are determined to "work," they are shared through widely distributed practitioner journals. A lesson study report includes descriptions of the original problem addressed, learning goals, the rationale for the lesson design, descriptions of activities, anticipated responses of students, and suggested responses by the teacher. The reports also include development and assessment data. Lesson study can be characterized as a system for continual, gradual, incremental, and measurable improvement through the method of multiple observation and replication (Stigler & Hiebert, 1999).

The lesson study structure is a dependable way of changing teaching, and it can and does do that in the service of both professional development and research needs. What the United States needs is its own national system of professional development—practitioners creating and sharing practice knowledge to improve their practice that will open up, we believe, new opportunities for educational research that requires the implementation of teaching changes.

Sketching an R & D Model for the United States

The idea that the United States could develop a national R & D system akin to lesson study has been proposed (e.g., Stigler & Hiebert, 1999) and elaborated elsewhere (Gallimore & Stigler, 2003; Hiebert et al., 2002; National Research Council, 2003). Our version of such a system envisions multiple purposes and communities being served, including the practitioners and researchers.

Implications of a New System for Practitioners

The potential of a national system for professional development and knowledge development was recommended by a National Commission chaired by former senator and astronaut John Glenn. To improve the quality of mathematics and science teaching in Grades K through 12, the commission urged that a "dedicated Internet Portal must be available to teachers so *they can make use of and contribute to an ever-expanding knowledge base*" (National Commission on Mathematics and Science Teaching for the 21st Century, 2001, n.p., italics added). A similar proposal was suggested by Al Shanker, a former leader of the American Federation of Teachers:

> With computer technology, we could have some of the best teachers figure out two or three of the best ways of teaching a lesson on the Gettysburg Address. They could offer a lesson plan that they had perfected of questions or examples that they know will work in presenting this topic. These suggestions could be put on a database available to teachers all over the country. (Shanker, 1997, p. 35)

Digital libraries enable teachers to not only learn from, but also contribute to, the knowledge base. The library could store and share practitioner knowledge that is detailed, concrete, and integrated and make it public and subject to verification. In due time, large national, regional, and specialty libraries of validated teaching knowledge could be built. These would serve to both help initiate and sustain a new national PD system.

Video technologies are crucial to the digital library concept. They are vital not only as a means of storing and sharing knowledge but also for the reasons highlighted by the TIMSS Video Study (Hiebert et al., 2003; Stigler & Hiebert, 1999). Emerging technologies now make it feasible to create multimedia digital libraries that include lesson videos, thereby increasing opportunities to observe alternatives to traditional practices that are so ubiquitous that they are taken for granted as the only way to teach.

The new system might also help educators to learn to be more discriminating consumers of research. Through researcher commentaries linked to specific practices being incorporated into video cases in the digital library, practitioners could learn about the principles and methods of scientific research. They would learn to make their knowledge public and develop a taste for validated knowledge and for participating in time-consuming, long-term, and challenging research projects.

Finally, the digital libraries would support and help build a national PD system akin to the Japanese lesson study model. From pre-, to early, to in-service, teachers could access multimedia libraries to observe and analyze multiple examples of content taught in diverse ways. Early programs capitalizing on emerging technologies are now being deployed to support teacher professional development at the local, state, regional, and national levels, and many organizations are building digital libraries of teaching knowledge (Gallimore & Stigler, 2003). Once established, an undergraduate entering the profession would participate in the national system at the beginning and for the rest of his or her teaching career.

Implications of a New System for Researchers

How do digital libraries and a national PD system solve the problems of researchers who must change teaching to successfully field their investigations? In several ways.

The emerging technology-enabled digital libraries provide a medium around and through which the research and practice communities could hold productive discussions to define researchable problems and plan major investigations. Digital libraries of lesson videos would enable shared study of classroom practice, assisting researchers to better link theories with practice, develop research plans more aligned with the National Research Council's (2003) vision of "'use-inspired' research and development," and yield designs with a greater chance of successful implementation.

Teachers accustomed to the production and validation of knowledge for digital libraries would represent an experienced pool of collaborators for researchers fielding ambitious projects. Like the teachers in Japan who change teaching by iterative testing of lessons, participants in a new R & D system would be better prepared, and perhaps more willing, to implement and sustain changes in practice as part of field experiments.

As the new system evolves and enlarges, more credible samples of teacher and schools might become available for experimental and quasi-experimental trials. Certainly, this is preferable to the current situation in which school districts and teachers willing to cooperate in randomized trials are hard to recruit (see many reasons cited by Cook, 2002), potentially creating self-selection biases and raising doubts about the "randomness" of volunteer samples. Having a large number of practitioners and districts routinely engaged in R & D, as is the case in Japan, is probably better than relying on recruiting reluctant volunteers. Once a new national system begins to develop, and teachers begin to regularly participate in iterative improvement efforts, the chances of fielding randomized or quasi-experimental trials ought to increase.

A national system would facilitate developmental work prior to the conduct of a field trial. This could temper the concern that the NCLB's emphasis on scientific research will crowd out support for iterative or design experiments needed to develop innovations to the point worthy of randomized trials (Kelly, 2003). It would also broaden participation in pilot studies prior to fielding a randomized trial, thereby allowing investigators in advance to identify contextual variations that might dilute an experimental intervention. Internet and video technologies offer researchers cost-effective ways to develop and refine robust, field-tested interventions. For example, clinical trials could be fielded nationally at lesser cost, and yet identical training using video could be provided to all participants through the Internet. The same system could support formative evaluations of field trials, by providing a means of collecting, sharing, and evaluating implementations of experimental treatments.

Another opportunity enabled by the R & D system sketched here is the addition of a powerful scientific methodology for validating promising practices: the process of multiple observation and replication that individual teachers have always used to learn to teach—by observing their own practice and revising it on the basis of students' feedback and progress (Hiebert et al., 2002). This process includes

- differentiating problems and developing a shared language for describing them;
- analyzing classroom practice in light of differentiated problems;
- envisioning alternative solutions; and
- recursively testing alternatives in the classroom, reflecting on their effects, and refining and reteaching until satisfied with the consequences.

This is essentially the same approach used by the U.S. agricultural extension system to aggregate annual crop results for review, indexing, and sharing with farmers seeking to improve yields. Such tests, conducted every year during the past century, helped create a highly productive system (Wilson & Daviss, 1994) that has the evidence-based qualities that the NCLB intends to secure for education (Whitehurst, 2002b).

With groups of practitioners around the nation working collaboratively to improve instruction in incremental ways, and with access to digital libraries of knowledge, another mechanism for bridging the research-to-practice gap would be available. And it would be one in which researchers could have a continuing role, beyond the publication of their findings. Indeed, when practitioners encounter implementation problems, the digital library will create a means by which video case examples of such problems can be deposited for joint analysis, discussion, and possible resolution by the two communities. As the libraries grow, they will also become vehicles for the dissemination of evidence-based practices, and a powerful tool for pre- and in-service teacher development.

Finally, the knowledge that makes it into the libraries needs to be rigorously evaluated, field tested, and sifted to provide a basis for the standards of practice that distinguish a profession (Yinger, 1999). It is essential that randomized trials become more frequently fielded to settle critical and nettlesome questions and that evidence based on multiple, rigorous methods—including those of practitioners as well as researchers—play an appropriate and prominent role. To achieve that end, however, will require overcoming a long tradition of disinterest and resistance to school-based research and, in particular, randomized trials (Cook, 2002). Changing this circumstance might be one of the benefits to follow from practitioner and researcher collaboration around the national digital libraries envisioned by the Glenn Commission. As the discussions proceed over the coming decades, the value of scientific studies may become more apparent to the public, policymakers, and practitioners.

Achieving Consensus Standards and Validating Educational Practices

Given the history of education, achieving consensus is no trivial matter, even when a minimally adequate evidence base begins to develop. There is a tradition in teaching that lesson and instructional planning is an individual creative act, and there is a history of resistance to standard practices. One goal of a national R & D system is an expansion of teachers' creative expression to the discovery and development of improved instruction through a "lesson study"-like process. Teacher creativity, in this new system, would be expressed in public contributions to the digital libraries of professional knowledge, not solely in unshared daily lessons.

We should not underestimate the difficulty of securing this shift. Al Shanker (1997) also addressed this issue in response to critics of practice standards.

> Doctors don't try to figure out a new technique or procedure for every patient who comes to their office, they begin by using standard techniques and procedures that are based on the experience of many doctors over the years. Nobody considers this a way of doctor-proofing medicine, although they have a name for the failure to use standard practices—it's *malpractice*. The standard practices that all doctors (and other professionals) use contain the wisdom of the profession. The same could come to be true of a national

database of lessons that have been polished and perfected by the most skillful members of the teaching profession. (p. 36)

There is at present no widely accepted structure or organization supporting analyses and discussions for reaching a consensus standards of practice. The hope is that mechanisms created as a result of the NCLB will emerge to fill this role (e.g., What Works Clearinghouse, http://www.w-w-c.org/), but that effort is in its infancy and is presently focused on vetting and posting research knowledge. It, or a structure like it, will be necessary for such a system, however.

Whatever evolves in the future, we suggest that technology-enabled digital libraries will not only facilitate collaboration between research and practice communities, as well as the work of such institutions as the What Works Clearinghouse, but also assist in the emergence of consensus on effective practices. Instructional approaches for which assessment-based effectiveness is well documented and verifiable, along with relevant assessment data, could be included as part of submissions to the digital libraries.

Final Thoughts

The proposal to create a national R & D system in which the work of practitioners contributes to the evidence base of education echoes a bit of 20th-century history.

> John Dewey and his laboratory school colleagues were planting the seeds of a school-based, teacher-engaged system of building professional knowledge. . . . Edward Thorndike had been developing a science of behavior . . . that ushered in a new era in educational knowledge building . . . knowledge often represented in forms that are relatively abstract . . . that cannot be easily reintegrated with interacting features of classrooms. . . . [This] approach to improvement meant the emergence of two professional communities. . . . Professional knowledge building became the province of researchers; applying the knowledge was left to the practitioners. . . .
>
> In our view, it is a mistake to interpret Thorndike's victory as one of scientific approaches over non-scientific approaches. . . . A more appropriate reading . . . is that Thorndike and colleagues successfully promoted some scientific methods over others. . . . Experimental, comparative methods . . . are not the only [ones] that yield dependable, trustworthy knowledge. Observation and replication across multiple trials can produce equally rigorous tests of quality and can, over time, produce dependable knowledge as well. (Hiebert et al., 2002, pp. 11–12)

The critics of the NCLB initiative see no sign that practitioners will be invited to play the kind of role envisioned in this chapter. Some fear that because "Edward L. Thorndike won and John Dewey lost" in the 20th century (Lagemann, 1989, p. 185), it will happen again. We, however, are cautiously optimistic that the sheer necessity of practitioners' participation in evidence building will lead the United States to a different choice in the 21st century—

one that capitalizes on new technologies to blend the methods of practitioners and researchers to achieve the goal of an evidence-based education.

References

Anderson, D. S., & Biddle, B. J. (Eds.). (1991). *Knowledge for policy: Improving education through research.* London: Falmer.

Berliner, D. C. (2002). Educational research: The hardest science of all. *Educational Researcher, 31*(8), 18–20.

Berliner, D. C., & Casanova, U. (1993). *Putting research to work in your school.* New York: Scholastic.

Berman, P., & McLaughlin, M. W. (1978). *Federal programs supporting educational change: Vol. 8. Implementing and sustaining innovations.* Santa Monica, CA: Rand Corporation.

Cazden, C. B. (1988). *Classroom discourse: The language of teaching and learning.* Portsmouth, NH: Heinemann.

Clark, C. M. (Ed.). (2001). *Talking shop: Authentic conversation and teacher learning.* New York: Teachers College Press.

Cochran-Smith, M., & Lytle, S. L. (Eds.). (1993). *Inside/outside: Teacher research and knowledge.* New York: Teachers College Press.

Cook, T. D. (2002). Randomized experiments in educational policy research: A critical examination of the reasons the educational evaluation community has offered for not doing them. *Educational Evaluation and Policy Analysis, 24,* 175–199.

Cuban, L. (1990). Reforming again, again, and again. *Educational Researcher, 19*(1), 3–13.

Doyle, W. (1997). Heard any really good stories lately? A critique of the critics of narrative in educational research. *Teaching and Teacher Education, 13,* 93–99.

Eisner, E. W. (1995). Preparing teachers for schools of the 21st century. *Peabody Journal of Education, 70*(3), 99–111.

Erickson, F., & Gutierrez, K. (2002). Culture, rigor, and science in educational research. *Educational Researcher, 31*(8), 21–24.

Feiman-Nemser, S., & Floden, R. (1986). The cultures of teaching. In M. Wittrock (Ed.), *Handbook of research on teaching* (3rd ed., pp. 505–526). New York: Macmillan.

Fernandez, C., Chokshi, S., Cannon, J., & Yoshida, M. (in press). Learning about lesson study in the United States. In M. Beauchamp (Ed.), *New and old voices on Japanese education.* Armonk, NY: M. E. Sharpe.

Feuer, M. J., Towne, L., & Shavelson, R. J. (2002). Scientific culture and educational research. *Educational Researcher, 31*(8), 4–14.

Figueredo, A. J., & Sechrest, L. B. (2001). Approaches used in conducting health outcomes and effectiveness research. *Evaluation and Program Planning, 25,* 41–59.

Fullan, M. (1991). *The new meaning of educational change.* New York: Teachers College Press.

Fullan, M. (1993). *Change forces.* London: Falmer.

Gallimore, R., & Stigler, J. (2003). Closing the teaching gap: Assisting teachers adapt to changing standards and assessments. In C. Richardson (Ed.), *Whither assessment* (pp. 25–36). London: Qualifications and Curriculum Authority.

Garet, M. S., Porter, A. C., Desimone, L., Birman, B. F., & Yoon, K. S. (2001). What makes professional development effective? Results from a national sample of teachers. *American Educational Research Journal, 38,* 915–945.

Goldenberg, C. N. (2004). *Settings for educational change: Achieving successful school improvement.* New York: Teachers College Press.

Goldenberg, C. N., & Gallimore, R. (1991). Local knowledge, research knowledge, and educational change: A case study of early Spanish reading improvement. *Educational Researcher, 20*(8), 2–14.

Hargreaves, D. H. (1998, August). *The knowledge-creating school.* Paper presented at the annual meeting of the British Educational Research Association, Belfast, Northern Ireland.

Hiebert, J., Gallimore, R., Garnier, H., Givvin, K. B., Hollingsworth, H., Jacobs, J., et al. (2003). *Teaching mathematics in seven countries: Results from the TIMSS 1999 Video Study* (NCES 2003-013). Washington, DC: U.S. Department of Education, National Center for Education Statistics.

Hiebert, J., Gallimore, R., & Stigler, J. W. (2002). A knowledge base for the teaching profession: What would it look like and how can we get one? *Educational Researcher, 31*(5), 3–15.

Hoetker, J., & Ahlbrand, W. (1969). The persistence of recitation. *American Educational Research Journal, 6,* 145–167.

Huberman, M. (1985). What knowledge is of most worth to teachers? A knowledge-use perspective. *Teaching and Teacher Education, 1,* 251–262.

Joyce, B., Wolf, J., & Calhoun, E. (1993). *The self-renewing school.* Alexandria, VA: Association for Supervision and Curriculum Development.

Kelly, A. E. (2003). Research as design. *Educational Researcher, 32*(1), 3–4.

Kennedy, M. (1999). Ed schools and the problem of knowledge. In J. D. Raths & A. C. McAninch (Eds.), *Advances in teacher education: Vol. 5. What counts as knowledge in teacher education?* (pp. 29–45). Stamford, CT: Ablex.

Lagemann, E. C. (1989). The plural worlds of educational research. *History of Education Quarterly, 29,* 185–214.

Leinhardt, G. (1990). Capturing craft knowledge in teaching. *Educational Researcher, 19*(2), 18–25.

Lewis, C., & Tsuchida, I. (1997). Planned educational change in Japan: The shift to student-centered elementary science. *Journal of Educational Policy, 12,* 313–331.

Lewis, C., & Tsuchida, I. (1998). A lesson is like a swiftly flowing river. *American Educator, 22*(4), 12–17, 50–52.

Little, J., & McLaughlin, M. (Eds.). (1993). *Teachers' work: Individuals, colleagues, and contexts.* New York: Teachers College.

Ma, L. (1999). *Knowing and teaching elementary mathematics: Teachers' understanding of fundamental mathematics in China and the United States.* Mahwah, NJ: Erlbaum.

Munby, M., Russell, T., & Martin, A. K. (2001). Teachers' knowledge and how it develops. In V. Richardson (Ed.), *Handbook of research on teaching* (4th ed., pp. 877–904). Washington, DC: American Educational Research Association.

National Commission on Mathematics and Science Teaching for the 21st Century. (2000). *Before it's too late: A report to the nation from the National Commission on Mathematics and Science Teaching in the 21st Century.* Washington, DC: U.S. Department of Education. Retrieved November 3, 2005, from http://www.ed.gov/americacounts/glenn/

National Education Research Policy and Priorities Board. (1999). *Investing in learning: A policy statement with recommendations on research in education by the National Educational Research Policy and Priorities Board.* Washington, DC: U.S. Department of Education.

National Research Council, Committee on a Feasibility Study for a Strategic Education Research Program. (1999). *Improving student learning: A strategic plan for education research and its utilization.* Washington, DC: National Academy Press.

National Research Council, Committee on Scientific Principles for Educational Research. (2002). *Scientific research in education.* Washington, DC: National Academy Press.

National Research Council, Committee on Strategic Education Research Partnership. (2003). *Strategic education research partnership.* Washington, DC: National Academy Press.

National Staff Development Council. (2001). *NSDC standards for staff development.* Oxford, OH: National Staff Development Council.

No Child Left Behind Act of 2001, Pub. L. No. 107–110, 107th Congress. Retrieved November 3, 2005, from http://www.ed.gov/legislation/ESEA02/

Olson, D. R., & Bruner, J. S. (1996). Folk psychology and folk pedagogy. In D. R. Olson & N. Torrance (Eds.), *Handbook of education and human development: New models of learning, teaching, and schooling* (pp. 9–27). Cambridge, MA: Blackwell.

Rice, J. M. (1893). *The public school system of the United States.* New York: Century.

Richardson, V. (1994). Conducting research on practice. *Educational Researcher, 23*(5), 5–10.

Rosenshine, B. (1986). Synthesis of research on explicit teaching. *Educational Leadership, 43,* 60–69.

Sarason, S. (1971). *The culture of the school and the problem of change.* Boston: Allyn & Bacon.

Sechrest, L. B., & Figueredo, A. J. (1993). Program evaluation. *Annual Review of Psychology, 44,* 645–674.

Sechrest, L. B., West, S. G., Phillips, M. A., Redner, R., & Yeaton, W. (1979). Some neglected problems in evaluation research: Strength and integrity of treatments. In L. B. Sechrest (Ed.), *Evaluation studies review annual* (Vol. 4., pp. 15–35). Beverly Hills, CA: Sage.

Shanker, A. (1997). A national database of lessons. *American Educator, 21*(1 & 2), 35–36.

Shimahara, N. K. (1998). The Japanese model of professional development: Teaching as craft. *Teaching and Teacher Education, 14,* 451–462.

Shimahara, N. K., & Sakai, A. (1995). *Learning to teach in two cultures: Japan and the United States.* New York: Garland.

Stein, M. K., & Lane, S. (1996). Instructional tasks and the development of student capacity to think and reason: An analysis of the relationship between teaching and learning in a reform mathematics project. *Educational Research and Evaluation, 2*(1), 50–80.

Stevens, R. (1912). Stenographic reports of high school lessons. *Teachers College Record, 11,* 1–66.

Stigler, J. W., & Hiebert, J. (1999). *The teaching gap: Best ideas from the world's teachers for improving education in the classroom.* New York: Free Press.

Takemura, S., & Shimizu, K. (1993). Goals and strategies for science teaching as perceived by elementary teachers in Japan and the United States. *Peabody Journal of Education, 68*(4), 23–33.

Tharp, R. G. (1982). The effective instruction of comprehension: Results and description of the Kamehameha Early Education Program. *Reading Research Quarterly, 17,* 503–527.

Tharp, R. G., & Gallimore, R. (1979). The ecology of program research and evaluation: A model of evaluation succession. In L. Sechrest, S. G. West, M. A. Phillips, R. Redner, & W. Yeaton (Eds.), *Evaluation studies review annual* (No. 4., pp. 39–60). Beverly Hills, CA: Sage.

Tharp, R. G., & Gallimore, R. (1989). *Rousing minds to life: Teaching, learning, and schooling in social context.* Cambridge, England: Cambridge University Press.

U.S. Department of Education. (1987). *What works: Research about teaching and learning* (2nd ed.). Washington, DC: U.S. Government Printing Office.

Wagner, T. (1994). *How schools change.* Boston: Beacon.

Whitehurst, G. J. (2002a, October). *Evidence-based education.* Paper presented at the Office of Elementary and Secondary Education's Student Achievement and School Accountability Conference, Washington, DC. Retrieved November 8, 2005, from http://www.ed.gov/offices/OERI/presentations/evidencebase.html

Whitehurst, G. J. (2002b, June). *The reauthorization of the Office of Educational Research and Improvement.* Retrieved November 8, 2005, from http://edworkforce.house.gov/hearings/107th/edr/oeri22802/whitehurst.htm

Whitehurst, G. J. (2002c, March). *Research on teacher preparation and professional development.* Paper presented at the White House Conference on Preparing Tomorrow's Teachers, Washington, DC. Retrieved November 8, 2005, from http://www.ed.gov/admins/tchrqual/learn/preparingteachersconference/whitehurst.html

Willinsky, J. (2001). The strategic educational research program and the public value of research. *Educational Researcher, 30*(1), 5–14.

Wilson, K. G., & Daviss, B. (1994). *Redesigning education.* New York: Holt.

Yinger, R. (1999). The role of standards in teaching and teacher education. In G. Griffin (Ed.), *The education of teachers: Ninety-eighth yearbook of the National Society for the Study of Education* (pp. 85–113). Chicago: University of Chicago Press.

Yoshida, M. (1999). *Lesson study: An ethnographic investigation of school-based teacher development in Japan.* Unpublished doctoral dissertation, University of Chicago.

2

Heroic Rescue During the Holocaust: Empirical and Methodological Perspectives

Elizabeth Midlarsky, Stephanie Fagin Jones,
and Robin K. Nemeroff

Benevolence is one of the pillars on which the world rests.

—Talmud

One of the most extraordinary forms of altruistic behavior in the 20th century was the heroic rescue of Jews performed by non-Jewish individuals living in Nazi-occupied Europe during World War II. The goal of this chapter is to describe research on these heroic rescuers—research for which the foundation was laid when the first author, Elizabeth Midlarsky, was a student of Lee Sechrest at Northwestern University.

The decision to pursue a PhD in clinical psychology at Northwestern University came from the desire to obtain the skill needed to provide competent professional help and to pursue knowledge on altruism and helping behavior. One of the most exciting and rewarding features of clinical PhD studies with Lee Sechrest was that there were no restrictions on the topics of inquiry. The primary "rules" were, first, that research was to be derived from a profound knowledge of the existing literature and that it was to be conducted systematically and with the utmost of rigor. Second, research was to proceed thoughtfully, remaining alert to possible sources of reactivity and to information in addition to that available through interviews and questionnaires. Most important, there was an expectation that methodological expertise be used in the service of one's creative capacities as a behavioral scientist.

In this milieu, a research program on altruism was launched. Over the years, this research has encompassed laboratory and field experiments on altruism and helping in children, adolescents, and older adults. The project described in this chapter, sponsored by the National Institutes of Health, was designed to investigate the personalities, current helping behavior, and subjective well-being of men and women who engaged in altruistic behavior during the Holocaust. Elizabeth Midlarsky was principal investigator on the project, and the two coauthors, Stephanie Fagin Jones and Robin Nemeroff, both began their extensive work on the data when they were clinical doctoral students of Midlarsky at Columbia University, and thus are second-generation Sechrest students.

Overview of the Rescuers Project

Genocide, mass murder, and persecution of populations with a specific ethnore-ligious identity have plagued the world, even into the 21st century (M. Midlarsky, 2005). Perhaps the most extensive genocide of the 20th century was the Holocaust. The cruelty and indifference that marked the behavior of the European population during World War II provide stunning challenges to the belief that humans have moral courage or the capacity for compassion. Even during the darkest period, however, a handful of non-Jews risked their lives to save Jews from annihilation. Rescue was far from a ubiquitous phenomenon. The highest estimate, of 1 million rescuers, represents less than one half of 1% of the total population under Nazi occupation (Oliner & Oliner, 1988). Nevertheless, the fact that rescue behavior did occur is as real as are the ovens of Auschwitz and therefore requires investigation.

Of course, the literature on rescue during the Holocaust provides sharp reminders that many rescues were not motivated by altruism (Huneke, 1981/1982; Oliner, 1984; Tec, 1986). Particularly in reading Huneke's analysis of archival data, one finds that even among those who were rescuers of the 200,000 Jews saved from the gas chambers, there were many quid pro quo rescues, typically motivated by the desire to fill one's coffers with the possessions of the victim. Among the remaining rescuers, there were those who helped as a means to some other end—for example, to harm the Nazis. The altruistic rescuers ranged widely in backgrounds and in the nature of their actions—from Raoul Wallenberg, member of an aristocratic Swedish family, who saved thousands of Jews from the death trains leaving Budapest (Bierman, 1981), to the Albanian clerk who rescued his Jewish employers (Paldiel, 2000), to the Ukrainian peasant woman who sheltered her neighbor (Eisenberg, 1982). The rescuers studied here are those for whom the rescue of Jews was reportedly an end in itself rather than a means to an end. They are people, many of whom appear "ordinary" rather than like mythical heroic figures (Fogelman, 1994). Nevertheless, their actions demonstrated the maintenance of standards of generosity under extreme stress.

This chapter is organized as follows. In the next section, we present methodological considerations. In the subsequent two sections, we present the results of two sets of analyses of the data, conducted to address hypotheses regarding (a) the current helpfulness and well-being of the aged Holocaust rescuers and (b) the current levels of proactive and altruistic personality traits of rescuers in comparison with bystanders and with prewar immigrants from Europe. In the final section, we discuss the implications of this work.

Methodology

Multifactor and, in some instances, multisource data (Webb, Campbell, Schwartz, Sechrest, & Grove, 1981) were systematically collected on the characteristics, historical and current helping behavior, and subjective well-being of Holocaust heroes, who helped in extremely high-risk situations. The study aimed to collect the rich and in-depth data yielded by qualitative interview procedures. However, in contrast to the preponderance of existing studies, which have relied on qualitative approaches, we included instruments with the best available psychometric properties and used statistical analyses.

We were, of course, keenly aware of the limitations in research design options for a study of this kind. It is not possible to use an experimental, quasi-experimental, or prospective study regarding events occurring well over 50 years ago (as in randomized controlled trials or observational cohort studies). Because of the centrality of an historical event (heroic rescue), combined with the lack of random assignment to conditions, the methodology is best characterized as retrospective, also known as case-control methodology. In case-control studies, people are assigned to groups on the basis of the presence (cases) or absence (controls) of some behavior or event (Horwitz & Feinstein, 1979; Lacy, 1997).

We hoped to guard against sources of bias inherent in studies of this general type, to the extent possible. First, to minimize bias in recalling whether and to what extent one was a rescuer, we relied on the identification of rescuers in accordance with detailed information provided by rescued survivors and, in many instances, also by archival data and accounts by eyewitnesses. Second, when inquiring about historical events, we asked specific, behaviorally anchored questions, which tend to be less subject to distortion than open-ended narratives, recollections about moods, and impressionistic accounts. For example, instead of asking, "Did you feel that _____ cared about the Jews whom she sheltered, and helped them wholeheartedly?" or "Tell me about the ways in which she showed that she cared for you," we asked a series of questions with Likert-like response formats, such as "How many times in a given week did _____ smile at you?" "How often did _____ say that you were eating too much of the food in the household?" and "How often did she ask, or in some other way act concerned, about your comfort and sense of security?"

Third, to make causal statements regarding, for example, the relationships between heroic efforts in the past, on the one hand, and helping and well-being, on the other, it is necessary to first establish the order of occurrence. In this instance, the establishment of temporal precedence was not a problem. However, we were cautious about drawing causal inferences regarding antecedents of the original heroism, precisely because of the problem of temporal sequence. Fourth, in studies of this kind, it is critical that clear standards for group membership be developed and used. Thus, the group of rescuers was, first of all, restricted to non-Jews who helped Jews, even though Jewish people also engaged in heroic rescue (e.g., Arieti, 1979; Kranzler, 1987; Moszkiewicz, 1987; Tec, 1993). Jews were doomed to annihilation whether or not they helped, whereas most of the non-Jewish rescuers could have avoided the risk of being murdered if they had simply avoided helping Jews. Therefore, although many Jewish rescuers may have acted on the basis of altruistic motives, fundamental differences in other motives, values, and anticipated consequences argue for studying them separately rather than as part of the group of rescuers studied here.

In addition to restricting the sample of rescuers to non-Jews, the rescuers consisted solely of those for whom there was verifiable evidence of the rescue and whose altruistic behaviors met the criteria for altruistically motivated heroism. (See Sample section, upcoming.) For each rescuer or group of rescuers, the contrast groups included verified nonrescuers—bystanders and immigrant "controls." (See Sample section.) The bystanders were similar to the rescuers in many respects and had very similar opportunities to help Jews. The inclusion of prewar immigrants to the United States and Canada permitted comparisons with a group that (a) had no exposure to the slaughter of Jews during World War II or opportunities to help persecuted Jews, but that (b) came from similar backgrounds and were currently living in a similar cultural milieu.

Thus, the research design allowed for consideration of both rescuers and nonrescuers on a comparative basis, a requirement often overlooked in naturalistic studies of altruism in general and of Holocaust heroes in particular. To explore the current helpfulness, well-being, and personalities of the rescuers, we asked participants to respond to an extensive interview that recorded both quantitative and qualitative data.

SAMPLE. The sample consisted of a total of 210 non-Jewish people who had lived in Europe earlier in their lives. In contrast to other studies of Holocaust rescue (Fogelman, 1994; Oliner & Oliner, 1988; Tec, 1993), the sample was not selected from people currently residing in Europe. Instead, it included 80 rescuers, 73 bystanders, and 57 people who left Europe before the onset of World War II, all of whom migrated to the United States or Canada between 1937 and 1950. The primary reason for studying people who are long-term residents of the United States and Canada was that we could use measures that had been used in other studies of altruism. When one administers measures that were developed for use in one group to an entirely different group, for whom the meaning may be different, questions are raised about validity and reliability. The scales that were used in this study have been found to be reliable when used with older adults, many of whom emigrated from Europe earlier in their lives (E. Midlarsky & Kahana, 1994; E. Midlarsky, Kahana, Corley, Schonbar, & Nemeroff, 1999). Thus, it was appropriate to choose a sample whose history is similar in this regard.

A second decision was to eschew the selection of rescuers who were known to Yad Vashem, the Holocaust Martyrs and Heroes' Remembrance Society and the authority in Israel for commemorating the Holocaust. The first author, Midlarsky, did begin her search for rescuers by traveling to Israel, where, with the gracious help of Mordecai Paldiel, she spent 2 weeks exploring the Yad Vashem archives and supplementing her own list of survivors and other informants. However, the rescuers who were rostered at Yad Vashem had been previously interviewed and, in most cases, honored in ways likely to evoke problems of reactivity.

The ability to locate respondents was enhanced by the fact that Midlarsky had devoted many years to clinical work with Holocaust survivors and their families, worked with the Oliners on their Altruistic Personality project, attended survivor meetings, and was an active participant in planning for and working with the Holocaust Memorial Center in West Bloomfield, Michigan. After the years of work with survivors and their families, many were ready to indicate rescuers (as well as bystanders) and to recount the details of their rescue efforts. In addition to giving verbal accounts, numerous survivors had kept diaries, letters, and other documentation from the period before, during, and after the war, which supported their recollections. As a professor in a Jesuit university, Midlarsky also had ready access to clerical and lay informants who willingly provided information about wartime activities by first-generation immigrants from countries such as Poland, Italy, Holland, Romania, Denmark, Germany, Lithuania, Hungary, and the former Soviet Union (principally the Ukraine).

As a result of these efforts, we discovered a total of 115 heroic rescuers in the United States and Canada, all of whom met the Yad Vashem inclusion criteria as altruists. These were people who intentionally helped one or more Jews at great risk to themselves and with no extrinsic reward. Of the 115 rescuers, 85 were discovered and verified by the research team for the first time and had never been interviewed or honored for their wartime activities. Five were unavailable because of extreme ill health, or they had died prior to a scheduled interview. All of the 80 who were available and met the study criteria participated in the project (100%).

Seventy-three bystanders were interviewed. Bystanders consisted of people who lived in Nazi-occupied Europe during the war, were not perpetrators, and did not participate in the rescue of Jews. The bystanders were randomly selected from lists of people who lived in the same geographic areas as the rescuers during the war—they were typically the rescuers' next-door neighbors in Europe. Following the war, they migrated and were now living in the same communities as the rescuers—once again, often as next-door neighbors. Many had the same parish priest in both places. Rescued survivors and their families were able to provide names of bystanders in some cases and, in others, verified names provided by other people (particularly by the priests). These survivor families recalled the bystanders as people who were not perpetrators or known informers and who "stayed out" of rescue activities. The bystanders interviewed here are people who reported that they offered no help even when they were asked for help (see Varese & Yaish, 2000).

A third group, included in some of the analyses, consisted of the prewar immigrants. These people were similar in demographic characteristics and were drawn from the same countries of origin and religious groups. They were similar in age to the rescuers and bystanders and were residing in the same geographic areas in both Europe and the Western hemisphere, as were the other two groups. They came to the United States or Canada prior to the onset of the war, between 1937 and 1939. Sixty such people were randomly selected to be part of the group of immigrants. Of the 60 selected, all agreed to be interviewed, and complete data were obtained for 57 people (95%).

We are aware of certain limitations on the sample for this study. We did not have a representative random sample of men and women who lived in Nazi-occupied Europe. However, a study of rescue during the Holocaust is a study of rare events, not readily identified in a random sample of an entire population. (Nor were we able to randomly assign people to "rescuer" and "bystander" groups, in the experimental tradition!) Our exclusion of officially recognized rescuers may have led to the omission of some of the most noble, or of those who rescued extraordinarily large numbers of people. Many of the more daring may have perished during the war. Also, the decision to study only those who migrated from their country of origin limited the generalizability of the findings. Hence our findings should be interpreted with reference to appropriate caveats reflecting these and other possible limitations on reliability and generalizability.

PROCEDURE. All of the data, including responses to scales and tests, were collected from the study respondents by means of face-to-face interviews. Whereas most of the scales were originally designed as self-report paper-and-pencil measures, interview administration has become standard in research on older adults (Kane & Kane, 2000). Interviews were conducted in the respondents' own homes and ranged from 1 to 3 hours for the immigrants to 3 to 5 hours for the bystanders and 4 to 7 hours for the rescuers. All of the measures used here have been used in prior research on altruism in late life and have been found to have good psychometric properties (E. Midlarsky & Kahana, 1994). In the very few cases (less than 10%) wherein help with language was needed, a translator was present.

Part 1 of the interview was administered to all of the study respondents. This part focused on the present, with questions about current demographics, perceived opportunities to help, personality variables, current helping, and well-being. Part 2 inquired about events and experiences during the prewar, wartime, and postwar periods and was administered to the rescuers and bystanders. Questions about the prewar period, but not about the wartime and postwar periods, were administered to the immigrant group. Responses were checked against written and oral testimony by others and written records from the periods under investigation (letters, diaries, and school records). Part 3 was administered to the rescuers alone. It included inquiries about the wartime rescue: the nature and degree of the help, the meaning of helping to the helper, and perceived consequences of the rescue. Once again, quantitative data and narratives were cross-checked, for consistency, against other sources. Further details of the study procedures can be found in the article by E. Midlarsky, Fagin Jones, and Corley (2005).

Current Helping and Well-Being Among Older Adult Holocaust Rescuers

Do heroic actions earlier in one's life predict behavior and well-being in older adulthood? An important aim of this study was to investigate whether historic helping would be related to current helping and to successful adaptation during later life. A central thesis is that adaptation is based not only on reactions to life events but also on one's own actions, including the actions undertaken earlier in life. Indeed, for some, the later years may be a period in which the focus is on the meaning of one's life and during which one emphasizes not just what one is, or is experiencing, but what one has been and done (Butler, Lewis, & Sunderland, 1990; E. Midlarsky & Kahana, 1994; Piliavin, 2003; Van Willigen, 2000). We expected that historic helping would predict current helping rather than serving as a nonrecurring response to an extreme situation. We predicted that, in contrast to the bystanders, the Holocaust rescuers would be more likely to perceive opportunities to help others, would have more positive recollections about their past actions, would be helping more, and would have a higher degree of well-being.

Perceived Opportunities to Help

Overall, the rescuers perceived significantly more opportunities to be of service to others than did the bystanders, $t(151) = 3.25, p < .001$. In response to a series of closed- and open-ended questions about needs for help in the community and among neighbors and friends, the Holocaust rescuers indicated awareness of many opportunities to help in response to the needs of others, $\chi^2(4, N = 153) = 17.72, p < .01$.

Current Helping

In general, as predicted, Holocaust-era rescuers are still engaged in more altruistic behavior than the bystanders over half a century after the end of World War II. In brief, the findings on current helping are as follows:

1. Rescuers reported that they gave greater amounts of help than did the bystanders on all measures of helping. For example, rescuers reported more helping than the bystanders on the Altruistic Scale for the Elderly (ASE; Kahana et al., 1998). Indeed, they reported a higher frequency of helping on every item on the scale, with differences found even on ordinarily infrequent helping behaviors, such as blood donation. When the behavioral rating scale version of this measure was given to observers and help recipients, the rescuers were rated as giving more help than the bystanders ($p < .001$ in every analysis).

2. The preponderance of rescuers (72%) reported current involvement in volunteer work, in contrast to 41% of the bystanders ($p < .001$). This greater involvement in volunteer work occurred despite the fact that, on average, the rescuers are 4 years older than the bystanders.

3. Anecdotal data from the interviewers indicate that the rescuers treated them kindly and generously, offering to give as much time and effort to the project as needed (despite obvious emotional pain in many instances). The rescuers were generally solicitous and hospitable, often offering refreshments and meals to the researchers during the lengthy interviews. Many of the bystanders, however, persistently requested money in exchange for the time and effort they expended, despite being told that no funds were budgeted for payments to participants. Most bystanders attempted to terminate interviews

Table 2.1. Predictors of Current Helping Among Holocaust Rescuers
and Bystanders

Variable	β	$t(151)$	p
Historic rescue	.35	5.57	.001
Perceived opportunity	.29	3.17	.01
Risk taking	.16	2.12	.05
Intrinsic religious motivation	.15	2.06	.05
Altruistic moral judgment	.15	2.03	.05
Authoritarianism	−.14	−1.99	.05

Note. $R^2 = .63$

until the project personnel acceded to requests to treat them to expensive
restaurant meals or to give them gifts.

4. We also checked to see which people had signed the agreement to donate
their organs upon their death. Of the rescuers, 44% had signed the organ
donation card, in contrast to 12.4% of the bystanders ($p < .001$).

Predictors of Current Helping

The results of a multiple regression analysis of the predictors of current helping
appear in Table 2.1. The best predictor of current helping was past helping,
followed by perceived opportunity. (It is interesting that, in other studies, such
as E. Midlarsky & Oliner, 1985, we found that the best predictor of perceived
opportunity to help is altruistic motivation, indicating that those predisposed
to help others are acutely aware of helping opportunities.) Other significant
predictors of current helping were intrinsic religious motivation, altruistic
moral judgment, and risk taking, with an inverse relationship found between
helping and authoritarianism–intolerance for others.

Predictors of Current Well-Being

In general, the rescuers were currently more satisfied with life than were the
bystanders. Thus, more rescuers than bystanders agreed that they are just as
happy as when they were younger ($p < .01$), and they have more positive
feelings about their reminiscences than do the bystanders.

We then tested hypotheses about the predictors of several aspects of well-
being. We were particularly interested in congruence, measured by means of
the Congruence subscale of the Life Satisfaction Index, a reputable measure
of well-being among older adults (Neugarten, Havighurst, & Tobin, 1961).
Congruence refers to the sense of "rightness" or the correspondence between
desired and achieved goals. It tends to be associated with a sense of deep inner
contentment rather than a more fleeting mood or affect (George, 1994).

In this study, the rescuers were higher in congruence than were the bystanders. As presented in Table 2.2, among the strongest predictors of congruence were involvement in historic rescue and two personality variables associ-

Table 2.2. Predictors of Congruence Among Holocaust Rescuers and Bystanders

Variable	β	$t(151)$	p
Historic rescue	.27	2.30	.05
Altruistic orientation	.38	2.69	.01
Altruistic moral judgment	.20	2.56	.01
Education	.15	2.18	.05
Autonomy	−.18	−1.92	.05
Internal locus of control	−.15	1.94	.05

Note. $R^2 = .59$

ated with altruistic behavior—altruistic orientation (E. Midlarsky & Kahana, 1994; Kahana et al., 1998) and altruistic moral judgment (E. Midlarsky et al., 1999).

In comparison with the bystanders, more rescuers agreed than disagreed that they feel satisfied when they look back on their lives ($p < .001$). The rescuers were more likely than were the bystanders to agree that they would not change the past if they could ($p < .0001$) and that they have pretty much gotten what they expect from life ($p < .0001$)

Heroic Rescue and the Altruistic Personality

In the context of human social behavior, the altruism exhibited by the Holocaust rescuers is difficult to comprehend. In the prevailing economic models of human behavior, such as rational choice theory (see Piliavin & Charng, 1990), high cost to the helper leads to a lower probability of helping (Schroeder, Penner, Dovidio, & Piliavin, 1995). In the context of World War II, when the preponderance of Europeans was constrained to obey a tyrannical authority (Milgram, 1974), how can one explain the behavior of rescuers who flouted authority and, in so doing, risked their lives and the lives of their loved ones? Specifically, are the Holocaust rescuers, whose altruistic behavior differentiated them from the preponderance of the Nazi-era European population, also different in regard to their personalities? Can these non-Jewish rescuers, identified as generous, risk-taking heroes by rescued survivors, be identified on the basis of measured personality traits?

Many scholars have expressed great interest in the altruistic personality. Within the field of psychology, this topic has been dominated by experimental studies in which relatively low-risk, low-cost altruistic behaviors or small acts of kindness have been studied (Dovidio, Allen, & Schroeder, 1990; Miller & Eisenberg, 1996), or the topic has involved potential helping in a hypothetical situation (Cialdini, Brown, Lewis, Luce, & Neuberg, 1997; E. Midlarsky & Hannah, 1985).

In the relatively sparse literature on the personalities of naturalistic helpers, some consistencies have been found. In his pilot study on the Holocaust rescuers, London (1970) concluded from his interview data that rescuers were autonomous people with strong moral principles and were willing to take risks.

The impressionistic data collected by Huston, Ruggiero, Conner, and Geis (1981) about Good Samaritans who intervened in crime episodes indicated that these Samaritans tended to be competent risk takers who acted in accordance with their sense of social responsibility. Oliner and Oliner (1988) described the Holocaust rescuers as high in internal locus of control, social responsibility, and empathy, on the basis of their scores on personality measures. Similarly, E. Midlarsky (1992) found that older naturalistic helpers are characterized by altruistic moral reasoning, empathy, and social responsibility.

The research on altruism and helping has indicated that certain personality variables do seem to distinguish helpers from nonhelpers across a wide spectrum of situations. Although only the data collected by Oliner and Oliner (1988) were based on the use of some psychometrically sound instruments (measures of internal locus of control, empathy, social responsibility, and self-esteem) in a study that also used comparison groups, these data do indicate that the personalities of rescuers differ from those of nonrescuers. The study described in this chapter used a wider range of personality measures and took the analysis of altruistic personality a step further. That is, it addressed the question of whether the Holocaust rescuers, in contrast to the bystanders and the prewar immigrants, are characterized by altruistic personality traits, above and beyond any proactive predispositions and demographic variables.

Methodology

The sampling and procedures were discussed earlier in the chapter. With regard to sample characteristics, 44% of the sample were men, and 56% were women. There were no gender differences among the three study groups. The mean age of the overall sample at the time of the study was 71.6 years. There was no significant difference in the current ages of the rescuers and immigrants. However, similar to the age composition of the study by Oliner and Oliner (1988), on the average, the rescuers were 4 years older than the bystanders. The educational backgrounds ranged from fewer than 7 years of education (8%) to graduate or professional training (13%). There were no educational differences between the rescuers and the bystanders or between the bystanders and the immigrants. However, the immigrants were significantly more educated than the rescuers, possibly because of the greater educational opportunities in the United States and Canada, where they grew up, or perhaps because their education was not interrupted by the war.

Three proactive personality variables (locus of control, autonomy, and risk taking) and four altruistic or prosocial personality traits (social responsibility, authoritarianism–tolerance, empathy, and altruistic moral reasoning) were included. The measures used in this study represented efforts to choose the best available instruments in regard to both meaning and psychometric properties. All were pretested in groups of older adult European immigrants, to ensure that they could be readily understood and were amenable to oral administration.

With regard to the proactive personality traits, our measure of internal locus of control was the Control subscale of the Life Attitude Profile (Reker & Peacock, 1981; $\alpha = .90$). Autonomy, defined as independence and the resistance to social controls, was measured by Kurtines's (1978) Autonomy Scale (α = .71). Risk taking was measured by a 7-item scale, including items such as, "If something seems important enough to me, I am often willing to take a risk to do it." Items were scored on a 5-point Likert-like scale (α = .82).

Among the altruistic personality variables, social responsibility was measured by Berkowitz and Lutterman's (1968) Social Responsibility Scale (α = .78). Authoritarianism ("F")–tolerance was measured by the Balanced F Scale (Athanasiou, 1968; α = .71). With regard to empathy, we used both the Empathic Concern (EC) scale and the Personal Distress (PD) scale of the Interpersonal Reactivity Index (Davis, 1980). EC is considered to reflect general concern for the other and is related to helping for the sake of the other (altruistically). Helping by people high in PD empathy is deemed to be motivated by the helpers' (egoistic) need to terminate their own distress. The alpha coefficients for EC and PD were .91 and .73, respectively. Altruistic moral reasoning was measured with our Altruistic Moral Judgment Scale (E. Midlarsky et al., 1999), for which the alpha in this study was .90.

Results

Table 2.3 presents the results of preliminary analyses, conducted to assess group differences in the eight personality variables, using one-way analyses of variance with Bonferroni's correction for multiple tests ($p < .006$). Results of the Scheffé post hoc range tests reveal that the rescuers scored higher than the bystanders on all of the proactive and altruistic personality variables except for personal distress empathy. The rescuers also scored higher than the immigrants on five of the eight personality variables (autonomy, risk taking, social responsibility, empathic concern, and altruistic moral reasoning) but did not differ from the immigrants in internal locus of control, authoritarianism–tolerance, or personal distress empathy. There were no significant differences between the bystanders and the immigrants.

We performed hierarchical discriminant function analysis (HDFA). The demographic variables entered into the HDFA were wartime age and gender. Wartime occupation and education were omitted because they were irrelevant for the prewar immigrants. Nine cases were omitted because of missing information on one or more discriminating variables. Five with missing data were rescuers and 4 were immigrants, resulting in sample sizes of 75 rescuers, 73 bystanders, and 39 immigrants. The prior probabilities for the three groups were .40 (rescuers), .39 (bystanders), and .21 (immigrants).

On the basis of all nine predictors, two significant discriminant functions were identified. The first function accounted for 89.7% of the variance and had an eigenvalue of 2.43 and a canonical correlation of .84. The second function accounted for 10.3% of the variance and had an eigenvalue of .28 and a canonical correlation of .47. Group centroids are shown in Table 2.4. As this table indicates, the rescuers and bystanders are more than three standard deviations apart on the first function, which is best defined by the variables associated with altruistic personality variables. The rescuers and the immigrants are approximately two-and-a-half standard deviations apart on the first function.

Table 2.3. Means and Standard Deviations, F Tests, and Post Hoc Range Comparisons

Variable	Rescuers		Bystanders		Immigrants		$F(2, 207)$	p^a	Scheffé^b $p < .006$
	M	SD	M	SD	M	SD			
Locus of control	36.41	7.00	30.74	7.58	32.38	7.19	11.80	.0001	1 > 2
Autonomy	10.29	2.53	7.42	2.76	7.62	1.96	27.99	.0001	1 > (2,3)
Risk taking	25.16	5.16	17.78	5.17	20.77	3.64	42.80	.0001	1 > (2,3)
Social responsibility	34.32	4.67	25.40	4.23	27.92	3.16	86.69	.0001	1 > (2,3)
Authoritarianism– tolerance	30.58	5.65	27.38	6.66	29.49	4.29	5.72	.004	1 > 2
Personal distress	16.71	5.85	15.77	4.23	18.33	5.97	2.95	.055	ns
Empathic concern	32.63	3.30	23.48	7.12	25.49	6.41	51.13	.0001	1 > (2,3)
Altruistic moral reasoning	10.91	4.56	4.14	.61	4.31	1.15	115.40	.0001	1 > (2,3)

Note. ^{a}Bonferoni's correction for multiple Fs was used; therefore, only those $ps < .006$ are considered significant. ^{b}Group 1 = rescuers; Group 2 = bystanders; Group 3 = immigrants. ns = nonsignificant.

Table 2.4. Group Centroids for Hierarchical Discriminant Analysis

Group	Function 1	Function 2
Rescuers	1.88	−.069
Bystanders	−1.42	−.447
Refugees	−.963	.969

On the second function, primarily reflecting age differences, the immigrants are approximately one standard deviation higher than the rescuers and one-and-a-half standard deviations higher than the bystanders. The structure matrix is presented in Table 2.5. It indicates that the first function, which separates the rescuers from both the bystanders and the immigrants, is best defined by altruistic moral reasoning and social responsibility, followed by empathic concern, risk taking, and autonomy. The second function, which separates the immigrants from the bystanders and with the rescuers falling in between, is best defined by wartime age.

The two demographic predictors, age in 1939 and gender, yielded statistically significant separation among the three groups ($p < .01$). At this step in the HFDA, 52.3% of the cases were correctly classified, indicating an improvement of approximately 12% over the prior probabilities for the rescuers and bystanders and 31% for the immigrants. After adding the proactive personality variables (locus of control, autonomy, and risk taking), 70.1% of cases were correctly classified, indicating an improvement of approximately 30% for the rescuers and the bystanders, and 50% for the immigrants. Addition of the proactive variables reliably separated the three groups ($p < .001$).

After addition of the altruistic personality variables (social responsibility, authoritarianism–tolerance, empathic concern, and altruistic moral reasoning), 83.4% of the cases were correctly classified, indicating an improvement

Table 2.5. Structure Matrix for Personality/Motivational Variables

Variable	Function 1 Structural coefficient	Function 2 Structural coefficient
Altruistic moral reasoning	.71*	−.19
Social responsibility	.62*	.23
Empathic concern	.48*	.10
Risk taking	.43*	.30
Autonomy	.35*	−.06
Locus of control	.22*	.09
Wartime age	.10	.78*
Authoritarianism–tolerance	.15	.21*
Gender	.02	.14*

Note. Pooled within-group correlations between discriminating variables and standardized canonical discriminant function. Variables ordered by absolute size of correlation with function.
*Largest absolute correlation between each variable and any discriminant function.

of approximately 44% over the prior probabilities for the rescuers and the bystanders, and 62.4% for the immigrants. Reliability in separation of the groups was achieved by the altruistic variables ($p < .001$), as was significant improvement in classification (13.4%) over and above the demographic and proactive predictors combined ($p < .001$). Correct classification rates were 84% for the rescuers, 91.8% for the bystanders, and 66.7% for the immigrants. All of the incorrectly classified immigrants were misclassified as bystanders, and only one bystander was misclassified as a rescuer.

Implications and Conclusions

Emerging from these analyses is a portrait of the Holocaust rescuers, or "Righteous Gentiles," that is different from the nonrescuers. In contrast to the view that rescuers are "ordinary people" for whom situational factors were often critical (Varese & Yaish, 2000), the rescuers whom we interviewed were quite distinctive. These Holocaust heroes exhibited high degrees of altruism and proactivity, and they are far more helpful than the nonrescuers many years after the Second World War and well into their older adulthood.

Who were these rescuers? Qualitatively, they were people who stood out in bas relief against the backdrop of all others who were interviewed. They told, with great modesty and often humor, of deeds performed under conditions that made us shudder. Many spoke with nostalgia of living for months and even years with people who had been sentenced to death—knowing that they had chosen to share in that sentence. Fully aware that they had been in extreme and avoidable danger of being murdered, they spoke with love of those whom they had sheltered. All whom we interviewed were also recalled with the greatest of fondness by the people whom they rescued and were described as remarkable people, "saints," and "heroes." Strikingly, however, despite this praise, the rescuers continually said that they deserved no special recognition, as they did no more than any decent person would have done.

By choosing a sample of verified rescuers who had never been previously interviewed about their wartime activities, we lessened reactivity to a certain extent. It was, however, impossible to erase the impacts of the wartime helping itself, the war traumas, and the many years and developmental stages that had passed since they had engaged in rescue behavior. Thus, it is virtually impossible to verify, empirically, the personality dispositions that differentiated the rescuers and nonrescuers during the Holocaust. However, it is possible that these personality predispositions represent traits that were present far earlier in the lives of the individuals whom we studied. Whereas some researchers believe that personality changes over the life course (Neugarten, 1968), evidence from longitudinal studies indicates that there may be continuity of personality over the life span (McCrae & Costa, 1984) and that "attitudes become crystallized and increasingly stable with age" (Alwin, Cohen, & Newcomb, 1991, p. 264).

Among the most gratifying findings was the similarity in important respects to those stemming from studies using very different methodologies. In framing hypotheses, especially about the personality predictors of rescue, we turned to field studies (Bierhoff, Klein, & Kramp, 1991) and laboratory experiments exploring relatively low-cost, short-term helping behavior (e.g., Dovidio et al., 1990). We were excited to find that the variables that distinguished helpers from nonhelpers in that work also differentiated Holocaust rescuers from nonrescuers.

Our study has certain limitations. All of the people studied here were interviewed many years after they made critical choices about whether to leave Europe before the war or to stay, and whether to intervene on behalf of a group of stigmatized neighbors. Our sample is relatively small, and the degree to which it represents the total group is unknown. All migrated from their countries of origin and have surely been affected by the stress associated with acculturation as well as by war trauma. Nevertheless, the fact that these findings concur with studies using a wide range of populations, situations, and research methodologies provides evidence for convergence that may indicate that we are capturing veridicality (Webb et al., 1981).

In sum, altruistic behavior seems to be associated with a unique configuration of proactive and altruistic variables. The importance of this knowledge is obvious. Evil and aggression are remarkably persistent phenomena, as is genocide. One of the oldest genocides in history, the Melian of the Peloponnesian War, was recorded as occurring approximately 25 centuries ago, whereas the Tutsi genocide in Rwanda occurred within the past decade. The 20th century alone witnessed three major genocides (M. Midlarsky, 2005). In a world in which evil exists, altruism is a necessity. Future research should focus on the development of compassion and action on behalf of others, to prevent violence and to cultivate altruism within human society.

References

Alwin, D., Cohen, R., & Newcomb, T. (1991). *Political attitudes and the life span.* New York: Wiley.

Arieti, S. (1979). *The parnas.* New York: Basic Books.

Athanasiou, R. (1968). Technique without mystique. *Psychological Measurement, 28,* 1181–1188.

Berkowitz, L., & Lutterman, K. (1968). The traditionally socially responsible personality. *Public Opinion Quarterly, 32,* 169–187.

Bierhoff, H. W., Klein, R., & Kramp, P. (1991). Evidence for the altruistic personality from data on accident research. *Journal of Personality, 59,* 263–280.

Bierman, J. (1981). *Righteous gentiles.* New York: Viking.

Butler, R., Lewis, M., & Sunderland, T. (1990). *Aging and mental health.* New York: Macmillan.

Cialdini, R., Brown, S., Lewis, B., Luce, C., & Neuberg, S. (1997). Reinterpreting the empathy–altruism relationship. *Journal of Personality and Social Psychology, 73,* 481–494.

Davis, M. (1980). Measuring individual differences in empathy. *JSAS Catalog of Selected Documents in Psychology, 10,* 85.

Dovidio, J., Allen, J., & Schroeder, D. (1990). Specificity of empathy-induced helping. *Journal of Personality and Social Psychology, 59,* 249–260.

Eisenberg, A. (1982). *The lost generation: Children in the Holocaust.* New York: Pilgrim.

Fogelman, E. (1994). *Conscience and courage.* New York: Anchor.

George, L. (1994). Multidimensional assessment instruments. In M. Lawton & J. Teresi (Eds.), *Annual review of gerontology and geriatrics* (Vol. 14, pp. 353–375). New York: Springer.

Horwitz, R. I., & Feinstein, A. R. (1979). Methodologic standards and contradictory results in case-control research. *American Journal of Medicine, 66,* 556–564.

Huneke, D. (1981/1982). A study of Christians who rescued Jews during the Nazi era. *Humboldt Journal of Social Relations, 9*(1), 144–160.

Huston, T., Ruggiero, M., Conner, R., & Geis, G. (1981). Bystander intervention into crime. *Social Psychology Quarterly, 44,* 14–23.

Kahana, E., Midlarsky, E., King, C., Chirayath, H., Schumacher, J., & Kercher, K. (1998, November). *Altruism in late life: Measurement, antecedents, and outcomes.* Paper presented at the meeting of the Gerontological Society of America, Washington, DC.

Kane, R. J., & Kane, R. A. (2000). *Assessing older persons.* New York: Oxford University Press.

Kranzler, D. (1987). *Thy brother's blood: The orthodox Jewish response during the Holocaust.* New York: Mesorah.

Kurtines, W. M. (1978). A measure of anatomy. *Journal of Personality Assessment, 42,* 253–257.

Lacy, M. G. (1997). Efficiently studying rare events: Case-control methods for sociologists. *Sociological Perspectives, 40,* 129–145.

London, P. (1970). The rescuers. In J. Macaulay & L. Berkowitz (Eds.), *Altruism and helping behavior* (pp. 241–250). New York: Academic Press.

McCrae, R., & Costa, P. (1984). *Emerging lives, enduring dispositions.* Boston: Little, Brown.

Midlarsky, E. (1992). Helping in late life. In P. Oliner, S. Oliner, L. Baron, L. Blum, D. Krebs, & Z. Smolenska (Eds.), *Embracing the other* (pp. 253–276). New York: New York University Press.

Midlarsky, E., Fagin Jones, S., & Corley, R. (2005). Personality correlates of heroic rescue during the Holocaust. *Journal of Personality, 73*(4), 1–28.

Midlarsky, E., & Hannah, M. (1985). Competence, reticence, and helping among children and adolescents. *Developmental Psychology, 21,* 534–541.

Midlarsky, E., & Kahana, E. (1994). *Altruism in later life.* Newbury Park, CA: Sage.

Midlarsky, E., Kahana, E., Corley, R., Schonbar, R. A., & Nemeroff, R. (1999). Altruistic moral judgment among older adults. *International Journal of Aging and Human Development, 49,* 39–53.

Midlarsky, E., & Oliner, S. P. (1985, August). *The aged Samaritan.* Paper presented at the 93rd Annual Convention of the American Psychological Association, Los Angeles, CA.

Midlarsky, M. (2005). *The killing trap: Genocide, realpolitik, and loss in the twentieth century.* Cambridge, England: Cambridge University Press.

Milgram, S. (1974). *Obedience to authority: An experimental view.* New York: Harper & Row.

Miller, P., & Eisenberg, N. (1996). Relations of moral reasoning and vicarious emotion to young children's prosocial behavior toward peers and adults. *Developmental Psychology, 32,* 210–219.

Moskiewicz, H. (1987). *Inside the Gestapo.* Reading, England: Sphere Books.

Neugarten, B. L. (1968). Adult personality. In B. L. Neugarten (Ed.), *Middle age and aging* (pp. 137–147). Chicago: University of Chicago Press..

Neugarten, B. L., Havighurst, R. J., & Tobin, S. S. (1961). The measurement of life satisfaction. *Journal of Gerontology, 16,* 132–143.

Oliner, S. P. (1984). The unsung heroes in Nazi-occupied Europe: The antidote for evil. *Nationalities Papers, XII* (1), 130.

Oliner, S. P., & Oliner, P. M. (1988). *The altruistic personality.* New York: Free Press.

Paldiel, M. (2000). *Saving the Jews.* Rockville, MD: Schreiber.

Piliavin, J. (2003). Doing well by doing good: Benefits for the benefactor. In L. M. Corey & J. Haidt (Eds.), *Flourishing: Positive Psychology and the Life Well-Lived* (pp. 227–247). Washington, DC: American Psychological Association.

Piliavin, J., & Charng, H. (1990). Altruism. *Annual Review of Sociology, 16,* 27–65.

Reker, G., & Peacock, E. (1981). The Life Attitude Profile (LAP). *Canadian Journal of Behavioral Science, 13,* 264–273.

Schroeder, D., Penner, L., Dovidio, J., & Piliavin, J. (1995). *The psychology of helping and altruism.* New York: McGraw-Hill.

Tec, N. (1986). *When light pierced the darkness: Christian rescue of Jews in Nazi-occupied Poland.* New York: Oxford University Press.

Tec, N. (1993). *Defiance: The Bielski partisans.* New York: Oxford University Press.

Van Willigen, M. (2000). Differential benefits of volunteering across the life course. *Journal of Gerontology, 55B*, S308–S318.

Varese, F., & Yaish, M. (2000). The importance of being asked: The rescue of Jews in Nazi Europe. *Rationality and Society, 12*, 307–334.

Webb, E. J., Campbell, D. T., Schwartz, R. D., Sechrest, L. B., & Grove, J. B. (1981). *Nonreactive measures in the social sciences.* Boston: Houghton Mifflin.

3

Understanding Social Contexts and Coping: Connections With Intervention Programs

Rudolf H. Moos

What are the primary domains of social context factors and coping strategies in people's lives? How do transitory and enduring life circumstances affect health and well-being, and can individuals' appraisal and coping skills alter their influence? What are the connections between community setting and intervention programs? Do life context and coping factors predict participation in, and the outcome of, treatment? How can new knowledge in these areas be applied in clinical practice? For more than three decades, my colleagues and I have tried to address these issues by formulating conceptual models, developing ways to measure key constructs, and using the models and measures to conduct long-term naturalistic studies.

The research we pursued and the questions we posed reflect a fundamental premise: To develop viable prevention and intervention programs, and to improve community settings and individuals' health and well-being, we must understand social contexts and the coping processes that shape their stability and evolution. In this sense, the study of social contexts and coping is part of the basic science that underlies the pursuit of new knowledge in the social and behavioral sciences.

Throughout his career, Lee Sechrest has exemplified profound thinking and inspiration about these issues. He had the vision more than 35 years ago to call for an integration of research and practice in clinical psychology (Goldstein, Heller, & Sechrest, 1966) and to emphasize the value of nonreactive measures of social and psychological phenomena (Webb, Campbell, Schwartz, & Sechrest, 1966). Later, he emphasized the need to assess the strength and integrity of intervention programs and described methods to do so (Sechrest & West, 1983; Yeaton & Sechrest, 1992), and he highlighted the importance

Preparation of this chapter was supported in part by the Department of Veterans Affairs Health Services Research and Development Service and by National Institute on Alcohol Abuse and Alcoholism Grant AA12718. The views expressed here are the author's and do not necessarily represent the views of the Department of Veterans Affairs.

of theory in program evaluation (Sechrest & Scott, 1992). His work has provided guidance and exemplars for basic psychological and health services research and for the application of new knowledge to practice.

In keeping with the spirit of Lee Sechrest's work, this chapter presents a conceptual model that may help us to understand how people use personal and social resources to confront life crises and how ongoing life contexts are closely connected with participation in, and the outcomes of, intervention programs. I illustrate applications of the model by updating our earlier work on these issues (Moos, 1995, 2002; Moos, Finney, & Cronkite, 1990) and setting out some propositions about context and coping.

A Guiding Conceptual Model

The emergence of a systems orientation and a focus on the social context of human development promise new insights into person–environment transactions and the design of more effective intervention programs. This systems orientation has led to a conceptual framework that can guide the search for new knowledge about social contexts, coping, and adaptation (Figure 3.1). The model depicts the *environmental system* (Panel I) as composed of relatively stable conditions in specific life domains, which include the social climate and ongoing life stressors and social resources. The *personal system* (Panel II) includes such personal resources as cognitive and intellectual abilities, self-confidence and social competence, and optimism and extroversion.

Panel I reflects relatively enduring aspects of the environment, whereas Panel III includes *transitory conditions*, such as new life events and participation in intervention and treatment programs. Considering these two sets of life circumstances together highlights the point that both sets reflect new contexts that provide opportunities for learning and the potential for personal development or decline. The model posits that ongoing environmental and personal factors foreshadow these transitory conditions and that these three sets of factors shape cognitive appraisal and coping skills (Panel IV) and, in turn, individuals' health and well-being (Panel V).

The paths in the model show that these processes are transactional, that mutual feedback can occur at each step, and that people select and shape the social contexts that influence them. The framework also reflects the belief that these processes are basically comparable among individuals who do and those who do not participate in intervention programs. It shows that stable and transitory life context factors and personal factors are determinants of participation in an intervention, which itself is a transitory life context. In turn, personal and contextual factors act in conjunction with coping skills to affect psychosocial functioning and maturation, which become part of the personal system at the next stage of development.

Propositions About Context and Coping

There are eight propositions about context and coping. Two propositions focus on how to conceptualize these domains and two consider their power. Four

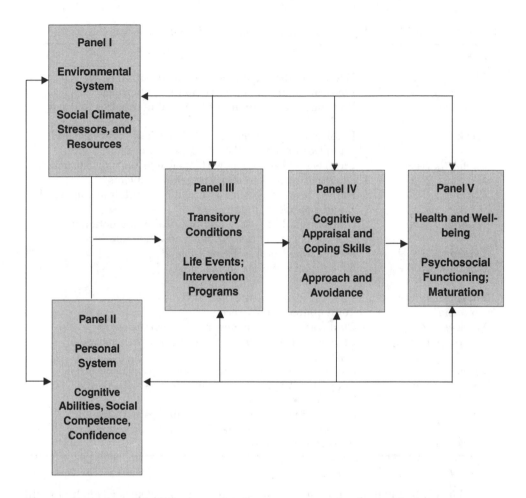

Figure 3.1. A model of the interplay between context, coping, and adaptation.

propositions consider the connections between ongoing life context and coping factors and intervention programs.

Proposition I: There are eight primary domains of life stressors and social resources in people's lives; these domains can be portrayed together in an integrated way.

On the basis of the idea that social contexts are composed of specific life domains, we developed the Life Stressors and Social Resources Inventory (LISRES), which taps life stressors and social resources in eight key areas. It assesses variables in Panels I and III of the model. In constructing the Adult Form of the LISRES, we used our framework to guide the measurement development process, formulated indices to cover individuals' ongoing life contexts and new life events, and applied both conceptual and empirical criteria to construct the indices. (For more information about the LISRES's psychometric and normative characteristics, see Moos & Moos, 1994a.)

Table 3.1. LISRES Adult Form: Life Stressors and Social Resources Subscales

Life stressors	Description
Physical health	Medical conditions and serious physical ailments
Home/neighborhood	Physical conditions of home and neighborhood
Financial	Problems such as inability to afford necessities and pay bills
Work	Problems with supervisor and coworkers: pressure and unpleasant physical conditions at work
Spouse/partner	Interpersonal problems with spouse or partner; spouse or partner's physical and emotional problems
Child	Interpersonal problems with children; children's physical and emotional impairment
Extended family	Interpersonal stressors and physical and emotional problems of mother, father, and other relatives
Friends	Interpersonal problems with friends
Negative events	New negative events in last year
Social resources	
Financial	Total annual family income
Work	Challenge, independence, and support at work
Spouse/partner	Support and empathy in relationship with spouse or partner
Child	Support and empathy in relationships with children
Extended family	Support and empathy in relationships with mother, father, and other relatives
Friends	Support and empathy in relationships with friends; number of friends; membership in social groups
Positive events	New positive events in last year

The Adult Form of the LISRES assesses ongoing stressors in each of eight domains: physical health, housing and neighborhood, finances, work, and the quality of relationships with spouse or partner, children, extended family, and friends (Table 3.1). It also measures the number of negative life events that occurred in these eight domains in the past year. In addition, the inventory measures ongoing social resources and positive events in six of the eight domains.

The indices of ongoing interpersonal stressors and resources are composed of between 5 and 15 items rated on 4-point or 5-point scales. To enhance comparisons among domains, we used similar items to tap the quality of relationships with spouse or partner, children, other family members, and friends. For example, the stressor item "Is he or she critical or disapproving of you?" is included in each domain. Each domain also includes the resource item "Does he or she respect your opinion?"

The Youth Form of the LISRES (Moos & Moos, 1994b) focuses on adolescents' life contexts and also measures life stressors and social resources in eight areas: the youth's physical health, home and money situation, and relationships with parents, siblings, extended family members, teachers and students at school, and a special boyfriend or girlfriend (Table 3.2).

Table 3.2.   LISRES Youth Form: Life Stressors and Social Resources Subscales

Life stressors	Description
Physical health	Medical conditions and serious physical ailments
Home and money	Physical conditions of home; money problems
Parental	Interpersonal problems with mother and father; Parental relationship problems
Sibling	Interpersonal problems with siblings
Extended family	Interpersonal problems with extended family members
School	Interpersonal problems with teachers and students
Friends	Interpersonal problems with friends
Boy- or girlfriend	Interpersonal problems with a special boy- or girlfriend
Negative events	New negative events in last year
Social resources	
Parental	Support and empathy in relationships with mother and father
Sibling	Support and empathy in relationships with siblings
Extended family	Support and empathy in relationship with extended family members
School	Support and empathy in relationships with teachers and counselors
Friends	Support and empathy in relationships with friends
Boy- or girlfriend	Support and empathy in a relationship with a special boy- or girlfriend
Positive events	New positive events in last year

This framework and the inventories enable a clinician to focus on specific transitions or crises in the context of an individual's overall life situation. A counselor can examine the potential consequences of a separation or divorce, the loss of a job, the sudden death of a loved one, or a natural disaster in light of information about an individual's health, housing, and relationships with family members and friends. Parents' and adolescents' life contexts can be considered in tandem. In addition, aspects of individuals' life contexts can be linked to their functioning and well-being.

Proposition II: Coping skills can be conceptualized with respect to their focus (approach or avoidance) and method (cognitive or behavioral).

Contemporary researchers have used two main conceptual approaches to classify coping responses. One approach emphasizes the *focus* of coping: a person's orientation and activity in response to a stressor. An individual can approach the problem and make active efforts to resolve it, or try to avoid the problem or focus on managing the emotions associated with it. A second approach emphasizes the *method* of coping; that is, whether a response entails primarily cognitive or behavioral efforts.

The Coping Responses Inventory (CRI), which measures variables in Panel IV of the conceptual model, combines these two approaches. The CRI first assesses relevant aspects of cognitive appraisal, such as the extent to which

Table 3.3. Underlying Dimensions of Coping Skills

Type of coping	Approach coping	Avoidance coping
Cognitive	Logical analysis	Cognitive avoidance
	Positive reappraisal	Acceptance or resignation
Behavioral	Seeking guidance and support	Seeking alternative rewards
	Problem solving	Emotional discharge

a situation is seen as challenging or threatening, expected or unexpected, and caused by the self, another person, or the external environment. It then considers an individual's orientation toward a stressor and divides coping into approach and avoidance responses, and further divides these domains into cognitive or behavioral coping efforts.

Thus, the CRI organizes coping responses into four domains (Table 3.3). Logical analysis and positive reappraisal reflect cognitive approach coping; seeking support and problem solving reflect behavioral approach coping. Cognitive avoidance and affective resignation exemplify cognitive avoidance coping; seeking alternative rewards and emotional discharge exemplify behavioral avoidance coping. (For more information about the psychometric and normative characteristics of the CRI—Adult and the CRI—Youth, see Moos, 1993a, 1993b.)

Each of the eight coping dimensions is composed of six items. Respondents select a recent (focal) stressor and rate their reliance on each of the 48 coping items on 4-point scales varying from *not at all* to *fairly often*. For example, the item "Did you think of different ways to deal with the problem?" assesses logical analysis, and the item "Did you talk with a friend about the problem?" taps seeking guidance and support. The item "Did you try not to think about the problem?" assesses cognitive avoidance, and the item "Did you cry to let your feelings out?" taps emotional discharge.

Proposition III: The cumulative role of transitory and enduring circumstances in these eight domains exemplifies the power of social contexts.

Any one aspect of life context may have only a limited influence on an individual, but the cumulative effect of life stressors in several domains can be quite extensive. For example, in a study of older adults, we found that negative life events explained 12% of the variance in depression. Consideration of financial stressors and conflict with a spouse or partner raised the explained variance to 24%. The presence of additional stressors, such as those associated with work, friends, children, and extended family members, raised it to 38%. These findings highlight the value of separately assessing negative life events and specific domains of ongoing stressors.

Our findings also emphasize the importance of assessing varied domains of social resources. In our studies of older adults, we found that financial resources, a supportive relationship with a spouse or partner, supportive relationships with friends, and the presence of additional resources in other life domains, such as those from coworkers, children, and extended family members, each raised the explained variance in self-confidence. Thus, to understand the full power of social contexts, it is important to examine the cumulative role of adversity and social resources.

Ongoing life stressors and social resources typically have more predictable and robust connections with health-related and functioning outcomes than do transitory life events. When a transitory, but fateful or powerful, event exerts a long-term influence on psychological maturation, it usually is because of an enduring change in an individual's life context (Dohrenwend, 2000). In this vein, childhood traumas and life events in adolescence and early adulthood often contribute to new acute and chronic stressors, which, in turn, may be independently or jointly related to development (Wachs, 2001).

Proposition IV: Appraisal and coping skills transmit and alter the influence of stable and transitory life context factors on health and well-being.

In general, individuals who rely on approach coping relative to avoidance coping are more likely to resolve stressors and to obtain some benefit from them, as well as to experience more self-confidence and less depression and dysfunction. Approach coping skills, such as seeking information and problem solving, can moderate the potential adverse influence of acute life crises and enduring role stressors on psychological functioning. In contrast, avoidance coping, such as refusing to think about a crisis and venting affect, typically is associated with distress and worse outcomes, especially when adjustment is assessed beyond the initial crisis period (Rohde, Lewinsohn, Tilson, & Seeley, 1990).

Although approach coping tends to be more effective than avoidance coping, individuals adapt best when their coping efforts match situational demands (Miller, 1992). The adaptive value of different coping skills depends on the interaction between personal and social resources and the requirements of a particular situation. For example, individuals who are more analytic and structured are likely to be more successful in dealing with situations that require logical analysis and self-reliance. Individuals who are more oriented toward social relationships may seek clues from the social context to help them solve interpersonal and other problems more effectively.

Less is known about the adaptive implications of the method of coping, but, contrary to prevailing wisdom, cognitive strategies seem to be at least as closely associated with adaptation as are behavioral strategies, perhaps because they are more under an individual's control and can be applied in circumstances in which behavioral options are unavailable. Even though coping skills are somewhat context dependent, they seem to capture a moderately stable aspect of personal reactions to life circumstances that is associated with long-term maturation and well-being.

As shown in Figure 3.1, social and personal resources (Panels I and II in the model) relate to subsequent functioning (Panel V) both directly and indirectly through coping skills (Panel IV). The relative strength of the predictive associations in the model should vary with the level of life stressors. Coping is a stabilizing factor that helps maintain psychological adjustment during stressful periods; accordingly, coping efforts should be most helpful when there is a high level of stressors.

In a test of this model, we found that self-confidence, an easygoing disposition, and family support operated prospectively over 4 years to protect individuals from becoming depressed (Holahan & Moos, 1991). The pattern of associations varied as predicted. Under high stressors, personal and social resources were indirectly related to lower depression, through their link to more reliance on approach coping. Under low stressors, these resources were directly related to psychological adjustment. Thus, when an individual is challenged by a high level of stressors, personal and social resources operate prospectively to enhance approach coping; in turn, approach coping is associated with more well-being.

Coping also plays a key role in confronting the adaptive demands of medical disorders. In an attempt to predict depressive symptoms among patients with chronic cardiac illness, we found that more social support at baseline predicted fewer depressive symptoms at a 4-year follow-up (Holahan, Moos, Holahan, & Brennan, 1997). Especially important conceptually, more reliance on approach coping mediated the influence of social support on fewer depressive symptoms. Social support enhanced reliance on approach coping; in contrast, social stressors, such as conflict and criticism from family and friends, were associated with more reliance on avoidance coping.

Proposition V: Conceptually comparable dimensions characterize and underlie the outcomes of community settings and intervention programs.

When individuals enter an intervention or prevention program, it becomes part of their life context. Ongoing life settings and intervention programs are comparable in that both establish a context for individual development or dysfunction, both involve person–environment matching processes, and both may be altered by the participants they seek to alter. In addition, both are environmental conditions that can be characterized by three common sets of social climate dimensions: relationship, personal growth, and system maintenance and change (Moos, 2003).

There are comparable linkages between these three sets of dimensions and the outcomes of community settings and intervention programs. Thus, just as in families and the workplace, when intervention programs emphasize independence and skills training, participants' social and vocational abilities tend to improve. When intervention programs emphasize self-understanding and expressiveness, participants tend to become more forthright and insightful. Just as in community settings, high expectations in an intervention program can enhance participants' personal growth but also can cause problems such as confusion and withdrawal (Moos, 1997).

In general, interventions that help individuals shape and adapt to their life circumstances are especially effective in alleviating behavioral and emotional problems. The most powerful modalities for the treatment of many psychological disorders involve cognitive–behavioral interventions, which focus primarily on enhancing clients' skills in coping with everyday life circumstances and on improving the match between clients' abilities and environmental demands (Nathan & Gorman, 2002). Moreover, self-help and mutual support groups are associated with positive long-term outcomes, primarily because they often become part of participants' life contexts and provide a stable social network that helps them shape and adapt to daily stressors.

Proposition VI: Life context and coping factors help predict entry into and participation in intervention and prevention programs.

There is an interplay between life context and coping factors and entry into and the process of mental health treatment. Researchers typically have focused either on life context or on treatment factors, but these two sets of factors are interrelated and should be considered together. Information about life context and coping can help one understand when individuals will seek treatment and the process of treatment, involvement in and the proximal outcomes of mutual help groups, and when individuals can resolve their problems without treatment.

In a study of late-life alcohol consumption, we examined how well life stressors and social resources predicted older problem drinkers' help-seeking. Problem drinkers who reported more negative life events (both health related and non-health-related) and more chronic health, spouse, and child-related stressors were more likely to have sought help for their drinking problems. This was also true of problem drinkers who had fewer financial, spouse, child, extended family, and friend-related resources, and whose friends disapproved more strongly of drinking (Moos, Brennan, & Schutte, 1998). These findings support the idea that health and interpersonal stressors may trigger help-seeking and that professional health care may temporarily substitute for informal social resources.

Coping responses also predict participation in treatment and self-help groups; in turn, participation in treatment and self-help groups is associated with changes in coping. For example, Timko and colleagues (Timko, Moos, Finney, & Lesar, 2000) found that individuals with alcohol use disorders who relied more on approach coping were more likely to seek out professional treatment and to participate in self-help groups. Patients who are more involved in treatment or in self-help groups tend to show an increase in approach coping and a decline in avoidance coping over time. An improvement in coping skills seems to be a general outcome of treatments that emphasize broad personal change, such as 12-step approaches, as well as of treatments that focus specifically on increasing coping skills, such as cognitive–behavioral approaches (Finney, Ouimette, Humphreys, & Moos, 2001).

Proposition VII: Information about life context and coping can help to predict clinically relevant outcomes.

There are robust relationships between life context factors and the course and progression of emotional and behavioral disorders. For example, in a study of clients in treatment for depression, more family independence, less family conflict, more close relationships, and more helpful friends and activities with friends predicted stable remission at a 10-year follow-up (Cronkite, Moos, Twohey, Cohen, & Swindle, 1998; Moos, Cronkite, & Moos, 1998). In contrast, stressful life circumstances and family members' expression of criticism or anger to an individual with a psychiatric disorder, including schizophrenia and borderline personality as well as depression, raise the likelihood of a relapse (Hooley & Gotlib, 2000).

Patients whose coping skills improve during treatment or shortly afterward tend to show better outcomes. Avants, Warburton, and Margolin (2000) found that patients who increased their reliance on approach coping and decreased their reliance on avoidance coping had better substance use outcomes during treatment, which, in turn, were associated with a higher likelihood of abstinence at a 6-month follow-up. Lemke and Moos (2003) found that patients who relied more on approach coping at discharge from the acute episode of treatment reported less alcohol consumption, fewer drinking problems, and less distress at both 1-year and 5-year follow-ups. Similarly, more behavioral approach coping and less cognitive avoidance coping predicted fewer alcohol-related problems in 6- and 12-month follow-ups of treated alcoholic patients (Chung, Langenbucher, Labouvie, Pandina, & Moos, 2001).

Even though coping responses are somewhat situation specific, they seem to capture an aspect of stable personal tendencies that is associated with long-term functioning and treatment outcome. In a long-term study of the outcome of treatment for depression, for example, we found that reliance on avoidance coping was associated with poorer 10-year outcomes (Cronkite et al., 1998). Similarly, among patients in treatment for alcohol use disorders, more reliance on cognitive approach coping as well as less reliance on avoidance coping was associated with better 2-year and 10-year treatment outcomes. Patients who relied more on cognitive approach coping at 2 years consumed less alcohol and reported fewer physical symptoms and less depression at 10 years (Moos et al., 1990).

Prior life context and coping factors may be as predictive of treatment outcome as are individuals' demographic characteristics and levels of functioning at intake to treatment. The fact that the evolving conditions of life play an essential role in the process of remission from relatively severe behavioral and emotional disorders is a hopeful sign. It implies that these disorders need not become chronic, that formal treatment and self-help groups can provide social resources, and that individuals who are able to establish and maintain relatively benign circumstances are likely to recover.

Proposition VIII: Just like other life contexts, intervention programs are characterized by risks as well as rewards and by fragility as well as power.

Overall, treatment for substance use and psychiatric disorders has a modest positive effect on outcome (Nathan & Gorman, 2002). Studies of a wide range of psychological and behavioral intervention programs have reached similar conclusions (e.g., Felner, Felner, & Silverman, 2000). Just as with any powerful context, however, intervention programs can have negative consequences, and, in fact, about 10% of patients in treatment for psychiatric or substance use disorders or both seem to deteriorate (Mohr, 1995).

We found that 13% of a sample of patients with substance use disorders who were in treatment experienced more substance use problems at follow-up than at baseline. Risk factors for symptom exacerbation included younger age, nonmarried status, and residential instability; long-term use of drugs, prior arrests, prior alcohol treatment, and psychiatric problems; and such interpersonal problems as severe conflicts with three or more individuals and a lack of any close friends. A longer duration of care was associated with a reduced likelihood of the exacerbation of symptoms, especially among high-risk patients (Moos, Nichol, & Moos, 2002).

Deterioration may stem from a diagnostic labeling process that elicits expectations of stigma and rejection (Link, Struening, Rahav, Phelan, & Nutt-brock, 1997). It may also be a consequence of the arousal of hope and subsequent unfulfilled expectations associated with brief intervention episodes, especially for individuals who have stressful life contexts and little or no social support, and of the resulting decline in self-worth and self-efficacy.

As noted earlier, the benefits of intervention programs seem to depend on the same conditions that impel positive outcomes in other settings: high-quality relationships, high expectations for personal growth, and a moderate level of structure. In contrast, significant risks are posed by interventions that are poorly implemented in these areas, such as those which emphasize confronta-tion and fail to establish an alliance with clients, and those which lack goal direction and clarity. Such programs have relatively high dropout rates, which may contribute to deterioration effects

Ineffective patient–treatment matching strategies may also contribute to deterioration effects. In this vein, Timko (2003) found that patients with more severe substance use and psychiatric problems improved more on substance use outcomes when they were treated in programs that provided more intensive services, whereas patients with a moderate level of problems did as well on substance use outcomes and improved more on psychiatric symptoms when they were treated in programs that provided less intensive services. Negative or iatrogenic effects of treatment may occur when patients are mismatched to receive an inappropriate intensity of treatment, such as when severely ill patients do not receive an adequate dose of treatment and when moderately ill patients receive overly intensive treatment that undermines their autonomy and makes it harder for them to adapt to life in the community. These findings highlight the value of Lee Sechrest's ideas: Ongoing evaluation is needed to ensure that intervention programs are implemented effectively with respect to their clients' needs.

Applications to Assessment and Intervention

Because each path in the framework shown in Figure 3.1 identifies a fluid process, the concepts and measures of life context and coping factors may be useful in clinical practice. From an applied perspective, the model has implications for clinical assessment, understanding the process of remission and relapse and the role of participation in mutual help groups, and explaining personal growth in the aftermath of adversity.

Clinical Assessment

Most traditional assessment procedures focus on obtaining an accurate diagno-sis. In contrast, clinicians should emphasize the extent to which assessment contributes to better treatment outcome, most often by enhancing treatment planning and the match between clients and treatment procedures. In this vein, assessment of clients' life contexts and coping preferences can help to increase their awareness of their life situation and coping abilities and to predict their responses to specific intervention procedures or styles of communication (Beutler, Moos, & Lane, 2003). The resulting information can be used to understand how clients manage specific stressful circumstances, to specify coping factors associated with symptom remission and relapse, to examine how new life events affect a person's ways of coping, and to identify how coping processes change an individual's life situation and functioning.

Stress and coping processes are inherently flexible and amenable to change. A high level of stressors and few social resources are not fixed characteristics of individuals but stem in part from personal characteristics and a lack of effective coping responses, which are both amenable to change. Coping efforts are relatively flexible responses that are affected by personal and contextual factors. Thus, individuals' health and well-being can be improved through interventions that target either the person, such as by strengthening reliance on approach coping, or his or her life context, such as by augmenting available social resources.

The Process of Remission and Relapse

An appreciation of life context and coping factors can broaden our understanding of the process of recovery from psychiatric and substance use disorders. Our model emphasizes that treatment is part of an open system, in which an intervention program is only one of multiple factors that influence psychiatric disorders and other aspects of adaptation. Many mental health care programs improve clients' psychosocial functioning in the short run, but these positive changes often fade quickly over time. In contrast, clients' life contexts and coping skills are associated with the long-term outcome of an intervention and with normalization of function among stably remitted individuals.

Consistent with research on the power of social contexts and coping skills, these findings show that context and coping factors shape the course of psychological and behavioral problems much more strongly than formal mental health treatment does. Clinicians should pay more attention to the extratreatment factors that most strongly influence the process of remission and recovery. These factors are thought to be extraneous to treatment, but they continue long after treatment, are more pervasive and intense, and have a stronger impact on outcome.

An important issue for clinicians is the relative emphasis to place on teaching clients general versus situation-specific coping skills. In a study of individuals with substance use disorders, Moggi, Ouimette, Finney, and Moos (1999) found that general approach coping and substance-specific coping skills increased during treatment and that both forms of coping were associated with 1-year abstinence. However, some deterioration occurred in both forms of coping between discharge from acute treatment and the 1-year follow-up. To guide clinical decisions in this area, more information is needed on the comparative effectiveness of general and situation-specific coping, on how well these skills can be maintained over time, and on how life context factors can promote generalization of the gains made during treatment.

Participation in Mutual Help Groups

The conceptual model we propose can help one understand the determinants and effects of participation in mutual help groups. Using such a model, Humphreys, Finney, and Moos (1994) found that individuals who had more social and coping deficits were more likely to enter a mutual help group and that participation in the group served to ameliorate these deficits. More specifically, individuals with alcohol use disorders who reported more stressors and fewer social resources, and who relied more on avoidance coping, were more likely to become involved in Alcoholics Anonymous (AA). In turn, involvement in AA predicted fewer subsequent financial stressors, more support from friends, and more reliance on approach coping and less on avoidance coping.

In a related project, Humphreys, Mankowski, Moos, and Finney (1999) found that self-help group involvement predicted increases in approach coping and the quality of friendships. Enhanced reliance on approach coping and better friendship networks mediated part of the effect of 12-step group involvement on reduced substance use. According to Bond, Kaskutas, and Weisner (2003), involvement in 12-step self-help groups, such as AA, strengthens social contacts that support reduced drinking and thereby contributes to better treatment outcome. Taken as whole, the findings in this area show that participation in mutual support groups promotes improvement in clients' life contexts and coping skills; they also highlight the need to better understand the processes that contribute to these beneficial effects.

Adversity and Personal Growth

Many people are remarkably resilient in the face of adversity. They may emerge from a crisis with greater self-confidence, new coping skills, closer relationships with family and friends, and a richer appreciation of life. The prevalence of life crises in which individuals have experienced positive outcomes and maturation has led to the concept of posttraumatic growth as a valuable counterpoint to the ubiquitous emphasis on learned helplessness and posttraumatic stress disorder (Tedeschi, Park, & Calhoun, 1998). To explain this phenomenon, we need a fundamental paradigm shift in how to construe and examine the aftermath of life crises.

Our conceptual framework is consistent with the idea that life crises often are "constructive confrontations" that challenge an individual and provide an opportunity for learning new skills and personal growth. These basic ideas were formulated more than 50 years ago when Erikson (1950) noted that normative developmental transitions have the potential for growth or for stagnation and decay. The process of managing transitions shapes new experiences and coping skills, and, if successful, contributes to a sense of mastery and self-confidence, which enhances the likelihood of continued maturation when new transitions occur. Caplan (1964) broadened the focus from normative transitions to unexpected life events and crises, and, relatively recently, researchers have begun to examine the positive consequences of adversity.

Key issues to address include the conditions under which successful crisis resolution leads to new coping skills; when prior stressors impel a hardening process that sets the stage for later growth; and whether lack of exposure to stressors eventuates in a dearth of learning experiences and deficient coping skills. Other related questions involve whether psychological distress is an essential catalyst for change; how cognitive coping strategies, such as positive reappraisal and a search for meaning help arouse positive affect in the presence of severe life crises; and the extent to which resilience exacts a cost of emotional insulation and an inability to form close relationships.

Conclusions and Future Directions

We have learned much about the characteristics of social contexts and the processes by which they evolve. Because each process is alterable and identifies a point of leverage for change, the findings have important implications for intervention. At the individual level, we can integrate information about every-day social contexts, such as the family, workplace, and neighborhood, into case descriptions, and thereby show how specific aspects of these settings may underlie an individual's distress and problem behavior. A snapshot of an individual's current situation can identify areas for intervention, such as those characterized by pervasive stressors or few resources, or those in which a pattern of elevated stressors and resources may signal a dangerous and volatile enmeshment.

From a broader perspective, we can use our knowledge about how settings develop and evolve to enhance the power of beneficial contexts and the fragility of harmful ones. In this vein, program evaluators and counselors have used information about actual and preferred social settings to improve the family context for youths, design effective workplaces for health care staff, enhance the quality of educational settings, and promote the positive outcomes of intervention programs (Moos, 2003).

As behavioral scientists, we have a unique role to play in this process: We contribute expertise about how contexts function and the interplay between contexts and individuals, the skill to promote ongoing assessment and participatory evaluation, and the wisdom to temper our own zeal and that of others in light of an understanding of the risks and casualties of powerful contexts. It is in these endeavors that we adhere most closely to the underlying ideals that have characterized Lee Sechrest's career: evidence-based participation in the process of social construction with the goal of enhancing personal relationships, task fulfillment, and social change.

References

Avants, S. K., Warburton, L. A., & Margolin, A. (2000). The influence of coping and depression on abstinence from illicit drug use in methadone-maintained patients. *American Journal of Drug and Alcohol Abuse, 26,* 399–416.

Beutler, L., Moos, R. H., & Lane, G. (2003). Coping, treatment planning, and treatment outcome. *Journal of Clinical Psychology, 59,* 1151–1167.

Bond, J., Kaskutas, L. A., & Weisner, C. (2003). The persistent influence of social networks and Alcoholics Anonymous on abstinence. *Journal of Studies on Alcohol, 64,* 579–588.

Caplan, G. (1964). *Principles of preventive psychiatry.* New York: Basic Books.

Chung, T., Langenbucher, J., Labouvie, E., Pandina, R., & Moos, R. (2001). Changes in alcoholic patients' coping responses predict 12-month treatment outcomes. *Journal of Consulting and Clinical Psychology, 69,* 92–100.

Cronkite, R., Moos, R. H., Twohey, J., Cohen, C., & Swindle, R. (1998). Life circumstances and personal resources as predictors of the ten-year course of depression. *American Journal of Community Psychology, 26,* 255–280.

Dohrenwend, B. P. (2000). The role of adversity and stress in psychopathology: Some evidence and its implications for theory and research. *Journal of Health and Social Behavior, 41,* 1–19.

Erikson, E. H. (1950). *Childhood and society.* New York. Norton.

Felner, R. D., Felner, T. Y., & Silverman, M. M. (2000). Prevention in mental health and social intervention. In J. Rappaport & E. Seidman (Eds.), *Handbook of community psychology* (pp. 9–42). New York: Kluwer Academic/Plenum Publishers.

Finney, J., Ouimette, P. C., Humphreys, K., & Moos, R. H. (2001). A comparative process-evaluation of VA substance abuse treatment. In M. Galanter (Ed.), *Recent developments in alcoholism: Services research in the era of managed care* (Vol. 15, pp. 373–391). New York: Kluwer Academic/Plenum Publishers.

Goldstein, A. P., Heller, K., & Sechrest, L. B. (1966). *Psychotherapy and the psychology of behavior change.* New York: Wiley.

Holahan, C. J., & Moos, R. H. (1991). Life stressors, personal and social resources, and depression: A four-year structural model. *Journal of Abnormal Psychology, 100,* 31–38.

Holahan, C. J., Moos, R. H., Holahan, C. K., & Brennan, P. (1997). Social context, coping strategies, and depressive symptoms: An expanded model with cardiac patients. *Journal of Personality and Social Psychology, 72,* 918–928.

Hooley, J. M., & Gotlib, I. A. (2000). A diathesis-stress conceptualization of expressed emotion and clinical outcome. *Applied and Preventive Psychology, 9,* 135–151.

Humphreys, K., Finney, J. W., & Moos, R. H. (1994). Applying a stress and coping perspective to research on mutual help organizations. *Journal of Community Psychology, 22,* 312–327.

Humphreys, K., Mankowski, E., Moos, R. H., & Finney, J. (1999). Enhanced friendship networks and active coping mediate the effect of self-help groups on substance abuse. *Annals of Behavioral Medicine, 21,* 54–60.

Lemke, S., & Moos, R. H. (2003). Treatment outcomes at 1-year and 5-years for older patients with alcohol use disorders. *Journal of Substance Abuse Treatment, 24,* 43–50.

Link, B. G., Struening, E. L., Rahav, M., Phelan, J., & Nuttbrock, L. (1997). On stigma and its consequences: Evidence from a longitudinal study of men with dual diagnoses of mental illness and substance abuse. *Journal of Health and Social Behavior, 38,* 177–190.

Miller, S. M. (1992). Individual differences in the coping process: What we know and when we know it. In B. N. Carpenter (Ed.), *Personal coping: Theory, research, and application* (pp. 77–91). New York: Praeger Publishers.

Moggi, F., Ouimette, P., Finney, J., & Moos, R. H. (1999). Dual diagnosis patients in substance abuse treatment: Relationships among general coping and substance-specific coping and one-year outcomes. *Addiction, 94,* 1805–1816.

Mohr, D. C. (1995). Negative outcome in psychotherapy: A critical review. *Clinical Psychology: Science and Practice, 2,* 1–27.

Moos, R. H. (1993a). *Coping Responses Inventory: Adult Form manual.* Odessa, FL: Psychological Assessment Resources.

Moos, R. H. (1993b). *Coping Responses Inventory: Youth Form manual.* Odessa, FL: Psychological Assessment Resources.

Moos, R. H. (1995). Development and application of new measures of life stressors, social resources, and coping responses. *European Journal of Psychological Assessment, 11,* 1–13.

Moos, R. H. (1997). *Evaluating treatment environments: The quality of psychiatric and substance abuse programs.* New Brunswick, NJ: Transaction.

Moos, R. H. (2002). The mystery of human context and coping: An unraveling of clues. *American Journal of Community Psychology, 30,* 67–88.

Moos, R. H. (2003). *Social Climate Scale user's guide* (3rd ed.). Redwood City, CA: Mind Garden.

Moos, R. H., Brennan, P., & Schutte, K. (1998). Life context factors, treatment, and late-life drinking behavior. In E. Gomberg, A. M. Hegedus, & R. A. Zucker (Eds.), *Alcohol problems and aging* (pp. 261–279). Washington, DC: National Institute on Alcohol Abuse and Alcoholism.

Moos, R. H., Cronkite, R., & Moos, B. (1998). Family and social resources and the 10-year course of treated depression. *Journal of Abnormal Psychology, 107,* 450–460.

Moos, R. H., Finney, J., & Cronkite, R. (1990). *Alcoholism treatment: Context, process, and outcome.* New York: Oxford University Press.

Moos, R. H., & Moos, B. (1994a). *Life Stressors and Social Resources Inventory—Adult Form manual.* Odessa, FL: Psychological Assessment Resources.

Moos, R. H., & Moos, B. (1994b). *Life Stressors and Social Resources Inventory—Youth Form manual.* Odessa, FL: Psychological Assessment Resources.

Moos, R. H., Nichol, A., & Moos, B. (2002). Risk factors for symptom exacerbation among treated patients with substance use disorders. *Addiction, 97,* 75–85.

Nathan, P. E., & Gorman, J. M. (2002). *A guide to treatments that work.* New York: Oxford.

Rohde, P., Lewinsohn, P. M., Tilson, M., & Seeley, J. R. (1990). Dimensionality of coping and its relation to depression. *Journal of Personality and Social Psychology, 58,* 499–511.

Sechrest, L. B., & Scott, A. G. (1992). Theory-driven approaches to cost–benefit analysis. In H. Chen & P. H. Rossi (Eds.), *Using theory to improve program and policy evaluations* (pp. 243–257). New York: Greenwood Press.

Sechrest, L. B., & West, S. G. (1983). Measuring the intervention in rehabilitation experiments. *International Annals of Criminology, 21*(1), 11–19.

Tedeschi, R. G., Park, C. L., & Calhoun, L. G. (Eds.). (1998). *Posttraumatic growth: Positive changes in the aftermath of crises.* Mahwah, NJ: Erlbaum

Timko, C. (2003, February). *Matching dual diagnosis patients' symptom severity to treatment intensity.* Paper presented at the Annual Health Services Research and Development Service Career Development Meeting, Washington, DC.

Timko, C., Moos, R. H., Finney, J., & Lesar, M. (2000). Long-term outcomes of alcohol use disorders: Comparing untreated individuals with those in Alcoholics Anonymous and formal treatment. *Journal of Studies on Alcohol, 61,* 529–540.

Wachs, T. D. (2001). *Necessary but not sufficient: The respective roles of single and multiple influences on individual development.* Washington, DC: American Psychological Association.

Webb, E., Campbell, D. T., Schwartz, R. D., & Sechrest, L. B. (1966). *Unobtrusive measures: A survey of nonreactive research in social science.* Chicago: Rand McNally.

Yeaton, W. H., & Sechrest, L. B. (1992). Critical dimensions in the choice and maintenance of successful treatments: Strength, integrity, and effectiveness. In A. E. Kazdin (Ed.), *Methodological issues and strategies in clinical research* (pp. 137–156). Washington, DC: American Psychological Association.

4

Stress, Coping, and Outcome in Cognitive Therapy

Lawrence H. Cohen, Kathleen C. Gunthert, and Andrew C. Butler

Translational research is defined as a program of empirical research, frequently interdisciplinary in nature, in which basic research findings inform the development of interventions and in which the evaluation of these interventions informs theory and the conduct of basic research (Hyman, 2000). The theme is that basic research and theory contribute to program development and that program evaluation contributes to basic research and theory.

There are many examples of interesting translational research programs. One example is especially relevant to our research. Teasdale et al. (2002) have conducted basic research on metacognitive awareness (the cognitive set in which negative thoughts and feelings are viewed as transitory mental events rather than core aspects of the self). They have also evaluated cognitive therapy's effects on metacognitive awareness and the predictive role of this awareness in depression relapse. Another example comes from the laboratory of Mary Dozier, a colleague at the University of Delaware. She has conducted descriptive research on the attachment relationship between foster parents and their foster infants and toddlers, and then used these data to develop prevention programs for foster families (Dozier, Higley, Albus, & Nutter, 2002).

Federal research agencies have made translational research a high priority in their funding agenda. Aware of this agenda, investigators now "package" their grant proposals with an emphasis on the translational implications of their research. Some proposals are specifically designed to develop translational (and usually interdisciplinary) research centers.

Translational research is obviously important and deserves its current status in the funding arena. Indeed, interventions are frequently developed without proper guidance from theory and basic research, and basic research is often unaffected by program evaluation findings. It is rare to find a researcher or team of researchers who is dedicated to the reciprocal development of both theory and

Research described in this chapter was supported in part by National Institute of Mental Health Grant R21-MH067825.

intervention for a specific topic. In fact, some individuals have championed translational research as a novel, ground-breaking concept. We disagree with this last point, however, because some researchers have recognized the importance of translational research for decades. The phrase "old wine in a new bottle" is admittedly a hackneyed one, but in this case it applies.

Psychotherapy and the Psychology of Behavior Change, by Arnold Goldstein, Kenneth Heller, and Lee Sechrest, was published almost 40 years ago, in 1966. The book's message was that theory and basic research findings from primarily social psychology and learning could contribute to the development of psychotherapeutic interventions. The authors specified a number of "translational" hypotheses. For example, one hypothesis was that "therapy group cohesiveness may be increased by intergroup competition" (p. 454). Another hypothesis was that "there will be greater transfer of learning from psychotherapy to extratherapy situations if therapy is provided by more than one therapist" (p. 454). Still another hypothesis was that "resistance in psychotherapy is reduced by messages which immunize the patient against subsequent counterargument" (p. 452).

The book is important not because of the validity of the hypotheses, some of which seem naïve by today's standards, but because it proposed a way of thinking about psychotherapy and intervention in general. Specifically, Goldstein et al. (1966) presented a translational research agenda for the field of psychotherapy. And that was almost 40 years ago! In our opinion, Goldstein et al.'s book is an underappreciated gem and a must-read for behavioral scientists interested in the conduct of translational research. The book foreshadowed later contributions by Lee Sechrest, all of which shared one major characteristic: They were years ahead of the field. (See Sechrest's early papers on unobtrusive measures, health psychology, treatment integrity, mental health quality assurance, and mental health research utilization, for example.) After the publication of his 1966 book, Sechrest continued to publish influential papers on the unfortunate schism between psychological science and psychotherapy research and practice (e.g., Sechrest & Smith, 1994).

Lee Sechrest is best known as a methodologist, for the development and application of unique methodological approaches to the study of important social problems. Our current research has been influenced by Sechrest insofar as it tackles an important social problem (psychotherapy outcome) by using a relatively novel methodology (daily process research) that we have borrowed from the personality and behavioral medicine fields. Specifically, our current research involves the application of a daily stress and coping paradigm to research on cognitive therapy for depression. We acknowledge that it does not meet all of the "criteria" for translational research, but it has been guided by translational principles that were presented by Goldstein et al. (1966)— specifically, the use of a basic research paradigm to further our understanding of process and outcome in cognitive therapy.

We are interested in how initial appraisals, cognitions, coping, and affective reactivity in response to everyday stressors of patients with depression are related to changes in depressive symptomatology over the course of cognitive therapy. We used a daily process design to assess the initial stress and coping variables. We predicted that, independent of their initial depression severity, patients with better initial ability to cope with daily stress would show greater symptom reduction during treatment than would patients with lesser initial ability to cope with daily stress (Rude & Rehm, 1991; Whisman, 1993). This hypothesis is consistent with a capitalization model of aptitude by treatment effects (Cronbach & Snow, 1977; Smith & Sechrest, 1991): Patients who come to treatment with relative strengths in treatment-related skills and resources should show the most improvement.

Daily Stress and Coping

As an introduction, we first present some general issues in research on stress and coping. For two decades, Lazarus and Folkman's (1984) transactional model has been the predominant model of stress and coping. They proposed the following sequence: (a) the occurrence of an event; (b) primary appraisal of the event, which involves evaluation of the event's stressfulness (e.g., threat, loss), and secondary appraisal, which involves evaluation of the individual's coping resources for that event (i.e., perceived coping efficacy); (c) the use of specific coping strategies to deal with the event—coping entails behavioral (e.g., direct action) and cognitive (e.g., positive reinterpretation) activities that are in response to the event; and finally, (d) an outcome, such as a change in mood or self-esteem. This description of the transactional model is admittedly simplistic. The model is dynamic and nonrecursive and unfolds over a period of time. Lazarus and Folkman's model is usually described as a cognitive one because it proposes that an event's stressfulness is determined by its *meaning* to the individual rather than the event's objective characteristics.

Until recently, the dominant methodology in coping research was the nomothetic or between-person approach, which examines relations among variables across individuals. For example, this approach involves correlations between number of negative life events and mood, or use of specific coping strategies and mood. However, the only inference that can be drawn from this approach is that individuals who report high numbers of negative events or the frequent use of a specific coping strategy also report high levels of a negative outcome. In the idiographic, or within-person, approach, the focus is on relations between variables over time in that person's life. This approach frequently relies on a daily process methodology. Specifically, an idiographic approach can examine whether an individual reports higher levels of negative affect on days when stress is high, compared with days when stress is low. In our research, we have relied on a combined idiographic–nomothetic approach. Specifically, we assess within-person processes and also evaluate the effects of between-person variables on these processes.

In a daily process design, stress, coping, and outcome variables are assessed repeatedly over days. There are several advantages to this design, including increased power and the ability to capture proximal stressors, appraisals, coping efforts, and outcomes closer in time to their actual occurrence, resulting in more valid assessment of these variables (Bolger, Davis, & Raraeli, 2003; Stone et al., 1998). For example, research by Stone and his colleagues has shown that retrospective reports of coping behavior correlate poorly with concurrent reports of coping behavior that span the same period (Stone et al., 1998).

Some daily studies have computed idiographic analyses of the relationship between number of daily stressors and daily negative affect (Suls, Martin, & David, 1998) and daily self-esteem (Butler, Hokanson, & Flynn, 1994), whereas other studies have computed idiographic analyses of the relationship between appraisals and coping strategies associated with daily stressors and daily negative affect (Gunthert, Cohen, & Armeli, 1999). All of these studies attempted to assess the intricacies of daily stress response processes by using a combined idiographic–nomothetic approach, and most have used multilevel modeling procedures (e.g., hierarchical linear modeling [HLM]; Bryk & Raudenbush, 1992) to capture within- and between-person effects.

In the context of an idiographic daily process design, affective reactivity can be conceptualized as a marker of *affect regulation*, broadly defined. Affect regulation is an extremely complex construct (Gross, 1998) and has been assessed in a variety of ways, including by measures of coping (Garber, Braafladt, & Weiss, 1995) and by laboratory-based mood induction procedures with resultant measures of coping and affect persistence (Gilboa & Gotlib, 1997). Recent research suggests that within-subject reactivity indices have significant potential to advance our understanding of affect regulation (Gunthert et al., 1999; Nezlek, 2002). These indices reflect an individual's day-to-day changes in mood as a function of number of daily stressors, severity of stress appraisals, or use of specific coping strategies (Bolger & Zuckerman, 1995; Gunthert et al., 1999). By definition, a highly reactive individual would show extreme fluctuations in daily negative affect or daily self-esteem as a function of the number of daily negative events or the severity of primary and secondary appraisals of daily stressors.

As mentioned previously, our current research applies a daily stress and coping paradigm to research on cognitive therapy for depression. Our daily measures were based on Lazarus and Folkman's (1984) transactional model, in that they assessed the occurrence of specific daily events and how those events were evaluated, coped with, and reacted to affectively. We used a combined idiographic–nomothetic approach. Reactivity indices were computed with HLM.

Cognitive Therapy for Depression

A fundamental component of Aaron Beck's cognitive theory and therapy of depression concerns how individuals evaluate and respond to their daily stressors. Specifically, Beck proposes that depression is maintained by negative thinking. When people are depressed, they interpret objectively negative events at the negative extreme. Beck's cognitive therapy of depression teaches patients to reduce their stress and negative affect by using adaptive cognitive and behavioral coping strategies to deal with daily stressors, change negative thoughts, and enhance their involvement in positive activities (Alford & Beck, 1997; A. T. Beck, Rush, Shaw, & Emery, 1979).

Cognitive therapy is an efficacious and effective treatment for depression and anxiety (Barlow, Raffa, & Cohen, 2002; DeRubeis & Crits-Cristoph, 1998). However, a significant percentage (perhaps 50%) of patients do not completely recover in cognitive therapy (Elkin et al., 1989). Despite a very large outcome literature, we know little about the patient factors that predict the effectiveness of cognitive therapy (Hamilton & Dobson, 2002). Identification of patient characteristics that predict outcome could point to patient factors that are malleable and can be addressed clinically, either through modification of cognitive therapy techniques, augmentation of cognitive therapy with additional interventions, or referral of specific patients to alternative treatments. Identification of patient characteristics that predict outcome could also contribute to an understanding of the mechanisms of treatment (Hamilton & Dobson, 2002).

Because of its cognitive orientation, Lazarus and Folkman's (1984) transactional model of stress and coping provides a compatible conceptual and methodological framework for our stress and coping research with patients in cognitive therapy. Specifically, in our research, we assessed patients' responses to daily stressors, including their primary and secondary appraisals, use of specific coping strategies, and daily affective reactivity (changes in daily mood), as well as their automatic thoughts associated with daily events. We then evaluated the predictive role of these daily stress and coping variables in outcome in cognitive therapy. Given cognitive therapy's emphasis on affect regulation, a capitalization model would predict that patients who begin treatment with better ability to regulate negative affect (independent of their initial level of depression) would have better outcomes than patients with worse initial ability to regulate negative affect. If obtained, this pattern would suggest the need to modify cognitive therapy for patients who begin treatment with poor ability to regulate negative affect, for example, by providing supplementary sessions on coping skills or by extending the length of treatment (Wells, 2000).

Several cognitive therapy prediction studies have included variables that are relevant to stress and coping. For example, some cognitive therapy studies have tested the predictive role of major life events (Simons, Gordon, Monroe, & Thase, 1995), the use of active coping behaviors (Burns & Nolen-Hoeksema, 1991), and cognitive vulnerability variables, such as dysfunctional attitudes (Sotsky et al., 1991) and a pessimistic explanatory style (Simons et al., 1995). Results from these studies have been inconsistent (Gunthert, Cohen, Butler, & Beck, 2005; Hamilton & Dobson, 2002). However, the predictor measures used in these studies were administered on a "one-shot" basis and therefore cannot capture the dynamic nature of the stress and coping process (Tennen & Affleck, 1996). Moreover, several researchers have criticized retrospective measures of stress and coping and dispositional measures of cognitive vulnerability as inadequate indices of affect regulation: The former are vulnerable to response biases and correlate poorly with concurrent measures of stress and coping (Stone et al., 1998), whereas the latter are vulnerable to current mood and lack sensitivity and specificity (Gotlib & Neubauer, 2000). In other words, no cognitive therapy study to date, with the exception of our research, has used "process" measures to directly assess patients' initial ability to regulate affect in response to daily stress and then evaluated this variable as a predictor of outcome.

Study 1

In our first study, patients receiving cognitive therapy for depression and anxiety completed daily measures of stress, appraisals, negative cognitions, and mood every day for 1 week at the beginning of treatment. At each treatment session, patients completed a measure of depressive symptoms. We were interested in the predictive role of daily stress and coping variables in outcome (depression reduction) in cognitive therapy.

Method

PARTICIPANTS. The participants were adult outpatients at the Beck Institute for Cognitive Therapy and Research in Bala Cynwyd, Pennsylvania (near Philadelphia). Patients who met the *Diagnostic and Statistical Manual of Mental Disorders* (4th ed.; *DSM–IV*; American Psychiatric Association, 1994) criteria for a depressive or anxiety disorder, or both, were included. Exclusionary criteria were coexisting active substance abuse or dependence and coexisting psychotic disorder. The sample consisted of 46 patients, which represented 54% of eligible patients. The most frequent diagnoses were major depression (52%), generalized anxiety disorder (13%), adjustment disorder with mixed features (9%), dysthymic disorder (7%), and adjustment disorder with depressed mood (4%). Sixty-five percent were women, 96% were Caucasian, and the average age was 39 years (*SD* = 11.15, range = 21–70 years). Approximately half of the sample was married. The participants were well educated, with 54% having an advanced or professional degree. The mean treatment length was approximately 12 sessions (*SD* = 6.93). Forty-six percent received concurrent pharmacotherapy during the course of the study. Only 4 patients (9%) terminated treatment prematurely.

All of the patients were seen once a week. Cognitive therapists were four women and three men, with a median of 10 years of experience with cognitive therapy. Although not explicitly manualized, cognitive therapy at the Beck Institute is provided by highly trained and experienced cognitive therapists who receive regular in-service supervision and consultation from Aaron and Judith Beck.

MEASURES. All of the measures were administered in a paper-and-pencil format. Patients completed the depression measure at the Beck Institute, and they completed the daily stress and coping measures at home. Patients' initial and weekly levels of depression were assessed with the 21-item Beck Depression Inventory—II (BDI–II; A. T. Beck, Steer, & Brown, 1996).

After their first treatment session, patients completed a modified version of Stone and Neale's (1984) Daily Coping Inventory at the end of the day for 7 consecutive days. Patients indicated their most stressful event of the day, and these events were coded as interpersonal, work related, somatic, emotional–cognitive (e.g., "I couldn't stop crying"), and other stressors. Patients then rated the day's most stressful event on the primary appraisal dimensions of controllability and undesirability and the secondary appraisal dimension of perceived coping efficacy (5-point scales).

Patients then indicated how they coped with the day's worst event, using the coping categories of distraction, positive reinterpretation, direct action, catharsis, acceptance, seeking social support, relaxation, and checked negative thoughts. Patients were instructed to check all of the coping strategies that they used for the day's worst event. Each coping strategy was followed by a brief definition to ensure that participants understood the strategies.

We assessed the frequency of depressive automatic thoughts in response to the day's most stressful event by using five items from A. T. Beck, Brown, Steer, Eidelson, and Riskind's (1987) Cognition Checklist (5-point scales). Cronbach's alpha in the present study was .88.

State negative affect at the end of the day was assessed with Watson and Clark's (1994) Positive and Negative Affect Schedule—Expanded Form (PANAS–X). For negative affect, we combined the 6-item anxiety subscale and the 5-item sadness subscale (5-point scales). Cronbach's alpha for this composite scale was .92.

Results

For this chapter, we summarize the major findings. Interested readers can find a full report of the study in Gunthert et al. (2005). Study compliance was good, with 76% of the patients completing all 7 days of daily assessments. The most frequent stressors were work and interpersonal events. Direct action and distraction were the most frequently used coping strategies, and catharsis was the least frequently used strategy.

To evaluate affective reactivity to negative appraisals and automatic thoughts associated with the worst event of the day, we used the within-person relationship between these variables and negative affect. We were interested in how negative affect changes as event appraisals become more negative and automatic thoughts become more frequent. Thus, for each person, we used his or her 7 days of daily ratings to compute regressions with appraisals and automatic thoughts predicting negative affect. For these analyses, we used HLM, in which each person has a unique empirical Bayes regression coefficient to indicate his or her relationship between negative appraisals (or cognitions) and negative affect. Individuals with steeper slopes are more emotionally reactive to increasingly negative appraisals and more frequent negative thoughts.

On the basis of the weekly assessments of depression (BDI–II), we used a longitudinal growth modeling approach to establish each patient's change trajectory in treatment and to identify individual differences in those trajectories. Specifically, we used the affective reactivity indices described earlier to predict individual differences in response to cognitive therapy when characterized as growth trajectories of weekly BDI–II scores. The word *growth* in this case reflects the vernacular of the statistical approach being used, longitudinal growth modeling, and is somewhat counterintuitive. We expected the actual trajectories to reflect a decrease in BDI–II scores.

When we plotted patients' depression scores as a function of time (i.e., treatment sessions), a visual inspection suggested that there was a curvilinear trend in the data. Patients' depression scores dropped rapidly during the first few sessions of treatment, but then tended to level off near the end of treatment. This pattern is consistent with the dose–response relationship frequently reported in the psychotherapy research literature (Lueger et al., 2001). Thus, we added a quadratic term to the Level 1 equation to model the curvilinear nature of the growth trajectory. In this chapter, we do not report findings from the intercept analyses—how individual differences in initial daily stress and coping related to initial status on depression (BDI–II scores). These findings can be found in Gunthert et al. (2005).

At Level 2, we predicted the growth parameters as a function of the initial daily stress and coping variables. We were particularly interested in the affective reactivity slopes described earlier. Specifically, we predicted that patients who were less reactive when they began cognitive therapy (those with flatter reactivity slopes) would show greater reduction in depression (have steeper trajectories of BDI–II scores) during treatment. In these analyses, we controlled for initial depression scores, total number of treatment sessions, and whether patients received concurrent pharmacological treatment.

Overall, the linear trend in the BDI–II trajectories (changes in depression over treatment sessions) was negative, indicating that depression decreased over time in cognitive therapy. Across the sample, the average intake BDI–II score (intercept of the growth model) was 21.78, and BDI–II scores dropped, on average, 1.26 points per session (slope of the growth model). Thus, over the course of 12 sessions, the typical patient's depression score decreased by approximately 15 points. The curvilinear trend was also significant, indicating that there was an acceleration in the rate of change at the beginning of treatment and that change tended to level off toward the end of treatment. Hence, depression tended to decrease relatively rapidly during the early phase of treatment, and the decrease was more gradual as treatment continued.

On the basis of the capitalization model, we expected that patients who began treatment with more adaptive stress and coping responses would show greater improvement over the course of therapy. As anticipated, there were a number of initial daily stress and coping variables that influenced patients' BDI–II trajectories in the expected direction. For example, the slope for patients with less frequent negative cognitions at the start of treatment was steeper; those with fewer negative cognitions responded to treatment more quickly. Individuals who had greater confidence in their coping ability (secondary appraisal scale) also had steeper slopes; that is, their rate of change in depression was faster compared with those with lower perceived coping efficacy. Another finding was that the greater use of direct action coping for patients' most stressful daily event was associated with better treatment response.

With respect to affective reactivity, patients who were less emotionally reactive to negative appraisals (associated with their most stressful daily events) were more responsive to treatment; that is, their BDI–II trajectories showed steeper reductions in depression. This finding was obtained independently of patients' initial level of depression. Moreover, the finding withstood the inclusion of additional control variables, including type of daily stressor, specific therapist, gender, marital status, depression versus anxiety diagnosis, and the presence of a coexisting Axis II disorder. However, affective reactivity to negative cognitions (associated with patients' most stressful daily events) was not a significant predictor of patients' BDI–II trajectories.

Discussion

In this study, we used a daily process design to evaluate the predictive role of initial stress and coping variables in outcome in cognitive therapy. As mentioned previously, previous attempts to evaluate the predictive role of these variables have yielded inconsistent results, which could be because of limitations in the assessment of coping and affect regulation. In addition, instead of a traditional pre–post comparison of symptom level to assess treatment outcome, we used a more powerful longitudinal growth modeling approach.

In our opinion, the most interesting analyses involve the predictive role of affective reactivity to increasingly negative appraisals and more frequent negative cognitions associated with the day's most stressful event. Results for negative cognitions were not significant, but they were significant for undesirability appraisals. Specifically, we found that patients whose end-of-day negative affect was closely associated with how undesirable they appraised the day's worst event showed a weaker response to treatment over time. Outcome was somewhat better for patients whose daily negative affect was less closely tied to their perceptions of the undesirability of the day's worst event.

This finding involving undesirability appraisals is novel. Our within-subject index of daily affect regulation (i.e., negative affective reactivity) circumvents many of the problems associated with cross-sectional, between-person analyses of stress, coping, and outcomes (Tennen & Affleck, 1996). Although a number of therapy researchers have evaluated the predictive role of stress and coping variables, broadly defined, none to our knowledge have collected stress and coping data on a daily basis and then used within-person analyses to evaluate affect regulation processes.

Our findings have some clinical implications for the practice of cognitive therapy. In standard cognitive therapy, the early phase of treatment focuses on coping skills training. Then, cognitive therapy focuses on the exploration and modification of underlying dysfunctional attitudes and beliefs. This second phase usually begins after five or six sessions (J. Beck, 1995). Perhaps for highly reactive patients, who have problems with daily affect regulation, the first phase of cognitive therapy should be extended. This might require longer or additional sessions in the early part of cognitive therapy, or perhaps the addition of an adjunctive skills training group.

We acknowledge that our study had several methodological limitations. First, there was no control group. It is unclear whether we would have obtained the same findings for patients in any kind of treatment, including pharmacotherapy and other types of psychotherapy. Second, our use of paper-and-pencil measures precluded corroboration of study compliance. Stone, Shiffman, Schwartz, Broderick, and Hufford (2003) documented the poor reliability of participants' daily completion of paper-and-pencil measures. Computer-assisted measurement, which tracks the time when reports are actually completed, is a superior measurement approach. Third, although the terms *affective reactivity* and *affect regulation* imply cause–effect relationships, the correlational nature of our data does not allow conclusions regarding causality or the direction of causality. Finally, we did not administer the daily stress and coping measures at the end of treatment, and therefore we were unable to evaluate changes in affect regulation as a result of cognitive therapy.

Study 2: Current Research

Our current research at the Beck Institute, funded by the National Institute of Mental Health, is based on Study 1. Our major objectives are (a) to determine whether cognitive therapy improves the ability of patients with depression to regulate daily negative affect and self-esteem in response to daily stress, and, (b) like Study 1, to determine whether patients with depression who begin cognitive therapy with relative strengths in daily affect regulation have better outcomes (i.e., depression reduction) in treatment than patients who begin cognitive therapy with relative weaknesses in daily affect regulation.

The study is ongoing. Daily stress and coping measures are administered before the first session of treatment and again six sessions later. At each time, data are collected nightly for 7 consecutive nights. Participants are approximately 60 patients with major depression who are receiving cognitive therapy at the Beck Institute. Daily data are collected via an interactive voice response (IVR) system developed by Healthcare Technology Systems in Madison, Wisconsin. Every night during Time 1 (right after intake) and Time 2 (after the sixth treatment session), patients call a dedicated 1-800 phone number and respond to automated questions using the numbers on their touch-tone telephone. The daily interview requires about 8 minutes. The measures and statistical analyses are similar to those described previously.

An IVR procedure has a number of strengths. It can document a patient's compliance with the study procedure, because the day and time of all phone calls are recorded. It can easily be integrated with a software program so that responses are immediately coded and stored in a database. In general, an IVR procedure achieves the same goals as sophisticated palm pilots while minimizing participant burden.

This project represents the first application of an IVR-based daily stress and coping methodology, and idiographic indices of daily affect regulation, to research on cognitive therapy. Our project is motivated by the belief that traditional nomothetic designs and methods used to date cannot capture the daily stress and coping processes that have been hypothesized to influence change in cognitive therapy. If successful, our methodology will have broad applicability to fundamental questions in psychotherapy research involving daily affect regulation—for example, the mediating role of affect regulation in treatment outcome, and the predictive role of posttreatment affect regulation in depression relapse.

Overall, our research is unique in its application of a daily stress and coping paradigm, borrowed from the personality and behavioral medicine fields, to research on cognitive therapy for depression. We believe that it is based on translational principles, insofar as we are studying a clinical intervention with methods that are usually associated with more basic research. We would like to think that our research is consistent with the spirit of Goldstein et al. (1966) and other papers by Lee Sechrest (e.g., Sechrest & Smith, 1994) that emphasize the reciprocal relationship between psychological science and the development and evaluation of psychotherapy.

References

Alford, B., & Beck, A. T. (1997). *The integrative power of cognitive therapy.* New York: Guilford Press.

American Psychiatric Association. (1994). *Diagnostic and statistical manual of mental disorders* (4th ed.). Washington, DC: Author.

Barlow, D., Raffa, S., & Cohen, E. (2002). Psychosocial treatments for panic disorders, phobias, and generalized anxiety disorders. In P. Nathan & M. Gorman (Eds.), *A guide to treatments that work* (pp. 301–335). London: Oxford University Press.

Beck, A. T., Brown, G., Steer, R., Eidelson, J., & Riskind, J. (1987). Differentiating anxiety and depression: A test of the content-specificity hypothesis. *Journal of Abnormal Psychology, 96,* 179–183.

Beck, A. T., Rush, A., Shaw, B., & Emery, G. (1979). *Cognitive therapy of depression.* New York: Guilford Press.

Beck, A. T., Steer, R., & Brown, G. (1996). *Beck Depression Inventory manual* (2nd edition). San Antonio, TX: Psychological Corporation.

Beck, J. (1995). *Cognitive therapy: Basics and beyond.* New York: Guilford Press.

Bolger, N., Davis, A., & Rafaeli, E. (2003). Diary methods: Capturing life as it is lived. *Annual Review of Psychology, 54,* 579–616.

Bolger, N., & Zuckerman, A. (1995). A framework for studying personality in the stress process. *Journal of Personality and Social Psychology, 69,* 890–902.

Bryk, A., & Raudenbush, S. (1992). *Hierarchical linear models.* Newbury Park, CA: Sage.

Burns, D., & Nolen-Hoeksema, S. (1991). Coping styles, homework compliance, and the effectiveness of cognitive–behavioral therapy. *Journal of Consulting and Clinical Psychology, 59,* 305–311.

Butler, A., Hokanson, J., & Flynn, H. (1994). A comparison of self-esteem lability and low trait self-esteem as vulnerability factors for depression. *Journal of Personality and Social Psychology, 66,* 166–177.

Cronbach, L., & Snow, R. (1977). *Aptitudes and instructional methods.* New York: Irvington.

DeRubeis, R., & Crits-Christoph, P. (1998). Empirically supported individual and group psychological treatments for adult mental disorders. *Journal of Consulting and Clinical Psychology, 66,* 37–52.

Dozier, M., Higley, E., Albus, K., & Nutter, A. (2002). Intervening with foster infants' caregivers: Targeting three critical needs. *Infant Mental Health Journal, 25,* 541–554.

Elkin, I., Shea, M., Watkins, J., Imber, S., Sotsky, S., Collins, J., et al. (1989). NIMH Treatment of Depression Collaborative Research Program: General effectiveness of treatments. *Archives of General Psychiatry, 46,* 971–983.

Garber, J., Braafladt, N., & Weiss, B. (1995). Affect regulation in depressed and nondepressed children and young adolescents. *Development and Psychopathology, 7,* 93–115.

Gilboa, E., & Gotlib, I. (1997). Cognitive biases and affect persistence in previously dysphoric and never-dysphoric individuals. *Cognition and Emotion, 11,* 517–538.

Goldstein, A., Heller, K., & Sechrest, L. B. (1966). *Psychotherapy and the psychology of behavior change.* New York: Wiley.

Gotlib, I., & Neubauer, D. (2000). Information-processing approaches to the study of cognitive biases in depression. In S. Johnson, A. Hayes, T. Fields, N. Schneiderman, & P. McCabe (Eds.), *Stress, coping, and depression* (pp. 117–143). Mahwah, NJ: Erlbaum.

Gross, J. (1998). The emerging field of emotion regulation: An integrative review. *Review of General Psychology, 2,* 271–299.

Gunthert, K., Cohen, L., & Armeli, S. (1999). The role of neuroticism in daily stress and coping. *Journal of Personality and Social Psychology, 77,* 1087–1100.

Gunthert, K., Cohen, L., Butler, A., & Beck, J. (2005). Predictive role of daily coping and affective reactivity in cognitive therapy outcome: Application of a daily process design to psychotherapy research. *Behavior Therapy, 36,* 79–90.

Hamilton, K., & Dobson, K. (2002). Cognitive therapy of depression: Pretreatment patient predictors of outcome. *Clinical Psychology Review, 22,* 875–893.

Hyman, S. (2000). Reshaping behavior science at NIMH. *APS Observer, 13,* pp. 3, 41.

Lazarus, R., & Folkman, S. (1984). *Stress, appraisal, and coping.* New York: Springer.

Lueger, R., Howard, K., Martinovich, Z., Lutz, W., Anderson, E., & Grisson, G. (2001). Assessing treatment outcome of patients using expected treatment response models. *Journal of Consulting and Clinical Psychology, 69,* 150–158.

Nezlek, J. (2002). Day-to-day relationships between self-awareness, daily events, and anxiety. *Journal of Personality, 70,* 249–275.

Rude, S., & Rehm, L. (1991). Response to treatments for depression: The role of initial status on targeted cognitive and behavioral skills. *Clinical Psychology Review, 11,* 494–514.

Sechrest, L. B., & Smith, B. (1994). Psychotherapy is the practice of psychology. *Journal of Psychotherapy Integration, 4,* 1–29.

Simons, A., Gordon, J., Monroe, S., & Thase, P. (1995). Toward an integration of psychologic, social, and biologic factors in depression. Effects on outcome and course of cognitive therapy. *Journal of Consulting and Clinical Psychology, 63,* 369–377.

Smith, B., & Sechrest, L. B. (1991). Treatment of Aptitude × Treatment interactions. *Journal of Consulting and Clinical Psychology, 59,* 233–244.

Sotsky, S., Glass, D., Shea, M., Pilkonis, P., Collins, J., Elkin, I., et al. (1991). Patient predictors of response to psychotherapy and pharmacotherapy: Findings in the NIMH Treatment of Depression Collaborative Research Program. *American Journal of Psychiatry, 148,* 997–1008.

Stone, A., & Neale, J. (1984). New measure of daily coping: Development and preliminary results. *Journal of Personality and Social Psychology, 4,* 892–906.

Stone, A., Schwartz, J., Neale, J., Shiffman, S., Marco, C., Hickcox, M., et al. (1998). A comparison of coping assessed by ecological momentary assessment and retrospective recall. *Journal of Personality and Social Psychology, 4,* 892–906.

Stone, A., Shiffman, S., Schwartz, J., Broderick, J., & Hufford, M. (2003) Patient compliance with paper and electronic diaries. *Controlled Clinical Trials, 24,* 182–199.

Suls, J., Martin, R., & David, J. (1998). Person–environment fit and its limits: Agreeableness, neuroticism, and emotional reactivity to interpersonal conflict. *Personality and Social Psychology Bulletin, 24,* 88–98.

Teasdale, J., Moore, R., Hayhurst, H., Pope, M., Williams, S., & Segal, Z. (2002). Metacognitive awareness and prevention of relapse in depression: Empirical evidence. *Journal of Consulting and Clinical Psychology, 70,* 275–287.

Tennen, H., & Affleck, G. (1996). Daily processes in coping with chronic pain: Methods and analytic strategies. In M. Zeidner & N. Endler (Eds.), *Handbook of coping* (pp. 151–177). New York: Wiley.

Watson, D., & Clark, L. A. (1994). *The PANAS–X: Manual for the Positive and Negative Affect Schedule—Expanded Form.* Iowa City: University of Iowa Press.

Wells, A. (2000). *Emotional disorders and metacognition: Innovative cognitive therapy.* New York: Wiley.

Whisman, M. (1993). Mediators and moderators of change in cognitive therapy of depression. *Psychological Bulletin, 114,* 248–265.

Part II

Methodology in Research and Evaluation

5

Mechanisms of Change in Psychotherapy: Advances, Breakthroughs, and Cutting-Edge Research (Do Not Yet Exist)

Alan E. Kazdin

The focus of this chapter is on psychotherapy research and a call for research on mechanisms of therapeutic change. The central theses, statement of the problem, and suggestions for redressing critical lacunae are in keeping with the work of Lee Sechrest, in whose honor this chapter was written. Sechrest has had many lines of work, one of which is psychotherapy. Examples of critical topics he has addressed include the importance of assessing and evaluating treatment integrity, evaluating and calibrating outcome measures, and understanding moderators of therapeutic change (Sechrest, McKnight, & McKnight, 1996; Sechrest, West, Phillips, Redner, & Yeaton, 1979; Sechrest, White, & Brown, 1979; Smith & Sechrest, 1991). We are all indebted to Sechrest for his many contributions and for his untiring insistence on high-quality research and assistance in improving our ways of thinking about and executing research.

The present chapter includes two themes or characteristics of Sechrest's writings. The first of these is that methodology makes a difference. We ought to care about research methods because they affect substantive and practical issues. For example, in one of his books he has shown that we know too little about how to rehabilitate criminal offenders, not because of the absence of creative ideas or even because of a lack of research (Sechrest, White, & Brown, 1979). Rather, the quality of research and pervasive lapses in the integrity of treatment at the time signaled that few of the creative ideas had been well or fairly tested. Similarly, the present chapter discusses deficits in research methods that materially affect the quality of treatment that is provided to patients.

Completion of this chapter was facilitated by support from the William T. Grant Foundation (98-1872-98) and the National Institute of Mental Health (MH59029).

A second characteristic of Sechrest's work is the constructive side. It is easy to review almost any body of research with methodological weapons of mass destruction (e.g., threats to validity) in a way that leaves a reader in despair. Sechrest has provided measured critiques and noted checkered practices in various substantive and methodological areas. Invariably, he provides constructive ways to redress the problems. For example, the case study is riddled with all sorts of problems as a way of drawing scientifically valid inferences. Sechrest has articulated ways in which strong inferences can be drawn and the conditions that can make the case study a valuable and valid source of knowledge (Sechrest, Stewart, Stickle, & Sidani, 1996). This chapter emulates the characteristic of providing constructive ways through seeming cul-de-sacs. There are limitations of research devoted to understanding psychotherapy and checkered research priorities currently in vogue. Beyond lamenting these, the chapter makes concrete suggestions on how to improve research.

Several forms of psychotherapy for children, adolescents, and adults have been shown to produce therapeutic change. Reviews of therapy research have concluded that many psychotherapies, when studied carefully, produce therapeutic change and greater changes than those which occur over time without a formal intervention (Kazdin, 2000; Lambert, 2004). Recent research has focused on delineating those treatments which are evidence based and distinguishing these from the hundreds of treatments that have yet to be studied or whose effects are not evident (e.g., Chambless & Ollendick, 2001; Kazdin & Weisz, 2003; Nathan & Gorman, 2002). Even with thousands of therapy studies, many questions remain to be answered; some of these are rather basic and absolutely pivotal. Arguably the most pivotal question is why and how does therapy work? That is, what are the processes and mechanisms through which changes are achieved in the individual? There has been scant attention to the question (Kazdin, 1999; Kazdin & Nock, 2003).

Interest in mechanisms of change in relation to social, emotional, and behavioral problems is not new. For example, Aristotle (384–322 BCE) emphasized the role of catharsis in tragic drama, comedy, and the arts more generally in arousing and alleviating emotional states (*Poetics*, 350 BCE; *Politics* VIII, 350 BCE). He spoke of how people experiencing emotional outbreaks could be cured by cathartic songs (*Politics* VIII, 7.1342a, 4–16). Aristotle's views have been used to explain the effects of psychotherapy. For example, Bernays (1857), a relative of Freud by marriage, drew on Aristotle to note that the cathartic benefits obtained via tragic drama are similar to the process of healing in psychotherapy.

Armchair discussions and theorizing about why treatment works are plentiful, but supportive evidence is quite rare. Moreover, the way research currently is designed and executed, even with exemplary studies (e.g., randomized controlled trials [RCTs], pretest–posttest designs), may not be able to identify why treatment works. This chapter focuses on the importance of studying mechanisms of therapy, limitations of existing data evaluation and design strategies, and what changes might be made in research to study how therapy produces change.

Exhibit 5.1. Key Terms and Concepts

Cause: The intervention that led to the change.

Mechanism or mediator: The basis for the effect; that is, the processes or events that are responsible for the change (used here interchangeably with mediator); the reasons that change occurred or how change came about.

Construct validity: In research methodology, construct validity encompasses the distinction between the cause (treatment effect) and the underlying basis (construct) for the effect (Cook & Campbell, 1979). For example, a randomized controlled clinical trial can show that treatment was responsible for (caused) the change but may or may not shed light on what facet of that treatment (mechanism, mediator) was responsible for the change and why the change occurred. That is, the construct underlying the change remains to be evaluated.

Study of Mechanisms

Critical Terms Defined

The focus of the chapter is on *mechanisms*, by which I mean those processes or events which lead to and are responsible for therapeutic change.[1] There are a few related terms that are important to distinguish and endless confusion and inconsistency in their use. Exhibit 5.1 provides a statement of key terms just to ensure that my own contribution to the confusion is explicit.

In psychotherapy research, and psychological research more generally, *mediator* is often used as the term intended to signify a cause or mechanism of change and distinguished from *moderator*, as evident in the now-classic paper by Baron and Kenny (1986). *Mediator* refers to the process(es) through which change occurs; *moderator* refers to any characteristic that influences the extent to which or, indeed, whether change occurs. Mediator and moderator are related. For example, if one finds sex differences in response to an intervention (e.g., treatment, harsh child-rearing practices), one can say that the sex of the child serves as a moderator for the intervention. The finding raises the prospect that different mediators may be at work. There are many such findings in the social and biological sciences in which moderators clearly suggest the likelihood that different mediators are at work. For example, aggressive

---

[1] I use the terms *mechanism, mediator,* and *process responsible for change* interchangeably, in keeping with their more frequent use (e.g., Baron & Kenny, 1986). In using these terms, I refer to the component, element, or feature that is the basis for the change or the reason that change occurs. Sometimes a distinction is made between mediators and mechanisms (e.g., Kraemer, Wilson, Fairburn, & Agras, 2002). *Mediators* refers to possible ways in which a treatment might have an effect. They are demonstrated through observation and correlation (e.g., multiple regression) to explain or account for the outcome. *Mechanism* is reserved for a demonstration in which a more stringent criterion is met. An experiment is required in which the mechanism is manipulated and shown to produce change. I combine the uses here because the distinction can be blurry and because the goal is to understand why and how treatment produces change. Strategies to address this goal serve the basis of this chapter.

behavior during elementary school years predicts later delinquency in adolescence for boys but not for girls (Tremblay et al., 1992). The finding raises the prospect that different mechanisms might be involved in the processes leading to delinquency for male and female adolescents. In short, moderators have implications for mediators, a topic of keen interest but one not included in this chapter.

In the context of this discussion, I refer to *mechanisms of change* to reflect the processes through which therapeutic change occurs. This requires showing a causal relation between an intervention and an outcome of interest. Yet a causal relation alone is not sufficient. For example, an RCT of treatment (e.g., comparing treatment vs. no treatment) can establish a causal relation between an intervention and a therapeutic change. Demonstrating a causal relation does not necessarily explain *why* the relation was obtained. The treatment may have caused the change, but was this due to specific or conceptually hypothesized components of treatment (e.g., cognitive restructuring, habituation) or some other construct or constructs (e.g., attention/placebo influences, stress reduction, mobilization of hope)?[2]

As an example, there are very few types of psychotherapies as well established as cognitive therapy (CT) as applied to depression among adults (American Psychiatric Association, 2000; Hollon & Beck, 2004). By all counts, this treatment is evidence based in light of the range of trials. But why does CT work? That is, through what mechanisms? In fact, little can be stated as to why treatment works. It is not obvious, clear, or established that changes in cognitions are the basis for therapeutic change (Burns & Spangler, 2001; Ilardi & Craighead, 1994; Whisman, 1993, 1999). Indeed, suitable studies are rarely done. Some studies have demonstrated that changes in cognitions during treatment predict symptom change (e.g., DeRubeis et al., 1990; Kwon & Oei, 2003). Yet, it has not been clear in such studies whether symptom change preceded changes in cognition, a point elaborated later in this chapter. In general, there is a firm basis for stating that CT can change depression but little empirical basis for stating why.

The distinction between the cause and the basis of the cause is readily illustrated from the extensive literature on cigarette smoking and lung cancer. Spanning decades, cross-sectional and longitudinal studies and research with humans and animals have established a causal role between cigarette smoking and lung cancer. Establishing a causal relation does not automatically explain the mechanisms, that is, the process(es) through which change has come about. The mechanism has only been demonstrated relatively recently. In specific, a chemical (benzo[a]pyrene) found in cigarette smoke induces genetic mutation (at specific regions of the gene's DNA) that is identical to the damage evident in lung cancer cells (Denissenko, Pao, Tang, & Pfeifer, 1996). This finding is considered to convey precisely how cigarette smoking leads to cancer at the molecular level. Thus, beyond the demonstration of a causal relation (smoking

---

[2] I use the term *causal relation* throughout the chapter. There are many conditions and requirements for inferring cause in science, as reviewed elsewhere (Kazdin & Nock, 2003). By *cause* in this chapter, I mean the demonstration that some intervention has been shown to produce change and that other influences are implausible as explanations of the effect.

leads to cancer), a fine-grained analysis of mechanisms conveys what happens to produce the outcome.

Why Study Mechanisms?

Evaluating mechanisms of therapeutic change is important for several reasons. (See Exhibit 5.2.) First, there is an embarrassing wealth of treatments in use. For example, in the context of child and adolescent therapy alone, leaving aside the much larger area of adult therapy, over 550 psychotherapies are in use (Kazdin, 2000). This count is conservative because it omits various combinations of treatments and eclectic hybrids and draws only on interventions that are documented within the English language. Even so, consider the number as a reasonable approximation. Presumably some large number of these produces changes; it is not likely that all of the different treatments produce change for different reasons. Understanding the mechanisms of change can bring order and parsimony to the current status of multiple interventions.

Second, therapy can have quite broad outcome effects, beyond the familiar benefits of reducing social, emotional, and behavioral problems (e.g., suicidal ideation, depression, and panic attacks). In addition, therapy reduces physical ailments (e.g., pain, blood pressure), improves recovery from surgery or illness, and increases the quality of life. (See Kazdin, 2000.) How do these effects come about? Understanding how therapy produces change in such a diverse array of outcomes would be important. Some effects may be direct (i.e., altered directly through the process of change in therapy), and others may be concomitant effects that result from improvements in symptoms or impairment. Revealing the mechanisms of therapy will clarify the connections between what is done (treatment) and what happens (outcomes).

Third, an obvious goal of treatment is to optimize therapeutic change. By understanding the processes that account for therapeutic change, one should be better able to foster and maximize improvements in clients. Consider the development and use of treatment manuals to convey the point. Treatment manuals consist of descriptions of the procedures used in therapy. The manuals codify what is done, by whom, and when. Manuals vary from explicit statements and transcripts of the therapist's presentations on a session-by-session basis to broad principles to guide the clinician in how to make decisions about what to do in treatment. The advance that treatment manuals represent is not at all in question here. However, without knowing how therapy works and what

Exhibit 5.2. Why We Need to Understand Mechanisms

---

1. Bring order to the vast number of treatments.
2. Explain the broad effects of therapy.
3. Maximize therapeutic change.
4. Enhance generalization of treatments to clinical practice.
5. Identify moderators to pursue.
6. Understand change processes more generally.

---

the necessary, sufficient, and facilitative ingredients are and within what "dose" range, it is difficult to develop optimally effective treatment.

Most treatment manuals probably include the following components:

- low doses of effective practices (i.e., factors that genuinely make a difference);
- ancillary but important facets that make delivery more palatable (e.g., the spoonful of sugar that makes the medicine go down);
- superstitious behavior on the part of those of us who develop manuals (e.g., factors that we believe make a difference or that we like); and
- factors that impede or merely fail to optimize therapeutic change.

The difficulty is that without understanding how treatment works, which element in a manual falls into which of these categories is a matter of surmise. If we wish to optimize therapeutic change, understanding the critical ingredients and processes through which they operate is essential.

Fourth, a priority of contemporary treatment research is to extend treatment to clinic settings (e.g., National Advisory Mental Health Council [NAMHC], 1999; NAMHC Workgroup on Child and Adolescent Mental Health Intervention Development and Deployment, 2001). Diverse terms have been introduced to describe these extensions, including *translational research, transportability,* and *tests of effectiveness* (in contrast to *efficacy*), to mention a few. The terms refer to a common question, namely, will treatments work in real-world settings? Obviously, we wish to extend findings from research to practice. Less obvious is that doing so without understanding how treatment works is quite problematic.

Extension and evaluation of treatment in clinic settings have all sorts of problems that can increase variability and reduce the ability to demonstrate therapeutic change (Kazdin, 2003). However, we enter the clinical arena with one hand tied behind our back if we apply an unspecified and possibly low dose of some treatment that we do not understand. To optimize the generality of treatment effects from research to practice, we would like to know the critical ingredients. This is related to the prior point about manuals. We want to know what is needed to make treatment work, what are the optimal conditions, and what we ought to and ought not to worry about as some components get diluted when treatment is moved from the lab to clinical practice.

Fifth, understanding how therapy works can help identify moderators of treatment, that is, variables on which the effectiveness of a given treatment may depend. There are an unlimited number of moderators that can plausibly influence outcome. Understanding the processes through which treatment operates can help sort through those facets which might be particularly influential in treatment outcome. For example, if changes in cognitive processes account for therapeutic change, this finding might draw attention to characteristics of these processes or their underpinnings at pretreatment. Pretreatment status of cognitive processes (abstract reasoning, problem solving, attributions), stages of cognitive development, and neurological or neuropsychological characteristics on which these cognitions might depend are just some of the moderators that might be especially worth studying, depending on the specific processes shown to mediate treatment effects. Other promising moderators that influence treatment might be proposed on theoretical grounds once the mechanisms of therapy are known.

Sixth, understanding the mechanisms through which change takes place is important beyond the context of psychotherapy because of its broader relation to psychological science. There are many therapeutic processes in everyday life. By therapeutic, I refer to interventions or experiences that improve adjustment and adaptive functioning, ameliorate problems of mental and physical health, help people manage and cope with stress and crises, and, more generally, navigate the shoals of life. As examples, participating in religion, chatting with friends, exercising, undergoing hypnosis, and writing about sources of stress all have supportive evidence in their behalf. Therapy research is not merely about techniques but rather about the broader question, namely, how does one intervene to change social, emotional, and behavioral characteristics? Mechanisms that elaborate how therapy works might have generality for understanding human functioning more generally. The other side is also true. Mechanisms that explain how other change methods work might well inform therapy. Basic psychological processes (e.g., learning, memory, perception, persuasion, social interaction) and their biological pathways (e.g., changes in neurotransmitters, responsiveness of receptors to transmitters) may be common to many types of interventions, including psychotherapy.

Current Methods for Studying Mechanisms of Change in Psychotherapy

Methods for studying mechanisms are available and indeed have been used in the context of treatment research (Hofmann, 2000; Weersing & Weisz, 2002). The ways in which mechanisms have been studied do not permit the empirical demonstration of processes that explain therapeutic change. I highlight current methods and why we have not been able to learn about mechanisms from them.

The Statistical Mediation Approach

OVERVIEW. Statistical evaluation can play a central role in addressing whether a particular construct accounts for change. Multiple regression techniques, path analysis, structural equation modeling, and bootstrap methods are prominent options to evaluate whether a given construct is likely to account for an outcome (Baron & Kenny, 1986; Holmbeck, 2002; Hoyle & Smith, 1994; Kenny, Kashy, & Bolger, 1998; Shrout & Bolger, 2002). Multiple regression analyses have been the most commonly used techniques, and an overview of the logic conveys the benefits as well as the problems. Consider a hypothetical outcome study in which we evaluate the following components:

> A = an intervention (the treatment)
> B = a mediator, mechanism, or process that explains why A works
> C = an outcome (therapeutic change)

The interrelations of A, B, and C, as evaluated statistically, are used to infer whether B might well be the reason that treatment works. In demonstrating mediation statistically, four conditions and tests are usually proposed.

1. The treatment or intervention (A) must be related to the therapeutic change (C).
2. The treatment must be related to the proposed mediator (B).
3. The proposed mediator (B) must be related to the therapeutic change (C).
4. The relation between the intervention (A) and the therapeutic change (C) must be reduced after statistically controlling for the proposed mediator (B).

The logic seems compelling because the many conditions, if met, suggest that the impact of treatment (A) on therapeutic change (C) really depends on some intervening processes or mechanism (B). There are many nuances that the description ignores. For example, the extent to which the ABC relationship depends on (is reduced by) controlling for B is a matter of degree, and there is no cut point to decide whether there is or is not support for a particular mediational view. More generally, the various statistical analyses are not free from controversy. In fact, whether mediation is shown even if central conditions are met can be challenged. (See Kraemer, Stice, Kazdin, Offord, & Kupfer, 2001; Kraemer, Wilson, Fairburn, & Agras, 2002.) I merely wish to convey the fact that the statistical analyses highlighted here are used to evaluate mechanisms of change in therapy.

LIMITATIONS. A key limitation in the use of many mediational analyses is the fact that the time line between the mediator and the outcome is not established. To establish a causal relation requires that the putative cause be shown to occur before the outcome. Most psychotherapy studies of mediation evaluate the mediator and symptoms at pretreatment and posttreatment. Change in the mediator (pre–post) is shown to correlate, predict, mediate, and account for variance in relation to the outcome. The statistical analysis alone cannot establish that one influence preceded and therefore possibly mediated the other.

The language of many data-analytic strategies lends itself to misconception in relation to the time line. For instance, regression analyses identify variables as *predictors,* or independent variables, and others as *outcomes,* or dependent variables. Yet, the statistical analyses make no assumption of a time line for the variables that are entered; the distinction between antecedent (independent) and outcome (dependent) variables, from the standpoint of the steps of the statistical analyses, is arbitrary. Even if the statistical analysis of mediation is included in a longitudinal study in which the proposed mediator is assessed before the outcome, the time line can still be a problem. This point is better explained by discussing assessment and design issues rather than statistical analyses.

Design Methods for Studying Mechanisms

OVERVIEW. *Design* refers to the plan or arrangement of the study and the strategies that will be used to rule out the various sorts of threats to validity, artifacts, and biases. RCTs remain the primary method of demonstrating a causal relation between treatment and therapeutic change, although there are other rigorous experimental methods (Kazdin, 2003). A causal relation between the intervention (as a whole) and therapeutic change is nicely addressed in an RCT, as mentioned previously.

LIMITATIONS. Identifying specific mechanisms of change, or what active ingredient is responsible for the observed effects, is not usually permitted by such designs. The proposed mechanism and outcome are usually assessed at the same time, namely, at pretreatment and posttreatment. Statistical analyses of the type referred to previously may show that change in cognitions mediated a change in symptoms. Yet, the timing of the assessments in relation to mediator and outcome does not permit one to conclude that change in cognitions mediated or was the causal mechanism of therapeutic change. It may even be generous to say that this pattern (change in symptoms and cognitions) is "compatible with" cognitions as a mediator, because the findings are also compatible with cognitions having no mediational role at all. The study of mechanisms of change in therapy, or the reasons that therapy produces effects, requires assessment during the course of treatment to establish the time line. Showing that the proposed process changed and that therapeutic change followed moves us closer to establishing that the process may be the mechanism involved.

The most common limitation of current techniques used to study mediation and mechanisms of change pertains to the failure to establish a time line. Consider the earlier example in more detail to convey two facets about the time-line problem. CT (A) might be administered to patients with depression, and we propose that change in cognitive processes is the mechanism (B) leading to therapeutic change (C). We assess depression and cognitions at pretreatment and posttreatment and conduct various statistical analyses to evaluate the relation of cognitive processes to treatment outcome. An obvious difficulty is that cognitive processes and symptom change were assessed at the same time (pre, post), and one cannot show whether one preceded the other. Symptom change could lead to changes in cognitions C → B, vice versa (B → C), or, of course, the "third-variable" problem (some D → B, C). We may know that A (treatment) was responsible for change, but strictly speaking we cannot tell why the change occurred, that is, what the mediator is.

Assessing proposed mechanisms during treatment is necessary but not sufficient to show the time line between mechanism and outcome. The assessment of symptom change is required during treatment as well. An example from a well-studied area of therapy conveys these requirements. A great deal of research has focused on the therapeutic alliance, that is, the extent to which the client and the therapist bond, work collaboratively, and have a positive relationship (e.g., Norcross, 2002). There are many measures, and views of alliance and their differences, important in other contexts, are not pertinent to the points made here.

One view has been that alliance leads to therapeutic change. That is, during the course of treatment, an alliance develops, and if this is a good alliance, it predicts and accounts for improvement in symptoms. To study this requires that one look at alliance during treatment. Usually, assessment is based on videotaping one or a few sessions early and mid treatment, coding alliance from the tapes, and showing that alliance predicts later therapeutic change. There are scores of excellent studies indicating that the therapist–patient relationship predicts therapeutic change (Norcross, 2002; Orlinsky, Rønnestad, & Willutzki, 2004).

To demonstrate that alliance is a critical mechanism requires that the putative cause (alliance) come before the outcome (therapeutic change). It is possible that alliance and symptoms both changed in the middle of treatment, and showing that alliance predicts later symptom change by itself does not show that alliance plays a causal role. Ideally, to show the temporal relation, one must show that alliance has changed and symptoms have not, but eventually will, change later. Merely because symptoms are not assessed in the middle of treatment does not mean they have not already changed. Indeed, it is conceivable that very early in treatment, clients get a little better (some symptom improvement) and *then* form a stronger or better alliance with the therapist as a result. That is, symptom change may mediate or lead to a strong alliance. Any demonstration that alliance predicts therapeutic change does not necessarily show that alliance is the basis for therapeutic change; symptom change may have already occurred before the putative mediator operated.

Actually, some research to help sort this situation out has been completed. A study of psychodynamically oriented supportive therapy showed that changes in alliance early in treatment predict symptom change at the end of treatment (Barber, Connolly, Crits-Christoph, Gladis, & Siqueland, 2000). This is in keeping with a large body of evidence. However, a critical addition was included. Both symptom change and alliance were assessed at multiple points. Symptom changes early in treatment predicted alliance, and alliance also predicted further symptom change. This suggests that symptom change and alliance mutually influence each other. Assessments of both symptom change and alliance were completed at multiple points during the course of treatment to identify these interesting relations. Other studies with assessments at multiple points have shown that improved alliance follows improvements in symptoms (Tang & DeRubeis, 1999). As a more general point, establishing the time line requires that assessment of the putative cause occur before the putative outcome. To accomplish this may require that both the "outcome" (e.g., symptoms) and proposed mechanisms be assessed during treatment.

Design Options in Outcome Research

Consider different types of outcome studies and how they address questions related to the mechanism of change. Table 5.1 lists five outcome designs that

Table 5.1. Outcome Study Designs and Evaluation of Mechanisms

Design variation	Mechanism assessment			Outcome assessment		
	Pre	During	Post	Pre	During	Post
1. Usual outcome design	0	0	0	X	0	X
2. Concurrent study of mechanisms and outcomes	X	0	X	X	0	X
3. Assessment of mechanisms during treatment	0	X	0	X	0	X
4. Assessment of mechanisms and outcomes during treatment	X	X	X	X	X	X
5. Assessment of mechanisms and outcomes all or most sessions	X	X, X, X,. . .	X	X	X, X, X,. . .	X

Note. X = assessment is conducted; 0 = no assessment.

vary in the assessment of potential mediators or mechanisms of change and treatment outcome. Assume all to be RCTs in which treatment is compared with no treatment. The table presents the assessment for each of the groups.[3] The first design variation, the most common form of psychotherapy outcome research, is a pre–post design. There is no assessment of potential mediators of change. Pre–post RCTs are excellent in demonstrating a causal relation between the intervention and therapeutic change; those designs which resemble the first variation can say nothing about mechanisms, even though we as authors often do. In the second design variation, symptoms and possible mechanisms are assessed at the same time at pretreatment and posttreatment. With this variation, conclusions cannot be reached about whether the symptoms changed the proposed mechanisms or vice versa, or, of course, whether both were altered by another variable.

The third design variation assesses symptoms at pretreatment and posttreatment. In addition, during the course of treatment (on one or more occasions), the proposed mediator is assessed. The data analyses then evaluate whether the process during treatment contributes to (predicts, accounts for) treatment outcome. This research gives a strong but misleading impression that a time line is established between some process (e.g., cognitions, alliance)

---

[3]There are many issues one can raise in studying mechanisms based on a comparison of groups that receive the intervention versus those which do not and how between-group data patterns can support or not support a particular model of mediation. In this context, the mediator is proposed and tested in the intervention group. No doubt, some people in the no-intervention group will show therapeutic changes also. These patterns of change in mediators and symptoms, even without treatment, can be pertinent to conclusions about the mediator in the intervention group. These issues are beyond the scope of the chapter.

and therapeutic change. The failure to measure symptoms at the same time or, indeed, before the mid-assessment of the supposed mediator precludes conclusions about whether the mediator comes before symptom change.

The fourth design variation makes a palpable improvement over prior variations. In this variation, the proposed mediator and the "outcome" (e.g., symptoms) are assessed during treatment. Ideally, there will be more than one assessment occasion during treatment. With this information, the investigator can evaluate the time sequence, that is, whether changes in the mediator preceded symptom change (and might be a plausible mechanism thereof), whether symptom change preceded change in the putative mediator (which may make the mediator an effect rather than a cause), or whether there is a reciprocal relation in which the proposed mediator is in some way both an outcome (i.e., influenced by symptom change) and a mediator (i.e., mechanism through which greater change occurs). To study mechanisms of changes, some variation of the fourth design is needed to establish the time line of predictor (mediator) and criterion (outcome).

A disadvantage of the fourth design variation is that it presumes that the course of change for both the mediator and the outcome is captured by measuring each at one or two fixed points during treatment (e.g., after Sessions 4 and 8). There could be great variation in when the change is made among patients receiving the same treatment. Both the mediator and symptoms may change at different points among a set of patients. The fifth design variation, an extension of the previous design, provides a more fine-grained analysis of change in mediator and symptoms and overcomes this concern. On a session-by-session basis, assessments are made so that one can examine the course of change of mediator and symptoms individually for each patient. Session-by-session evaluation permits evaluation of the relation of proposed mediators and symptom change and can take into account individual differences in when the changes occur.

The design variations—particularly the last two—can greatly enhance conclusions about the relations between mediators and outcome. Of course, merely using the suggested designs is not sufficient. Conceptual analyses about mediation and statistical analyses are no less central to the demonstration. (See Shrout & Bolger, 2002.) For example, a recent study of CT for depression assessed the proposed cognitive mediators and therapeutic change at pretreatment, at posttreatment, and on two occasions during treatment (Kwon & Oei, 2003). This is an excellent illustration of one of the design variations (Design 4). The study evaluated whether changes in cognitive processes (mediator) might explain changes in symptoms (outcome). Changes early in treatment in both cognitions and depression (pretreatment to Session 4) were interpreted as suggesting that changes in cognitions lead to symptom change. However, the data analyses did not rule out the possibility that changes in symptoms (depression) changed cognitions or that both cognitions and depression were altered by some other variable. In short, to study mechanisms, designs are needed in which assessment during treatment permits evaluation of the proposed mediator. At the same time, the data analyses and models used to test the effects are pivotal as well.

Exhibit 5.3. Recommendations for Research

1. Include measures of potential mechanisms of change.
2. Establish a time line of proposed mechanisms and outcomes.
3. Assess more than one potential mechanism.
4. Assess whether there is a gradient (dose–response relation).
5. Intervene to change the proposed mechanism of change.
6. Examine consistency across different types of studies.
7. Use theory as a guide to select potential mechanisms for study.

Recommendations for Research

A plea for studying mechanisms of change is old wine, but there are reasons to put this in a new bottle and to pass it off as a new research priority. First, there is now a heightened interest in transporting gains of therapy research to clinical practice. The appeal for more work on mechanisms is in part a response to this interest. It is still the case that the very best practice will come from the best science. By best science, I refer to the development of theory and the evaluation of theory in ways that lead to understanding of how and why therapy achieves its effects. The difficulties with, and lamentable features of, controlled laboratory (so-called efficacy) studies of therapy are not the failure to study "real" patients, with "real" clinicians, in "real" clinics. Indeed, these features are the strengths of these studies. The difficulty is that the experimental control of the laboratory has not been used to do what such research does best, namely, to understand how something works.

Second, there may be a widespread belief that mechanisms are being studied and that methods currently in place will allow us to isolate mechanisms. (See Kazdin & Nock, 2003; Weersing & Weisz, 2002.) The vast majority of studies of mediation in psychotherapy have not demonstrated neither a time line between the proposed mediator and outcome nor that the outcome could not have changed before the mediator. In any study proposed to evaluate mechanisms, the reader must ask, could the outcome have occurred before the proposed cause? Statistical analyses can contribute enormously to answering the question; however, there are additional assessment and design requirements.

In general, the investigation of mechanisms of therapy can be improved in several ways. Exhibit 5.3 provides recommendations to enhance our understanding of the mechanisms of therapeutic change. Each is highlighted and illustrated here.

Include Measures of Potential Mediators in Treatment Studies

The study of mechanisms requires the investigator to propose the possible bases for change. This is an obvious precondition for studying mechanisms. In many therapy studies, authors discuss mechanisms in the Introduction and Discussion sections of the article, but there is nothing in the Method or Results sections to provide evidence. The discussion of mechanisms often serves as a point of departure and rationale for executing the study or for using a particular treatment with a particular clinical problem. Typical of such studies is a conceptual view that problem x might be conceived of as a deficit, distortion, or excess of y (e.g., y = disastrous cognitions) and that treatment x is perfect for this because it targets y. More is needed than conceptual points of departure.

The mechanism ought to be specified so that it can be measured. Measures for assessing constructs over the course of treatment have been described elsewhere (Eddy, Dishion, & Stoolmiller, 1998). Studies occasionally include such measures to study mechanisms (Hofmann, 2000; Weersing & Weisz, 2002). The inclusion of such measures is a requirement for studying mechanisms, but other design features are needed as well.

Address the Time Line

It is important to establish the fact that the proposed mediator is changing before the outcome. This is obvious in principle. Yet, the failure to establish a time line is the Achilles' heel of research completed to date. The time line has two requirements. First, the proposed mediator must be assessed before the proposed outcome; this would be mid-treatment assessment of the mediator and posttreatment assessment of the outcome. Second, the "outcome" must also be assessed at mid-treatment as well as posttreatment. Even during the middle of treatment, long before the investigator may be interested in therapeutic change, it is quite possible that improvements occur in the client and these improvements lead to (i.e., come before) change in the putative mediator. Also, symptom change may occur at the same time as the change in mediator, both of which might have changed because of some other influence.

Assessment is the main change needed in research. I have suggested assessment during the course of treatment as an essential addition to treatment research interested in evaluating mechanisms. Assessment on multiple occasions during treatment can provide information on the time line of mechanisms and outcomes and the possibility of bidirectional changes; that is, each one influences the other in some way and at different points. Assessment on a session-by-session basis (i.e., every occasion over the course of treatment) permits evaluation of the mechanism(s) of change and symptom reduction and considers individual differences in the course of these changes.

Assess More Than One Mediator

The accumulation of evidence would profit from the assessment of more than one mediator in a given study. It is rare that even one mediator is studied, and hence there may be little value in raising the bar yet higher by recommending the assessment of two or more mediators. Assessing one mediator requires that pre–post treatment designs be modified to include additional assessment occasions during treatment. Recommending the assessment of more than one mediator during treatment means that the assessment battery (e.g., how many measures) will increase as each mediator is added to the design. In laboratory (efficacy) studies of therapy, the addition of one or two measures during the course of treatment may not be particularly onerous. Increasing the assessment battery in clinical settings invariably has a cost in patient and therapist reactions. Also, in clinical settings, usually there is little or no reimbursement of clinician time and clinic time for sessions devoted in whole or in part to assessment. These are the sorts of practical issues that the laboratory is likely to surmount.

The assessment of multiple mediators in a given study has enormous benefits. If two or more mediators are studied, one can identify whether one is more plausible or makes a greater contribution to the outcome. In addition, the assessment of multiple potential mediators within individual studies is economically efficient, given the tremendous amount of time and resources needed for any treatment investigation. Across many studies, some mediators may repeatedly emerge as possible contenders while others fall by the wayside. The survival of some mechanisms more than others over the course of research would be an important advance.

Assess Whether There Is a Gradient (Dose–Response Relation)

Another option for elucidating mechanisms is evaluating whether there is a dose–response relation, that is, whether more of the mediator is related to greater therapeutic change. For example, if the therapeutic relationship or repeated practice and rehearsal are the critical ingredients (mediators), is a better relationship or more practice related to greater change? Dose–response relations are "naturalistic" studies in the context of this discussion. That is, dose is not experimentally manipulated.

Searching for and interpreting dose–response relations can raise many problems. For example, the assumption is that more of the mechanism is better in relation to outcome. A linear relationship is assumed but might not capture the actual relation. Also, more of the mechanism is not randomly distributed across participants and hence might be confounded with a selection factor. For example, people whose cognitions changed to the greatest extent (proposed mediator) may show the greatest therapeutic change (dose–response relation). However, people whose cognitions changed may have some other characteristic that accounts for the relation. Finally, variations in responses among different subgroups (moderator effects) may mask a dose–response relation.

Caveats aside, a dose–response relation between the proposed mechanism and outcome can add considerably to the overall argument that a particular mechanism may play a central and causal role. In medicine, epidemiology, and public health, the evaluation of dose–response relations often has directed research to a plausible or likely mechanism related to disease (e.g., lung cancer, lead poisoning). Evidence of a dose–response relation is consistent with the view that a particular mechanism may be involved and often is an excellent first step toward demonstrating the relation more persuasively.

Intervene to Change the Proposed Mediator

An excellent strategy is to conduct an experiment in which the proposed mediator is in fact altered or varied across groups. Groups randomly composed might
be assigned to low, high, and medium levels of a proposed mediator. Results
showing that outcome varies directly as a function of levels of the mediators,
assessed during treatment, would be quite powerful support. Of course, it is
possible that changing some mediator actually works for a reason different
from the one proposed by the investigator. For example, changing level of
expectations (a proposed mediator) or alliance (bonding statements of the therapist) might work because of other constructs (e.g., how much hope is developed
in the patients). For other findings, replication and the accumulation of studies
are needed in which the proposed mediator, rather than some other influence,
becomes the most parsimonious explanation.

Intervening to change a mediator is an excellent strategy. Here, too, assessing more than one mediator would be helpful in understanding why change
occurred. Intervening to alter the mediator and assessing the level of that
mediator (as a check on the manipulation) and of two or more plausible other
mediators that are not manipulated would be an elegant way of evaluating
mechanisms. In such a study, one can rule out or make implausible some
mediators while providing evidence in behalf of another mediator. The less
elegant study would still be an enormous contribution, namely, intervening to
change one mediator and assessing that mediator and outcome within the
study.

Examine Consistencies Across Different Types of Studies

Understanding mechanisms through which therapeutic change occurs could
profit from different types of studies, beyond those which might be construed
as part of therapy research. Conclusions from these studies may be consistent
and converge in making a particular process plausible. Consider some of the
options.

NATURALISTIC STUDIES. If one is proposing a mediator of change, is there a
sample, population, or setting in which this mediator may be expected to vary
naturalistically? For example, if changing parenting style is proposed to explain
why a parent- or family-based treatment of a child's clinical problem is effective,
naturalistic studies examining families with and without these practices and
the short- and long-term child behaviors with which these are associated are
relevant.

Naturalistic studies by themselves may not permit strong causal conclusions. Yet, such evidence can be enormously helpful. For example, advances
in understanding long-term exposure to low levels of lead as a predictor of
hyperactivity and diminished IQ in children came from naturalistic studies
(Needleman, 1988; Needleman, Schell, Bellinger, Leviton, & Alldred, 1990).
Many advances in understanding cancer, heart disease, and stroke began by
looking for variation in putative mechanisms (e.g., in health habits, diet) among

individuals with varied outcomes (e.g., morbidity, mortality). Observing processes that may be operative in the natural environment and their short- and long-term correlates can be very useful, both for generating and for testing hypotheses about mechanisms.

QUALITATIVE RESEARCH. Research that is based on comparisons of groups, testing of the null hypothesis, and statistical analyses to reject these hypotheses, usefully referred to here as quantitative research, characterizes the vast majority of therapy studies. *Qualitative research* is a readily distinguishable methodology that could be quite useful to the study of mechanisms of therapy. Qualitative research is an approach to the subject matter of human experience and focuses on narrative accounts, description, interpretation, context, and meaning. Among the key characteristics is the in-depth study of the phenomena of interest. Individual participants or cases are focused on intensely to examine processes, meaning, characteristics, and contexts. Qualitative research encompasses many different disciplines and diverse design, assessment, and data-analytic strategies, well beyond the scope of the present chapter (e.g., Berg, 2001; Kazdin, 2003). It is important to note that qualitative design is a rigorous, verifiable, empirical, and replicable methodology. (Too often, and quite unfortunately, "case studies," loose descriptions, and aversion to data are characterized as qualitative research.)

Among the strengths of qualitative research is its ability to generate as well as test hypotheses. In the context of the present discussion, a careful analysis of the process of therapy, how that process is experienced by the patient and therapist, and what might be critical actions, cognitions, and beliefs at different points and how they relate to improvement might be studied in qualitative research. Qualitative research might provide a fine-grained analysis of the phenomenon of interest by intensively evaluating the richness and details of the process, including who changes and how change unfolds, and who does not change and what might be operative there.

LABORATORY STUDIES OF THERAPEUTIC PROCESSES. Laboratory studies of therapy encompass many types of research. Efficacy studies refer to outcome studies under well-controlled situations. Such studies are viewed with ambivalence because they do not show whether treatment works in "real settings." Efficacy studies are now more important than ever before. As mentioned earlier, if we are really interested in extending research findings to practice and helping patients, we ought to understand how and why therapy works.

Controlled studies of therapy outside of the context of clinics are in the best position to study mechanisms. The careful control afforded such research is precisely what is needed. The problem with efficacy studies has been their almost exclusive focus on outcome questions under highly controlled situations. Naturally, after such a study, one wants to ask, "But will these outcomes generalize to the 'real world'?" This is a legitimate question and one prompted by the narrow focus of most controlled outcome studies. However, more studies are needed with the high levels of control that investigate potential mechanisms. The study of mechanisms is precisely why we want laboratory research; the shift of focus needed in efficacy studies is to underscore processes and mediators that are likely to explain treatment. Studying mechanisms in real-world settings is possible but much less advisable than in the laboratory.

ANIMAL LABORATORY RESEARCH. It is worth commenting separately on animal studies, even though these would fall under laboratory research. Granted, many mediators of therapy may not be amenable to mouse models. Also, some of the interventions that might be of interest to a therapy researcher cannot easily be studied or modeled outside the context of human interaction. For example, in my own lab, we have been unable to evaluate the Gestalt therapy empty-chair technique with mice. Also, our alleged failure to complete our well-funded study of structural family therapy with Planaria is pending litigation with the funding agency (Planarian Institute of Mental Health) and cannot be commented on at this time. Notwithstanding my own limited research skills, the principle is one that warrants much more attention.

Some of the mechanisms of therapy might be studied in the lab, and we ought not to be shy about them or shy away from them. Perhaps, the most well-known example is in the area of flooding for the treatment of anxiety. Animal and human tests of this intervention to overcome anxiety and avoidance bear conceptual similarity that makes plausible the translation of one demonstration to the other. Mechanisms related to stress, arousal, habituation, and problem-solving abilities might well be studied in animal research. Moreover, critical processes (e.g., changes in the structure or function of the brain) might further elaborate plausible underpinnings to support the conceptual view of the mechanism and how it operates. Such tests, far removed from therapy settings, provide important tests of principle.

Theory as a Guide to Study Mechanisms

Whenever possible, theory is useful to guide research. Theory refers to an explanatory statement that is intended to account for, explain, and understand relations among variables, how they operate, and the processes involved. Conceptualization of treatment would consist of explicit views about what treatment is designed to accomplish and through what processes. How will the procedures used in treatment influence the processes implicated in the dysfunction or counteract these influences by developing new repertoires? It may be that treatment directly addresses those processes considered to be involved in the development of the problem. For example, inept discipline practices influence the development of aggressive behavior in children (Dodge, Pettit, & Bates, 1994; Patterson, Reid, & Dishion, 1992). Parent management training is an evidence-based treatment that directly alters these practices and alters aggressive child behavior. That is, the conceptual model of what factors contribute to the problem overlaps with the conceptual model of the treatment.

In other treatments, the conceptual model of therapeutic change may be unrelated to and distinguishable from the processes considered to be involved in the development of the problem. For example, aspirin is effective as a treatment for headaches, but headaches are not due to the lack of aspirin in one's system, nor does aspirin necessarily work, because of the effects in getting at the underlying or original cause of the problem. More pertinent to the present discussion, specific actions on the part of the therapist may be seen as critical to therapeutic change. A demonstration that these actions occur before symptoms change and that they influence outcome moves us closer to identifying what might be critical processes underlying change (e.g., Feeley, DeRubeis, & Gelfand, 1999).

The guiding question is, how does this treatment achieve change? The answer may involve basic psychological processes (e.g., memory, learning, information processing) or a broader theory (e.g., motivation). It is no longer sufficient to provide global conceptual views that foster a treatment approach or orientation toward what to do in the sessions. Rather, to ensure progress, specific conceptual models are needed to explain those processes (e.g., psychodynamic, cognitive, or familial) which are responsible for therapeutic change. The conceptual model and operationalization for purposes of assessment would greatly advance research on mechanisms.

In research, there is often a strong demand for the investigator to begin with a theory or conceptual model. The study that follows is a test of that theory. However, the goal of research is to end up with an understanding of how therapy works. This goal can be achieved by research that generates hypotheses and theories in addition to research that tests hypotheses. There is far too little research that focuses on generating hypotheses from careful observation and on building theory that can be tested subsequently (Kazdin, 2003; McGuire, 1997).

Mind Fields in Studying Mechanisms

I have implied that adding a few assessments to outcome studies will solve key problems and finally allow us to understand how therapy operates. There are conceptual problems and dangers as one walks through the field of research on mechanisms of therapy (i.e., "mind fields"). Let me mention some of these briefly to convey the greater challenges facing us.

First, a key challenge is defining and specifying the mechanisms of therapeutic change. A mechanism of therapy—that is, the process through which change occurs—may depend on some facet of treatment delivered by the therapist, an emergent process during treatment (e.g., alliance), or something received and experienced by the patient. It is useful to consider medication for a moment to convey a seemingly straightforward model of presenting a critical therapeutic agent. The medication depends on the delivery of some agent that is therapeutic but also on the ingestion, metabolization, and uptake of the treatment. Analogously, in therapy something must be delivered, but it also must be received. In studying mechanisms of change, one must specify what a given mechanism is and what it means for the mechanism to have been invoked and fairly tested.

If all patients in a treatment condition receive the intervention, it may not be suitable to evaluate the mechanisms of change for the group as a whole.

The mechanism may not have been invoked, occurred, or taken effect for all of the patients. Indeed, even in the case of medication, a "standard" dose (e.g., for clinical depression) can be an overdose or underdose for people of different ethnicities and countries (Lin, Poland, & Nakasaki, 1993). For the underdose groups, it may not be meaningful to ask, did the medication work? In many ways, the test was not appropriate because a subtherapeutic dose was provided. Analogously, if mechanism x is proposed to be responsible for therapeutic change, one must specify what it means for the conditions of mechanism x to be met, present, and appropriately tested.

In some treatment and prevention trials, investigators are interested in whether integrity of treatment makes a difference—that is, whether individuals who experienced the treatment as intended make a greater change than those who did not. Investigators may analyze the data with only those individuals who received the intervention or who received some minimal dose. This might be evaluated by omitting cases that did not receive the intervention as defined or by including all cases and by showing a correlation between how well treatment was implemented and therapeutic change. These well-intended analyses are not easily interpretable. Receiving the appropriate levels of treatment is not randomly distributed and may well be confounded with participant characteristics. For example, getting more, better, or more carefully implemented treatment may relate to the personality of the client (or therapist), severity of his or her problems, match of values and interests between the therapist and patient, and more. Similarly, in the study of mechanisms of therapy, the investigator may wish to assess only those individuals for whom the mechanism was invoked or occurred. This approach raises issues about when to conclude that the mechanism occurred and was fairly tested and how to analyze the data.

Second, conceptualization of mechanism of change and outcome warrants a more in-depth analysis. I have emphasized that a cause must precede an effect, such an obvious claim that it was easy to glide over. In general, but perhaps not invariably, one must show that there is temporal precedence— that is, change in the proposed mechanism followed by change in the symptoms. Yet, it is conceivable that the proposed mechanism may change and immediately bring with it a change in symptoms. There may be no delay, because, as the putative mechanism changes (e.g., cognitions for depression), so do the symptoms (e.g., the patient feels a little better instantaneously, interests have returned to their predepression levels). In principle, some mechanisms may be so intertwined with outcome effects as to make their delineation almost impossible.

Third, the discussion of mediation throughout the chapter neglected the sister concept of moderation. As noted previously, a moderator is a characteristic that may influence the relation between two other variables. Sex, age, ethnicity, culture, and social class are moderators often studied outside the context of therapy. It is possible that the mechanism of change varies as a function of a moderator variable. It may be that the critical mechanism or process in therapy changed and was followed by a change in symptoms for some individuals but not others. This suggests that a moderating influence might be identifiable. Yet, searching for moderators (a priori or post hoc), testing them (statistical power from multiple divisions of the sample), and interpreting them (e.g., is the moderator a proxy for some other variable?) have their own special challenges. I mention the issue here because the search for a mechanism of change, in prior sections of this chapter, implied a main effect across all participants. Yet, it is possible and indeed likely that there will be an interaction (effect that is influenced by another variable) with some preexisting characteristic. The mediator may look weak in any demonstration because of the undetected and unanalyzed influence of a moderator.

Fourth, measurement of mechanisms of change raises multiple challenges. Measures to evaluate therapeutic change are often well developed and standardized. There is no parallel set of measures that are validated to assess various mechanisms of therapy. Measurement development is needed. Ideally, mechanisms of change, like any other construct, would be measured through multiple strategies with different methods. Which method of assessment is appropriate or ideal may well depend on the nature of the mechanism (e.g., self-report and subjective evaluation to assess expectancies or critical beliefs, biological measures of stress, psychological indices of expectancies, or neuro-imaging changes).

In developing a measure of a mechanism, the relation of the measure to outcome measures raises issues. Some mechanisms (e.g., cognition) may be related to the symptoms quite closely (e.g., cognitions that are part of clinical depression). Some measures of mechanisms may include items that overlap with the items included in the outcome measures. The measurement challenges alone are potentially daunting, depending on the mechanisms. One must develop valid measures of mechanisms and ensure that they are correlated at the Goldilocks level so as not to be confounded with outcome measures but not to be completely orthogonal either.

Fifth, the emergence or occurrence of the mechanism raises critical issues. Assume for a moment that 10 patients receive identical treatment over the course of 20 sessions and that treatment works for each of them for the identical reason; that is, the same mechanism or process is responsible for change. It is not likely that the process of change will follow the identical time course so that, by Session 8, for example, the mechanism has changed in a critical way and symptom change is under way. The mechanism or process of change may have a different time course for individuals. Some patients may make rapid or sudden gains at a particular point in treatment (e.g., Tang & DeRubeis, 1999). One could say that, at a given point, some have and some have not made change in some qualitative or categorical fashion. Alternatively, one could consider that the point of therapeutic change for all individuals is normally (or close to normally) distributed with a certain mean and standard deviation. In either scenario (sudden gains but not at the identical point or normally distributed changes across several points), assessment of the mechanism is a challenge. Assessment of the mechanism at any one or two points in the study may not capture when change in the mechanism has occurred. Conceptualization of the mechanism and how it unfolds and the ability to detect the pattern of unfolding are nuances not yet well articulated.

Finally, interpretation of the data poses challenges when mechanisms and outcomes are studied. Consider a 2×2 matrix (four cells) that includes the combination of these categories.

1. Showing change in the mechanism (two levels: those who do vs. those who do not).
2. Achieving therapeutic change (two levels: those who show therapeutic change vs. those who do not).

I have provided the categories (do vs. do not) for simplicity of illustration, but, of course, change in the mechanism and symptoms are likely to reflect continua. In any case, consider the cells generated by the matrix. One of the four cells includes individuals who showed that the mechanism was operative and who improved. Another cell includes individuals for whom the mechanism was not invoked or did not occur and who did not improve. These two cells seem to be consistent with the importance of the proposed mechanism. Then there are these other two "annoying" cells, namely, individuals who experienced or received the mechanism but who did not show therapeutic change, and those who did not experience or receive the mechanism but who showed therapeutic change. Understanding all of the cells in the matrix is critical. In general, one cannot expect the clarity I have implied throughout the chapter, namely, that one specifies and assesses the mechanism, establishes the time line to ensure that symptom change did not precede change in the mechanism, and shows the relation of the mechanism to treatment outcome.

Conclusions

Understanding how psychotherapy works can serve as a basis for maximizing treatment effects and ensuring that critical features of treatment generalize to clinical practice. There has been enormous progress in psychotherapy research (Lambert, 2004; Nathan & Gorman, 2002). This has culminated in the recognition of several treatments that have strong evidence in their behalf. Despite this progress, research advances are sorely needed in studying the mechanisms of therapeutic change. It is remarkable that after decades of psychotherapy research, we as clinical researchers cannot confidently provide an evidence-based explanation for how or why even our most effective interventions produce change. More surprising is the infrequency with which this issue, or research addressing this issue, appears in the research literature. There are few studies, and of these, almost none meets the criteria of establishing the time line between the mechanism and behavior change (Hofmann, 2000; Weersing & Weisz, 2002, for review).

A potential exception is the rather large body of research on the therapeutic relationship. Many of the studies are designed to explain how therapy works, but they rarely establish the time line between the proposed mediator and the outcome. Studies rarely rule out the possibility that the relationship is the result of symptom change or some other variable rather than a mechanism responsible for it. I am not quibbling with the importance of the relationship—

I have tried one or two relationships myself. This is a quarrel about the necessary assessment and design requirements that are infrequently included in research.

Although prior research has not succeeded in demonstrating the operation of potential mechanisms of change, it has provided important groundwork on which future studies can build. For instance, an increasing number of studies are including assessments during the course of treatment (e.g., Eddy & Chamberlain, 2000; Kolko, Brent, Baugher, Bridge, & Birmaher, 2000; Kwon & Oei, 2003). The designs used in these investigations represent a great improvement over prior studies and signal progress in research on mechanisms of change. Existing studies have attempted to evaluate only a handful of potential mechanisms of change. Most of my examples drew on the rich literature on the CT for depression. Although it is not clear why that treatment works, this literature is the furthest along among therapies in attending to the question of mechanism.

The scientific study of mechanisms of change is certainly not an easy path on which to embark. A given treatment might work for multiple reasons. Just as there is no simple and single path to many diseases, disorders, or social, emotional, and behavioral problems (e.g., lung cancer, attention-deficit/ hyperactivity disorder), there may be analogous complexity in mechanisms for a given treatment technique or therapeutic outcome. Two patients in the same treatment conceivably could respond for different reasons. The complexities are critically important to understand because of a point made previously, namely, that the best patient care will come from ensuring that the optimal variation in treatment is provided. Understanding mechanisms of treatment is the path toward improved treatment.

References

American Psychiatric Association. (2000). Practice guideline for the treatment of patients with major depressive disorder (revision). *American Journal of Psychiatry, 157*(Suppl. 4), 1–45.

Barber, J. P., Connolly, M. B., Crits-Christoph, P., Gladis, L., & Siqueland, L. (2000). Alliance predicts patients' outcome beyond in-treatment change in symptoms. *Journal of Consulting and Clinical Psychology, 68*, 1027–1032.

Baron, R. M., & Kenny, D. A. (1986). The moderator–mediator variable distinction in social psychological research: Conceptual, strategic, and statistical considerations. *Journal of Personality and Social Psychology, 51*, 1173–1182.

Berg, B. L. (2001). *Qualitative research methods for the social sciences* (4th ed.). Needham Heights, MA: Allyn & Bacon.

Bernays, J. (1857). *Zwei Abhandlungen über die Aristotelische Theorie des Drama: I. Grundzüge der verlorenen Abhandlung des Aristoteles über Wirkung der Tragödie; II. Ergänzung zu Aristoteles' Poetik* [Two essays on the Aristotelean theory of drama: I. Main feature of Aristotle's lost treatise on the properties of tragedy; II. Supplement to Aristotle's Poetics]. Berlin, Germany: Breslau.

Burns, D. D., & Spangler, D. L. (2001). Do changes in dysfunctional attitudes mediate changes in depression and anxiety in cognitive behavioral therapy. *Behavior Therapy, 32*, 337–369.

Chambless, D. L., & Ollendick, T. H. (2001). Empirically supported psychological interventions: Controversies and evidence. *Annual Review of Psychology, 52*, 685–716.

Cook, T. D., & Campbell, D. T. (Eds.). (1979). *Quasi-experimentation: Design and analysis issues for field settings*. Chicago: Rand McNally.

Denissenko, M. F., Pao, A., Tang, M., & Pfeifer, G. P. (1996, October 18). Preferential formation of benzo[a]pyrene adducts at lung cancer mutational hotspots in P53. *Science, 274,* 430–432.

DeRubeis, R. J., Evans, M. D., Hollon, S. D., Garvey, M. J., Grove, W. M., & Tuason, V. B. (1990). How does cognitive therapy work? Cognitive change and symptom change in cognitive therapy and pharmacotherapy for depression. *Journal of Consulting and Clinical Psychology, 58,* 862–869.

Dodge, K. A., Pettit, G. S., & Bates, J. E. (1994). Socialization mediators of the relation between socioeconomic status and child conduct problems. *Child Development, 65,* 649–655.

Eddy, J. M., & Chamberlain, P. (2000). Family management and deviant peer association as mediators of the impact of treatment condition on youth antisocial behavior. *Journal of Consulting and Clinical Psychology, 68,* 857–863.

Eddy, J. M., Dishion, T. J., & Stoolmiller, M. (1998). The analysis of intervention change in children and families: Methodological and conceptual issues embedded in intervention studies. *Journal of Abnormal Child Psychology, 26,* 53–69.

Feeley, M., DeRubeis, R. J., & Gelfand, L. A. (1999). The temporal relation of adherence and alliance to symptom change in cognitive therapy for depression. *Journal of Consulting and Clinical Psychology, 67,* 578–582.

Hofmann, S. G. (2000). Treatment of social phobia: Potential mediators and moderators. *Clinical Psychology: Science and Practice, 7,* 3–16.

Hollon, S. D., & Beck, A. T. (2004). Cognitive and cognitive behavioral therapies. In M. J. Lambert (Ed.), *Bergin and Garfield's handbook of psychotherapy and behavior change* (5th ed., pp. 447–492). New York: Wiley.

Holmbeck, G. N. (2002). Post-hoc probing of significant moderational and mediational effects in studies of pediatric populations. *Journal of Pediatric Psychology, 27,* 87–96.

Hoyle, R. H., & Smith, G. T. (1994). Formulating clinical research hypotheses as structural equation models: A conceptual overview. *Journal of Consulting and Clinical Psychology, 62,* 429–440.

Ilardi, S. S., & Craighead, W. E. (1994). The role of nonspecific factors in cognitive–behavior therapy for depression. *Clinical Psychology: Science and Practice, 1,* 138–156.

Kazdin, A. E. (1999). Current (lack of) status of theory in child and adolescent psychotherapy research. *Journal of Child Clinical Psychology, 28,* 533–543.

Kazdin, A. E. (2000). *Psychotherapy for children and adolescents: Directions for research and practice.* New York: Oxford University Press.

Kazdin, A. E. (2003). *Research design in clinical psychology* (4th ed.). Needham Heights, MA: Allyn & Bacon.

Kazdin, A. E., & Nock, M. K. (2003). Delineating mechanisms of change in child and adolescent therapy: Methodological issues and research recommendations. *Journal of Child Psychology and Psychiatry, 44,* 1116–1129

Kazdin, A. E., & Weisz, J. R. (Eds.). (2003). *Evidence-based psychotherapies for children and adolescents.* New York: Guilford Press.

Kenny, D. A., Kashy, D. A., & Bolger, N. (1998). Data analysis in social psychology. In D. Gilbert, S. T. Fiske, & G. Lindzey (Eds.), *Handbook of social psychology* (4th ed., Vol. 1, pp. 233–265). Boston: McGraw-Hill.

Kolko, D. J., Brent, D. A., Baugher, M., Bridge, J., & Birmaher, B. (2000). Cognitive and family therapies for adolescent depression: Treatment specificity, mediation, and moderation. *Journal of Consulting and Clinical Psychology, 68,* 603–614.

Kraemer, H. C., Stice, E., Kazdin, A. E., Offord, D. R., & Kupfer, D. J. (2001). How do risk factors work together? Mediators, moderators, independent, overlapping, and proxy-risk factors. *American Journal of Psychiatry, 158,* 848–856.

Kraemer, H. C., Wilson, G. T., Fairburn, C. G., & Agras, W. S. (2002). Mediators and moderators of treatment effects in randomized clinical trials. *Archives of General Psychiatry, 59,* 877–883.

Kwon, S., & Oei, T. P. S. (2003). Cognitive processes in a group cognitive behavior therapy of depression. *Journal of Behavior Therapy and Experimental Psychiatry, 34,* 73–85.

Lambert, M. J. (Ed.). (2004). *Bergin and Garfield's handbook of psychotherapy and behavior change* (5th ed.). New York: Wiley.

Lin, K., Poland, R. E., & Nakasaki, G. (Eds.). (1993). *Psychopharmacology and psychobiology of ethnicity.* Washington, DC: American Psychiatric Press.

McGuire, W. J. (1997). Creative hypothesis generating in psychology: Some useful heuristics. *Annual Review of Psychology, 48*, 1–30.

Nathan, P. E., & Gorman, J. M. (Eds.). (2002). *Treatments that work* (2nd ed.). New York: Oxford University Press.

National Advisory Mental Health Council. (1999). *Bridging science and service* (NIH Publication No. 99-4353). Washington, DC: National Institutes of Health.

National Advisory Mental Health Council Workgroup on Child and Adolescent Mental Health Intervention Development and Deployment. (2001). *Blueprint for change: Research on child and adolescent mental health.* Washington, DC: National Institutes of Health.

Needleman, H. L. (Ed.). (1988). *Low level of lead exposure: The clinical implications of current research.* New York: Raven Press.

Needleman, H. L., Schell, A. S., Bellinger, D., Leviton, A., & Alldred, E. N. (1990). The long-term effects of exposure to low doses of lead in childhood: An 11-year follow-up report. *New England Journal of Medicine, 322,* 83.

Norcross, J. C. (Ed.). (2002). *Psychotherapy relationships that work: Therapist contributions and responsiveness to patients.* New York: Oxford University Press.

Orlinsky, D. E., Rønnestad, M. H., & Willutzki, U. (2004). Fifty years of psychotherapy process–outcome research: Continuity and change. In M. J. Lambert (Ed.), *Bergin and Garfield's handbook of psychotherapy and behavior change* (5th ed., pp. 307–389). New York: Wiley.

Patterson, G. R., Reid, J. B., & Dishion, T. J. (1992). *Antisocial boys.* Eugene, OR: Castalia.

Sechrest, L. B., McKnight, P., & McKnight, K. (1996). Calibration of measures for psychotherapy outcome studies. *American Psychologist, 51,* 1065–1071.

Sechrest, L. B., Stewart, M., Stickle, T. R., & Sidani, S. (1996). *Effective and persuasive case studies.* Cambridge, MA: Human Services Research Institute.

Sechrest, L. B., West, S. G., Phillips, M. A., Redner, R., & Yeaton, W. (1979). Some neglected problems in evaluation research: Strength and integrity of treatments. In L. B. Sechrest, S. G. West, M. A. Phillips, R. Redner, & W. Yeaton (Eds.), *Evaluation studies: Review annual* (Vol. 4, pp. 15–35). Beverly Hills, CA: Sage.

Sechrest, L. B., White, S. O., & Brown, E. D. (Eds.). (1979). *The rehabilitation of criminal offenders: Problems and prospects.* Washington, DC: National Academy of Sciences.

Shrout, P. E., & Bolger, N. (2002). Mediation in experimental and nonexperimental studies: New procedures and recommendations. *Psychological Methods, 7,* 422–445.

Smith, B., & Sechrest, L. B. (1991). Treatment of aptitude × treatment interactions. *Journal of Consulting and Clinical Psychology, 59,* 233–244.

Tang, T. Z., & DeRubeis, R. J. (1999). Sudden gains and critical sessions in cognitive–behavioral therapy for depression. *Journal of Consulting and Clinical Psychology, 67,* 894–904.

Tremblay, R. E., Masse, B., Perron, D., LeBlanc, M., Schwartzman, A. E., & Ledingham, J. E. (1992). Early disruptive behavior, poor school achievement, delinquent behavior, and delinquent personality: Longitudinal analyses. *Journal of Consulting and Clinical Psychology, 60,* 64–72.

Weersing, V. R., & Weisz, J. R. (2002). Mechanisms of action in youth psychotherapy. *Journal of Child Psychology and Psychiatry, 43,* 3–29.

Whisman, M. A. (1993). Mediators and moderators of change in cognitive therapy of depression. *Psychological Bulletin, 114,* 248–265.

Whisman, M. A. (1999). The importance of the cognitive theory of change in cognitive therapy of depression. *Clinical Psychology: Science and Practice, 6,* 300–304.

6

Treatment Strength and Integrity: Models and Methods

David S. Cordray and Georgine M. Pion

In 1979, Sechrest, West, Phillips, Redner, and Yeaton edited Volume 4 of the *Evaluation Studies Review Annual*. During the *Annual's* relatively short history, its various editors opted to either reprint a collection of exemplary evaluation studies or organize their respective volume around important methodological and technological themes underlying the conceptualization and execution of evaluation studies. Lee Sechrest and his fellow editors chose the latter course of editorial action, highlighting the importance of incorporating *treatment strength and integrity* into evaluation endeavors as their major theme. Labeling it as one of the "neglected problems in evaluation research," they argued that evaluation researchers had typically shortchanged the role of the treatment in their studies. In brief, treatment strength referred to the *a priori intensity* of the planned intervention, and treatment integrity referred to the *fidelity* with which the treatment was actually delivered. Building on earlier work (Sechrest & Redner, 1979), this theme was reiterated and expanded on by Sechrest and other collaborators (Scott & Sechrest, 1989; Sechrest, 1982; Sechrest & Yeaton, 1981; Yeaton & Sechrest, 1981a, 1981b).

Taken together, the ideas in these papers make up an important part of the intellectual foundation underlying many conceptual, methodological, and technical advances in evaluation research. This chapter recounts Sechrest et al.'s (1979) original notions of treatment strength and integrity. More recent work that was inspired, directly and indirectly, by their thinking also is summarized. Overall, their call for paying more attention to adequately assessing treatment integrity did not fall on deaf ears; new implementation measures have been developed, and an increasing number of intervention efficacy and effectiveness studies now include evidence on treatment integrity. The same conclusion is not justified for treatment strength as it was conceptualized in Sechrest et al.'s (1979) chapter. In reading subsequent papers citing their works, the two constructs were not often distinguished, being discussed as a single construct—*strengthandintegrity*. Many conceptual and methodological developments in evaluation and intervention research have emerged (see Lipsey & Cordray, 2000; Shadish, Cook, & Campbell, 2002) over the past 2 decades, making it is possible to restore the separate status of their original two constructs. Now, a stronger argument for the a priori consideration of treatment strength is possible. Before engaging in those discussions, we summarize the main ideas raised by Sechrest and his colleagues in several important papers.

Treatment Strength and Integrity *a la* Sechrest and Colleagues

Sechrest et al.'s (1979) interest in treatment strength and integrity is clearly understandable if we place their ideas in a historical context. When their edition of the *Annual* was published, program evaluation research was still in its infancy, having begun, in earnest, in the mid-1970s. By 1979, these efforts had produced a succession of "no-difference" findings as reported in the literature. These disappointing results, along with the implication that "nothing works," prompted an industrywide, critical investigation of the circumstances surrounding the conduct of evaluation efforts.

Sechrest and his colleagues made at least two important contributions to the debate about the reasons for prior treatment failures. First, they made several key observations about the nature of treatments: (a) They are delivered in real settings and are rarely standardized; (b) they often are multifaceted, composed of multiple components or stages; (c) they are sometimes delivered by poorly trained, unmotivated, or resistant program staff; and (d) their delivery can be heavily influenced by events in the real world, many of which are not under the provider's or researcher's control. Each can engender potential problems with treatment delivery. Under such "messy" circumstances, Sechrest et al. (1979) concluded that "the failure of an actual treatment to produce a significant effect may tell us nothing about the potential effect had the treatment been correctly implemented" (p. 16).

Their second observation is perhaps better classified as a nonobservation. In classic "Sechrestian" style, they asked, "What is missing within these evaluation studies?" Their answer identified the absence of any compelling rationale, model, or theory underlying the programs that were tested. To make this point crystal clear, they grounded their concern about questionable treatment–outcome linkages by using a real evaluation study as an example. They asked,

> On what *a priori theoretical basis* could [these] researchers have expected that an hour or two a week of counseling by poorly trained correctional officers would have any detectable effect on the response [subsequent criminal activity] of the offenders to parole over a period of three years? (Sechrest et al., 1979, p. 23, italics added)

In other words, how could such a seemingly weak intervention produce an effect in a behavior that is notoriously difficult to change? The emphasis on treatment strength was to avoid developing and testing interventions that had no obvious chance for success.

To formalize their concerns, Sechrest and his colleagues offered two somewhat different definitions of treatment strength and integrity. Initially, they defined treatment strength as *"the intensity with which the researcher intends that the treatment be delivered"* (Sechrest et al., 1979, p. 16, italics added). Integrity of treatment was defined as *"the fidelity* with which the treatment is *actually delivered"* (p. 16, italics added). Two years later, Yeaton and Sechrest (1981a) made the connection between the theory underlying the treatment and fidelity by referring to integrity as "the degree to which treatment is *delivered as intended"* (p. 160, italics added).

Treatment Strength: A Multifaceted Concern

There are at least four benefits to an increased concern about determining treatment strength that can be deduced from the discussions provided by Sechrest and his colleagues: (a) specifying the amount or "magnitude" of the treatment to be delivered, (b) understanding the coherence of the intervention or treatment, (c) enhancing the validity of inference that can be derived from studies of treatment effectiveness, and (d) optimizing the use of the results to guide interventions or clinical practices.

The Magnitude of Treatment

Treatments can differ in quantifiable ways. Sechrest et al. (1979) offered several dimensions of treatments that imply the possibility of differential levels of strength. In particular, they noted that treatments can vary with regard to the *number of sessions* that are to be provided, the *duration* over which they are to be provided, and the intended *intensity* (units per time interval) of the scheduled sessions.

Yeaton and Sechrest (1981a) stated that "strong treatments contain large amounts in pure form of those ingredients leading to change" (p. 156). Not to be confused with a general notion that more is always better, optimal treatment strength is viewed as the preferable target. Optimality depends on the detail with which the problem is specified, the magnitude of the problem to be allevi- ated, the differential responsiveness of individuals (e.g., Treatment × Partici- pant interactions), and political realities.

The Theoretical Coherence of Treatments

Inspired by research and practice in medicine, Sechrest et al. (1979) pointed out that optimal treatments depend on knowledge about the conditions under which treatments (notably, drugs) produce desired outcomes. That is, medical practitioners need to know which drugs "work" on which medical conditions, the mechanisms that are at work, and the appropriate dosage adjustments in the presence of other attributes (e.g., weight, age, gender, and comorbid condi- tions of the patient). A similar network of knowledge is required for nonmedical interventions. Sechrest et al. argued that the treatment plan needs to be well grounded in a theory that links the type of intervention that is proposed, the specific population that is involved, and the anticipated outcomes. Strong treatments have an acceptable theoretical rationale, treatment plan, and specification of the mechanisms or processes that are expected to produce the desired outcomes. Their definition stresses the a priori consideration of treatment strength, emphasizing its role in the initial conceptualization of the intervention.

Assessing the a priori strength of a treatment can be accomplished by asking experts to rate: (a) the likelihood that the treatment, as described, will produce the desired changes in the outcome; (b) its clarity; and (c) the extent to which it is focused on the intended problem. Strength estimates also can be developed in reference to the strongest possible treatment (e.g., a substantial fraction of the available time) and the attributes of standard treatments or norms about customary care.[1] The prior experiences of potential clients in standard treatments can serve as a basis for rating the strength of an innovative form of treatment. Sechrest et al. (1979) also hinted at the potential role of meta-analytic methods in parametric studies.

Improving Causal Inference

Another "Sechrestian" feature of the published discussions concerning treatment strength and integrity is an emphasis on enhancing the validity of causal inferences about the effects of interventions. As such, it is not surprising that the role of strength and integrity of treatment is discussed in terms of Cook and Campbell's (1979) definition of *construct validity* (of the cause)—the proper understanding of the true meaning of the treatment. Again, placing these discussions in historical context, construct validity had previously received little or no attention relative to the concerns expressed over internal validity (the proper attribution of an observed effect). Applying Cook and Campbell's threats to construct validity, inappropriate inferences about the treatment effects could be due to confounding variables, nonspecific effects (e.g., expectancy, placebo effects), inadequate theoretical formulation of the treatment, and inadequate description of the treatment and control conditions. To this list, they added "inadequacy of the planned strength of the treatment and the integrity with which it is delivered" (p. 18).

Improving Clinical Practice

Research and evaluation are undertaken for a variety of reasons. Throughout the collection of papers issued by Sechrest and his colleagues runs the assumption that research results should serve as an important basis for improving practitioners' delivery of social and behavioral treatments. In large measure, this concern is a natural extension of their emphasis on construct validity. The careful explication of treatment rationales, specification of the conditions necessary for their delivery, and description of the mechanisms that link treat-

---

[1]A year is equal to 8,760 hours; any treatment that approached that dose per year could be considered a strong treatment.

ment components and processes to outcomes (intended and unintended) serve as important bases for the development of practice guidelines. Improving clinical practice will be seriously hampered if we do not direct explicit attention to (a) treatment parameters that are plausibly linked to treatments; (b) the relative effects produced and outcomes achieved by treatments (e.g., improvement rates and achieved levels of functioning); and (c) the conditions under which effects and outcomes are produced as well as their differential effects on subgroups of clients.

An obvious question concerns the extent to which their concerns registered with the scientific and practitioner communities and prompted efforts to strengthen the evidence base on the nature and effectiveness of interventions. Recognizing that the discussion which follows falls seriously short of a comprehensive review, we nevertheless attempt to summarize some of the progress that has been made. Where possible, we also highlight issues that have not attracted the level of attention that they warrant.

Models for Linking the Strength of Causes With Their Effects

In the series of papers just described, Sechrest and his colleagues focused mainly on explicating the critical and, in their view, neglected aspects of the purported cause (treatment) within studies of treatment effectiveness. In most of their papers, Sechrest and his colleagues left the effect undefined. Because little attention had been directed at treatment strength, discussions of methods for measuring strength were suggestive, and following the highly original framework of field research captured in the book *Unobtrusive Methods* (Webb, Campbell, Schwartz, & Sechrest, 1966), the methods were creative. The past 2 decades of research and development have witnessed a surge of interest in the role of theories in intervention research (e.g., Chen, 1990; Chen & Rossi, 1992; Lipsey, 1993; Yin, 1997) and, in turn, interest in defining treatments, mechanisms by which treatments operate, and their linkages to outcomes. With these advances came the possibility of more explicit consideration of the original ideas developed by Sechrest and his colleagues about treatment strength and integrity.

Across a broad spectrum of intervention research (e.g., clinical psychology, psychosocial rehabilitation, substance abuse, and homelessness), causal analysis and evaluation methods reveal at least three models of how causes (treatments) can be linked to their expected effects. The first model stems from the literature on human judgment processes. We refer to it as the *cause–effect congruity model* because it focuses explicitly on a priori conceptions of the correspondence between the size (or strength) of the cause and the size (or magnitude) of the resulting effect. Second, the *counterfactual model* is derived from the experimental research and evaluation traditions. Here, the effect is defined as a relative, average difference between groups. As a consequence, the cause (treatment) has to be defined as a relative difference between treatment conditions. Moreover, the methodological underpinnings of the counterfactual model can provide the soundest basis for causal attribution. The third approach to linking treatment strength to outcomes is the *dose–response model*. This

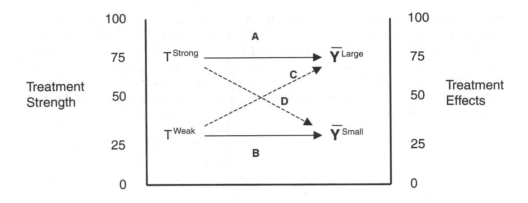

Figure 6.1. Cause–effect congruity and incongruity. T = treatment; Y = outcome.

model examines the form of the relationship between differing strengths of treatment and levels of outcomes.

The Cause–Effect Congruity Model

In their paper titled "Judging Probable Cause," Einhorn and Hogarth (1986) provided a set of rules that, they argued, people use to make judgments of causality. In addition to the usual cues-to-causality used in causal research (i.e., the appropriate temporal order or X→Y, covariation of the cause and effect, and the absence of rival explanations for the observed X and Y relationship), Einhorn and Hogarth introduced the idea of cause–effect *congruence* as another important cue-to-causality. As depicted in Figure 6.1, two treatments are scaled according to their treatment strength (e.g., through expert ratings).[2] Congruence occurs when strong treatments (e.g., rated at the 75th percentile of all relevant treatments) produce large effects (mean^Y = 75, where 100 is a maximum level of performance) and small causes (weak treatments, e.g., a treatment rated in the 25th percentile of all relevant treatments) produce, on average, small effects (mean^Y = 25). These different scenarios are designated as Paths A and B, respectively, in Figure 6.1. In practice, routine a priori assessment of treatment strength should minimize the implementation of a weak treatment, pressuring program developers to bolster treatment models in ways that strengthen the treatment and increasing the likelihood of success.

Incongruity occurs when it is thought that a small cause can produce a big effect or the reverse occurs. Incongruence motivates a search for additional mechanisms to explain the apparent mismatch between treatment and outcome strength (Cordray, 1986, 2000). As seen in Figure 6.1, Path C requires the specification of mechanisms that transform a weak treatment into a strong

---

[2]Consistent with the simple view of cause–effect congruence, the hypothetical examples shown in the figures assume a direct correspondence between the size of the effect and the size of the cause. This, of course, is too simplistic inasmuch as there are no constraints on this correspondence.

effect. At the planning stage, Path C probably reflects the "wishful thinking" bias in intervention research implied by Sechrest et al. (1979). However, with a priori acknowledgment that the planned intervention is weak, specification of the mechanisms needed to link a weak treatment to a large outcome and assessment of the plausibility of those linkages might avert further attacks of major social problems with treatments guided by wishful thinking.[3]

Path D requires an explanation of the factors that "dampened" the influence of an initially strong treatment. In the language of Sechrest and his colleagues, one plausible explanation is the lack of treatment integrity—in reality, the presumed strong treatment degraded into a weak one that produced small (or null) treatment effects.

JUDGING A PRIORI TREATMENT STRENGTH. Other aspects of Einhorn and Hogarth's (1986) notions of ordinary human judgments of causality comport nicely with ideas described by Sechrest and his colleagues. In particular, in Einhorn and Hogarth's terms, causal relations are customarily viewed within a specifiable complex *causal field*. The causal field described by Sechrest and his colleagues recognizes that treatment strength is to be judged in the context of the specific problem to be resolved, the presence of contextual factors, and attributes of the agents (e.g., people) to be affected. However, given the weak theoretical and empirical foundations for most social programs (Lipsey, 1993), we may have to accept a priori judgments of treatment strength that are cruder than implied earlier in this chapter.

MODELING TREATMENT COHESIVENESS. The specification of a cohesive model that links the treatment to mechanisms of change and then the linking of these mechanisms to outcomes for a subclass of clients amounts to articulating a causal field of action. Although a normal part of naïve causal inference (Einhorn & Hogarth, 1986) and a necessary part of intervention research (Sechrest et al., 1979), deriving and judging the cohesiveness of an intervention is challenging, to say the least. Fortunately, within evaluation research and in causal modeling, a host of "methodological tools" and heuristics have been developed to aid in the specification of these models of the causal field.

In particular, explication of what activities and services constitute a program theory is often aided by the creation, refinement, and use of program logic models (Brekke, 1987; Brekke & Test, 1992; Cordray & Pion, 1993; Julian, 1997; Yin, 1997) and program templates (Scheirer, 1996) that depict the program activities in relation to each other and to the expected outcomes for service recipients. A handful of formal measures of strength, based on formal and informal program theories, have been reported in the literature (e.g., Brandt, Kirsch, Lewis, & Casey, 2004; Carroll et al., 1998; McGrew, Bond, Dietzen, & Salyers, 1994; Orwin, Sonnefeld, Cordray, Pion, & Perl, 1998).

---

[3] Note that, if substantively interesting mechanisms had been known a priori, the treatment would have been rated as a strong treatment under Sechrest et al.'s scheme. As research accumulates, once-weak treatments could be better understood as strong ones.

JUDGING STRENGTH OR COHESIVENESS. Program articulation (e.g., through a logic model), however, represents half the task. Sechrest et al. (1979) required a second step, an explicit judgment of cohesiveness or strength. We know of no instance in which logic models have been systematically reviewed for their implied strength. However, explanatory models in meta-analysis (see Cook et al., 1992) and in other forms of model-driven synthesis (Cordray & Fischer, 1995) hold some promise. For example, the Prospective Evaluation Synthesis, developed within the Program Evaluation and Methodology Division of the U.S. General Accounting Office (1990), has been used to determine whether the models underlying congressional legislation are likely to work if implemented. After conceptual and operational models are developed for a proposed piece of legislation, evaluation literature is consulted and synthesized to determine whether there is empirical support for each "causal" link in the models.

DIRECT ANALYSES OF A PRIORI TREATMENT STRENGTH. Sechrest et al. (1979) were clear about the distinction between treatment strength and treatment integrity. Integrity is to be assessed in light of the parameters specified by a priori judgments or assessments of the planned strength of the treatment. As such, treatment strength is awarded priority over treatment integrity.

However, a search of abstracts catalogued by PsycINFO produced only 14 documents that contained the words *treatment strength* in either the titles or abstracts. Of this group, only a handful possessed any relevance to the ideas articulated by Sechrest and his colleagues. After reviewing the available literature on treatment strength in physical medicine (e.g., rehabilitation from stroke), Keith (1997) concluded that there was a paucity of information about the nature and theory of these treatments and argued that an accumulation of research data on dose specificity, treatment effectiveness, and the mechanisms underlying effective treatments not only was feasible but also would greatly benefit the field in such ways as the development of practice guidelines. Two other articles involved empirical efforts to examine strength. Northup, Fisher, Kahang, Harrell, and Kurtz (1997) attempted to empirically ascertain the levels of two labor-intensive procedures (differential reinforcement of an alternative behavior and brief time-outs) that were necessary to achieve the desired reductions in severe behavior problems in 3 individuals with severe developmental disabilities. Braden, McGlone, and Pennington (1993) examined the relationship between the amount of time spent in a self-help class designed to teach coping skills, problem solving, and cognitive reframing and outcomes among 313 individuals with systemic lupus erythematosus.

The Counterfactual Model

The counterfactual model (Holland, 1986; Rosenbaum, 2002; Rubin, 1974) begins with the specification of the purest form of causal inference: the effect of the cause on the same individual.[4] As such, the effect of a cause on Person i

---

[4]Proponents of the counterfactual model consider causes to be only those variables for which an individual *could* experience all levels (e.g., treatment = 1; no treatment = 0) of the variable.

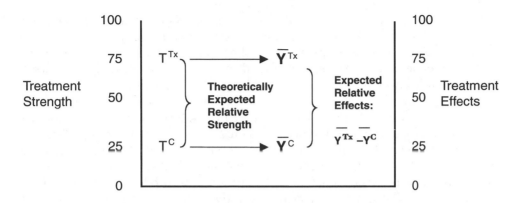

Figure 6.2. Theoretically expected relative treatment strength and effects. Y= outcome; Tx = treatment condition; C = counterfactual condition.

can be simply represented as the difference between his or her score on an outcome (Y_i) under the treatment (represented as Tx) condition (Y_i^{Tx}) and the outcome under the counterfactual (non-Tx, or c) condition (Y_i^c). Under this model of causality, Holland (1986) and Rubin (1974) argued that the treatment effect—the causal parameter of interest—would be expressed as T = (Y_i^{Tx}) − (Y_i^c). This definition of the causal parameter requires an individual to be exposed simultaneously to both conditions. For obvious reasons, such a requirement cannot be met. To circumvent this fundamental problem of causal inference, Holland (1986) described a series of approximations to causal analysis.

DEFINING THE EFFECT. Figure 6.2 provides a schematic overview of the linkage between the each level of the causal variable and the effects. Starting with the right-hand side of the figure, rather than observing the responses of an individual to both the treatment and counterfactual conditions (Y_i^T and $Y_{i,}^c$ respectively), the average responses of a group of individuals who experienced the treatment are compared with the responses of another group of individuals who did not experience the treatment. If groups are composed at random, Holland's (1986) first approximation to causal analysis is the classic randomized experiment (Boruch, 1997).

As shown in Figure 6.2, the casual effect of treatment is actually a relative effect, which can be estimated as RE = E(Y^{Tx}) − E(Y^c), or the difference between the expected values for each group. In practical terms, this translates into the differences between group averages. In the simple example illustrated in the figure, it is expected that the T^{Tx} will produce an average outcome of 75 units of well-being and T^C will produce an average outcome of 25 units. The relative

---

Naturally, a host of individual difference, or organismic, variables would be excluded from consideration. Because treatment conditions can be actively manipulated, treatments can be regarded as causes.

effect of T^{Tx} is an increase of 50 units of well-being.[5] For this to be an adequate approximation, a number of conditions and statistical assumptions must hold. In any given comparative causal study, these assumptions may be important or trivial, depending on the specific details of the research design that is used (Rosenbaum, 2002).

DEFINING THE CAUSE. If the effect in a cause–effect relationship is defined as the relative, average difference between the means of the groups (Tx and C) on the outcome (Y), the cause also needs to be regarded as the difference between the treatment conditions (e.g., number of sessions, strength as assessed by cohesiveness). As shown in Figure 6.2, to produce a relative effect [RE = $E(Y^T) - E(Y^c)$], there must be a relative difference between groups on the essential causal variables (Cordray & Pion, 1993; Mackie, 1974).[6]

RELATIVE STRENGTH. Differences with respect to a causal variable reflect the *relative strength* (or RS = [$T^{Tx} - T^C$]) of the contrast. This can be expressed in both qualitative and quantitative terms. Qualitatively, the focus is on the presence/absence of causal elements or the alternative configuration of causal elements. Quantitative scales emphasize differences in the levels of causal variables within the groups. In Figure 6.2, T^{Tx} and T^C are 75 and 25 treatment strength units, respectively, with the relative strength being 50 treatment strength units. Orwin et al. (1998) used the number of program elements that were possible and received to index the strength of each innovation in a multi-site evaluation of programs for homeless substance abusers.

TREATMENT DIFFERENTIATION: AN ADDED COMPLEXITY. Assessing the relative strength of treatment conditions is comparatively simple in the dose–response models developed by Howard, Kopta, Krause, and Orlinsky (1986). As the treatment conditions become more complex, so does the assessment of treatment differentiation. Although Waltz, Addis, Koerner, and Jacobson (1993) cast their discussion of treatment differentiation in terms of assessing therapist adherence and competence, their ideas are quite general. Their scheme for treatment differentiation includes the assessment of items that reflect (a) treatment components and therapist behaviors that are unique to the treatment modality and essential to it, (b) treatment components and therapist behaviors that are essential to the treatment but not unique to it, (c) treatment compo-

---

[5] Alternatively, the relative effect can be indexed as a statistic defined by Cohen (1988): the effect size. An effect size is a descriptive statistic that expresses the difference between the means of the treatment (M_Y^T) and counterfactual condition (M_Y^C) on an outcome in standard deviation units, or ES = (M_YT – M_Y^C)/ SD_{pooled}, where the pooled standard deviation is the weighted average of the standard deviations within each condition. Cohen posited that effect sizes of .20, .50, and .80 can be interpreted as representing small, medium, and large effects, respectively. The ES index is particularly useful as a means of establishing a statistical association (covariation) when the study sample sizes are small and, as a consequence, statistical precision (or power) is low.

[6] For the purposes of statistical analysis, each causal condition is represented by a group-assignment variable (G). Each causal condition is assigned a value (e.g., if t, then G = 1, if c, then G = 0) on a group-assignment variable to test whether group means on Y differ after exposure to the conditions.

nents and therapist behaviors that are compatible with the treatment model but not unique or needed, and (d) components and behaviors that are not supposed to be provided (*proscribed*).

Following the scheme proposed by Waltz et al. (1993), Carroll et al. (2000) developed and validated a 55-item measure (the Yale Adherence and Competence Scale) that is designed to be used by most behavioral programs that target drug addicts. Similarly, the Dartmouth Assertive Community Treatment Scale is designed to obtain program fidelity (integrity) information on programs that use the assertive community treatment (ACT) model for people with serious mental illness. Administered by interviewers, this 28-item instrument not only measures implementation of ACT (characterized by a team approach with shared caseloads, frequent staff meetings, intensive community-based services, and assistance with daily living skills) but also discriminates it from other types of case management programs and has shown to be related to certain client outcomes (McGrew et al., 1994; McHugo, Drake, Teague, & Xie, 1999; Salyers et al., 2003; Teague, Bond, & Drake, 1998).

The Dose–Response Models

One of the most intuitively appealing models of the relationship between the magnitudes of the treatment and the outcome is the dose–response model. Although it has a well-established place in psychotherapy research (Howard et al., 1986), it has been less investigated in other areas or has been found to yield no strong evidence for a relationship (e.g., National Institute of Child Health and Human Development Early Child Care Research Network, 2003).

Originating in the biological sciences to investigate the potency of stimuli with living participants, this research focuses on examining the impact of different doses of a stimulus on a specific response variable (Hansen, Lambert, & Forman, 2002). Unlike the contiguity model, which emphasizes the a priori consideration of strength, the dose–response model seeks to answer the question, "How much treatment is enough?" A prototypical pattern for the relationship is shown in Figure 6.3, in which treatment strength, as measured by treatment contact (or exposure) hours, is linked to treatment outcomes as a negatively accelerated curve. In our hypothetical example, 10 contact hours corresponds to a success rate of $P = 0.20$ (20% of clients report no symptoms), 30 hours is associated with a success rate of $P = 0.55$, and 60 sessions corresponds to a success rate of $P = 0.85$. Not surprisingly, this example mirrors empirical results in psychotherapy (e.g., Howard et al., 1986; Kadera, Lambert, & Andrews, 1996; Lambert, Hansen, & Finch, 2001). As intuitively appealing as the dose–response relationship appears, it is not without some difficulties. In particular, it relies on results for clients with different levels of exposure to the treatment, raising questions about the internal validity of the claim describing the functional form of the relationship. However, the logic of the dose–response model is not restricted to naturally occurring variation in treatment receipt. For example, Barkham et al. (1996) used the counterfactual model by randomly assigning individuals to receive different doses (8 or 16 sessions) of two types of time-limited psychotherapy. The encouraging news,

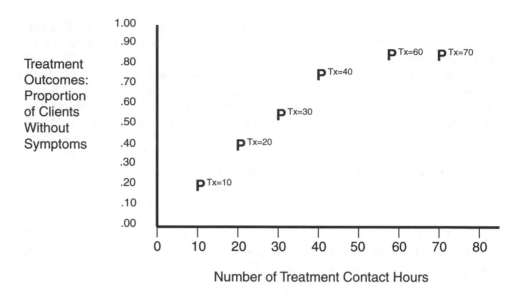

Figure 6.3. Linking treatment (Tx) strength to outcomes: the dose–response model.

at least to our untrained eyes, is that over the range of treatment strength (up to 16 sessions), their results are not inconsistent with the negatively accelerated functions previously reported, and their model has the additional benefit of examining treatment integrity (therapist adherence) to the two therapy models being tested.

The dose–response model appears to have an advantage over the counterfactual model when data are available on a broad range of treatment strengths. Specifically, exclusive reliance on the counterfactual model, with its emphasis on relative strength and relative effects, could yield results that are less useful to practitioners than is desired (Yeaton & Sechrest, 1981b). In some extreme instances, very potent treatments could be ruled ineffective when their success rates are very high. In Figure 6.4, we array the hypothetical results of three studies that investigated the effects of a treatment model. Study 1 compared 10 versus 20 contact hours of the treatment, with success rates of 0.21 and 0.40, respectively (effect size = 0.42). Study 2 contrasted 30 versus 40 contact hours, exhibiting success rates of 0.50 and 0.70 (effect size = .41). By conventional standards, both studies revealed moderate relative effects. However, interpreting just the effect size ignores valuable information about the effectiveness of treatments. Specifically, although the effect sizes are roughly equivalent, without taking into account the level of success for each treatment, we would overlook the fact that the success rates of both conditions in Study 2 greatly exceed those in Study 1. In the extreme, a study in which both conditions involved substantial doses of the treatment (Study 3) might produce an effect size that is neither statistically nor practically meaningful, yet the success rates of both noticeably exceed those in all conditions of Studies 1 and 2.

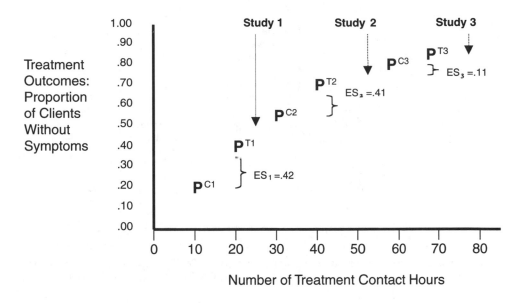

Figure 6.4. Relative effects and treatment outcomes for three hypothetical studies. T = treatment; C = counterfactual condition; ES = effect size.

Treatment Integrity

Unlike treatment strength, as defined by Sechrest and his colleagues, the literature on treatment integrity is voluminous. Concern about treatment integrity—the extent to which the treatment is carried out according to its model, plan, or theoretical specifications—dates back to the 1950s in psychotherapy (Bond, Evans, Salyers, Williams, & Kim, 2000; Moncher & Prinz, 1991). Indeed, there is little doubt that concern over integrity could not be traced back to the earliest moments of civilization. For example, major German beer makers proudly advertise that their product is brewed in accordance with the German Purity Law of 1516! In this section, we focus on (a) a proposed connection between treatment strength and integrity, (b) the relationship of treatment integrity to similar constructs, (c) the prevalence assessment of treatment integrity in effectiveness studies, and (d) what is known about factors influencing the integrity with which treatments are delivered and received.

Bridging Treatment Strength and Integrity: Achieved Relative Treatment Strength

According to Sechrest et al. (1979), the relationship between treatment strength and treatment integrity is reasonably straightforward. Whereas treatment strength is the a priori magnitude of the treatments (T^{Tx} and T^{C}), integrity refers to departures from their intended strengths. Departures can result from

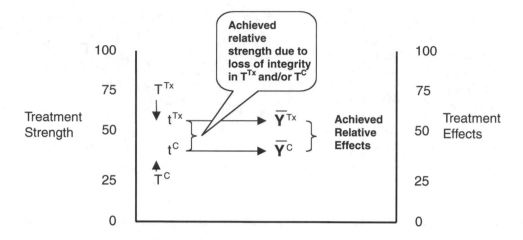

Figure 6.5. Achieved relative treatment strength and effects. T = conceptual condition; t = achieved condition; Y = outcome; C = counterfactual condition; Tx = treatment condition.

numerous factors, including contextual, organizational, staffing, and participant variables.

Although it is theoretically possible that treatment strength could exceed original expectations on implementation in the field, the more likely scenario is that it is eroded by these departures. However, a variety of processes described by Shadish et al. (2002) can operate to transform the counterfactual treatment to more closely resemble the target treatment condition. If elements of the treatment condition are also provided to participants in the counterfactual group (e.g., compensatory equalization, treatment diffusion) or through other mechanisms (e.g., compensatory rivalry, crossing over of participants), the counterfactual condition, as realized in practice, could resemble the theoretical form (T^C) less and the target treatment condition (T^{Tx}) more than was intended.

Accordingly, relative strength becomes *achieved relative strength* at the study's conclusion because of factors that influence the integrity of both T^{Tx} and T^C. To capture the distinction between relative strength and achieved relative strength, Figure 6.5 adds t^{Tx} and t^C to represent the achieved strength of each group in relation to T^{Tx} and T^C, respectively. Achieved relative strength (ARS) can be specified as ARS = [t^{Tx} and t^C]. In our hypothetical example diagrammed in Figure 6.5, ARS is 20 strength units (60 – 40), rather than the 50 strength units that were expected a priori. (See Figure 6.3.) The relative effect then shrinks, on average, to 20 well-being units.

The factors discussed in this section are thought to account for, in part, the transformation of $T^{Tx} \rightarrow t^{Tx}$ and the conversion of $T^C \rightarrow t^C$ or the treatments as planned (T's) versus the treatments as experienced (t's). Whereas relative treatment strength refers to the differences between T^{Tx} and T^C, the net effect of problems associated with a loss of treatment integrity is the achieved relative treatment strength, or $t^{Tx} - t^{C.}$ We suspect that part of the reason that treatment integrity has received so much more attention in the literature than has treatment strength is because, at the end of the study, it is the achieved relative treatment strength that matters most in explaining the presence or magnitude of treatment effects. Lipsey (1990) provides guidance on how to maximize the statistical power of an intervention study.

The loss of statistical power from the reduction in treatment strength represents a main concern of Sechrest et al. (1979). We might speculate that one reason for their repeated advice to first test the strongest possible treatment was to maximize the achieved relative strength between conditions. Boruch and Gomez (1977) provided a truly elegant analysis of the consequences resulting from the loss of treatment integrity for statistical power.

Comparable Concepts

Naturally, during its long history in the sciences, the notion of treatment integrity has been captured under a number of different labels. Our quick literature search (in PsycINFO) uncovered nearly 5,000 references to treatment integrity and its related concepts. Some of these alternative labels include *treatment fidelity, compliance,* and *implementation.* For example, Moncher and Prinz (1991) defined treatment fidelity in terms of the experimental tradition of a "manipulation check." Compliance refers to the extent to which clients accept treatment services, and implementation is a broad term associated with the installation of an intervention (Lipsey & Cordray, 2000). Other terms focus on specialized aspects of the treatment implementation process. These include the *adherence* of practitioners to the treatment protocol and *competence. Adherence* generally refers to whether a practitioner uses treatment approaches prescribed in the treatment manual and avoids the use of approaches that are proscribed (Waltz et al., 1993). Adherence, then, is similar to the notion of treatment purity described by Scott and Sechrest (1989). *Competence* refers to the skill of the practitioner in delivering the treatment.

Elements of Integrity Assessments

Several excellent reviews of the elements of treatment integrity are available (e.g., Carroll et al., 2000; Waltz et al., 1993). In particular, Carroll et al. (2000) identified the "technology model of psychotherapy research" as characterizing the state-of-the-art approach to assessing aspects of treatment integrity. According to Carroll et al. (2000), the technology model

> requires the specification of behavioral therapies in terms of their "dose" (the frequency and number of sessions), their active and inert ingredients (clarification of the unique and common elements of the therapy), the conditions under which they are administered, and assessment of whether the treatment was adequately delivered to all patients (compliance). (p. 225)

Consistent with suggestions made by Sechrest et al. (1979), Carroll et al. (2000) suggested that certain study features have become "virtual requirements" in clinical trials. Efforts to promote treatment integrity include (a) the specification of treatments in manuals, (b) the training and supervision of implementers, and (c) the monitoring of treatment delivery.

Integrity Assessment in Effectiveness Studies

Historical reviews of treatment fidelity in drug abuse prevention (Dusenbury, Brannigan, Falco, & Hansen, 2003), psychiatric rehabilitation (Bond et al., 2000), and other helping professions (Moncher & Prinz, 1991) point to the slow but steady growth of empirical assessment of treatment integrity. Several reviews of the extent to which treatment integrity has become a focal feature within outcome and effectiveness research have used Carroll et al.'s (2000) three dimensions to track methodological progress in various fields (e.g., clinical psychology, behavior therapy, marital and family therapy, parent training, drug prevention, alcohol treatment). For example, Moncher and Prinz (1991) examined 359 treatment outcome studies in clinical psychology, behavior therapy, psychiatry, and marital and family therapy appearing between 1980 and 1988. In defining assessment of fidelity, they focused on the use of procedures to promote fidelity (manuals and supervision) and whether aspects of treatment delivery were verified (adherence checks). Over time, the use of manuals increased from 28% (1980–1982) to 39% (1986–1988). Similarly, the use of supervision to promote fidelity increased from 17% to 34%. Adherence checks were conducted more frequently in 1986 through 1988 (31.7%) than in the earliest period of their review (13%, in 1980–1982). Although progress had been made, 55% of the studies ignored issues of fidelity entirely. Moreover, only about 13% of the studies incorporated all three fidelity assessments.

Dane and Schneider (1998) reviewed 162 evaluations in primary and early secondary prevention published between 1980 and 1994. Again, they found similar increases in the use of integrity checks (17% between 1980 and 1987 and 31% between 1988 and 1994).

These two reviews confirm the claims made by Sechrest and his colleagues. About the time their first papers were published, less than 20% of studies attended to issues of treatment integrity. In the interim, progress has been made, but there is still a long way to go before treatment integrity becomes a routine part of the portfolio of research practices in studies of treatment effectiveness.

Factors Affecting Treatment Integrity or Relative Treatment Strength

Cataloguing the potential influences on treatment integrity is greatly facilitated by the fact that factors are often nested or hierarchically organized. Behaviors of clients are influenced by the behavior of intervention staff; intervention staff can be influenced by policies and practices of their organization; and organizations can be influenced by other organizations (at the same level of operation) or at higher levels in the structure (e.g., rules, regulations, and laws of local, state, and federal governments). The cumulative influence of integrity problems emanating at higher levels of this hierarchy can have dramatic effects on services received by groups of clients. If treatment integrity is breeched at the clinic level (by policy or lack of support for component X), the actions of all therapists will be constrained and the services will not be delivered and received by all clients. Similarly, if clients refuse to participate, the strength of the treatment law, regardless of whether the staff are willing and able to provide services, will be diluted. As such, there are multiple ways to adversely affect treatment integrity.

PARTICIPANT COMPLIANCE AND ENGAGEMENT. The literature on treatment integrity focuses a great deal of attention on aspects of the treatment delivery process that the researcher has some hope of controlling through training, supervision, or treatment reengineering (e.g., Duan, Braslow, Weisz, & Wells, 2001). The behavior of participants plays an equally important role in determining the overall achieved relative strength of an intervention or treatment. In particular, their compliance with and engagement in the treatment protocol can dramatically affect how much treatment is received. Stecher et al. (1994) reported that 40% of clients assigned to (residential or nonresidential) treatment failed to become engaged (in the treatment) even for 1 day. Less than 10% of clients graduated from the treatment conditions. In another example, in assessing the discriminability conditions and integrity of Project MATCH treatments, Carroll et al. (1998) found that clients completed between 60% and 80% of the potential outpatient and aftercare treatment sessions. Although there were no between-condition differences in integrity, the noncompletion rates suggest that, on average, the conditions were not as strong as they might have been had all participants completed their full package of care.

ORGANIZATIONAL FACTORS. Implementation of interventions is not always a smooth process within established or new organizations. Consequently, the strength of the treatment can vary over time. It may take a new or revamped program literally years to be up and running at full strength if, indeed, that ever occurs. Moreover, mature programs are vulnerable to periods when they deliver services incompletely, inconsistently, or not at all to a noticeable proportion of their target clients. For example, Stecher et al. (1994) compared residential and nonresidential treatments for dually diagnosed homeless adults. Both interventions involved two phases; the first had eight goals (e.g., client engagement, retention, assessment, and treatment planning) and an intended duration of 3 months. On the basis of interviews with treatment administrators and staff, it was found that less than 20% of the goals were accomplished for the nonresidential program during its first 9 months of operation. However, implementation had reached 75% by the 15th month and then remained stable. Even though the residential treatment had been operational for 4 years prior to the study, it was not until the 18th month that all eight program goals had been achieved. Orwin et al. (1998) showed that treatment strength and relative strength ebbs and flows over the course of a program's time line. It is not unreasonable to believe that different client cohorts attained differential levels of outcomes. The dose–response model for linking outcomes to differential experiences within programs may provide a useful approach to capitalizing on this natural variation within programs.

The idea of investigating dose–response relationships is not confined to individuals or individuals within programs: The "dosages" provided by different sites with the same treatment model also may differ. For example, McGrew et al. (1994) measured the fidelity (the achieved strength) of 18 assertive community treatment programs and found variability in fidelity that correlated with a program-level client outcome. Similar achieved strength and outcome relationships have been found by Becker, Smith, Tanzman, Drake, and Tremblay (2001), and Yeaton (1994).

OUTSIDE SERVICES. Because some community-based interventions rely on services outside the direct control of a treatment, assessing achieved strength requires the inclusion of these outside (or wraparound) services. An observational measure has been developed to measure the key elements of the wraparound approach for children with serous emotional disturbance and their families within a system of care (Nordness & Epstein, 2003). Wraparound services can also reduce the achieved relative strength of treatment conditions by enhancing the amount of treatment provided to participants in the control condition. Carroll et al. (1998) found that 28% to 38% of outpatient clients had involvement in at least one significant outside treatment session.

THE POTENTIAL INFLUENCE OF CHANGES IN THE POLICY CONTEXT. Experimental assessments of interventions can take years to plan and execute. At the same time, changes in reimbursement policies and shifts in priorities of administrations can increase or decrease the availability of treatment resources that can affect the strength of the target treatment, the counterfactual treatment, or both. McHugo et al. (1999) reported that state-based changes in reimbursement for community outreach created incentives for traditional case managers to increase outreach (enhancing the strength of the control condition). Federal Medicaid changes for psychiatric hospitalization altered the payment structure, reducing the strength of treatment for both groups because the cap on the length of stay was reduced.

CHANGES IN TECHNOLOGY. If the public sector (policy context) can interject its influence on the integrity or strength of treatments, so can the private sector. Again, McHugo et al. (1999) noted that clozapine emerged at the same time that their interventions were being tested, creating a competitor to their treatment theory. Shifts in economic circumstances can certainly affect the potential effects of interventions that rely on work or have employment as an outcome.

The foregoing discussion of treatment integrity was intended as a "snapshot" of progress and issues that have emerged since the time Sechrest et al. (1979) called for greater attention to the nature and strength of interventions. Given the volume of material that has appeared, our summary has attempted to highlight the contextual, organizational, and individual (both clients and implementers) factors that can and do exert an influence on treatments, as realized in the field.

Status of Treatment Strength and Integrity

Sechrest and his colleagues framed intervention research from two perspectives: (a) At the conceptual level, they stressed the a priori magnitude and theoretical cohesiveness of the treatment, referring to this as treatment strength; and (b) at the operational level, they defined treatment integrity as the extent to which the theoretically grounded treatment was implemented as planned. In the two decades since they issued these definitions, the field has witnessed increasing attention being directed at dimensions of treatment integrity. The question implied by the definition of treatment strength—"How much treatment is enough and how should it be optimally organized?"—has received less direct attention. Indirectly, however, many of the ideas underlying treatment strength have been incorporated into research practices through the development of theory-driven evaluations, logic models, program templates, and treatment manuals.

In its most intuitive form, the idea of treatment strength is quite appealing and understandable. In the context of models of treatment effectiveness research, the notion of relative treatment strength probably fits better. Furthermore, because the net influence of factors that dampen treatment integrity represents the achieved relative treatment strength in a comparative study, the distinction between strength and integrity may have been lost. We continue to believe that the a priori consideration of the strength of each treatment condition remains a fundamental question in intervention research.

Although nearly 5,000 references related to treatment integrity were uncovered in preparing this chapter, the most up-to-date reviews of effectiveness studies still suggest that the measurement of strength or integrity is not yet universal. In particular, assessing treatment integrity is dependent on having adequate measurement tools. Unless one simply relies on client participation data (e.g., length of stay, number of therapy sessions, or class attendance), the development of such measures is labor intensive and often the result of a lengthy program of research. This is particularly true for interventions that are complex or multifaceted. Given the number of dimensions that are to be assessed, data collection is labor intensive, often involving interviewers, observers, or multiple sets of respondents (e.g., clients, practitioners, and parents).

Much of the impressive work done to date on features of treatment integrity is the result of a program of research conducted on treatments with well-articulated theories, manuals, training materials, established measures, and so on. The majority of programs (interventions) in local organizations are not nearly as sophisticated. For these researchers, the "high-end" methods reported in this chapter are likely to be of little consequence.

Returning to the issues raised by Sechrest and his colleagues, there are three fundamental questions pertaining to treatment strength and integrity: (a) Is there a compelling enough rationale for the intervention to produce the desired effects? (b) Is the intervention sufficiently different from what would have been received had it not been installed? and (c) Did participants in the treatment condition get more services or treatment than those in the counterfactual condition? At a minimum, answering the first two questions involves critical thinking, not an elaborate assessment package. Finding simple indicators of treatment receipt (e.g., number of treatment sessions attended) may be enough to answer the third question. To the extent that expected outcomes are confirmed, important rival explanations are ruled out, and the achieved relative strength is adequate (the cause is "ruled in"), the particular intervention would become a candidate for a longer and more intensive program of research. Studies need to be done "well enough" to avoid overlooking an intervention that has promise.

Sechrest and his collaborators, by framing the questions concerning strength and integrity of treatments the way they did and so early in the history of evaluation research, have contributed greatly to the search for effective ways of discovering how to ameliorate adverse social conditions.

References

Barkham, M., Rees, A., Stiles, W. B., Shapiro, D. A., Hardy, G. E., & Reynolds, S. (1996). Dose–effect relations in time-limited therapy for depression. *Journal of Consulting and Clinical Psychology, 64,* 927–935.

Becker, D. R., Smith, J., Tanzman, B., Drake, R. E., & Tremblay, T. (2001). Fidelity of supported employment programs and employment outcomes. *Psychiatric Services, 52,* 834–836.

Bond, G. R., Evans, L., Salyers, M. P., Williams, J., & Kim, H. W. (2000). Measurement of fidelity in psychiatric rehabilitation. *Mental Health Services Research, 2,* 75–87.

Boruch, R. F. (1997). *Randomized experiments for planning and evaluation: A practical guide.* Thousand Oaks, CA: Sage.

Boruch, R. F., & Gomez, H. (1977). Sensitivity, bias, and theory in impact evaluations. *Professional Psychology, 8,* 411–434.

Braden, C. J., McGlone, K., & Pennington, F. (1993). Specific psychosocial and behavioral outcomes from the systemic lupus erythematosus self-help course. *Health Education Quarterly, 20,* 29–41.

Brandt, P. A., Kirsch, S., Lewis, F. M., & Casey, S. M. (2004). Assessing the strength and integrity of an intervention. *Oncology Nursing Forum, 31,* 833–837.

Brekke, J. S. (1987). The model-guided method for monitoring implementation. *Evaluation Review, 11,* 281–299.

Brekke, J. S., & Test, M. A. (1992). A model for measuring implementation of community support programs: Results from three sites. *Community Mental Health Journal, 28,* 227–247.

Carroll, K. M., Connors, G. J., Cooney, N. L., DiClemente, C. C., Donovan, D. M., Kadden, R. R., et al. (1998). Internal validity of the Project MATCH treatments: Discriminability and integrity. *Journal of Consulting and Clinical Psychology, 66,* 290–303.

Carroll, K. M., Nich, C., Sifry, R. L., Nuro, K. F., Frankforter, T. L., Ball, S. A., et al. (2000). A general system for evaluating therapist adherence and competence in psychotherapy research in the addictions. *Drug and Alcohol Dependence, 57,* 225–238.

Chen, H.-T. (1990). *Theory-driven evaluations.* Newbury Park, CA: Sage.

Chen, H.-T., & Rossi, P. H. (Eds.). (1992). *Using theory to improve program and policy evaluations.* New York: Greenwood Press.

Cohen, J. (1988). *Statistical power analysis for the behavioral sciences* (2nd ed.). Hillsdale, NJ: Erlbaum.

Cook, T. D., & Campbell, D. T. (1979). *Quasi-experimentation: Design and analysis issues for field settings.* Chicago: Rand McNally.

Cook, T. D., Cooper, H., Cordray, D. S., Hartmann, H., Hedges, L. V., Light, R. J., et al. (1992). *Meta-analysis for explanation: A casebook.* New York: Russell Sage Foundation.

Cordray, D. S. (1986). Quasi-experimental analysis: A mixture of methods and judgment. *New Directions for Program Evaluation, 31,* 9–27.

Cordray, D. S. (2000) Expanding the scope of social experimentation. *Crime and Delinquency, 46*, 401–424.

Cordray, D. S., & Fischer, R. (1995). Evaluation synthesis. In J. Wholey, H. Hatry, & K. Newcomer (Eds.), *Handbook of Practical Program Evaluation*. San Francisco: Jossey-Bass.

Cordray, D. S., & Pion, G. M. (1993). Psychosocial rehabilitation assessment: A broader perspective. In R. L. Glueckauf, L. B. Sechrest, G. R. Bond, & E. C. McDonel (Eds.), *Improving assessment in rehabilitation and health* (pp. 215–241). Newbury Park, CA: Sage.

Dane, A. V., & Schneider, B. H. (1998). Program integrity in primary and early secondary prevention: Are implementation effects out of control? *Clinical Psychology Review, 18*, 23–45.

Duan, N., Braslow, J. T., Weisz, J. R., & Wells, K. B. (2001). Fidelity, adherence, and robustness of interventions. *Psychiatric Services, 52*, 413.

Dusenbury, L., Brannigan, B., Falco, M., & Hansen, W. B. (2003). A review of research on fidelity of implementation: Implications for drug abuse prevention in school settings. *Health Education Research, 18*, 237–256.

Einhorn, H. J., & Hogarth, R. M. (1986). Judging probable cause. *Psychological Bulletin, 99*, 3–19.

Hansen, N. B., Lambert, M. J., & Forman, E. M. (2002). The psychotherapy dose–response effect and its implications for treatment delivery services. *Clinical Psychology: Science and Practice, 9*, 329–343.

Holland, P. (1986). Statistics and causal inference. *Journal of the American Statistical Association, 81*, 945–970.

Howard, K. I., Kopta, S. M., Krause, M. S., & Orlinsky, D. E. (1986). The dose–response effect in psychotherapy. *American Psychologist, 41*, 159–164.

Julian, D. A. (1997). The utilization of the logic model as a system level planning and evaluation device. *Evaluation and Program Planning, 20*, 251–257.

Kadera, S., Lambert, M. J., & Andrews, A. A. (1996). How much therapy is really enough? A session-by-session analysis of the psychotherapy dose–effect relationship. *Journal of Psychotherapy Research and Practice, 5*, 132–151.

Keith, R. A. (1997). Treatment strength in rehabilitation. *Archives of Physical Medicine and Rehabilitation, 78*, 1298–1304.

Lambert, M. J., Hansen, N. B., & Finch, A. E. (2001). Patient-focused research: Using patient outcome data to enhance treatment effects. *Journal of Consulting and Clinical Psychology, 69*, 159–172.

Lipsey, M. W. (1990). *Design sensitivity: Statistical power for experimental research*. Newbury Park, CA: Sage.

Lipsey, M. W. (1993). Theory as method: Small theories of treatment. *New Directions for Program Evaluation, 57*, 5–38.

Lipsey, M. W., & Cordray, D. S. (2000). Evaluation methods in intervention assessment. *Annual Review of Psychology, 51*, 345–375.

Mackie, J. L. (1974). *The cement of the universe: A study of causation*. New York: Oxford University Press.

McGrew, J. H., Bond, G. R., Dietzen, L. L., & Salyers, M. P. (1994). Measuring the fidelity of implementation of a mental health program model. *Journal of Consulting and Clinical Psychology, 62*, 670–678.

McHugo, G. J., Drake, R. E., Teague, G. B., & Xie, H. (1999). Fidelity to assertive community treatment and client outcomes in the New Hampshire Dual Disorders Study. *Psychiatric Services, 50*, 818–824.

Moncher, F. J., & Prinz, R. J. (1991). Treatment fidelity in outcome studies. *Clinical Psychology Review, 11*, 247–266.

National Institute of Child Health and Human Development Early Child Care Research Network. (2003). Does quality of child care affect child outcomes at age 4½? *Developmental Psychology, 39*, 451–469.

Northup, J., Fisher, W., Kahang, S. W., Harrell, R., & Kurtz, P. (1997). An assessment of the necessary strength of behavioral treatments for severe behavioral problems. *Journal of Developmental and Physical Disabilities, 9*, 1–16.

Nordness, P. D., & Epstein, M. H. (2003). Reliability of the Wraparound Observation Form— Second Version: An instrument designed to assess the fidelity of the wraparound approach. *Mental Health Services Research, 5*, 89–96.

Orwin, R. G., Sonnefeld, L. J., Cordray, D. S., Pion, G. M., & Perl, H. I. (1998). Constructing quantitative implementation scales from categorical services data: Examples from a multisite evaluation. *Evaluation Review, 22,* 245–288.

Rosenbaum, P. R. (2002). *Observational studies* (2nd ed.). New York: Springer-Verlag.

Rubin, D. B. (1974). Estimating the causal effects of treatments in randomized and non-randomized studies. *Journal of Educational Psychology, 66,* 688–701.

Salyers, M. P., Bond, G. R., Teague, G. B., Cox, J. F., Smith, M. E., Hicks, M. L., et al. (2003). Real-world examples of evaluating the degree of implementation for Assertive Community Treatment. *Journal of Behavioral Health Services and Research, 30,* 304–320.

Scheirer, M. A. (1996). A template for assessing the organizational base for program implementation. *New Directions for Evaluation, 72,* 61–80.

Scott, A. G., & Sechrest, L. B. (1989). Strength of theory and theory of strength. *Evaluation and Program Planning, 12,* 329–336.

Sechrest, L. B. (1982). Program evaluation: The independent and dependent variables. *The Counseling Psychologist, 10,* 73–74.

Sechrest, L. B., & Redner, R. (1979). Strength and integrity of treatments in evaluation studies. In *Evaluation reports.* Washington, DC: National Criminal Justice Reference Service.

Sechrest, L. B., West, S. G., Phillips, M. A., Redner, R., & Yeaton, W. (1979). Some neglected problems in evaluation research: Strength and integrity of treatments. In L. B. Sechrest, S. G. West, M. A. Phillips, R. Redner, & W. Yeaton (Eds.), *Evaluation studies review annual* (Vol. 4, pp. 15–35). Beverly Hills, CA: Sage.

Sechrest, L. B., & Yeaton, W. H. (1981). Empirical bases for estimating effect size. In R. F. Boruch, P. M. Wortman, & D. S. Cordray (Eds.), *Reanalyzing program evaluations: Policies and practices for secondary analysis of social and educational programs* (pp. 212–224). San Francisco: Jossey-Bass.

Shadish, W., Cook, T. D., & Campbell, D. T. (2002). *Experimental and quasi-experimental designs for generalized causal inference.* Boston: Houghton Mifflin.

Stecher, B. M., Andrews, C. A., McDonald, L., Morton, S., McGlynn, E. A., Petersen, L. P., et al. (1994). Implementation of residential and nonresidential treatment for dually diagnosed homeless. *Evaluation Review, 18,* 689–717.

Teague, G. B., Bond, G. R., & Drake, R. E. (1998). Program fidelity of implementation of a mental health program model. *American Journal of Orthopsychiatry, 68,* 216–232.

Waltz, J., Addis, M. E., Koerner, K., & Jacobson, N. S. (1993). Testing the integrity of a psychotherapy protocol: Assessment of adherence and competence. *Journal of Consulting and Clinical Psychology, 61,* 620–630.

U.S. General Accounting Office. (1990). *Prospective evaluation methods: The prospective evaluation synthesis.* Washington, DC: Author.

Webb, E. J., Campbell, D. T., Schwartz, R. D., & Sechrest, L. (1966). *Unobtrusive measures: Nonreactive research in the social sciences.* Chicago: Rand McNally.

Yeaton, W. (1994). The development and assessment of valid measures of service delivery to enhance inference in outcome-based research: Measuring attendance at self-help group meetings. *Journal of Consulting and Clinical Psychology, 62,* 686–694.

Yeaton, W. H., & Sechrest, L. (1981a). Critical dimensions in the choice and maintenance of successful treatments: Strength, integrity, and effectiveness. *Journal of Consulting and Clinical Psychology, 49,* 156–167.

Yeaton, W. H., & Sechrest, L. B. (1981b). Meaningful measures of effect. *Journal of Consulting and Clinical Psychology, 49,* 766–767.

Yin, R. K. (1997). Case study evaluation: A decade of progress? *New Directions for Evaluation, 76,* 69–78.

7

Random Assignment: A Systematic Review

Souraya Sidani

Evaluating the effectiveness of interventions in producing desired outcomes is critical for developing a sound knowledge base to guide practice in various applied disciplines such as psychology, medicine, and nursing. The experimental or randomized controlled trial (RCT) design is viewed as the "gold standard" for effectiveness research (Norquist, Lebowitz, & Hyman, 1999; Shadish, Cook, & Campbell, 2002). The features of the RCT design are careful participant selection, random assignment of participants to the study groups, and manipulation of the intervention implementation. The features of the RCT make it the most appropriate design to demonstrate the causal relationship between the intervention and the outcomes (Cook, 1993). Yet, it is these features that render the RCT results of limited applicability and relevance to the real world of everyday practice (e.g., Goldfried & Wolfe, 1996; Hollon, 1996; Newman & Tejeda, 1996). This state of the science has led some to question the assumptions underlying the experimental approach (e.g., Kunz & Oxman, 1998; Sidani & Braden, 1998) and to suggest alternative designs and research methods that would enhance the clinical relevance of effectiveness research (e.g., Clarke, 1995; Norquist et al., 1999; Schwartz, Chesney, Irvine, & Keefe, 1997; Sidani, Epstein, & Moritz, 2003). The debate around the use of different research designs and methods relies primarily on logic or rhetoric rather than on evidence (Kunz & Oxman, 1998). Sechrest (1998) pointed out that in the literature on research methods, different methodological features are considered as essential for enhancing the validity of conclusions in intervention evaluation studies. This literature, however, falls short of providing empirical evidence demonstrating the extent to which these features actually maintain the validity of study results. It, therefore, is important and timely to generate empirical evidence to inform methodological decisions.

This chapter is funded by the Nursing Effectiveness, Utilization, and Outcomes Research Unit, Faculty of Nursing, University of Toronto, Ontario, Canada. The opinions expressed in this chapter represent those of the author and may not reflect the views of the Nursing Effectiveness, Utilization, and Outcomes Research Unit.

Random assignment is the cornerstone of the experimental, or RCT, design and is the methodological feature that has received attention in recent debates. Although random assignment is regarded as the most critical safeguard of internal validity, its use in effectiveness research has been critiqued on several grounds. In addition, the results of meta-analyses showed that under some conditions, the effect size (ES) estimates in randomized experiments approximate those in nonrandomized experiments. This finding challenges the belief that experimental designs produce correct and "trustworthy" results (Concato, Shah, & Horwitz, 2000). It also questions the utility of random assignment in effectiveness research and the extent to which random assignment is effective in producing initially equivalent groups. In this chapter, these questions are addressed by critically reviewing the role and limitations of random assignment and by presenting the results of a systematic, quantitative review of intervention evaluation studies. The systematic review was designed to provide empirical evidence of the extent to which randomization is successful in achieving comparable groups.

Role of Random Assignment

Random assignment involves the application of chance-based procedures (e.g., the toss of a coin) for allocating participants to study groups. It is considered instrumental for minimizing selection bias associated with the process of assigning participants to groups (Cook & Campbell, 1979; Schulz, Chalmers, Hayes, & Altman, 1995). Specifically, allocating participants to study groups on the basis of chance alone eliminates selection bias that results from systematically assigning participants on the basis of preferences, desires, and expectancies (Horwitz, 1987; Weinberger et al., 2002). The participants' strong preferences for treatment options and desire to receive care, the therapists' preferences for treatment options, and the researchers' expectancies may interfere with the assignment process, yielding unequal or noncomparable groups. Initial group nonequivalence presents a major threat to internal validity. Between-groups differences in baseline characteristics may confound the intervention effects on the expected outcomes.

Random assignment enhances equivalence or comparability on measured and unmeasured variables between the study groups, prior to the implementation of the intervention under investigation. Chance-based allocation of participants leads to a situation in which participants with given idiosyncrasies assigned to one group will, on the average, be counterbalanced by participants with comparable (but not necessarily identical) idiosyncrasies assigned to the other group (Cook & Campbell, 1979). The end result of random assignment is an even or balanced distribution of participants with similar characteristics that could influence the outcomes between the study groups. Thus, the average scores of participants in one group do not differ from the average scores of participants in the other group on variables measured prior to treatment implementation (Abel & Koch, 1999; Demissie, Mills, & Rhoads, 1998; McKee et al., 1999). Initial group equivalence decreases the variability in the posttest outcomes that is not attributable to the treatment and increases the chance of detecting unbiased treatment effects (Heinsman & Shadish, 1996; Lipsey, 1990). It is important to clarify that the group equivalence achieved by random assignment is probabilistic. This implies that random assignment increases the likelihood, but does not guarantee, that the two groups are exactly comparable. The groups' mean scores will not be identical and may differ; however, such difference is due to chance alone (Cook & Campbell, 1979; Rossi, Freeman, & Lipsey, 1999; Yeaton & Sechrest, 1981).

Limitations of Random Assignment

Random assignment has been considered the most effective means for achieving initial group equivalence and therefore for enhancing the validity of the causal relationship between the intervention and the outcomes. Arguments challenging this belief have been presented recently. They are based on empirical evidence and on logical analysis.

Limitations Based on Empirical Evidence

In multiple meta-analyses aimed at determining the effects of various interventions on relevant outcomes, the ESs obtained from RCT were compared with those obtained from nonrandomized studies, such as quasi-experiments and observational, case-control, or historical control studies. The results of the comparisons were inconsistent across meta-analyses. In some, the mean ES for randomized experiments did not differ significantly from the mean ES for nonrandomized studies. In other meta-analyses, the mean ES differed between randomized and nonrandomized studies. The differences did not reveal any consistent pattern in which randomized experiments underestimated the intervention effects in some instances and overestimated the effects in other instances.

Smith, Glass, and Miller (1980) and Lipsey and Wilson (1993) found minimal differences in the mean ES of randomized and nonrandomized studies examining the benefits of psychotherapy. Lipsey and Wilson reported a .05 mean value for the difference. Demissie et al. (1998) indicated that the summary risk estimates of RCT and case-control studies that evaluated the effectiveness of screening mammography were not significantly different for a subgroup of the target population (i.e., women ages 40–49 years). Similarly, Concato et al. (2000) reported similar pooled relative risk values for RCT and case-control or observational studies that evaluated a variety of medical treatments, including tuberculosis vaccine, screening mammography, cholesterol-lowering drugs, and antihypertensive medications. Several researchers found differences in the ES estimates between randomized and nonrandomized studies. Sacks, Chalmers, and Smith (1982, 1983) found that the results of historical control trials tend to be more positive, supporting the benefits of the treatment being evaluated, than those of RCTs. Heinsman and Shadish (1996), Shadish and Ragsdale (1996), and Shadish, Matt, Navarro, and Phillips (2000) reported that, on average, nonrandomized studies of different psychoeducational therapies significantly underestimated intervention effects, compared with randomized studies.

In contrast, Knownacki (1997, cited in Shadish, 2000) found that the ESs for quasi-experimental studies were larger than those for randomized studies of alcohol treatment. McKee et al. (1999) reported a similar trend of a larger mean ES for nonrandomized studies. Additional analyses showed that the difference in the ES between the randomized and nonrandomized studies is related to aspects of the research study, including ES of the outcomes measured at pretest, participants' self-selection into a study group, attrition, nature of the control condition (Heinsman & Shadish, 1996; Shadish et al., 2000; Shadish & Ragsdale, 1996), client selection criteria, and control of potential prognostic factors that influence outcomes (McKee et al., 1999).

In summary, the empirical evidence showed no clear bias (i.e., under- or overestimation) for nonrandomized experiments. The evidence also implies that the presence or lack of random assignment is not the only design feature responsible for the variability in the results across studies. Nonexperimental studies that are well designed to minimize or account for potential threats to validity may produce results that approximate those of randomized experiments (Chen & Rossi, 1987; Concato et al., 2000; McKee et al., 1999).

Limitations Based on Logical Analysis

The methodological arguments against the use of random assignment in effectiveness research are based on its inherent limits and its potential to pose other threats to the validity of the study conclusions. Although the points are interrelated, they are discussed separately.

INHERENT LIMITS OF RANDOM ASSIGNMENT. Random assignment increases the probability that the study groups are equivalent on known and measured, or unknown and unmeasured, variables prior to the implementation of the intervention. This statement has two methodological implications. First, it implies that random assignment does not guarantee that the study groups will be exactly matched on all characteristics that may affect the outcomes (Kraemer & Fendt, 1990). Therefore, the groups should be compared on all baseline variables, such as demographic and health- or illness-related characteristics, as well as outcomes assessed at pretest to determine the extent to which randomization was successful in equalizing the groups. Yet, any between-groups difference on any variable is viewed as a chance occurrence, even if it is statistically significant (Rossi et al., 1999). Such difference in a baseline variable is considered of little consequence to internal validity when the variable is weakly correlated with the outcomes. Initial between-groups differences, however small, cannot be ignored, as they can be clinically meaningful.

The second implication is that random assignment maintains initial equivalence at the group and not the individual participant level. As Cook and Campbell (1979) stated, random assignment "does not, of course, remove the idiosyncrasy from any one unit" (p. 340). That is, it does not deal with interindividual differences in the baseline variables. Initial interindividual differences, therefore, are not controlled for, and they may still exert their influence on posttest outcome achievement. They may contribute to increased error variance (i.e., variance in posttest outcomes that is not attributable to the intervention), which reduces the power to detect significant intervention effects (Chen & Rossi, 1987; Costner, 1989). The impact of interindividual differences is exacerbated with attrition. In fact, random assignment enhances group comparability prior to the implementation of the intervention; however, it does not guarantee that this comparability will be maintained at posttest outcome measurement, in light of attrition (Abel & Koch, 1999; Howard, Krause, & Lyons, 1993). The groups should be comparable on all baseline measures at the time when the posttest outcomes are assessed. This is critical for making valid inferences about the treatment effects.

THREATS POSED BY RANDOM ASSIGNMENT. Although random assignment minimizes selection bias, which is a major threat to internal validity, it can pose other threats to the validity of the study conclusions. Participants resent random assignment to the treatment options under investigation. They are not willing to leave the choice of treatment to chance alone (Bradley, 1993); rather, they prefer to be involved in treatment-related decision making. For instance, O'Reilly, Martin, and Collins (1999) found that only 1 of 20 participants accepted being randomized to either of two radical treatments for prostate cancer. They reported that patients who were well informed about the two treatments refused randomization and preferred to make their own decision as to which treatment they wanted. Similarly, Coward (2002) found that only 6 of 41 women were willing to be randomized to the study groups (i.e., support group for breast cancer survivors and control groups). Individuals who are not willing to be randomized may decline participation in the study. Llewellyn-Thomas, McGreal, Thiel, Fine, and Erlichman (1991) explained that patients who refused to enroll in a cancer trial demanded more participation in treatment decision making. Therefore, people who take part in an RCT differ from those who do not. Thus, the study sample consists of individuals who do not mind receiving treatment based on chance, which poses a threat to external validity.

Initial empirical evidence indicates that participants who accept randomization differ on several baseline characteristics from those who do not. McKay et al. (1998) compared male veterans seeking treatment for cocaine abuse who were willing to be randomized to inpatient or day-hospital rehabilitation with those who were not willing to be randomized. They found that randomized participants were less educated, reported more days of cocaine use, and had more severe drug and psychiatric problems at baseline than nonrandomized participants. Thus, participants in an RCT form a sample that is not representative of the various subgroups composing the target population, which potentially limits the generalizability of the findings (Bradley, 1993; Man-Son-Hing, Hart, Berquist, O'Connor, & Laupacis, 2001; Schwartz et al., 1997).

Participants may have a strong preference for one of the treatment options under investigation. Through the process of obtaining consent, participants are informed of the treatment options. They may perceive the options as unequally attractive, suitable, or optimal, and they may favor a particular treatment option. Some participants may decline enrollment in the study if they strongly prefer one of the treatment options and are aware that they have just a 50% chance of receiving it (Bradley, 1993; Droitcour, 1997). Llewellyn-Thomas et al. (1991) found that only a small number of patients (2 of 22) with a preference for the standard treatment agreed to participate in an RCT, whereas a larger number (22 of 36) with a preference for the experimental treatment agreed. Some participants may enroll in the study with the hope that they will receive the treatment option of their preference (Brewin & Bradley, 1989). However, random assignment does not take their preference into account, resulting in a mismatch between the participants' preferred and allocated treatment options, and subsequently in dissatisfaction with the allocated treatment. Dissatisfied participants may react in different ways. Some will drop out of the study, potentially leading to nonequivalence or noncomparability of the study groups on baseline characteristics (Bradley, 1993). Others will have low motivation to comply with the treatment or will become demoralized, which contributes negatively to outcome achievement (Anderson, Firschein, & Meenan, 1989; Bottomley, 1997; Brewin & Bradley, 1989; Coward, 2002; Hicks, 1998; Torgerson, Klaber-Moffett, & Russell, 1996). Still, some dissatisfied participants will show compensatory rivalry, leading to positive outcomes (Nield-Anderson, Dixon, & Lee, 1999). Participants could be randomly assigned to their treatment of preference. These participants are satisfied with the allocated treatment. They show enthusiasm for the treatment, which is demonstrated by active and continued engagement in treatment, high expectations of the treatment, improved psychological adjustment, and high compliance with the treatment. All these reactions contribute to the achievement of positive outcomes (Brewin & Bradley, 1989). In brief, random assignment creates two subgroups within the study sample: those who are satisfied, and those who are disappointed, with the allocated treatment. The location of these subgroups within the study groups (i.e., experimental and control) will bias the estimates of the intervention effects (i.e., under- or overestimation), thereby threatening the validity of conclusions regarding the effectiveness of the intervention. For example, Gale, Kirk, and Davis (1994) found that patients randomly assigned to their treatment of preference tended to report improvement in the outcomes, whereas those not assigned to their treatment of preference showed no significant change in the outcomes.

In summary, random assignment has been considered a key feature of experimental or RCT designs for achieving initial group equivalence on all measured and unmeasured variables, and therefore, for minimizing the influence of these variables on outcome achievement. Yet, random assignment does not guarantee initial group equivalence. It has inherent limits in controlling for interindividual differences in baseline characteristics, and those limits may have direct or indirect effects on the outcomes expected of an intervention. In addition, participants' resentment of randomization and strong preferences for treatment options present threats to internal and external validity. Furthermore, results of meta-analytic studies showed that the mean ES for experimental studies was not much different from the mean ES for nonexperimental studies. These findings challenge the belief that random assignment is the most critical feature for maintaining the validity of the causal relationship between the intervention and the outcomes.

The literature review pointed to the strengths and limitations of random assignment. However, it fell short of providing the empirical evidence demonstrating the extent to which randomization actually achieves initial group equivalence. A systematic review of intervention evaluation studies, using a quantitative analysis, was undertaken to address this gap in the methodological literature.

Systematic Review of Intervention Evaluation Studies

The overall purpose of this systematic review of intervention evaluation studies was to examine the extent to which random assignment of participants to the study groups is effective in producing initially equivalent groups. Published reports of studies that used random assignment to allocate participants to groups were reviewed to (a) determine whether the groups were compared at baseline for the purpose of checking on the success of randomization in producing initially comparable groups and (b) delineate the results of such comparisons. The report of nonsignificant between-group differences and the magnitude of between-group differences (estimated with the standardized mean difference, or ES) at baseline were considered appropriate criteria for determining the effectiveness of randomization in equalizing the groups. Small sample size and attrition are identified as conditions that interfere with the success of randomization (Chen & Rossi, 1987; Kraemer & Fendt, 1990; Yeaton & Sechrest, 1981). Therefore, the influence of these two conditions on between-group differences at baseline was explored. Differences between the groups at baseline are associated with similar differences at posttest, which may confound the intervention effects on the expected outcomes (Cook & Campbell, 1979; Heinsman & Shadish, 1996). The relationship between baseline and posttest differences was also examined in this systematic review.

Method

SAMPLE. The sample for the systematic review consisted of 100 published reports of intervention evaluation studies. The studies were included if they met the following criteria: (a) The study was concerned with evaluating the effects of a treatment on expected outcomes, and (b) the study design was experimental, in which random assignment was used to allocate participants to groups. The sample was randomly selected from refereed, research-based journals within the disciplines of psychology, medicine, and nursing. The studies were selected from the three disciplines to enhance the representativeness of the sample and to avoid any potential bias that might be present in a particular field of study. Within each discipline, a list of journals was generated. For each journal, the volumes issued in the period extending from 1980 to 2002 were identified. A random sample of the volumes was chosen and reviewed for reports of intervention evaluation studies. The abstract of each study report was read carefully to determine whether the study met the selection criteria. Of those, 100 studies were randomly selected for inclusion in the systematic review.

VARIABLES CODED. For each study, data were extracted for the following variables of interest.

Sample size. The sample size consisted of the reported total number of eligible individuals who consented to participate in the study and were allocated to the study groups.

Comparisons on baseline variables. The baseline variables were categorized into demographic characteristics and pretest outcome variables. This distinction was maintained for conceptual and analytic purposes. Demographic characteristics may not correlate significantly with the outcome variables. Therefore, between-group differences in demographic characteristics may not influence posttest outcome achievement. In contrast, the scores on the outcomes measured at pretest tend to correlate with the scores on the outcomes measured at posttest. Thus, differences in pretest outcomes may confound the treatment effects and present a major threat to making valid causal inferences. Information on whether or not baseline comparisons were made (coded 0 = not done and 1 = done) was extracted from either the researchers' report indicating that the groups did or did not differ on any baseline variable or tables presenting the results of descriptive statistics for each group and of analyses comparing the groups.

Results of baseline comparisons. The results of baseline comparisons were gathered for each demographic characteristic and pretest outcome variable included in the study. The results were recorded in two forms. The first form consisted of reporting whether or not there was a statistically significant difference between the groups on the variable in question (coded as 0 = no statistically significant difference and 1 = statistically significant difference). The second form for recording the results of baseline comparisons aimed at determining the magnitude of initial group differences and involved computing the ES. The ES was computed as the standardized difference between the means of two groups (formula used: mean of control group – mean of experimental group / pooled standard deviation) when the mean and standard deviation values were available. In situations in which the study involved more than two groups, the results of the baseline comparisons between a randomly selected treatment group and the control group were used in this review. Two values for the ES were recorded. The first was the actual value, which could be either positive (indicating that the control group had the highest mean) or negative (indicating that the experimental group had the highest mean). Although the sign of the ES is important in determining the effects of an intervention on the expected posttest outcomes, it is of little consequence in examining group differences at baseline. In the latter case, the interest is in finding out the extent to which the groups are similar or different, represented by the magnitude of the difference. Therefore, the second value was the absolute value of the ES (i.e., regardless of which group had the highest mean), which was calculated for the demographic and pretest outcome variables included in the selected studies.

Attrition. To explore the influence of attrition on initial group comparability, data were extracted from each study on the sample used in the baseline comparative analyses. In studies in which the initial sample (i.e., those participants allocated to the groups) was used in the comparisons, this variable was coded as 0. For studies in which the comparisons were made on the subset of participants who completed the study (i.e., excluding those who dropped out), this variable was coded as 1 (hereafter referred to as attrition sample).

Results of posttest comparisons. The results of posttest comparisons were recorded in two forms similar to those used for baseline comparisons (a) whether there was a statistically significant difference in the outcome between the two groups (same outcomes as those included in the baseline comparisons) and (b) the ES, computed as the standardized difference between the groups' means. The actual ES value (positive or negative) was used.

ANALYSES. The analyses were done at two levels: the level of the study and the level of the variable included in the baseline and posttest comparisons. At the study level, the analyses aimed at describing the number of studies in which baseline comparisons were made, the average number of baseline variables found to differ between groups, and the mean ES across variables measured at baseline. At the variable level, the descriptive analyses provided a detailed account of the extent to which the groups were comparable. Chi-square tests and Pearson correlation coefficients were used to examine the relationships between sample size and attrition and baseline differences, and between baseline and posttest differences.

Results

The results are presented in relation to the characteristics of the studies reviewed and to the objectives set for this systematic review. Where appropriate, the results are described at the study and variable levels. The actual and absolute values of the baseline effect sizes are reported separately.

CHARACTERISTICS OF THE STUDIES REVIEWED. The studies were selected from various journals in nursing ($n = 41$), medicine ($n = 38$), and psychology ($n = 21$). They were published over a 20-year period extending from 1982 to 2002. Eight studies were published between 1982 and 1989, 15 between 1990 and 1995, 62 between 1996 and 2000, and 15 between 2001 and 2002.

The number of groups included in the study varied from two to eight. Most ($n = 69$) studies involved two groups; 21 studies had three groups, 7 studies had four groups, 2 studies had five groups, and 1 study included eight groups. The reported sample size ranged from as low as 12 to as high as 7,705, with a mean of 333. Specifically, the sample size was less than or equal to 30 in 10 studies, 31 to 60 in 26 studies, 61 to 90 in 15 studies, 91 to 120 in 5 studies, 121 to 150 in 6 studies, and greater than 150 in 38 studies. In 70 studies, the initial sample size was reported, and in 30 studies, the attrition sample size was used in the analyses. The practice of reporting and using the initial sample size in the analysis is consistent with the principle underlying intention-to-treat analysis, which is widely accepted in health disciplines.

BASELINE COMPARISONS. Baseline comparisons were made in the majority of the studies reviewed. Comparisons on the demographic characteristics were done in 87 studies, and comparisons on the pretest outcomes were done in 70 studies. In some studies in which group differences in pretest outcomes were not examined, the outcome of interest, such as the relation between mortality rate and adverse drug effects, was not measured prior to treatment implementation. The observed trend of comparing the groups on baseline variables attests to the realization that randomization does not guarantee initial group equivalence and conforms with the recommendation to test for initial group comparability on measured variables (Rossi et al., 1999).

Within studies, the comparisons were done on a number of demographic characteristics that ranged from 1 to 20, with a mean of 7. In about half of the studies (48%), the comparisons were made on 6–10 demographic characteristics. The number of pretest outcomes compared varied between 1 and 15, with a mean of 5. In 64% of the studies, the comparisons were done on 1 to 5 pretest outcomes.

RESULTS OF BASELINE COMPARISONS. The results of baseline comparisons are presented for the demographic characteristics first and the pretest outcomes second.

Demographic characteristics. Of the 87 studies reporting comparisons on demographic characteristics, 57 studies (65.5%) indicated that there was no statistically significant difference in these variables between the groups, and 30 studies (34.5%) indicated that there was. In 19 of these 30 studies, a significant difference was found in 1% to 20% of the demographic characteristics compared; in 11 studies, a difference was found in 21% to 60% of the variables.

The actual ES for the demographic characteristics was computed in 51 studies in which required data were published. The ESs within each study were averaged to the study level. They ranged from –1.46 to .52, with a mean of .02 (±.27). The average actual ES was of a small (±.01 to .10) magnitude in 51%, moderate–low (±.11 to .25) in 29.3%, moderate–high (±.26 to .50) in 9.7%, and high (> ± .50) in 3.8%, of the studies (Table 7.1). More specifically, between-group comparisons were done on 617 demographic variables across the 87 studies reporting on such comparisons. The majority (88.8%) of these comparisons showed no statistically significant differences between the groups. The ES could be computed for 168 demographic characteristics. The actual ESs (i.e., assuming positive and negative values) ranged from –2.70 to 0.89, with a mean of .02 (±.37). Of the 168 ESs, 29.1% were of a low, 33.3% moderate–low,

Table 7.1.   Study-Level Effect Sizes

Category of effect size	Demographic characteristic	Pretest outcome	Posttest Outcome
0	3 (5.9%)	4 (6.3%)	3 (5.3%)
±.01 to .10	26 (51.0%)	31 (49.2%)	13 (23.2%)
±.11 to .25	15 (29.3%)	20 (31.7%)	11 (19.6%)
±.26 to .50	5 (9.7%)	5 (7.9%)	12 (21.4%)
±.50	2 (3.8%)	3 (4.7%)	17 (30.3%)

Table 7.2. Variable-Level Actual Effect Sizes

Category of effect size	Demographic characteristic	Pretest outcome	Posttest outcome
≤ –.50	8 (4.8%)	8 (2.7%)	21 (8.5%)
–.49 to –.25	13 (7.7%)	28 (9.6%)	18 (7.3%)
–.24 to –.10	32 (19.0%)	46 (15.7%)	19 (7.7%)
–.09 to –.01	21 (12.5%)	46 (15.7%)	29 (11.7%)
0	10 (6.0%)	24 (8.2%)	5 (2.0%)
.01 to .10	22 (13.1%)	48 (16.4%)	28 (11.4%)
.11 to .24	27 (16.1%)	32 (10.9%)	31 (12.5%)
.25 to .49	23 (13.7%)	46 (15.7%)	37 (15.0%)
> .50	12 (7.1%)	15 (5.1%)	64 (25.9%)

19.6% moderate–high, and 11.9% high, magnitude (Table 7.2). A similar pattern was observed for the absolute ES (i.e., absolute standardized mean difference). The mean absolute ES was .24 (±.28, range = .00 to 2.70). Most were categorized as of a low or moderate–low magnitude (Table 7.3).

Pretest outcomes. Of the 70 studies reporting comparisons on the pretest outcome measures, 58 (82.8%) indicated that there was no statistically significant difference in these variables between the groups, and 12 (17.2%) indicated that there was. In these 12 studies, the percentage of variables that showed a significant difference ranged from 1% to 100%. In particular, the percentage was 1% to 20% in 6 studies, 21% to 40% in 3 studies, 41% to 50% in one study, and 91% to 100% in two studies.

The actual ES was calculated in 63 studies, on the basis of the availability of the required data. The average study-level ES varied between –0.64 and 1.02. The mean value was .05 (±.22). Most (about 89%) of the average actual ESs were of a low-to-moderate magnitude (Table 7.1). The groups were compared on 352 pretest outcome variables across the 70 studies selected for the review. The vast majority (96.3%) of these comparisons showed no statistically significant differences between the study groups on the outcomes measured at pretest. A total of 293 ESs were computed, reflecting the magnitude of the between-groups differences on pretest outcomes. The actual ESs varied between –1.50 and 1.11, with a mean of .03 (±.30). About a third were of a low, 27.3% moderate–

Table 7.3. Variable-Level Absolute Effect Sizes

Category of effect sizes	Demographic characteristic	Pretest outcome
0	10 (6.0%)	24 (8.2%)
.01 to .10	49 (29.1%)	100 (34.1%)
.11 to .25	56 (33.4%)	80 (27.3%)
.26 to .50	33 (19.6%)	67 (22.9%)
> .50	20 (11.9%)	22 (7.5%)

low, 22.8% moderate–high, and 7.5% high magnitude (Table 7.2). The absolute ESs for pretest outcomes ranged from .00 to 1.50, with a mean of .20 (±.22). Most were considered of low or moderate–low magnitude (Table 7.3).

In summary, the results of analyses comparing the study groups at baseline indicated that for the most part, the comparisons showed no statistically significant differences between the groups on demographic and pretest outcome variables. Nonetheless, the magnitude of the between-group differences was of a small-to-moderate level. These findings imply that the results of determining the comparability of the groups by using tests of statistical significance could be misleading. Nonsignificant differences could be achieved with large within-group variance (Lipsey, 1990). The findings also support the notion that randomization does not guarantee initial group equivalence. The groups and participants within groups may still differ on several variables. Such a difference, although believed to be due to chance, is of a low-to-moderate size, which could be clinically meaningful.

RESULTS OF POSTTEST COMPARISONS. Comparisons between groups on the posttest outcomes were reported in almost all studies. The average study level ES for posttest outcome comparisons was computed for only 56 studies. It ranged from −1.33 to 4.87, with a mean value of .39 (±.78). Most implied that the treatment under investigation had a moderate-to-high effect on the expected outcomes (Table 7.1).

The groups were compared on 420 posttest outcomes across the 100 studies reviewed. Statistically significant differences were found in 46.9%, and nonsignificant differences in 53.1%, of the comparisons. The ES was computed for 247 outcome variables measured posttreatment. The actual ES varied between −3.10 and 5.33, with a mean of .28 (±.96). About half of the ESs were of a moderate-to-high magnitude (Table 7.2).

INFLUENCE OF SAMPLE SIZE AND SAMPLE USED ON THE SUCCESS OF RANDOMIZATION. The influence of sample size on the effectiveness of randomization in producing initially equivalent groups was examined by analyzing the direction and magnitude of the correlation between the sample size reported for the study and the calculated ES. At the study level, sample size did not correlate significantly with the ES for demographic and pretest variables (all $rs \leq .10$, $p > .05$). At the variable level, sample size showed no significant correlation with the actual ES for the demographic and pretest outcome variables. However, sample size was weakly, but negatively, related to the absolute ES for demographic ($r = -.20, p = .007$) and pretest ($r = -.28, p = .000$) outcome variables. It is interesting that sample size did not correlate with the ES for posttest outcomes.

The influence of the sample used on the success of randomization was explored by comparing the results of baseline comparisons of cases in which the initial sample was used with cases in which the attrition sample was used. At the study level, there was no statistically significant difference in the ES for demographic (means = .04 and −.00 for initial and attrition samples, respectively) and pretest (means = .05 and .05) variables when the initial or attrition sample was used. At the variable level, the analyses consisted of (a) comparing the number of variables found to differ statistically between groups, using the

Table 7.4. Percentage of Variables With and Without Between-Group Differences by Sample Used

Variable	Between-group difference	Initial sample used	Attrition sample used
Demographic	Nonsignificant	86.7%	92.9%
	Significant	13.3%	7.1%
	Mean (SD)	.04 (.29)	−.04 (.53)
Pretest outcomes	Nonsignificant	95.8%	96.9%
	Significant	4.2%	3.1%
	Mean (SD)	.04 (.25)	.01 (.34)
Posttest outcomes	Nonsignificant	52.7%	53.7%
	Significant	47.3%	46.3%
	Mean (SD)	.34 (1.02)	.21 (.89)

chi-square test; and (b) comparing the ES computed for the variables of interest. A statistically significant difference, $\chi^2(1, N = 617) = 5.73$, $p = .017$, was found for the number of demographic variables compared. Larger percentages of demographic variables with significant between-group differences were reported when the initial sample was used than when the attrition sample was used. The percentage of pretest outcomes with a significant between-group difference did not differ when the initial or attrition sample was used. Similarly, no difference was found for posttest outcomes (Table 7.4). The mean values for the actual ES computed for the demographic, pretest outcome, and posttest outcome variables were not significantly different when the initial and attrition samples were used. In contrast, statistically significant differences were found in the mean values of the absolute ES for demographic, $t(166) = -2.56$, $p = .011$, and pretest $t(291) = -2.58$, $p = .010$, outcomes. The mean values were slightly larger when attrition samples were used (.33 for demographic, and .23 for pretest, outcomes) than when initial samples were used (.20 and .17, respectively).

These findings are inconclusive, because no specific or definite pattern was observed at the different levels of analysis. However, they suggest that randomization tends to be slightly more effective in producing comparable groups in studies in which a large initial (i.e., actual number of participants allocated to groups) sample is used than in studies using a smaller sample comprising participants who completed the study. The findings imply that sample size and attrition are conditions that interfere, minimally, with the success of randomization.

CORRELATION BETWEEN BASELINE AND POSTTEST VARIABLES. The correlation among the ESs for the demographic characteristics, pretest outcomes, and posttest outcomes was examined at the study and variable levels. At the study level, the ESs for demographic variables were positively and moderately correlated with those for pretest outcomes ($r = .62$, $p = .000$) but not with those for posttest outcomes ($r = -.02$, $p > .05$). The pretest and posttest outcome ESs were also positively and moderately correlated ($r = .35, p = .018$). At the variable level, the correlation among the actual ESs for the three categories of variables was very small (< .20) and statistically nonsignificant. In contrast, the absolute ESs for the demographic characteristics were positively and moderately correlated with the absolute ESs for pretest outcomes ($r = .45, p = .000$) and weakly related with posttest outcomes ($r = .07, p > .05$). The absolute ESs for pretest outcomes showed a positive but small correlation with those for posttest outcomes. The relationship between the pretest and posttest outcome ESs is similar in direction and magnitude to that reported by Heinsman and Shadish (1996).

On the basis of these findings, it can be concluded that large between-groups differences in demographic characteristics are correlated with large differences in outcome variables measured at pretest. The latter, in turn, are associated with large differences in the same outcome variables measured at posttest. These interrelationships among the variables imply that baseline differences in demographic and outcome variables will confound the effects of the intervention on the posttest outcomes.

Conclusions

The findings of this systematic review and analysis of 100 reports of intervention evaluation studies provide preliminary evidence supporting the hypothesis that random assignment increases the likelihood, but does not ensure, initial group equivalence in a particular study. Sample size and attrition seem to interfere minimally with the effectiveness of randomization in equalizing the study groups on baseline variables. Comparison of the study groups on variables measured at baseline is highly recommended. However, researchers should recognize that, although the results of statistical tests may demonstrate nonsignificant differences, the groups may still differ. The magnitude of the between-group differences, even if small, could be clinically meaningful. The baseline differences occur at the level of individual participants as well, as indicated by large standard deviation values reported for the demographic characteristics and pretest outcomes. Increased within-group variance may have reduced the power to detect statistically significant differences and have been somewhat reflected in the small-to-moderate effect sizes for baseline variables. As pointed out by Cook and Campbell (1979) and Costner (1989), randomization does not eliminate interindividual differences at baseline. These differences still operate after randomization and will influence outcome achievement at posttest. Baseline differences at the group or individual participant level are interrelated and associated with differences in the outcomes measured at posttest. The relationships between baseline and posttest outcomes present a major threat to the validity of causal inferences about treatment effects. To minimize their potential confounding effects, baseline differences should be routinely accounted for in intervention evaluation studies. Several strategies can be used to account for baseline differences, including adjustment or residualization of their effects on posttest outcomes, subgroup analyses, and the use of propensity scores. In particular, the results of subgroup analyses are clinically relevant, as they delineate the profile of participants who benefit most from the intervention (Lipsey & Cordray, 2000; Sidani et al., 2003).

In conclusion, the utility of random assignment in effectiveness research remains questionable, particularly in studies with a small sample size and a high attrition rate. Increasing the sample size is, in most instances, not a viable solution. Although various strategies can be implemented to prevent attrition, only one seems promising in reducing attrition related to dissatisfaction with the allocated treatment option: taking patient treatment preferences into consideration when assigning participants to study groups. The impact of treatment preferences on the validity of causal inferences has not been evaluated systematically. The work is still ahead to develop the empirical base to guide methodological decisions in effectiveness research.

References

Abel, U., & Koch, A. (1999). The role of randomization in clinical studies: Myths and beliefs. *Journal of Clinical Epidemiology, 52,* 487–497.

Anderson, J. J., Firschein, H. E., & Meenan, R. F. (1989). Sensitivity of a health status measure to short-term clinical changes in arthritis. *Arthritis and Rheumatism, 32,* 844–850.

Bottomley, A. (1997). To randomise or not to randomise: Methodological pitfalls of the RCT design in psychosocial intervention studies. *European Journal of Cancer Care, 6,* 222–230.

Bradley, C. (1993). Designing medical and educational intervention studies. *Diabetes Care, 16,* 509–518.

Brewin, C. R., & Bradley, C. (1989). Patient preferences and randomized clinical trials. *British Medical Journal, 299,* 313–315.

Chen, H. T., & Rossi, P. H. (1987). The theory-driven approach to validity. *Evaluation and Program Planning, 10,* 95–103.

Clarke, G. N. (1995). Improving the transition from basic efficacy research to effectiveness studies: Methodological issues and procedures. *Journal of Consulting and Clinical Psychology, 63,* 718–725.

Concato, J., Shah, N., & Horwitz, R. I. (2000). Randomized, controlled trials, observational studies, and the hierarchy of research designs. *New England Journal of Medicine, 342,* 1887–1892.

Cook, T. D. (1993). A quasi-sampling theory of the generalization of causal relationships. *New Directions for Program Evaluation, 57,* 39–82.

Cook, T. D., & Campbell, D. T. (1979). *Quasi-experimentation: Design and analysis issue for field settings.* Boston: Houghton Mifflin.

Costner, H. L. (1989). The validity of conclusions in evaluation research: A further development of Chen and Rossi's theory-driven approach. *Evaluation and Program Planning, 12,* 345–353.

Coward, D. (2002). Partial randomization design in a support group intervention study. *Western Journal of Nursing Research, 24,* 406–421.

Demissie, K., Mills, O. F., & Rhoads, G. G. (1998). Empirical comparison of the results of randomized controlled trials and case-control studies in evaluating the effectiveness of screening mammography. *Journal of Clinical Epidemiology, 51*(2), 81–91.

Droitcour, J. A. (1997). Cross-design synthesis. Concept and application. In E. Chelimsky & W. R. Shadish (Eds.), *Evaluation for the 21st century: A handbook* (pp. 360–372). Thousand Oaks, CA: Sage.

Gale, F. M., Kirk, J. C., & Davis, R. (1994). Patient education and self-management: Randomized study of effects on health status of a mail-delivered program. *Arthritis & Rheumatology, 37,* 197.

Goldfried, M. R., & Wolfe, B. E. (1996). Psychotherapy practice and research: Repairing a strained alliance. *American Psychologist, 51,* 1007–1016.

Heinsman, D. T., & Shadish, W. R. (1996). Assignment methods in experimentation: When do nonrandomized experiments approximate the answers from randomized experiments? *Psychological Methods, 1,* 154–169.

Hicks, C. (1998). The randomised controlled trial: A critique. *Nurse Researcher, 6*(1), 19–32.

Hollon, S. D. (1996). The efficacy and effectiveness of psychotherapy relative to medications. *American Psychologist, 51,* 1025–1030.

Howard, K. I., Krause, M. S., & Lyons, J. (1993). When clinical trials fails: A guide to disaggregation. In L. S. Onken, J. D. Blaine, & J. J. Boren (Eds.), *Behavioral assessments for drug abuse and dependence* (NIDA Research Monograph No. 137, pp. 291–302). Washington, DC: National Institute for Drug Abuse.

Horwitz, R. I. (1987). Complexity and contradiction in clinical trial research. *American Journal of Medicine, 82,* 498–510.

Kraemer, H. C., & Fendt, K. H. (1990). Random assignment in clinical trials: Issues in planning (infant health and development program). *Journal of Clinical Epidemiology, 43,* 1157–1167.

Kunz, R., & Oxman, A. D. (1998). The unpredictability paradox: Review of empirical comparisons of randomized and non-randomized clinical trials. *British Medical Journal, 317,* 1185–1190.

Lipsey, M. W. (1990). *Design sensitivity: Statistical power for experimental research.* Newbury Park, CA: Sage.

Lipsey, M. W., & Cordray, D. S. (2000). Evaluation methods for social intervention. *Annual Review of Psychology, 51,* 345–375.

Lipsey, M. W., & Wilson, D. B. (1993). The efficacy of psychological, educational, and behavioral treatment: Confirmation from meta-analysis. *American Psychologist, 48,* 1181–1209.

Llewellyn-Thomas, H. A., McGreal, M. J., Thiel, E. C., Fine, S., & Erlichman, C. (1991). Patients willingness to enter clinical trials: Measuring the association with perceived benefit and preference for decision participation. *Social Science & Medicine, 32,* 35–42.

Man-Son-Hing, M., Hart, R. G., Berquist, R., O'Connor, A. M., & Laupacis, A. (2001). Differences in treatment preferences between persons who enrol and do not enrol in a clinical trial. *Annals CRMCC, 34,* 292–296.

McKay, J. R., Alterman, A. I., McLellan, T., Boardman, C. R., Mulvaney, F. D., & O'Brien, C. P. (1998). Random versus nonrandom assignment in the evaluation of treatment for cocaine abusers. *Journal of Consulting and Clinical Psychology, 66,* 697–701.

McKee, M., Britton, A., Black, N., McPherson, K., Sanderson, C., & Bain, C. (1999). Interpreting the evidence: Choosing between randomised and non-randomised studies. *British Medical Journal, 319,* 312–315.

Newman, F. L., & Tejeda, M. J. (1996). The need for research that is designed to support decisions in the delivery of mental health services. *American Psychologist, 51,* 1040–1049.

Nield-Anderson, L., Dixon, J. K., & Lee, K. (1999). Random assignment and patient choice in a study of alternative pain relief for sickle cell disease. *Western Journal of Nursing Research, 21,* 266–274.

Norquist, G., Lebowitz, B., & Hyman, S. (1999). Expanding the frontier of treatment research. *Prevention & Treatment, 2,* Article 0001a. Retrieved November 8, 2005, from http://journals. apa.org/prevention/volume2/pre0020001a.html

O'Reilly, P. H., Martin, L., & Collins, G. (on behalf of the CRASH Oncology Group). (1999). Controversy in managing patients with prostate cancer. *British Medical Journal, 318,* 126.

Rossi, P. H., Freeman, H. E., & Lipsey, M. W. (1999). *Evaluation: A systematic approach* (6th ed.). Thousand Oaks, CA: Sage.

Sacks, H. S., Chalmers, T. C., & Smith, H. (1982). Randomized versus historical controls for clinical trials. *American Journal of Medicine, 72,* 233–240.

Sacks, H. S., Chalmers, T. C., & Smith, H. (1983). Sensitivity and specificity of clinical trials. Randomized vs. historical controls. *Archives of Internal Medicine, 143,* 753–755.

Schulz, K. F., Chalmers, I., Hayes, R. J., & Altman, D. G. (1995). Empirical evidence of bias: Dimensions of methodological quality associated with estimates of treatment effects in controlled trials. *Journal of the American Medical Association, 273,* 408–412.

Schwartz, C. E., Chesney, M. A., Irvine, J., & Keefe, F. J. (1997). The control group dilemma in clinical research: Applications for psychosocial and behavioral medicine trials. *Psychosomatic Medicine, 59,* 362–371.

Sechrest, L. B. (1998, November). *Threats to validity of causal inference are not always plausible.* Paper presented at the American Evaluation Association Conference, Chicago.

Shadish, W. R. (2000). The empirical program of quasi-experimentation. In L. Bickman (Ed.), *Research design: Donald Campbell's legacy* (Vol. 2, pp. 13–36). Thousand Oaks, CA: Sage.

Shadish, W. R., Cook, T. D., & Campbell, D. T. (2002). *Experimental and quasi-experimental design for generalized causal inference.* Boston: Houghton-Mifflin.

Shadish, W. R., Matt, G. E., Navarro, A. M., & Phillips, G. (2000). The effects of psychological therapies under clinically representative conditions: A meta-analysis. *Psychological Bulletin, 126,* 512–526.

Shadish, W. R., & Ragsdale, K. (1996). Random versus nonrandom assignment in psychotherapy experiments: Do you get the same answer? *Journal of Consulting and Clinical Psychology, 64,* 1290–1305.

Sidani, S., & Braden, C. J. (1998). *Evaluating nursing interventions: A theory-driven approach.* Thousand Oaks, CA: Sage.

Sidani, S., Epstein, D. R., & Moritz, P. (2003). An alternative paradigm for clinical nursing research: An exemplar. *Research in Nursing and Health, 26,* 244–255.

Smith, M. L., Glass, G. V., & Miller, T. I. (1980). *The benefits of psychotherapy.* Baltimore: Johns Hopkins University Press.

Torgerson, D. J., Klaber-Moffett, J., & Russell, I. T. (1996). Patient preferences in randomised trials: Threat or opportunity? *Journal of Health Services Research and Policy, 1,* 194–197.

Weinberger, M., Oddone, E. Z., Henderson, W. G., Smith, D. M., Huey, J., Giobbie-Hurder, A., & Feussner, J. R. (2002). Multisite randomized controlled trials in health services research: Scientific challenges and operational issues. *Medical Care, 39,* 627–634.

Yeaton, W. H., & Sechrest, L. B. (1981). Critical dimensions in the choice and maintenance of successful treatments: Strength, integrity, and effectiveness. *Journal of Consulting and Clinical Psychology, 49,* 156–167.

8

Propensity Scores and Quasi-Experiments: A Testimony to the Practical Side of Lee Sechrest

William R. Shadish, Jason K. Luellen, and M. H. Clark

A hallmark of Lee Sechrest's career has been his emphasis on practical methods for field research. Sechrest once drove this point home in a comment on the first author's presidential address to the 1997 Annual Convention of the American Evaluation Association (Shadish, 1998). The title of that address was "Evaluation Theory Is Who We Are," and the address included a 10-item test on evaluation theory given to the entire audience. Those who failed the test were informed that their credentials as evaluators were in serious question—a rhetorical point in many respects, but one that was clearly controversial. After the address, Sechrest took Shadish aside and said "You really need to get out and *do* more evaluations." We hope it is belatedly responsive to this suggestion that, in this chapter, we focus on a very practical recent development in field research, one that Sechrest and his colleagues have both used and criticized—propensity score analysis of quasi-experimental data.

Quasi-experiments share many of the characteristics of randomized experiments, except they never use random assignment. Quasi-experiments are widely viewed as more practical than randomized experiments, especially when random assignment is not feasible or ethical. The latter might occur, for example, if the researcher is asked to design a study after a treatment is implemented, or if practitioners judge that treatment cannot be denied to needy clients. In such cases, it is common for participants in a quasi-experiment to select which treatment they want to have, or to have their treatment selected for them on a nonrandom basis by, say, administrators or treatment providers. Quasi-experiments have other desirable features as well. For example, the participants, treatments, outcome measures, and settings in quasi-experiments may be more representative of real-world conditions than are randomized experiments. Often, for example, randomized experiments can include only participants who agree to be randomly assigned or settings that agree to have their clients randomly assigned, and these are likely to be an unrepresentative subset of all participants and settings.

However, the major practical and theoretical disadvantage of quasi-experiments is that the estimates of treatment effects that they yield may not be unbiased. The reason is that the nonrandom selection process may result in differences between the groups that can be mistaken for treatment effects. Many recent attempts to address such selection bias have focused on modeling the selection process so that it can be removed from the estimate of treatment effects. Rosenbaum and Rubin (1983a, 1983b) presented one such approach that involves propensity scores. Many examples of propensity score analysis exist in medicine and epidemiology (Connors et al., 1996; Smith, 1997; Stone et al., 1995), economics (Czajka, Hirabayashi, Little, & Rubin, 1992; Lechner, 2002), and education (Rosenbaum, 1986). However, propensity score analysis is neither widely known nor widely used in psychology. In this chapter, we describe propensity scores and give an example of their use that compares results of a quasi-experiment that has been adjusted by propensity score analysis with results from an equivalent benchmark randomized experiment. We focus in particular on certain practical problems that emerge in the construction of propensity scores, showing how they can affect results in nontrivial ways.

Propensity Scores

A propensity score is the conditional probability that a person will be in one condition rather than another (e.g., get a treatment rather than be in the control group), given a set of observed covariates used to predict which condition he or she in (Rosenbaum & Rubin, 1983b). As a probability, a propensity score ranges from 0 to 1. Nearly all work with propensity scores has been done comparing two groups, and that is our focus here. However, in principle it is possible to do propensity score analysis with more than two groups (Imbens, 2000; Rubin, 1998).

Although propensity scores are almost never used in randomized experiments (but see Hill, Rubin, & Thomas, 2000), discussing what they would be for participants in a randomized experiment might help clarify their nature. In a randomized experiment, a participant's true propensity score is simple. If an equal probability assignment mechanism (e.g., a coin toss) was used to assign people to one of two conditions, each person has a 50% chance of being in one or the other condition. Thus, each person's true propensity score is .50. If participants are assigned randomly with unequal probabilities (e.g., using the roll of a die to place 4 participants in treatment for every 2 in control), then the true propensity score of each treatment group participant is .67 and that of each control group participant is .33.

With a quasi-experiment, however, the true propensity score is not known and must be estimated. The probabilities of receiving treatment (i.e., the propensity scores) are correlated with individual characteristics that influence treatment selection and are likely to vary from .50. For instance, if the researcher dummy-codes treatment as 1 and control as 0, then a propensity score above .50 would mean that the person was more likely to be selected into treatment than control, and a score below .50 would mean the opposite.

Given this description, it is clearly crucial to include covariates that may affect treatment selection in designing a quasi-experiment. Probably the worst applications of propensity scores use only covariates that happen to be conveniently available (e.g., sex, age, race, marital status), with little thought to what actually brings participants to each condition. The latter are, of course, never known exactly, but reasonable guesses can often be made. For example, a person who is afraid of mathematics might be less likely to enroll in an elective math course; fear of mathematics would be a productive covariate to measure at the start of the quasi-experiment, so that it can be used later in the propensity score analysis. Omitting such relevant covariates results in hidden bias that propensity scores cannot adjust. Rosenbaum (2002) offered other practical advice for designing quasi-experiments in ways that facilitate propensity score analysis.

Once propensity scores are constructed (in a manner we illustrate shortly), researchers can use them to balance nonequivalent groups by means of matching, stratification, or covariance adjustment (analysis of covariance [AN-COVA]). The idea is that participants who have the same propensity score but who are in different conditions are comparable because the distributions of their covariates are balanced (Rosenbaum & Rubin, 1983b, 1984). In this chapter, we focus on doing such balancing using stratification, which Rosenbaum and Rubin (1983b) preferred for two reasons. First, unlike covariance analysis, matching and stratification do not require the researcher to model correctly any nonlinearities in the relationship between propensity scores and outcomes. Second, stratification eliminates 90% of the bias that would have been eliminated by matching.

Illustrative Data

We illustrate propensity score analysis by using data from a study conducted in our laboratory and presented in detail elsewhere (Clark, 2000; Shadish & Clark, 2003). The study included 454 undergraduate introductory psychology students at a major southern university in the United States during 1998 and 1999. Of these, 445 students completed the study and are used for further analyses. Pretests assessed demographics, school achievement, various measures of mathematics and vocabulary aptitude, various personality tests, math anxiety, and depression. The 445 participants were then randomly assigned to be in either a randomized experiment or a quasi-experiment. Those participants who were randomly assigned to participate in the randomized experiment ($n = 235$) were then randomized to either mathematics ($n = 119$) or vocabulary training ($n = 116$). Those randomly assigned to participate in the quasi-experiment ($n = 210$) were allowed to choose either mathematics ($n = 79$) or vocabulary training ($n = 131$)—not surprisingly, more chose vocabulary than math training. Figure 8.1 summarizes the design. Participants in the quasi-experiment then described why they selected one treatment condition over another in a brief open-ended response. All of the participants then simultaneously attended

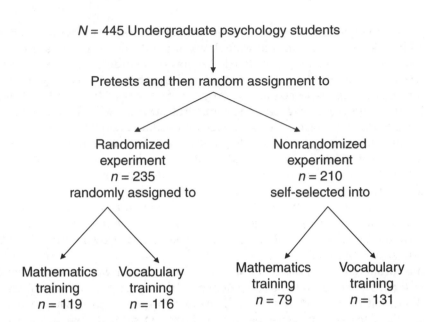

Figure 8.1. The design of a randomized experiment comparing randomized with nonrandomized experiments.

the same training sessions, at the end of which they completed a posttest with 20 mathematics items and 30 vocabulary items. We begin here by describing the unadjusted results, then discuss the construction of propensity scores and how well propensity score adjustments corrected bias in the quasi-experimental results.

Without propensity score analysis, the results of the quasi-experiment were clearly not the same as the results from the randomized experiments, so we presume that the quasi-experimental results may be biased. On the mathematics outcome, those who participated in the randomized experiment and received mathematics training scored an average of 3.92 points higher ($M = 10.61$) than those who received vocabulary training ($M = 6.69$), $F(1, 233) = 85.41, p < .001$. By comparison, those who participated in the quasi-experiment and received mathematics training scored an average of 4.65 points higher on the mathematics outcome ($M = 11.61$) than those who received vocabulary training ($M = 6.96$), $F(1, 208) = 79.65, p < .001$. To judge from a content analysis of quasi-experimental participants' answers to the open-ended question about the reasons for their choice of training condition, the slightly larger effect in the quasi-experiment is due to the fact that those who self-selected mathematics training did so mostly because they liked math and did better in it than those who chose vocabulary. In any case, the difference between the randomized and quasi-experimental results ($\Delta = 3.92 - 4.65 = -.73$) represents the bias in the mathematics outcome for the quasi-experimental group, where $\Delta = 0$ would indicate no bias. Only the absolute value of Δ is important to bias reduction.

A negative value of Δ implies that the adjusted results of the quasi-experiment approached those of the randomized experiment but that the effect in the adjusted quasi-experiment was still larger than the effect in the randomized experiment. A positive value of Δ indicates that the adjusted results of the quasi-experiment slightly overadjusted compared with the results of the randomized experiment, in that the effect from the adjusted quasi-experiment was slightly smaller than the effect in the randomized experiment. In all cases, however, the treatment group performed better than the comparison group, and there were no instances in which propensity score adjustments reversed this finding

Similarly, on vocabulary outcome, those who participated in the randomized experiment and received vocabulary training had a mean posttest vocabulary score that was 8.11 points higher than those who received mathematics training (16.19 vs. 8.08), $F(1, 233) = 336.71$, $p < .001$. Those who participated in the quasi-experiment and received vocabulary training had a mean score 9.00 points higher on that same outcome than those who received mathematics training (16.75 vs. 7.75), $F(1, 208) = 313.21$, $p < .001$. Again, content analysis of the open-ended question suggests that participants in the quasi-experiment who chose vocabulary did so because they avoided and disliked math, so may have been worse at it. As before, the difference in these results ($Δ = 8.11 - 9.00 = -0.89$) represents the bias in the vocabulary outcome for the quasi-experimental group.

Propensity Score Analysis

Researchers have used several methods for computing estimated propensity scores. Here we use logistic regression because it is the most common method for doing so.[1] However, before starting, we did not fully appreciate all the choices that have to be made in doing this logistic regression. In retrospect, we better understand that small variations in those choices can yield different levels of bias reduction. Here we focus on one choice that has not been made explicit before, a choice that concerns the underlying rationales that might be assumed in the regression, for that choice of rationale affects many other choices as well. We refer to the two rationales to be discussed here as the *balancing strata rationale* and the *maximum prediction rationale*. These two rationales lead to different implementations of the logistic regression. Hence,

---

[1] A less widely used method for computing estimated propensity scores is classification tree analysis (Pruzek & Cen, 2002; Stone et al., 1995). The classification tree approach has two advantages over the more commonly used logistic regression procedure: (a) The algorithms automatically detect interactions in the data so that those interactions do not have to be discovered and modeled explicitly, as they do in logistic regression, and (b) the tree's terminal nodes automatically supply the researcher with strata. The disadvantages of classification trees lie mostly in the difficulty and unfamiliarity of their implementation and the general lack of specific guidelines for executing the analysis. Luellen, Shadish, and Clark (in press) presented detailed instructions for using classification trees in propensity score construction, including computer script using the free program R (Version 1.7.0 for Windows) provided by the R Development Core Team (2003; see also Becker, Chambers, & Wilks, 1988).

we construct propensity scores and compare results under both rationales. Our treatment of missing data was, however, the same for both rationales: Following Rosenbaum and Rubin (1984), we created separate logistic regression models for those with complete versus incomplete data (though multiple imputation methods are theoretically possible; see D'Agostino & Rubin, 2000). Table 8.1 presents all the basic results of the unadjusted and adjusted analyses for this chapter, and Figure 8.2 graphically portrays the key bias reduction results. We now describe all the results in more detail.

The Maximum Prediction Rationale

We started with this approach, though we were not explicitly aware that we had done so until a careful reading of Rosenbaum and Rubin (1984), and e-mail correspondence with Rosenbaum made us realize that the implicit rationale we were using was different from theirs. The maximum prediction rationale conceptualizes the task of the logistic regression as obtaining the best possible prediction of group membership. After all, predicting group membership seems to be the obvious reason for doing this logistic regression, so predicting as well as possible seemed an obvious goal. The criterion we used to maximize prediction was the percentage correct classification of participants into conditions, using a backward stepwise regression that began with including all variables but then eliminating them one by one, stopping when the percentage correct prediction of each group was maximized.

This rationale has a second underlying logic as well. Quasi-experimental designs can yield unbiased estimates of treatment effects if the selection model is fully known and perfectly measured. The best illustration of this is the regression discontinuity design. (Indeed, we nearly called this rationale the regression discontinuity rationale rather than the maximum prediction rationale.) In the simplest pertinent version of that design, participants are assigned to treatment or control according to a cutoff score on an assignment variable that is measured before treatment. As long as assignment (selection) to conditions strictly follows this rule (just as randomized experimentation requires following the results of the random assignment process with no exceptions), the selection model is fully known and perfectly measured, and the researcher would have perfect prediction of group membership based solely on knowledge of the participant's score on the assignment variable. Inclusion of that assignment variable in a regression equation along with a treatment dummy variable will yield an unbiased effect estimate as long as all nonlinear relationships between the assignment variable and outcome are properly modeled (Rubin, 1977). Shadish, Cook, and Campbell (2002) provided further details about the logic and implementation of the regression discontinuity design.

Applying this logic, propensity score analysis could be conceptualized as an effort to create the equivalent of that perfect assignment variable in a regression discontinuity design. Hence, the goal is to create a set of propensity scores in which all treatment participants have a propensity score greater than .50 and all control participants have a score less than .50. Doing so would yield

Table 8.1. Percentage Bias Reduction in Quasi-Experimental Results by Various Adjustments

	Mathematics training mean	Vocabulary training mean	Mean difference	Bias	% Bias reduction
Mathematics outcome					
Unadjusted randomized experiment	10.61	6.69	3.92	0.00	
Unadjusted quasi-experiment	11.61	6.96	4.65	−0.73	
Maximum prediction propensity scores (PS_{mp})					
Stratification omitting stratum with an empty cell	11.41	7.31	4.10	−0.18	75%
Stratification using all strata (with adjusted cut points)	10.29	7.15	3.14	0.78	(7%)
ANCOVA	11.31	7.14	4.17	−0.25	65%
Balancing strata propensity scores (PS_{bs})					
Stratification omitting stratum with an $N = 1$ cell	11.44	7.71	3.73	0.19	74%
Stratification using all strata	11.75	7.40	4.35	−0.43	41%
ANCOVA	11.07	7.29	3.78	0.14	81%
Vocabulary outcome					
Unadjusted randomized experiment	16.19	8.08	8.11		
Unadjusted quasi-experiment	16.75	7.75	9.00	−0.89	
Maximum prediction propensity scores (PS_{mp})					
Stratification omitting stratum with an empty cell	16.14	7.70	8.44	−0.33	63%
Stratification using all strata (with adjusted cut points)	16.48	7.40	9.08	−0.97	(9%)
ANCOVA	16.41	8.31	8.10	−0.01	99%
Balancing strata propensity scores (PS_{bs})					
Stratification omitting stratum with an $N = 1$ cell	16.26	8.08	8.18	−0.07	93%
Stratification using all strata	16.46	8.27	8.19	−0.08	91%
ANCOVA	16.43	8.28	8.15	−0.04	96%

Note. ANCOVA = analysis of covariance.

150   SHADISH, LUELLEN, AND CLARK

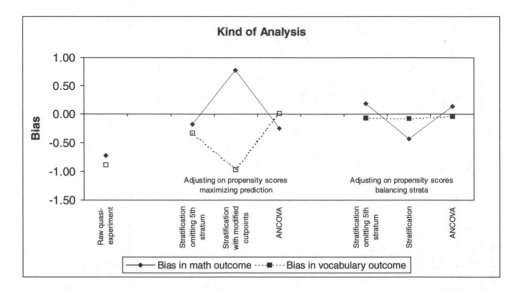

Figure 8.2. Bias reduction achieved by various different propensity score adjustment analyses compared with unadjusted quasi-experimental results. ANCOVA = analysis of covariance.

perfect prediction of group membership, which is approximated in propensity score analysis by maximizing prediction as much as possible. However, as we will see shortly with the results, success with this rationale creates a problem: The better the prediction, the less overlap exists between propensity scores of the treatment group and propensity scores of the control group, but overlap is required to use stratification on propensity scores as a method for adjusting quasi-experimental results. Here we illustrate how well propensity score analysis reduces bias using both stratification and ANCOVA—the former being Rosenbaum and Rubin's (1984) preferred approach and the latter being the analysis used in a regression discontinuity design.

We created maximum prediction propensity scores as follows. The initial logistic regression included all 29 available covariates that participants had completed at pretest. Backward stepwise regression then eliminated covariates one at a time until the percentage of participants correctly classified was at its maximum, in this case 82.2%. Propensity scores were then estimated for each participant on the basis of only those 26 covariates that yielded this maximum prediction. (The predicted probabilities of group membership that can be obtained as optional output from logistic regression are the propensity scores.)

Stratification on propensity score quintiles, however, yielded one empty cell because no one who chose mathematics training had a propensity score above the 80th percentile, a stratum that would indicate a propensity to choose vocabulary training. This result can be handled in one of three ways. First, the analyst can conclude that overlap between those who chose mathematics and those who chose vocabulary training is insufficient to support a useful propensity score adjustment—that is, the nonequivalent comparison group is too nonequivalent to get a good estimate of treatment effect. In this sense, an advantage of propensity score analysis is that it can lead to such a conclusion, providing a decision rule for how much selection bias is too much in any given case. We do not pursue this option here because (a) we want to illustrate the other two ways to handle empty cells and (b) general knowledge about the practical aspects of propensity score analysis is still preliminary enough that it is worth exploring such matters empirically.

The second option for handling an empty cell is to eliminate the stratum containing that cell. Doing so in the present case eliminated the 42 participants who chose vocabulary training and had a propensity score above the 80th percentile. To estimate the effects of treatment with a propensity score adjustment, we computed treatment and control group means as the unweighted average of the cell means over the four remaining strata for each group. Following this procedure with the quasi-experimental data in our example, we submitted the vocabulary and mathematics outcome measures (separately) to a two-way (2 [conditions] × 4 [strata]) analysis of variance (ANOVA). For the mathematics outcome, the initial difference between the randomized experiment and quasi-experiment ($\Delta = -.73$) was reduced 75% to $\Delta = -.18$ after stratification on propensity scores. For the vocabulary outcome, the initial difference between the randomized experiment and quasi-experiment ($\Delta = -.89$) was reduced 63% to $\Delta = -.33$ after stratification on propensity scores.

The third option for handling empty cells is to adjust the cut points defining the strata to eliminate empty cells. Procedurally, the analyst must decide how much of an adjustment to make and how many units per cell should be the minimum, both points about which little advice or evidence appears in the literature. In the present case, we experimented with a variety of adjustments that added progressively more participants to the low sample size stratum by borrowing them from the adjacent stratum. In Table 8.1 and Figure 8.2, we present only the adjusted cut point that ensured at least $N = 1$ in each cell. We then submitted the vocabulary and mathematics outcome measures (separately) to a two-way ANOVA (2 [conditions] × 5 [strata]). For the mathematics outcome, the initial difference between the randomized experiment and quasi-experiment ($\Delta = -.73$) was increased 7% to $\Delta = .78$. For the vocabulary outcome, the initial difference between the randomized experiment and quasi-experiment ($\Delta = -.89$) was increased 9% to $\Delta = .97$. By adjusting the cut point further to add more participants to the low-frequency cell, adjustment of the mathematics outcome improved considerably, but adjustment of the vocabulary outcome remained poor.

Instead of using stratification, the analyst might include propensity scores as a covariate in an ANCOVA, similarly to how the assignment variable is treated in the regression discontinuity design. When we did so in the present case, for the mathematics outcome, the initial difference between the randomized experiment and quasi-experiment ($\Delta = -.73$) was reduced 65% to $\Delta = -.25$ after covarying propensity scores. For the vocabulary outcome, the initial difference between the randomized experiment and quasi-experiment ($\Delta = -.89$) was reduced 99% to $\Delta = -.01$ after covarying propensity scores.[2]

In summary, then, Figure 8.2 shows that propensity score adjustments using the maximum prediction rationale tended to perform very well with ANCOVA, consistent with the analysis and rationale of the regression discontinuity design. Such adjustments also performed well with stratification done by eliminating strata with an empty cell, but quite poorly with stratification using adjusted cut points to eliminate empty cells—actually increasing bias in the latter case.

The Balancing Strata Rationale

The problems we encountered with empty cells when we used the maximum prediction rationale led us to contact Paul Rosenbaum for advice on how to handle those cells. After reviewing what we did, Rosenbaum suggested that we redo the analysis with more careful attention to the guidelines provided in Rosenbaum and Rubin (1984). Upon reading that article more closely, and after further correspondence with Rosenbaum, we realized that the underlying rationale in the article was very different from the maximum prediction rationale and led to very different procedures in the logistic regression, which yielded a set of propensity scores that were not perfectly correlated with those produced under the maximum prediction rationale ($r = .71$).

Under Rosenbaum and Rubin (1984), any propensity score that balances predictors over groups will do. Accuracy of predicted group membership is unimportant. In fact, it is perfectly satisfactory for each participant to have a propensity score of .50, the same propensity score that would occur in a randomized experiment. This would also produce maximum overlap between the propensity scores of the treatment and control groups, reducing the likelihood of encountering the empty-cell problem created under the maximum prediction rationale. The criteria for a good set of propensity scores is therefore also quite different, maximizing not the percentage correct prediction of group membership, but rather how well the propensity scores balance predictors over conditions, using tests described shortly.

The procedure is to start with all predictors entered into a logistic regression and use backward stepwise regression to eliminate variables, but with a very liberal tolerance level such as .50, so as not to rely overly on statistical significance as a criterion for retaining predictors (see Rosenbaum, 2002, for an explanation). Next, test the adequacy of the resulting propensity scores by stratifying on propensity score quintiles, then conducting 2×5 (Conditions $\times$ Strata) ANOVAs, using as dependent variables both the propensity scores

---

[2] Given that a key problem in the regression discontinuity design is to correctly model any nonlinearities in the relationship between assignment and outcome, we explored nonlinearities in the relationship between the maximum prediction propensity scores and outcome. Neither inspections of scatterplots nor the addition of various nonlinear terms suggested that nonlinearities were a problem in the present data.

themselves and each predictor individually. This step has two purposes. First, it shows whether all 10 cells contain cases; if empty or very sparse cells exist, the overlap between groups in their propensity score distributions may not be adequate to support an analysis. Second, the resulting interaction F ratio indicates whether treatment and control cases have equivalent propensity scores within each stratum, thereby obtaining an overall balance between groups over all the strata. If more than roughly 5% of these analyses yield a significant Condition × Strata interaction (the percentage expected by chance, assuming a Type I error rate of $\alpha = .05$), then the researcher should add more terms until the 5% criterion is met. The new terms are typically (a) predictors that had been excluded by the stepwise regression but yield a significant Condition × Strata interaction, (b) nonlinear transforms of any of the predictors in the equation, and (c) product terms representing interactions between predictors. There are no formal guidelines for identifying which nonlinear and interaction terms to include. The procedure is stopped either when balance is achieved or when the researcher decides that balance cannot be achieved with any more changes to the model. In the latter case, a virtue of this balancing strata rationale is that it indicates when group overlap is too poor to support a good propensity score adjustment of the quasi-experimental results.

Applying the balancing strata approach to the present data led to the following procedures and results. We entered all of the predictors we had measured at pretest and then used backward stepwise regression with a tolerance for exclusion of .50 to eliminate predictors. We divided the resulting propensity scores by quintiles and tested how well those scores succeeded in balancing covariates over conditions by using the 2 × 5 ANOVAs suggested earlier in this chapter. No empty cells occurred. However, one cell had a frequency of $N = 1$, so we report results both with and without the stratum containing this cell. The initial set of tests for interactions for the propensity scores themselves was nonsignificant; but 4 of 28 (14%) interactions using the predictors as dependent variables were significant. (Prior to propensity score stratification, 9 of 28 predictors yielded significant differences between conditions.) So we added several predictors that were out of balance but had been excluded by the stepwise regression, after which only 1 of 28 interactions (4%) were significant. At that point, we concluded that stratifying on propensity scores did achieve reasonable balance across groups on these covariates.

To estimate the effects of treatment with a propensity score adjustment, we again computed treatment and control group means as the unweighted average of the cell means over strata for each group. Following this procedure, we first submitted the vocabulary and mathematics outcome measures (separately) to a 2 × 4 ANOVA—that is, omitting the stratum with the $N = 1$ cell. For the mathematics outcome, the initial difference between the randomized experiment and quasi-experiment ($\Delta = -.73$) was reduced 74% to $\Delta = .19$ after stratification on propensity scores. For the vocabulary outcome, the initial difference between the randomized experiment and quasi-experiment ($\Delta = -.89$) was reduced 93% to $\Delta = -.07$ after stratification on propensity scores.

Second, we also submitted the vocabulary and mathematics outcome measures to a 2 × 5 ANOVA—that is, one that included the $N = 1$ cell. For the mathematics outcome, the initial difference between the randomized experiment and quasi-experiment ($\Delta = -.73$) was reduced 41% to $\Delta = -.43$ after stratification on propensity scores. For the vocabulary outcome, the initial difference between the randomized experiment and quasi-experiment ($\Delta = -.89$) was reduced 91% to $\Delta = -.08$ after stratification on propensity scores.

Finally, we again analyzed propensity scores as a covariate in an ANCOVA. For the mathematics outcome, the initial difference between the randomized experiment and quasi-experiment ($\Delta = -.73$) was reduced 81% to $\Delta = .14$ after covarying propensity scores. For the vocabulary outcome, the initial difference between the randomized experiment and quasi-experiment ($\Delta = -.89$) was reduced 96% to $\Delta = -.04$ after covarying propensity scores.

In summary, Figure 8.2 shows that all of the adjustments that used propensity scores designed to balance strata succeeded in reducing bias. As before, the best bias reduction occurred both with ANCOVA and with stratification that eliminated the fifth stratum. Including a stratum with a very low cell size performed worst, just as before. In both propensity score analyses—based on either the maximizing prediction or the balancing strata rationales—these results with stratification may have occurred because of poor overlap in propensity score distributions between treatment and comparison groups. It may be that propensity score stratification would have performed better over all the analyses if overlap had been better to begin with. In view of this inconsistent performance with stratification, the consistent bias reduction achieved with the use of propensity scores as a covariate is attractive. In all these cases, of course, the results could be unique to the data set we used here and might not be the same in other data sets. So further study of propensity score performance with other data sets (and other methodologies) is needed.

Discussion

Consider some observations about the methodology used in this study—that is, randomly assigning participants to being in a randomized or nonrandomized experiment. It has considerable benefits compared with the two major alternatives that have been used to date. One alternative is computer simulations on artificial data sets of how well propensity scores can adjust quasi-experimental data. They offer the advantage of sample sizes that can be virtually as large as the researcher wishes and systematic control of multiple variables that might be related to the question at hand. The problem with computer simulations is that selection biases are, by their very nature, inherently unknown, but computer simulations require known variables to program. Hence, the capacity of computer simulations to study real selection bias is inherently limited.

The second alternative methodology is to obtain data from a pair of randomized and nonrandomized experiments on the same intervention (e.g., Heckman, Ichimura, & Todd, 1997) and then to examine whether an adjustment to the raw quasi-experimental data can yield a result which approximates that from the randomized experiment. Compared with computer simulation, this methodology has the advantage of studying real as opposed to simulated selection biases; its disadvantages are that it requires access to raw data and that it is the captive of the differential peculiarities of substance and methodology that happened to be used in the two original studies. Of special concern is the fact that the particular randomized study used is likely to have many known and unknown features that systematically differ from those of the particular non-randomized study used. For example, it may have been conducted in a different setting, with different treatment providers, using different operationalizations of the outcome construct, and so forth. As a result, if the propensity score adjustment does not yield results similar to those of the randomized experiment, we cannot know if this is due to a failure of the analysis or to those different study features.

The methodology used in the present study combines many of the best features, and avoids many of the worst features, of both these alternative methodologies. It studies real selection biases, allows access to raw data, and ensures that both the participants and the methods in the nonrandomized experiment are similar to those in the randomized experiment. The disadvantages of the present methodology are that it cannot generate the large number of data sets and sample sizes available to computer simulations, it cannot systematically vary as many variables as in computer simulations, and its procedures use analogue treatments (e.g., brief vocabulary training) that may not well approximate treatments of policy interest.

Conclusion

We draw three tentative conclusions from the results reported in the present study. First, when constructed following the procedures recommended by Rosenbaum and Rubin (1984), propensity scores always reduced bias. However, when we deviated from those recommendations, bias increased in one of the two stratification adjustments we tried. Second, using propensity scores as a covariate in ANCOVA performed very well, and did so no matter how the propensity scores were created. This deserves further exploration, given that ANCOVA is not the usually recommended method. Third, bias reduction was much better when we eliminated a stratum with an empty or low-frequency cell than when we tried to include that stratum. Whether any of these three conclusions is replicated in other data sets remains to be seen.

To judge from the present results, however, propensity score analysis provides a practical approach to dealing with selection bias in quasi-experiments. This is not to minimize the potential problems with propensity score analysis, of course. For example, such analyses benefit from large sample sizes, they ultimately cannot adjust for hidden biases created by covariates that are not used in the creation of the propensity scores, and the conditions under which they seem to work best or worst remain mostly unexplored. However, the results reported here should encourage other researchers to continue to study the conditions under which propensity score adjustments reduce bias in quasi-experiments.

References

Becker, R. A., Chambers, J. M., & Wilks, A. R. (1988). *The new S language: A programming environment for data analysis and graphics.* Pacific Grove, CA: Wadsworth & Brooks/Cole Advance Books & Software.

Clark, M. H. (2000). *A laboratory experiment comparing assignment methods using propensity scores.* Unpublished master's thesis, University of Memphis.

Connors, A. F., Jr., Speroff, T., Dawson, N. V., Thomas, C., Harrell, F. E., Jr., Wagner, D., et al. (1996). The effectiveness of right heart catheterization in the initial care of critically ill patients. *Journal of the American Medical Association, 276,* 889–897.

Czajka, J. L., Hirabayashi, S. M., Little, R. J. A., & Rubin, D. B. (1992). Projecting from advance data using propensity modeling: An application to income and tax statistics. *Journal of Business and Economic Statistics, 10,* 117–131.

D'Agostino, R. B., & Rubin, D. B. (2000). Estimating and using propensity scores with partially missing data. *Journal of the American Statistical Association, 95,* 749–759.

Heckman, J. J., Ichimura, H., & Todd, P. E. (1997). Matching as an econometric evaluation estimator: Evidence from evaluating a job training programme. *Review of Economic Studies, 64,* 605–654.

Hill, J. L., Rubin, D. B., & Thomas, N. (2000). The design of the New York School Choice Scholarship program evaluation. In L. Bickman (Ed.), *Validity and social experimentation: Donald Campbell's legacy* (Vol. 1, pp. 155–180). Thousand Oaks, CA: Sage.

Imbens, G. W. (2000). The role of the propensity score in estimating dose–response functions. *Biometrika, 87,* 706–710.

Lechner, M. (2002). Program heterogeneity and propensity score matching: An application to the evaluation of active labor market policies. *Review of Economics and Statistics, 84,* 205–220.

Luellen, J. K., Shadish, W. R., & Clark, M. H. (in press). Propensity scores: An introduction and experimental test. *Evaluation Review.*

Pruzek, R. M., & Cen, L. (2002, October). *Propensity score analysis with graphics: A comparison of two kinds of gallbladder surgery.* Paper presented at the annual meeting of the Society for Multivariate Experimental Psychology, Charlottesville, VA.

R Development Core Team. (2003). *R 1.7.0 for Windows* [Computer software and manuals]. Retrieved May 27, 2003, from http://www.r-project.org/

Rosenbaum, P. R. (1986). Dropping out of high school in the United States: An observational study. *Journal of Educational Statistics, 11,* 207–224.

Rosenbaum, P. R. (2002). *Observational studies.* (2nd ed.). New York: Springer-Verlag.

Rosenbaum, P. R., & Rubin, D. B. (1983a). Assessing sensitivity to an unobserved binary covariate in an observational study with binary outcome. *Journal of the Royal Statistical Society, Series B (Methodological), 45,* 212–218.

Rosenbaum, P. R., & Rubin, D. B. (1983b). The central role of the propensity score in observational studies for causal effects. *Biometrika, 70,* 41–55.

Rosenbaum, P. R., & Rubin, D. B. (1984). Reducing bias in observational studies using subclassification on the propensity score. *Journal of the American Statistical Society, 79,* 516–524.

Rubin, D. B. (1977). Assignment to treatment group on the basis of a covariate. *Journal of Educational Statistics, 2,* 1–26.

Rubin, D. B. (1998). Estimation from nonrandomized treatment comparisons using subclassification on propensity scores. In U. Abel & A. Koch (Eds.), *Nonrandomized comparative clinical studies* (pp. 85–100). Dusseldorf, Germany: Symposion.

Shadish, W. R. (1998). Evaluation theory is who we are. *American Journal of Evaluation, 19,* 1–19.

Shadish, W. R. (2002). Revisiting field experimentation: Field notes for the future. *Psychological Methods, 7,* 3–18.

Shadish, W. R., & Clark, M. H. (2003). *A randomized experiment comparing randomized to nonrandomized experiments.* Manuscript in preparation.

Shadish, W. R., Cook, T. D., & Campbell, D. T. (2002). *Experimental and quasi-experimental designs for generalized causal inference.* Boston: Houghton Mifflin.

Smith, H. L. (1997). Matching with multiple controls to estimate treatment effects in observational studies. *Sociological Methodology, 27*, 325–353.

Stone, R. A., Obrosky, D. S., Singer, D. E., Kapoor, W. N., Fine, M. J., & the Pneumonia Patient Outcomes Research Team (PORT) Investigators. (1995). Propensity score adjustment for pretreatment differences between hospitalized and ambulatory patients with community-acquired pneumonia. *Medical Care, 33*, 56–66.

9

Seeing Your Data: Using Modern Statistical Graphics to Display and Detect Relationships

Stephen G. West

"You can observe a lot by watching."

—Yogi Berra (2005)

"The greatest value of a picture is when it *forces* us to notice **what we never expected to see."**

—John Tukey (1977, p. vi, bold and italics in original)

"Tools matter."

—William Cleveland (1993, p. 6)

During much of the 1970s, I was a colleague of Lee Sechrest at Florida State University. He was then a professor reaching the height of his career; I was then a young assistant professor with the particular good fortune of having an office directly across the hall from Lee's. This gave me the privilege of several years of just hanging out, listening to, and being stimulated by one of the most creative minds in our field. Indeed, a central challenge of my assistant professor years was to limit my focus to only a few of the provocative ideas that Lee presented. Lee and the group of faculty and graduate students around him during that period helped define my ideal of what a great university experience should be like—constant open, critical, yet supportive, discussion of the full array of ideas on the method and substance of psychology. The diversity and creativity of the topics presented in this Festschrift are testimony to Lee's similar influence at multiple universities throughout his career. This ideal of a great university experience that I learned from Lee is certainly a richer and more productive one than anything emerging from the developing modern university where an idea that leads to a $2 million grant is worth exactly twice as much as one that leads to a $1 million grant—so long as there is full indirect cost recovery.

One of the methodological ideas that drew our attention during the late 1970s was exploratory data analysis. Tukey (1977) and Mosteller and Tukey

(1977) had just published their seminal texts in this area, and their ideas led to considerable discussion by the field and by members of Lee's group. At the time, I thought these ideas were creative and exciting, but I ended up dismissing them because I firmly believed researchers could not feasibly implement the procedures in practice. Now, 25 years later, I freely admit that I was wrong. Yet, attaining feasibility required a revolution in computer technology. As Wainer and Thissen (1993) reminded us, what in 1980 took a room-sized mainframe computer, several days of programming, followed by additional days of patient "bug" detection (finding errors in computer code when the program failed to run), and access to specialized plotting equipment can now be accomplished in minutes on a desktop computer and a laser printer—with far better results. Specialized computer programs such as ARC, Data Desk, JMP, S-PLUS (and its freeware version R), and ViSta now make graphical exploratory data analysis easily available to users. Even general statistical packages that reside on nearly everyone's desktop, such as SPSS, now also incorporate some tools that facilitate graphical exploratory data analysis.

I begin this chapter by briefly reviewing some basic ideas from traditional hypothesis-driven analysis and exploratory data analysis. I then consider how some of these ideas may apply in one of the simplest contexts, multiple regression in which the central interest is in the influence of one predictor variable. These ideas are illustrated through analyses of one ideal (artificial) data set in which all assumptions are met and then three real data sets in which the central assumptions underlying regression analysis are violated. Along the way, I illustrate the use of a number of the wonderful tools that are now available in statistical packages to help researchers visualize their data. Finally, the conclusion briefly revisits issues in hypothesis-driven and exploratory data analysis. All statistical and graphical analyses presented here were performed in ARC (Cook & Weisberg, 1999), which can be downloaded without charge from http://www.stat.umn.edu/arc/.

Two Data Analysis Strategies: A Brief Overview

Hypothesis-Driven Research

Traditionally, researchers in many areas of psychology conduct research to test a priori hypotheses. In the context of one predictor regression model, the hypothesis virtually always takes the form of the independent variable, X, having a directional relationship (+ or −) with the dependent variable, Y. For example, a researcher might hypothesize that the number of major stressful life events in children has a positive relationship to the number of days missed from school. Such hypotheses do not typically specify the exact functional form of the relationship but rather implicitly accept the default of regression analysis that the relationship is linear. Nor do they specify the magnitude of the relationship (e.g., for each additional major stressful event, the child will miss 2 additional days of school). The directional hypothesis is tested by estimating a simple regression equation, $Y = b_0 + b_1X + e$, in which b_0 is the intercept, b_1 is the slope of the linear relationship between X and Y, and e is the residual (error of prediction). The significance test of b_1 provides the test of the hypothesis, and, if b_1 is positive and the null hypothesis that the slope in the population is 0 can be rejected, the data are interpreted as being consistent with the hypothesis. This approach of testing directional hypotheses with null hypothesis significance tests has been the focus of considerable recent debate in psychology. (See Harlow, Mulaik, & Steiger, 1997.) On the basis of work by Wilkinson and the APA Task Force on Statistical Inference (1999), the American Psychological Association's (2001) most recent *Publication Manual* (5th ed.) now also encourages the reporting of effect sizes and confidence intervals. These refinements are clearly useful, but they do not materially alter the fundamental logic of hypothesis-driven research.

The use of regression (or any other statistical procedure) as a method for testing a priori hypotheses rests on a set of underlying assumptions. Cohen, Cohen, West, and Aiken (2003, chap. 4) presented an extensive discussion of the assumptions that underlie ordinary least squares (OLS) regression analysis. Historically, on the basis of the results of early simulation studies done in the 1970s, researchers in psychology have taken the perspective that even fairly major violations of these assumptions are typically of little consequence and can be safely ignored. In contrast, recent work (e.g., McClelland, 2000; Wilcox, 2001) suggests that the early simulations were quite limited in scope and that violations of assumptions can materially alter the conclusions of hypothesis-testing research. Cohen et al. (2003, chap. 4) presented a detailed description of graphical and statistical methods for detecting violations of assumptions, and statistical remedies that facilitate accurate inference when such violations occur.

Exploratory Data Analysis

Exploratory data analysis takes a different and complementary tack. The general approach is to use graphical and tabular displays to examine the data, to generate tentative statistical models that appear to describe the relationship between the independent variables and the dependent variable, and to fit one or more of these potential statistical models to the data. Now the residuals come to be of central interest. Careful examination of graphical displays of residuals can detect weaknesses of the potential regression models or suggest alternative models that may provide a better account of the data. New (or revised) regression models are fit and the residuals of these new models are examined, possibly suggesting additional refinements to the models that should be explored. This iterative process continues, with each step potentially revealing new features of the data, until the analyst is satisfied that one or more of the models provides a good description of the data.

Four fundamental principles, sometimes termed the "4 Rs," underlie exploratory data analysis (Hoaglin, Mosteller, & Tukey, 1983).

1. *Revelation.* Exploratory data analysis emphasizes the use of graphical displays to reveal patterns and relationships in the data. Each graphical display has its own strengths and limitations, so multiple displays are encouraged. The set of graphical displays should ideally be capable of capturing both expected and unexpected relationships.

2. *Residuals*. Residuals represent the difference between the data and the model, $e = Y - \hat{Y}$, where $\hat{Y}$ is the value predicted by the regression model. Residuals magnify any remaining systematic variation in the data that is not captured by the current model. As more complete models are developed, increasingly subtle forms of systematic variation in the data may become apparent.

3. *Reexpression*. Reexpression, typically termed *transformation* in psychology, involves changing the scale of the data to simplify data analysis. Reexpression may be performed in an attempt to achieve any of several goals (Cohen et al., 2003, chaps. 4 and 6), including (a) to make nonlinear relationships linear, (b) to eliminate ordinal (weak) interactions between variables, (c) to make the variability of the residuals constant (homoscedasticy), (d) to make the distribution of the residuals normal, (e) to make univariate distributions of the variables symmetric, or (f) to make outliers more consistent with the bulk of the data. Often, but not always, a reexpression may be chosen that achieves several of these goals simultaneously. In some well-developed areas of science, reexpressed scales have become standard (Hoaglin, 1988), as in the measurement of earthquakes by means of the Richter scale (a logarithmic transformation), measurement of sound in decibels (another logarithmic transformation), and measurement of speed in kilometers per hour (a reciprocal transformation).

4. *Resistance*. Exploratory data analysis uses resistant methods that attempt to minimize the impact of outliers. Outliers are atypical observations that can lead to serious problems in OLS regression (Cohen et al., 2003, chap. 10; McClelland, 2000). The specific model that is fit to the data may be determined by a few (even one) cases, rather than the majority of observations. Dropping the outlying cases from the analysis can lead to profound changes in the values of the regression coefficients. One approach to this problem is to use robust regression methods that give little or no weight to outlying cases. A second approach is to identify the outliers, model the remaining body of the data, and then reexamine the outliers, treating them as an additional feature of the data that is to be understood.

The Complementary Value of the Two Approaches

The strength of hypothesis-testing research is that it leads directly to inferences about the existence of the predicted relationship in the population. The weakness of hypothesis-testing (confirmatory) research as typically practiced is that it investigates only the support for the proposed model. Careful consideration of the evidence supporting the proposed versus other alternative models can lead to much stronger inferences (Meehl, 1997; Platt, 1964; Shadish, Cook, & Campbell, 2002). In contrast, the strength of exploratory data analysis is that it seeks to develop one or more statistical models that adequately describe the relationship in the current sample. Comparison of the predictions of such models with the originally hypothesized model in future research can then serve as the basis for much stronger inferences. The weakness of exploratory data analysis is that it may capture chance relationships that exist only in the specific sample, thereby leading to incorrect inferences about relationships in the population. Yet both approaches are useful; as Tukey (1977) noted, "Today, exploratory and confirmatory can—and should—proceed side by side" (p. xii). The conclusion of the present chapter and Behrens and Ho (2003) provide a fuller consideration of the complementary strengths and weaknesses of the two approaches.

A Textbook Example: Faculty Salary Data

Suppose a researcher wishes to test the hypothesis that faculty salaries are positively related to years since the PhD degree. Cohen et al. (2003, pp. 81–82) presented an artificial data set ($N = 62$) that permits an idealized test of this hypothesis. Estimating the regression equation, $Salary = b_0 + b_1 Years + e$, yields the results shown in Table 9.1. The results indicate that for each 1-year increase in time since the PhD, salary was predicted to increase by \$1,379, $r = .61$, $R^2 = .37$, a statistically significant effect that is large in magnitude.

Figure 9.1 is divided into five panels and takes a more graphical approach. It introduces five plots that can be useful in understanding the data and in providing checks on the assumptions of multiple regression. Embedded in this presentation, several plotting tools that are helpful in the process of exploratory data analysis are introduced. These plots and the associated tools will serve as the basis for the exploratory data analysis of real data sets later in this chapter.

Panels A and B in Figure 9.1 are plots of the marginal distributions for each variable. Each plot presents a histogram of the distribution, as well as an overlaid kernel density estimate. Histograms have the advantage of being familiar from introductory statistics classes. However, data can appear to have markedly different distributions, depending on the analyst's choice of the number of bins (class intervals) and the range of scores that are covered by the histogram. (See Behrens & Ho, 2003, for a striking illustration.) An important tool known as a *kernel density estimate* attempts to improve on the histogram's representation of the underlying distribution in the population. In essence, the data are smoothed continuously over their actual range to minimize the influence of sampling error in each specific interval. (For details, see Cohen et al., 2003, pp. 105–109; Fox, 1990.) The result is that the data are represented as a smooth continuous curve that minimizes the influence of local sampling error on the appearance of the distribution. The central problem faced by the analyst is to determine the optimal amount of smoothing, an issue I like to term the "Goldilocks and the three bears problem." Too little smoothing leads to "lumpy" curves that overemphasize small, typically unimportant features of

Table 9.1. Regression Analysis: Years Since PhD and Faculty Salaries (Artificial Data)

Coefficient	Estimate	SE	$t(60)$	p
b_0. Intercept	45,450.1	1,862.3	24.41	<.0001
b_1. Years	1,379.3	232.6	5.93	<.0001

164   STEPHEN G. WEST

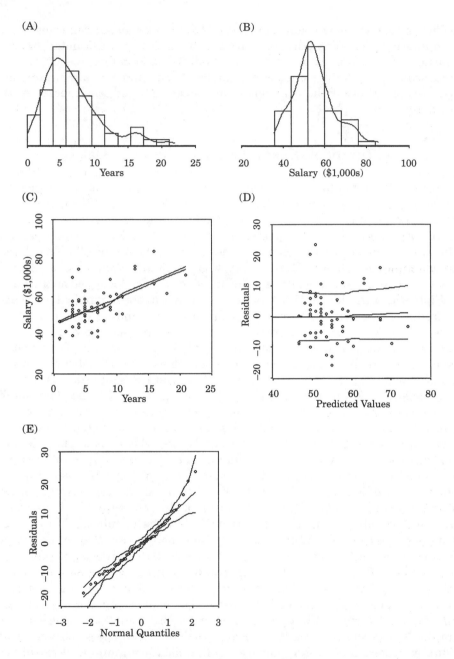

Figure 9.1. Five plots of the faculty salary data (artificial data). (A) Distribution of years since PhD: histogram with superimposed kernel density estimate. (B) Distribution of faculty salaries: histogram with superimposed kernel density estimate. Values of salary are in 1,000s of dollars. (C) Scatterplot of years since PhD versus salary. The best-fitting straight line and the lowess curve are overlaid. Salary is in 1,000s of dollars. (D) Scatterplot of predicted values versus residuals. The horizontal line represents 0 residual. The mean lowess curve and values at ±1 *SD* are overlaid. All values are in 1,000s of dollars. (E) Normal q-q plot of residuals. The straight line is the best-fitting straight line. The envelope is a simulated 95% confidence interval.

the data, whereas too much smoothing leads to curves that may miss important features of the data. The problem is to pick the amount of smoothing that gets it "just right." Modern exploratory data analysis packages such as ARC allow easy manipulation of the amount of smoothing with a pointer (computer mouse). As the pointer is moved, the kernel density estimate is continuously redisplayed, thus making it possible to identify a near-optimal amount of smoothing through manipulation and simple visual inspection. Inspection of the distribution of years since PhD in Panel A shows a moderately skewed distribution, characterizing a relatively young department with a mode of about 5 years, a range from roughly 0 to 22, and a tail to the right. Inspection of the distribution of salary in Panel B shows a roughly symmetrical distribution (a slight right skew is present) with a mode about $55,000 and a range of roughly $38,000 to $84,000. The fixed-effects regression model that is typically used in psychology does not make assumptions about the distribution of the independent and dependent variables, but highly skewed distributions can often be associated with violations of critical assumptions about the residuals.

Panel C presents a scatterplot of salary versus years since PhD. Unless another function is specified by the analyst, regression makes a strong default assumption that there is a linear (straight line) relationship between the independent and dependent variables. In Panel C, the straight line depicted is the best-fitting straight line. The overlaid wavy line is the lowess[1] curve that represents the best-fitting nonparametric function relating the independent to the dependent variable in the sample data. Details of the lowess calculation are presented in Cohen et al. (2003, pp. 111–114). As with kernel density estimates, the central problem facing the analyst is to determine the optimal amount of smoothing to best capture the form of the relationship. This task is easily accomplished with modern exploratory data analysis packages through visual inspection of continuous redisplays of the lowess curve as the analyst moves a pointer. The optimal lowess curve will resemble a child's freehand drawing of the "true" relationship, with the approximation to the relationship becoming better as the sample size increases. Panel C suggests that a linear relationship is appropriate for these faculty salary data.

Panel D plots the residuals against the predicted values. This plot provides a second check on the assumption of a linear relationship between the independent and dependent variables, as deviations from linearity can become magnified after the relationship has been removed from the data. The horizontal line in the middle of the plot (0-line) indicates where the value of the residual is 0. The superimposed wavy lowess line approximates the 0-line, indicating that the linear relationship is adequate. The other two wavy lines represent the value of the lowess function one standard deviation (SD) above and one SD below the central (mean) lowess line. These lines are roughly parallel to the central lowess line, providing evidence that the assumption of constant variance of the residuals around the regression line (homogeneity of variance) is adequately met.

Finally, tests of significance and the construction of confidence intervals in regression assume that the residuals should be normally distributed. Panel

---

[1]Lowess is an acronym for locally weighted scatterplot smoother.

E presents a normal q-q plot of the residuals from the analysis of the faculty salary data. In brief, the values of the n residuals are ordered from lowest to highest, and the percentile rank of each residual is computed. Normal quantiles, which are the z scores from a standard normal distribution that correspond to each percentile rank, are computed (e.g., percentile rank = .50, $z = 0$; percentile rank = .95, $z = 1.65$). The values of the residuals are then plotted on the Y-axis, and the values of the normal quantiles are plotted on the X-axis. To the extent that the residuals have a normal distribution, the residuals will follow a straight line. Panel E shows that the residuals for the faculty salary data generally closely follow a straight line. Also superimposed is a simulated 95% confidence interval around the straight line. Both of these plot enhancement tools suggest that the assumption of normality of the residuals is not violated for these data. Further details on the normal q-q plot can be found in Cohen et al. (2003, pp. 137–141) and Gnanadesikan (1977).

In summary, several plots and new plotting tools have been introduced for examining the assumptions of regression and have been applied to the faculty salary data. Likely new to the reader are the kernel density estimate for estimating the marginal distribution of each variable, the lowess curve for examining the form of the relationship between two variables, and the normal q-q plot for examining the normality of the residuals. Application of these plots and tools showed that the original linear form of the regression model adequately captured the form of the relationship in the sample, the variance of the residuals was homoscedastic, and the residuals were normally distributed. Such a result was not surprising, as the faculty salary data are an artificial textbook example—they were specifically created to have these features. We now turn to three real-world data sets that illustrate the utility of these specialized plots tools to facilitate data exploration when the assumptions of the hypothesized regression model are not met.

Real Data Example 1: Brain Weight Data in Mammals

Stephen Jay Gould (1973) hypothesized that the mean body weight for species of mammals would be positively related to brain weight. Of interest, Gould believed that positive residuals may represent extra brain capacity that would permit animals to perform more "intelligent" behaviors. Weisberg (1985, pp. 144–145) presented the mean body weight (in kilograms) and mean brain weight (in grams) for 62 species ranging in size from mice to elephants. Following standard hypothesis-testing procedures using species as the unit of analysis, he estimated the regression equation, Brain weight = $b_0 + b_1$Body weight + e. The results (see Table 9.2) indicate that for each 1-kg increase in body weight, brain weight was predicted to increase 0.97 gram, $r = .93$, $R^2 = 0.873$, a statistically significant effect that is very large in magnitude.

Let us now reexamine the data from the perspective of exploratory data analysis. The present analysis builds on prior work by Cleveland (1993) and Cook and Weisberg (1999). Figure 9.2 presents four of the plots introduced in the previous section. Panels A and B are histograms of the marginal distributions of brain weight and body weight, respectively. Both distributions are highly right

Table 9.2. Initial Regression Analysis: Body Weight and Brain Weight in Mammals

Coefficient	Estimate	SE	t(60)	p
b_0. Intercept	91.01	43.56	2.09	.04
b_1. Body weight	0.97	0.05	20.28	<.0001

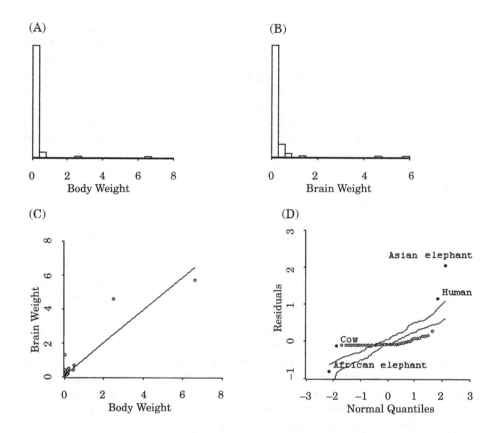

Figure 9.2. Body weight–brain weight data. (A) Histogram of body weight. Values are in 1,000s of kilograms. (B) Histogram of brain weight. Values are in 1,000s of grams. (C) Scatterplot of brain weight versus body weight. Values of body weight are in 1,000s of kilograms. Values of brain weight are in 1,000s of grams. The best-fitting straight line is overlaid. (D) Normal q-q plot of residuals. The two largest (Asian elephant and human) and two smallest (African elephant and cow) are identified. A simulated 95% confidence interval is overlaid.

skewed. Nearly all species are concentrated at the low end of the distribution, with a few outliers trailing off to the right. Panel C presents the scatterplot of brain weight versus body weight. This plot further enhances the impression from the first two panels, as nearly all of the cases are concentrated in the lower left corner of the plot. The two outliers depicted (the Asian elephant and the even larger African elephant) have a great potential to influence the results of the regression equation. Indeed, for the African elephant, a diagnostic measure of influence known as Cook's D (see Cohen et al., 2003, chap. 10; Cook, 1977) has a value of 130.6 compared with an often suggested rule-of-thumb cutoff of 1, indicating that this one data point is having an enormous impact on the results of the regression analysis. Finally, Panel D indicates that the residuals are clearly nonnormally distributed, so the results of significance tests and confidence intervals will be questionable. The normal q-q plot also identifies the smallest and largest residuals, information that will prove useful later in this analysis. The four largest positive outliers (two are shown) are the Asian elephant, human, chimpanzee, and okapi. The four largest negative outliers are the African elephant, cow, pig, and lesser short-tailed shrew. These two clusters of outliers do not help identify any obvious subspecies of mammals.

The initial analysis of the data yields a very large R^2 of .87—an effect size that we can aspire to, but only rarely attain, in psychology. Nonetheless, the model does not provide a very good representation of the data. The results are being driven by a few large mammals. If we delete the African elephant from the data and rerun the analysis, the Asian elephant now becomes hugely influential. If we now delete the Asian elephant, the giraffe becomes influential. And so on. Little progress can be made in this data set by deleting outlying observations. Our original analysis of the brain weight data leads to serious violations of the assumptions of multiple regression and will be abandoned in favor of a more exploratory approach.

Thus far, we have used three of the four Rs of exploratory data analysis (revelation, residuals, and resistance) but have not yet used reexpression. Is there a transformation of this highly skewed data set that would simplify the analysis? Exploratory data analysis packages make it easy to reexpress data. For example, a commonly used set of transformations is known as the Box–Cox family (Box & Cox, 1964; see also Cohen et al., 2003, chap. 6), in which $X_{\text{transformed}}$ may conceptually be thought of as the original value of X raised to a power, that is, $X_{\text{transformed}} = X^\lambda$, where λ is a value nearly always chosen to be between –2 and +2. Some commonly used values of λ are –1 ($1/X$), 0.5 ($\sqrt{X}$), and 2 (X^2), but any value in the range can be used.[2] When $\lambda = 0$, $X_{\text{transformed}}$ is defined as the log of X. Several graphical and statistical methods exist for selecting the optimal transformation (see Cook & Weisberg, 1999), but visually observing how the marginal distribution and the scatterplot change as the value of λ is changed is often sufficient.

Mosteller and Tukey (1977) suggested that when the ratio of the highest to the lowest value in a distribution exceeds 100, a logarithmic transformation should be considered. Following their advice, I applied a log (base 2) transformation to both the brain weight and body weight data. The first three panels presented in Figure 9.3 show histograms and kernel density estimates for body

---

[2]The Box–Cox tranformation is actually a scaled power transformation. In this scaling, $X^\lambda = (X^\lambda - 1)/\lambda$ if $\lambda \neq 0$ and $X^\lambda = \log(X)$ if $\lambda = 0$. Mathematically, this scaling adds logarithms to the family of transformations and preserves the same ordering of the scores for both positive and negative values of λ.

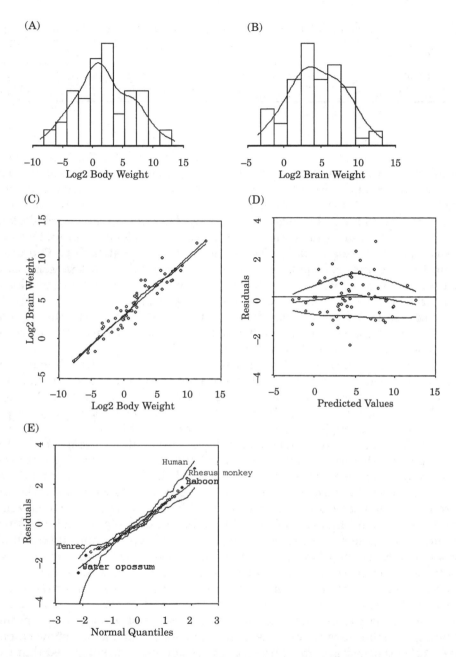

Figure 9.3. Log base 2 transformed body weight–brain weight data. (A) Log base 2 of body weight (kg): histogram with superimposed kernel density plot. (B) Log base 2 of brain weight (g): histogram with superimposed kernel density plot. (C) Scatterplot of log base 2 brain weight versus log base 2 body weight. Best-fitting straight line and lowess curve are overlaid. (D) Scatterplot of residuals versus predicted values. The horizontal line represents 0 residual. The mean lowess curve and values at ±1 *SD* are overlaid. (E) q-q plot of the residuals. The species corresponding to the three most positive (human, rhesus monkey, and baboon) and two most negative (tenrec and water opossum) residuals are identified. The straight line is the best-fitting straight line. The envelope is a simulated 95% confidence interval.

Table 9.3. Regression Analysis: Body Weight and Brain Weight in Mammals

Coefficient	Estimate	SE	$t(60)$	p
b_0. Intercept	3.08	0.14	22.23	<.0000
b_1. Log2 body weight	0.75	0.03	26.41	<.0000

Note. Both variables have now been log base 2 transformed.

weight, brain weight, and the brain weight versus body weight scatterplot for the transformed data, respectively. These panels correspond directly to Panels A to C in Figure 9.2 for the untransformed data. As can be seen, the marginal distributions for log2 body weight and log2 brain weight are no longer skewed but are approximately symmetrical in form. The scatterplot of log2 brain weight versus log2 body weight now shows a much clearer relationship. The best-fitting straight line and the lowess curve that are overlaid both indicate that the two variables appear to have a linear relationship following the logarithmic transformation. In general, the data seem much improved.

On the basis of this initial examination of the transformed data, the original regression equation was reestimated with the use of the log base 2 transformed data. The results are shown in Table 9.3.

These results show a strong, statistically significant, positive linear relationship between body weight and brain weight in the log metric. For each 1 log unit change in body weight, brain weight increases by 0.75 log unit. Drawing on the properties of base 2 logs, the results indicate that each time body weight doubles (a 1-unit change in log base 2 units), brain weight increases by a factor of 1.5 (0.75 × 2). The R^2 is now .92, although this value cannot be directly compared with the original analysis because the dependent variable has been rescaled by a nonlinear transformation. (See Cohen et al., 2003, p. 248.) Panel D indicates that the variance of the residuals is relatively constant, although there is some indication that the variance of the residuals may be somewhat smaller for low and high predicted values of log brain weight. Finally, Panel E indicates that the residuals now appear to be relatively normally distributed. A few of the largest and smallest residuals are shown. The five largest negative residuals appeared to represent diverse animals: the water opossum, tenrec (a spiny insect eater), musk shrew, pig, and Brazilian tapir. In contrast, the five largest residuals, in decreasing order from the largest positive residual, were human, rhesus monkey, baboon, owl monkey, and chimpanzee—species all falling into the class of primates. Inspection of the full data set showed that nearly all of the primates had large positive residuals. This suggested that the regression model might be further improved by including a dummy variable for primates (primate = 1, nonprimate = 0). A new regression equation was estimated in which log brain weight and primate were now the predictor variables, with the results shown in Table 9.4.

As is evident, the inclusion of primate in the equation yielded a substantially increased prediction of log brain weight, with R^2 now reaching .95. Because both the present and the previous regression equations used log base 2 brain weight as the dependent variable, the values of R^2 = .95 in the present

Table 9.4. Regression Analysis: Log Body Weight and Log Brain Weight in Mammals

Coefficient	Estimate	SE	$t(59)$	p
b_0. Intercept	2.85	0.12	24.75	<.0000
b_1. Log2 body weight	0.74	0.02	32.69	<.0000
b_2. Primate	1.75	0.29	6.13	<.0000

Note. Primate has been added as a second predictor.

and R^2 = .92 in the previous regression equations are directly comparable. These results illustrate how the process of exploratory data analysis can help improve the regression model over the initial linear model with the original data. Additional improvements in the regression equation may be possible by using substantive biological knowledge in combination with exploratory data analysis to identify other groups of mammals having similar values of the residuals.

Real Data Set 2: Infant Mortality Data

Researchers in the area of international health believe that better economic conditions in a country can help improve the quality of health care in that country. In addition, there is considerable interest in factors that may lead to unusually good or poor health care in countries having similar economic conditions. Rouncefield (1995) merged diverse economic and health-related data from the early 1990s to create a data set that permitted examination of some of these questions. The countries included in the data set were diverse in economic conditions, ranging from Afghanistan to Switzerland. For the present purposes, the gross national product (GNP) per capita is taken as a measure of economic condition and is expressed in units of $1,000s per capita. The infant mortality (IM) rate is taken as the measure of the quality of health care and is expressed in units of number of deaths of infants less than 1 year old per 1,000 of population. The initial hypothesis is that the GNP per capita will be negatively related to IM rates. The present analysis builds on prior unpublished work by Steiger (2002).

Beginning with a traditional hypothesis-testing approach, the regression equation IM = b_0 + b_1GNP + e is estimated for countries with complete data (n = 91), with the results shown in Table 9.5.

Table 9.5. Initial Regression Analysis: Gross National Product and Infant Mortality

Coefficient	Estimate	SE	$t(89)$	p
b_0. Intercept	75.0421	4.78891	15.67	<.0000
b_1. GNP	−0.0034	0.00048	−7.11	<.0000

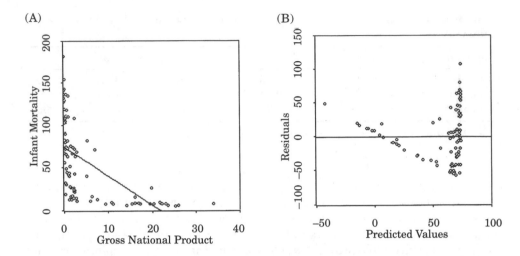

Figure 9.4. Infant mortality data. (A) Scatterplot of infant mortality versus gross national product. Infant mortality is number of infant deaths per 1,000 population. Gross national product is in 1,000s of dollars per capita. (B) Scatterplot of residuals versus predicted values.

The relationship between GNP and IM is statistically significant, $r = .60$ and $R^2 = .36$, again a large effect size, particularly in the area of health research. It is easy on the basis of such results to conclude that there is a strong linear relationship between GNP and IM and to claim that the hypothesis has received strong support. However, Figure 9.4 presents the scatterplot of IM versus GNP in Panel A and the scatterplot of the residuals versus predicted values in Panel B. In Panel A, the best-fitting regression line does not appear to fit the data well, with the predicted values of IM dropping below 0 for several of the wealthiest countries. In Panel B, the systematic variation is amplified following the removal of the linear relationship. For low predicted values up to about 60, the value of the residuals seems to be decreasing slowly. However, above this value, the residuals appear to increase rapidly. This observation suggests that these two parts of the data may be characterized by different regression functions. On the basis of an examination of the data, a predicted value of 60 occurs when the GNP is very roughly about $4,000 per capita. Fortuitously, a gap in the data occurs, with no countries having a GNP between $3,020 (Iraq) and $5,220 (Oman) per capita, so I divide the data into two parts: a group of lower-income countries with a GNP less than $3,021 per capita and a group of higher-income countries with a GNP greater than $5,219 per capita.

Considering first the group of lower-income countries, we rescale the scatterplot of IM versus GNP and then replot the data in Figure 9.5. This scatterplot suggests a much better fit to the data. However, the scatterplot of the residuals against the predicted values indicates that some systematic curvilinearity may remain in this portion of the data. Ignoring this potential curvilinearity for the moment, we find the results in Table 9.6 for the linear regression of IM

(A)

(B)

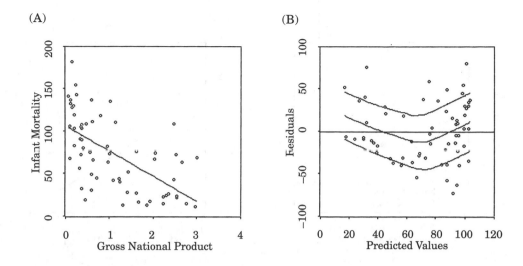

Figure 9.5. Infant mortality data for lower-income countries. (A) Scatterplot of infant mortality versus gross national product. Infant mortality is number of infant deaths per 1,000 population. Gross national product is in 1,000s of dollars per capita. (B) Scatterplot of residuals versus predicted values.

Table 9.6. Regression Analysis: Gross National Product and Infant Mortality in Poorer Countries

Coefficient	Estimate	SE	$t(61)$	p
b_0. Intercept	106.31	6.99	15.22	<.0000
b_1. GNP	−0.030	0.0048	−6.09	<.0000

on GNP for the poorer countries ($n = 63$). Once again, the relationship is large in magnitude and statistically significant.

Turning now to the wealthier countries, Figure 9.6, Panel A presents the scatterplot of IM versus GNP following rescaling of the plot. The bulk of these data appear to have low IM rates, but several appear to be possible outliers with higher values than we would predict on the basis of their GNP. I have identified these countries in the figure; each is a Middle Eastern or North African country with a relatively small population but high per capita income from oil revenues.[3] The oil countries were temporarily removed from the data.

---

[3] Input from substantive content experts would be critical here in deciding how best to define the boundaries of the construct characterizing these countries. There are other countries with some characteristics that overlap with the identified group that would or would not be included in the construct, depending on the definition. For example, Indonesia is another predominantly Muslim country with oil revenues, but with a very large population. Norway is another European country with substantial oil revenues, but with a relatively small population.

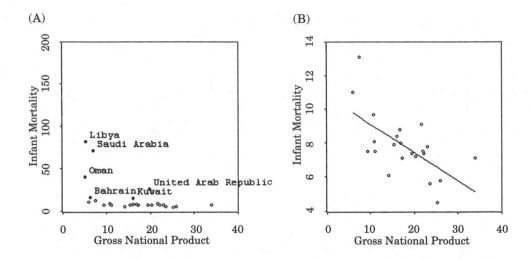

Figure 9.6. Infant mortality data for wealthier countries. (A) Scatterplot of infant mortality versus gross national product. A set of outlying countries is identified. (B) Scatterplot of infant mortality versus gross national product. Outlying countries have been removed from the data set, and the plot has been rescaled. The best-fitting straight line is overlaid.

Panel B presents the relationship for the remaining countries ($n = 22$), which are the wealthy industrial countries in Europe, North America, and Asia. Note that the y-axis of this plot has been rescaled so that the magnitude of the relationship appears to be much stronger than it would if the y-axis still represented the full range of IM from 0 to 200. The results of the regression analysis for the wealthier countries (excluding oil countries) are presented in Table 9.7. The decline in IM for each one-unit increase in GNP is still statistically significant. However, the rate of decrease in IM with increased GNP is markedly less for the wealthier countries, changing from an approximate 3% decline for each additional $1,000 in per capita income in the poorer countries to a 0.02% decline for each additional $1,000 in per capita income in the wealthier countries.

Putting the parts together, we see that the results of the initial exploratory approach suggest a piecewise regression equation with a breakpoint somewhere in the gap between $3,020 and $5,220 (Neter, Kutner, Nachtsheim, & Wasserman, 1996, pp. 474–478) and a dummy variable for Middle Eastern oil coun-

Table 9.7. Regression Analysis: Gross National Product and Infant Mortality in Wealthier Countries

Coefficient	Estimate	SE	$t(20)$	p
b_0. Intercept	10.81	0.88	12.289	<.0001
b_1. GNP	−0.00017	0.000046	−3.598	<.002

Note. Middle Eastern oil countries have been excluded.

Table 9.8. Piecewise Regression Analysis: Gross National Product and Infant Mortality

Coefficient	Estimate	*SE*	*t*(87)	*p*
b_0. Intercept	108.16	5.55	19.49	<.0001
b_1. GNP	−0.0329	0.0036	−9.11	<.0001
b_2. (GNP − 3021)Wealth	0.0327	0.0040	8.20	<.0001
b_3. Oil	42.59	10.82	3.945	.0002

Note. Different slopes are estimated for poorer and wealthier countries. Middle Eastern oil country has been added as a predictor.

tries. I arbitrarily selected the beginning of the gap ($3,021) as the breakpoint. The regression equation estimated is IM = b_0 + b_1GNP + b_2(GNP − 3021)Wealth + b_3Oil + e. Wealth is a dummy variable that is 0 for the poorer countries and 1 for the wealthier countries. Oil is a dummy variable that is 1 for Middle Eastern and North African oil countries and 0 for all others. This approach forces the two pieces of the regression equation to join at $3,021, a constraint that was not imposed in the exploratory analyses. The results of this regression equation are presented in Table 9.8. In this equation, b_0 is the predicted number of deaths per 1,000 infants when GNP = 0, b_1 = −0.0329 is the slope for the poorer countries, b_1 + b_2 = −.0002 represents the slope for the wealthier countries, and b_3 is the increase over the predicted number of infant deaths in the oil countries. The R^2 was .64, compared with the R^2 of .36 for the original linear model.

This model is a clear improvement over the original linear model. A final examination of the two plots that provide checks on the residuals is needed. Figure 9.7, Panel A, displays the residuals versus the predicted values with a

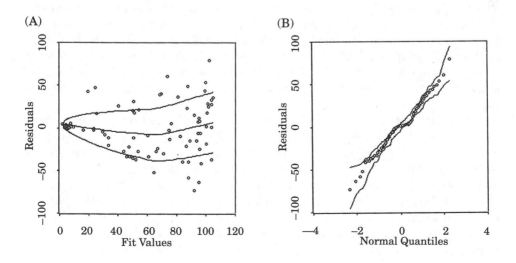

Figure 9.7. Residual plots for piecewise regression model. (A) Scatterplot of residuals versus predicted values. The mean lowess curve and values at ±1 *SD* are overlaid. (B) The q-q plot of the residuals. The envelope is a simulated 95% confidence interval.

lowess curve for the mean residual values and ±1 standard deviation from the mean value overlaid. The middle lowess curve (mean residual for each predicted value) indicates that there is some small additional curvature that is not captured by the piecewise model. The lowess curves at ±1 standard deviation from the predicted values indicate that the variance increases with the magnitude of the predicted value, so that the assumption of homoscedasticity is not met. Panel B presents the normal q-q plot of the residuals that indicates only a very modest discrepancy from a normal distribution. (The peak is slightly higher than expected.) Additional modifications of this piecewise approach, such as representing each piece of the regression equation as a curvilinear function that joins at the breakpoint, could also be undertaken. Or an entirely different tack, such as attempting to find reexpressions of GNP and IM that linearize the relationship, could be undertaken. An initial exploration taking logs of both variables led to a far more linear relationship between IM and GNP than the original analysis. However, there was still evidence of some curvilinearity and some nonconstant variance in the scatterplot of the residuals versus predicted values. Careful examination of the residuals may identify other possible groupings. Several of the largest positive residuals (e.g., Afghanistan, Angola, Sierra Leone) appear to be associated with countries at war in the early 1990s; several of the largest negative residuals (e.g., China, Ukraine) were countries with socialized medical systems. Exploration of such modifications, particularly with input from substantive content specialists in international health, may lead to further material improvements in the model.

Real Data Set 3: The Donner Party

The final example illustrates how graphical exploratory data analysis can be used when the dependent variable is dichotomous. Dichotomous dependent variables create major problems for standard OLS regression analysis (Cohen et al., 2003, chap. 13) and necessitate the use of specialized procedures such as logistic regression (Agresti, 2002). Nonetheless, many of the strategies and tools of graphical exploratory data analysis can be directly extended to logistic regression problems.

The data set for the example is taken from information collected about the Donner Party (Johnson, 1996). The Donner Party was a group of pioneer families that were caught by a heavy snowfall while attempting to cross the Sierra Nevada mountains in California during the winter of 1846–1847. The tragic decision to cross the mountains so late in the year resulted in the death of 46% of the group. The present analyses investigate the hypothesis that age is related to the chances of survival, using all cases for which both the age and survival status of the person are known ($n = 88$ of 91 total). Following standard hypothesis-testing procedures, a logistic regression equation $\hat{Y} = b_0 + b_1$ age was estimated. (See Table 9.9.)

As discussed in Cohen et al. (2003, chap. 13) and Agresti (2002), the interpretation of the coefficients in a logistic regression equation is more complex than in linear regression. $\hat{Y}$ is the natural log of the odds of survival and

Table 9.9. Initial Regression Analysis: Age and Mortality in the Donner Party

Coefficient	Estimate	SE	Est/SE	p
b_0. Intercept	0.979173	0.374549	2.614	.0089
b_1. Age	−0.0368882	0.0149224	−2.472	.0134

is known as the logit (logit =ln[$\hat{p}$/(1 − $\hat{p}$)], where $\hat{p}$ is the probability of survival). The ratio is known as the odds. The intercept is the predicted value of the logit when age = 0; here, the predicted logit = 0.98, which corresponds to a survival probability of .73. The slope = −.037 is the decrease in the predicted logit for each 1-year increase in age. Figure 9.8 shows a scatterplot of survival probability versus age, with the estimated logistic function overlaid. As can be seen, the logistic function roughly approximates a linear function for this example, because the predicted probabilities all fall in the range from 0.2 to 0.8. If the predicted probabilities were more extreme within the range of the data ($\hat{p}$ closer to 0.0 or 1.0), then the logistic function would appear to be more S-shaped in form.

The depiction of the data in the scatterplot in Figure 9.8, Panel A, is not very informative about the distribution of the cases. Given that there are only two possible values of the dependent variable for each person (1 = alive, 0 = dead), multiple cases having the same age will be overplotted. One solution is to jitter the values of survival—a small amount of random error is added to the values of survival to provide a better sense of the distribution. The jittered plot presented in Panel B gives us a rough sense of the data. Approximately half of the children younger than 10 years of age survive, a larger percentage of the people between about 10 and 25 years survive, and the probability of survival slowly decreases with further increases in age. An even better portrayal of the data is provided in Panel C, in which a lowess curve is fit to the original (nonjittered) data. The lowess curve indicates that the predicted probability of survival is about .50 at age 0 (the youngest children were 1 year old) and that this probability increases up to about age 18, following which the predicted probability of survival declines. Finally, Panel D presents another perspective on the same data; a histogram of age of the members of the Donner Party. Overlaid are two kernel density estimates, one for survival and one for death. The two curves are about the same height at age 0, indicating roughly a .50 probability of survival, or equivalently, odds (survival/death) = 1. The survival curve is higher than the death curve in adolescence, indicating that the probability of survival is greater than .50. At about age 25 the probability of survival is again about .50, and this probability continues to decrease from that point with the survival curve lower than the death curve.

This relationship can be estimated as a piecewise logistic regression equation. I chose the value of age = 18, suggested by the lowess curve, as the point at which the logistic function for children joins the function for adults. A dummy variable for adult was created that has a value of 0 when age has a value of 18 or less and 1 when age is greater than 18. Following the same general procedures as in the infant mortality example, a piecewise logistic regression equation was estimated. (See Table 9.10.)

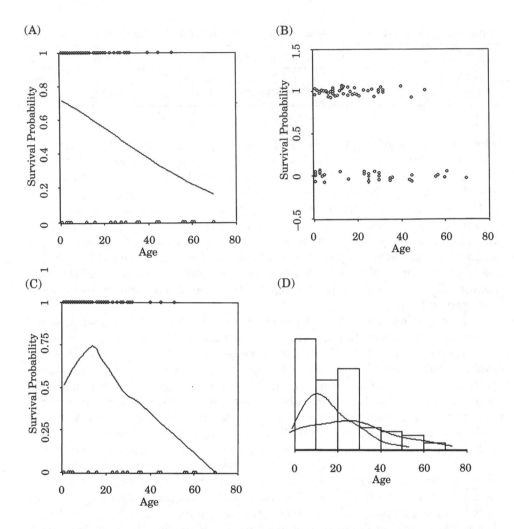

Figure 9.8. Donner Party data. (A) Scatterplot of survival probability versus age. The best-fitting logistic curve is overlaid. (B) Jittered scatterplot of survival probability versus age. Jittering reduces overplotting and makes the age distribution clearer within each outcome group. (C) Scatterplot of survival probability versus age. The lowess curve is overlaid. (D) Histogram of ages of members of the Donner Party. Two kernel density estimates are superimposed. The line that reaches its peak during adolescence is survival. The line that reaches its maximum value at approximately age 30 is death. The ratio of the heights of the two kernel density estimates at each age portrays the odds.

In this equation, $b_0 = 0.11$ represents the predicted value of the logit when age = 0. This value corresponds to a survival probability of 0.53. The b_1 indicates that, for each 1-year increase in age in the children who are 18 or younger, the predicted value of the logit increases by 0.06. The b_2 indicates that the slope changes by –0.15 at age 18; this change in slope is statistically significant. For the adult part of the function, the predicted value of the logit decreases by –0.09 (0.06 – 0.15) for each 1-year increase in age. The general form

Table 9.10. Piecewise Logistic Regression Analysis: Age and Mortality in the Donner Party

Coefficient	Estimate	SE	Est/SE	p
b_0. Intercept	0.11	0.508	0.221	.82
b_1. Age	0.06	0.044	1.365	.17
b_2. (Age − 18) × Adult	−0.15	0.069	−2.221	.03

Note. Different logistic regression equations are estimated for children and adults.

of the relationship is indicated by the lowess curve presented in Figure 9.8, Panel C. The piecewise logistic regression model appears to provide a far better description of the data than the original regression model. More advanced plots of the residuals to provide additional checks on the fit of the logistic regression model are available and are described in Cook (1998) and Cook and Weisberg (1999). Close examination of such plots may suggest further revisions of the model.

Extensions to More Complex Models

This chapter has provided an introduction to exploratory data analysis in the context of regression models. To convey the fundamental ideas of the approach and to introduce some of the modern tools that are available, the presentation was limited to cases in which there was only one predictor and, possibly, other grouping variables present in the data. The ideas presented in this chapter extend directly to exploratory data analysis in regression contexts with two or more predictor variables. A variety of additional tools is available to help visualize more complex relationships such as partial (conditional) relationships and complex interactions between independent variables. A variety of other, more advanced model-checking tools is also available. As we saw with Real Data Example 3, graphical tools are becoming available with which to examine data fit with nonlinear regression models and variants of the generalized linear model (McCullagh & Nelder, 1989). More advanced presentations of many of these tools and techniques can be found in Behrens and Ho (2003); Brillinger, Fernholtz, and Morgenthaler (1997); Cleveland (1993); Cook (1998); Cook and Weisberg (1999); Wilkinson (1999); and Young, Valero-Mora, and Friendly (in press). Such tools permit researchers to quick and efficiently apply the methods of exploratory data analysis to their own data sets.

Conclusion

You should look at your data. It's fun. You will learn something about your data that is often more fun and more useful than simply calculating *p* values. Graphical procedures can be used to display the data, the statistical model, or both. Each display is useful. Each display has its own strengths and weaknesses in revealing underlying relationships in the data. Displays that allow the researcher to see both the model and the data simultaneously are often of particular value. Displays that examine the characteristics of residuals highlight features of the data that have not been adequately captured in previously considered models.

Hypothesis-testing research remains the best method of testing a priori theoretical predictions and making inferences about population values. This general approach protects against Type I error when the assumptions are met. In regression analysis, these assumptions include linear relationships, homoscedasticity of residuals, and normally distributed residuals. However, many researchers in psychology fail to check the assumptions. Graphical methods provide an excellent way of doing so. In addition, hypothesis-testing methods can be further strengthened by moving from directional to more precise hypotheses. Hypotheses that make specific predictions about the exact functional form of the relationship or the exact value of a parameter permit much stronger inferences (Meehl, 1997). In addition, comparing the ability of competing models to account for the same data can also lead to stronger inferences (Platt, 1964; Shadish et al., 2002). Meehl (1978, 1997) strongly argued that theoretical progress in "soft" psychology can be accelerated through the use of more precise predictions that put scientific hypotheses at greater risk of disconfirmation. He also encouraged careful examination of the auxiliaries associated with hypothesis testing, including the assumptions underlying the statistical test.

Graphical methods provide a particularly strong approach to discovering new relationships in data. The ease with which graphical methods can now be implemented on one's desktop computer is permitting the early promise of exploratory data analysis to be fulfilled. New and interesting findings have come out of careful graphical analysis, as I have illustrated in the examples here. (For other examples, see Cleveland, 1993; Cook & Weisberg, 1999.) Graphical methods complement traditional hypothesis-testing methods by specifying the form of the relationship between variables and by suggesting alternative models with which the original hypothesis may be compared. Yet graphical methods describe only relationships that are present in the particular sample at hand. They do not permit direct statistical inference, and they may capitalize on chance relationships. Diaconis (1985) discussed these issues and described a variety of methods that can strengthen the inferences made from exploratory data analysis. Of these, the most important are replication techniques that should be used whenever possible. Or, as Steiger (2002) noted in another context, "An ounce of replication is worth a ton of inferential statistics" (p. 176). When the initial sample is large, the sample may be split, and the exploratory findings obtained in the first subsample can be replicated on the holdout subsample. Even better, an entirely new sample may be collected, and the findings may be replicated in the new sample, now treating the initial exploratory model as the a priori hypothesis. Particularly valuable are data for which the originally hypothesized model and the model(s) developed with exploratory data analysis make different new predictions (Behrens & Ho, 2003). In some cases, replication may not be possible because the data represent a unique event, the data are expensive to collect, or the sample may represent all or a large portion of the available data in the population (e.g., a study of the 50

U.S. states). In such cases, applications of several modern statistical procedures such as simulation, bootstrapping, and model development with repeated cross-validation in multiple resamples from the data set may be used to strengthen statistical inferences. Such procedures can help minimize the risk that the findings developed with exploratory data analysis methods are limited to the specific data set.

References

Agresti, A. (2002). *Categorical data analysis* (2nd ed.). New York: Wiley.

American Psychological Association. (2001). *Publication manual of the American Psychological Association* (5th ed.). Washington, DC: Author.

Behrens, J. T., & Ho, C.-H. (2003). Exploratory data analysis. In J. A. Schinka & W. F. Velicer (Eds.), *Handbook of psychology: Vol. 2. Research methods in psychology* (pp. 33–66). Hoboken, NJ: Wiley.

Berra, Y. (2005). *Yogi-isms*. Retrieved March 12, 2005, from www.yogiberra.com/yogi-isms.html

Brillinger, D. R., Fernholz, L. T., & Morgenthaler, S. (Eds.). (1997). *The practice of data analysis: Essays in honor of John W. Tukey*. Princeton, NJ: Princeton University Press.

Box, G. E. P., & Cox, D. R. (1964). An analysis of transformations. *Journal of the Royal Statistical Society, Series B, 26*, 211–246.

Cleveland, W. (1993). *Visualizing data*. Summit, NJ: Hobart Press.

Cohen, J., Cohen, P., West, S. G., & Aiken, L. S. (2003). *Applied multiple regression/correlation analysis for the behavioral sciences* (3rd ed.). Mahwah, NJ: Erlbaum.

Cook, R. D. (1977). Detection of influential observations in linear regression. *Technometrics, 19*, 15–18.

Cook, R. D. (1998). *Regression graphics: Ideas for studying regression through graphics*. New York: Wiley.

Cook, R. D., & Weisberg, S. (1999). *Applied regression including computing and graphics*. New York: Wiley.

Diaconis, P. (1985). Theories of data analysis: From magical thinking through classical statistics. In D. C. Hoaglin, F. Mosteller, & J. W. Tukey (Eds.), *Exploring data tables, trends, and shapes* (pp. 1–36). New York: Wiley.

Fox, J. (1990). Describing univariate distributions. In J. Fox & J. S. Long (Eds.), *Modern methods of data analysis* (pp. 58–125). Newbury Park, CA: Sage.

Gould, S. J. (1973). The shape of things to come. Allometry and size in ontogeny and phylogeny. *Biological Reviews, 41*, 587–640.

Gnanadesikan, R. (1977). *Methods for statistical analysis of multivariate data*. New York: Wiley.

Harlow, L. L., Mulaik, S. A., & Steiger, J. H. (Eds.). (1997). *What if there were no significance tests?* Mahwah, NJ: Erlbaum.

Hoaglin, D. C. (1988). Transformations in everyday experience. *Chance, 1*(4), 40–45.

Hoaglin, D. C., Mosteller, F., & Tukey, J. W. (Eds.). (1983). *Understanding robust and exploratory data analysis*. New York: Wiley.

Johnson, K. (1996). *Unfortunate emigrants: Narratives of the Donner Party*. Logan: Utah State University Press.

McClelland, G. H. (2000). Nasty data: Unruly, ill-mannered observations can ruin your analysis. In H. T. Reis & C. M. Judd (Eds.), *Handbook of research methods in social and personality psychology* (pp. 393–411). New York: Cambridge University Press.

McCullagh, P., & Nelder, J. A. (1989). *Generalized linear models* (2nd ed.). New York: Chapman & Hall.

Meehl, P. E. (1967). Theory testing in psychology and physics: A methodological paradox. *Philosophy of Science, 34*, 103–115.

Meehl, P. E. (1978). Theoretical risks and tabular asterisks: Sir Karl, Sir Ronald, and the slow progress of soft psychology. *Journal of Consulting and Clinical Psychology, 46*, 806–834.

Meehl, P. E. (1997). The problem is epistemology, not statistics: Replace significance tests by confidence intervals and quantify accuracy of risky numerical predictions. In L. L. Harlow, S. A. Mulaik, & J. H. Steiger (Eds.), *What if there were no significance tests?* (pp. 393–425). Mahwah, NJ: Erlbaum.

Mosteller, F., & Tukey, J. W. (1977). *Data analysis and regression.* Reading, MA: Addison-Wesley.

Neter, J., Kutner, M. H., Nachtsheim, C. J., & Wasserman, W. (1996). *Applied linear regression models* (3rd ed.). Chicago: Irwin.

Platt, J. R. (1964, October 16). Strong inference. *Science, 146,* 347–353.

Rouncefield, M. (1995). The statistics of poverty and inequality. *Journal of Statistics Education, 3*(2). Retrieved November 8, 2005, from www.amstat.org/publications/jse/v3n2/datasets. rouncefield.html

Shadish, W. R., Cook, T. D., & Campbell, D. T. (2002). *Experimental and quasi-experimental designs for generalized causal inference.* Boston: Houghton-Mifflin.

Steiger, J. H. (2002). *A tale of two regressions: Exploratory piecewise regression analysis of poverty and infant mortality.* Unpublished laboratory manual, Vanderbilt University, Nashville, TN.

Tukey, J. W. (1977). *Exploratory data analysis.* Reading, MA: Addison-Wesley.

Wainer, H., & Thissen, D. (1993). Graphical data analysis. In G. Keren & C. Lewis (Eds.), *A handbook for data analysis in the behavioral sciences: Statistical issues* (pp. 391–457). Hillsdale, NJ: Erlbaum.

Weisberg, S. (1985). *Applied linear regression* (2nd ed.). New York: Wiley.

Wilcox, R. R. (2001). *Fundamentals of modern statistical methods: Substantially improving power and accuracy.* New York: Springer.

Wilkinson, L. (1999). *The grammar of graphics.* New York: Springer.

Wilkinson, L., & the APA Task Force on Statistical Inference. (1999). Statistical methods in psychology journals: Guidelines and explanations. *American Psychologist, 54,* 594–604.

Young, F. W., Valero-Mora, P. M., & Friendly, M. (in press). *Visual statistics: Seeing data with dynamic interactive graphics.* New York: Wiley.

Part III

Validity and Measurement in Evaluation

10

How to Fool Yourself With Experiments in Testing Theories in Psychological Research

Werner W. Wittmann and Petra L. Klumb

The Northwestern school, as Glass (1983) coined it, no longer resides in the Department of Psychology at Northwestern University, Evanston, Illinois. Its members are now spread throughout the United States, and its international reputation and recognition is outstanding. Campbell and Stanley (1966), followed by Cook and Campbell (1979), and now by Shadish, Cook, and Campbell (2002), are all the sources that have to be studied, learned, and digested by every student worldwide who wants to do serious research in social sciences. The Northwestern school's influence and impact are still growing. Boruch and colleagues have founded the Campbell Collaboration to promote and foster research synthesis based on randomized experiments and quasi-experiments, especially in the context of education, the field most resistant to experimentation. Cook (2002) analyzed these reasons for resistance. The *American Journal of Evaluation* (2003), in its section "The Historical Record," gives voice to former Northwestern alumni to describe their experiences while being at the university. The number of challengers and critics is also a good indicator of the impact of a school of thought. The Northwestern school has attracted many critics, most importantly, Cronbach (1982; Cronbach et al., 1980), who challenged the preference and emphasis the school has placed on internal validity instead of focusing more on external validity or generalizability of results. Cronbach argued for correlational studies and designs, which may not give the same information about cause-and-effect relationships as the experimental and quasi-experimental designs, but whose predictions are better tailored to real life and give better generalizability. So, the differences between Campbell and Cronbach can be regarded as differences in the emphasis one places on different standards of quality of research designs.

We have been influenced by the debates between the Northwestern school and its critics and have tried to synthesize them into an overall framework.

We thank Guido Makransky and Tobias Bothe for their help with grammar and style.

This allows us, once we know of an evaluation project, to choose between different approaches.

The Five-Data-Box Conceptualization: A Comprehensive Framework for Research and Program Evaluation

For this purpose, we have developed a framework called the *five-data-box conceptualization* (Wittmann, 1985, 2002; Wittmann & Walach, 2002), which refers to five different sources of information one must consider and gather in the process of basic or applied research. Figure 10.1 distinguishes between an evaluation data box (EVA), a criterion box (CR), the experimental treatment box (ETR), the nonexperimental treatment box (NTR), and the predictor box (PR). All data boxes are conceptualized as Cattellian data boxes or covariation charts with their three dimensions: subjects, variables, and situations/time (Cattell, 1988).

The data boxes PR to CR are ordered according to the process of research on a time path. The EVA box on the left contains the stakeholders as subjects.

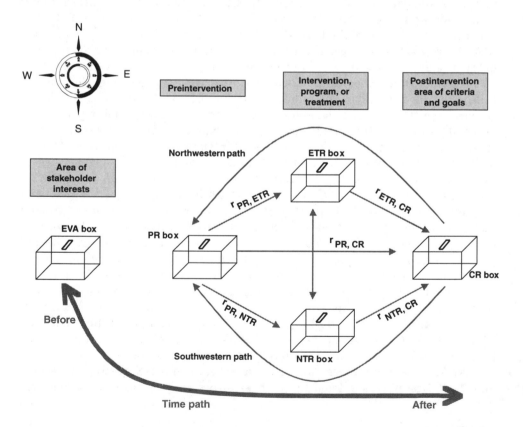

Figure 10.1. The five-data-box conceptualization. EVA box = evaluation data box; CR box = criterion box; ETR box = experimental treatment box; NTR box = nonexperimental treatment box; PR box = predictor box.

Stakeholders are subjects interested in the results—that is, the baseline, the process, the program or intervention, and the impact—of the research. The variables in that box are often fuzzy and vague constructs, which have to be translated into precise measurements by the researcher in program evaluation. In basic research, the subject is the researcher, who is free to choose his or her area of interest. Implicitly, a researcher also must consider one's peers, because difficulties result when there is a lack of interest in the topic that could lead to difficulties in the research being published. The PR box encompasses all variables as baseline data before any intervention. These variables are used for predictions, to control the status before research, and to answer any questions about selection effects regarding the population of interest. The ETR box maps the actively manipulated treatment variables and the members of the randomized experimental and control groups as subjects. In analysis of variance (ANOVA) parlance, these are the independent variables called fixed or random factors and their interactions. The NTR box contains all treatment aspects that could not be randomized—for example, factors mapping nonequivalent comparison groups, such as compliance, dosage, strength, integrity, and fidelity of the intervention. The CR box subsumes all criterion variables, which are used for a summative evaluation of the program or intervention. These variables must map the stakeholder interests and should correspond to what was done as an intervention. Different schools of research and evaluation concentrate on different data boxes and their possible relationships. If we regress the CR box on the ETR box and the PR box, we follow the Northwestern path. If we regress the CR box on the NTR box and the PR box, we follow the Southwestern path. The geographical wind rose at the upper-left corner of Figure 10.1 serves as a guide to reading the data-box conceptualization as a geographic map to facilitate our understanding of the contrast between the Northwestern schools and the Stanford evaluation consortium (with Lee Cronbach as the main spokesman) in what they consider important and feasible in program evaluation.

Suchman (1967), in the first systematic textbook on evaluation research, put the highest priority on the Northwestern school. He considered Campbell and Stanley (1966) as the "bible" of the researcher. Unfortunately, many evaluation studies showed low or zero effects. Rossi (1978) referred to that state of affairs as the iron law of program evaluation. The stately mansion of evaluation research and program evaluation rests on three strong pillars, namely, research design and the related data-analytic tools of assessment methods and decision aids.

Lee Sechrest has contributed to assessment (Sechrest, 1986; Sechrest, Schwartz, Webb, & Campbell, 1999), to debates about quantitative versus qualitative research, and to the problems related to treatment integrity, fidelity, implementation, and strength (Sechrest, West, Phillips, Redner, & Yeaton, 1979; Sechrest & Yeaton, 1981, 1982; Yeaton & Sechrest, 1981). Lack of treatment integrity or failures in implementing a program can easily explain why the program did not show the effects its stakeholders hoped. Boruch and Gomez (1977), in the same sense, proposed a small measurement theory in the field and pointed to the problem of overlap between treatment and its outcome measures as an explanation for low or zero-order effects.

The debates about adequate research designs and its data-analytic strategies have a long history in psychological science. In the 1950s, there was a heated debate between proponents of experimental design and those of representative design. Egon Brunswik (1955), who proposed the representative design, was heavily criticized, especially by Hilgard (1955). Brunswik's data-analytic tool was regression/correlation. It is well known that correlations are only a necessary, but not sufficient, prerequisite for causal explanations. Yet when the time paths are known, we can use regression analysis as path analysis (Wright, 1921) to search for true causal relationships, even in nonexperimental designs, distinguishing between direct and indirect effects and false causal claims as spurious. We can control for selection into treatment effects but still have to face the problem of generalizability and the possible consequences of unmeasured causes. Experiments are traditionally analyzed with Fisher's ANOVA, and many researchers believe that doing an ANOVA brings them all the virtues of a randomized experimental design. Cohen (1968), in his seminal paper, demonstrated that all designs, whether experimental, quasi-experimental, or plain correlational, can be analyzed by the general linear model—that is, multiple regression/correlation. His paper was expanded into a full textbook (Cohen & Cohen, 1975), which has seen its third edition (Cohen, Cohen, West, & Aiken, 2003).

The four boxes on the right-hand side of Figure 10.1 are related with directed arrows mapping the time paths between them. Only the relationship between the ETR box and the NTR box is denoted with a double-headed arrow, indicating the gradual decline from a fully randomized design to a more quasi-experimental and correlational one. It is interesting to note that the title of Cook and Campbell (1979) already was *Quasi-Experimentation*, demonstrating that the Northwestern school was fully aware of the problems associated with doing research in field settings (i.e., real life). Nevertheless, Cronbach (1982) accused the Northwestern school of putting too much emphasis on internal validity and neglecting external validity or generalizability. Cook (1993) and Matt (2003) are Northwesterners most open to Cronbach's challenges, and Shadish et al. (2002), in the latest completely reworked edition of the "research bible," integrate ideas about generalizability and how to better balance conflicts between internal and external validity.

Brunswik Symmetry: A Key Concept for Successful Psychological Research

Looking for reasons that natural sciences like physics, chemistry, and biology have been so successful, we often find references to the experimental methods and good falsifiable theories. It is no wonder that those ambitious enough to change psychology from literature and art to science insisted so much on the experimental approach. However, psychologists have neglected another key concept for success in science, namely, the ubiquitous concepts and principles of symmetry. Zee (1989) described symmetry, and we have learned that the successes in physics of Michael Faraday, Murray Gell-Mann, and Richard Feynman, among many others, would not have occurred without capitalizing

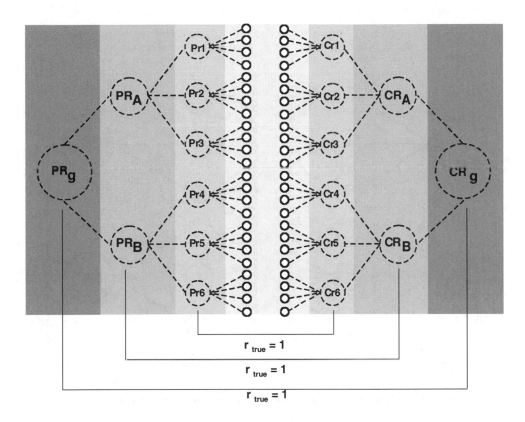

$$r_{true} = 1$$

$$r_{true} = 1$$

$$r_{true} = 1$$

Figure 10.2. The true Brunswik symmetrical latent structure of nature. PR = predictor; CR = criterion.

on symmetry. Brunswik's main conceptual breakthroughs—the representative design and the lens model for human perception and judgment—have not been appreciated by most of his peers, but his ideas have survived with the help of Hammond (1966, 1996; Hammond & Stewart, 2001). We focus on his lens model and use it to look at the relationship between our data boxes. Figure 10.2 visualizes the PR–CR box relationship.

The Gestalt principles immediately force us to consider symmetry principles in amount of aggregation, level of generality, and correspondence between predictor and criterion constructs. Only when these principles hold can we hope to get maximum validity in terms of correlation coefficients or variance accounted for. Variants of violations of symmetry give us hints to how and when our research might fool us. Figure 10.3 distinguishes four variants of asymmetry.

Figure 10.3a shows the case of full asymmetry, which is the case in which nothing works. Predictors and criteria do not overlap; it is the extreme case when what is taught and what is tested do not correspond. The reliability of the predictor and the criterion constructs may be perfect, but we have no

(A)

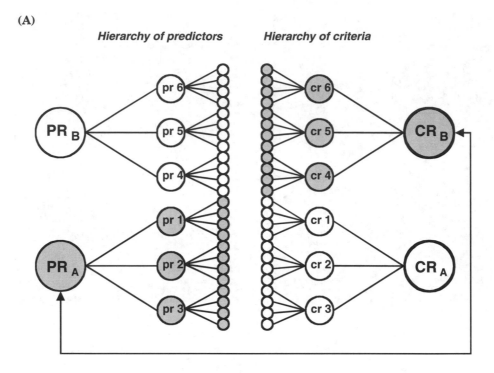

All correlations between predictors and criteria are zero!

(B)

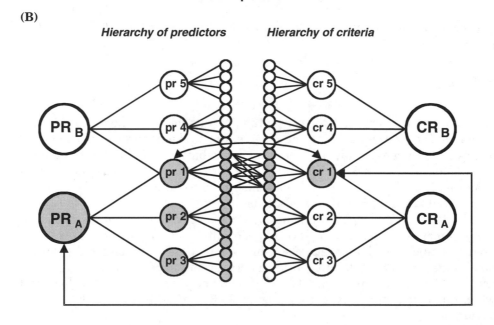

Predictor and a narrower lower level criterion.

(C)

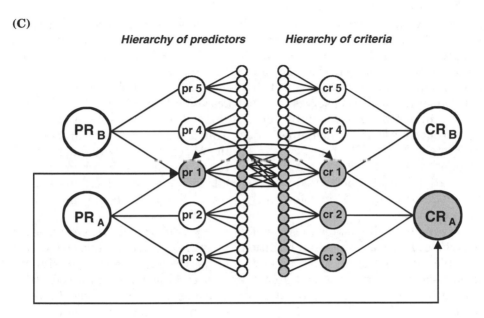

Predictor and a broad higher level criterion.

(D)

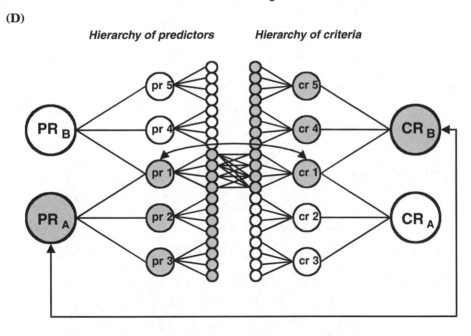

Mismatch at the same level of generality!

Figure 10.3. (A) Full asymmetry: the case in which nothing works. (B) Asymmetry because of a broad higher level predictor. (C) Asymmetry because of a narrower lower level predictor. (D) The hybrid case of asymmetry. PR = predictor; CR = criterion.

predictive validity. This case happens by choosing assessments according to their psychometric reliability only and not in terms of their construct relevance, or, as we call them, their construct reliability. Nevertheless, it is an interesting case because, according to Campbell and Fiske (1959), we have perfect discriminant validity. Knowing what something is not is very helpful for falsification in a Popperian sense and serves for construct validation. Figure 10.3b denotes the case in which we have a broad predictor construct and a narrow criterion; they do not correspond in nomothetic span. This case illustrates the problems in the Epstein–Mischel debate about the validity of personality trait dispositions. Epstein (1980, 1983; Epstein & O'Brien, 1985) focused on the importance of aggregation and demonstrated that he could boost on validity, but Mischel (Mischel & Peake, 1982) insisted on the predictability of behavior in the specific situation.

Figure 10.3c illustrates the case of narrow predictor and broader criterion constructs. This case has a sad tradition in psychology. Applying construction principles of homogeneity in assessment via Cronbach alpha or Kuder–Richardson estimates, we drill a smaller and smaller hole into a construct, gaining internal consistency reliability but losing nomothetic span. Many of our assessment tools derived this way later show chronically low validity because they have lost the nomothetic span of criteria we are interested in. Figure 10.3d is the hybrid case, in which we have a mismatch at the same level of generality (i.e., only partial overlap). Validity is different from zero, but is this an indication of convergent or discriminant validity?

This visualization is immediately evident, and it is easy to find examples in which we might have fooled ourselves. We can apply the same principles to the relationship between the treatment boxes and the criterion box. Doing this, we ask how the intervention is operationalized or assessed. Figure 10.4 shows the ETR box.

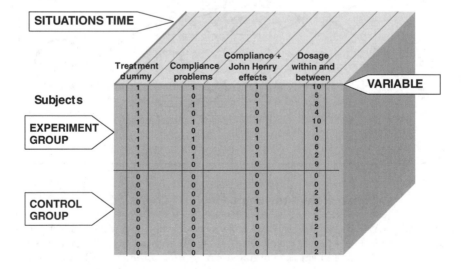

Figure 10.4. A closer look at the experimental treatment box.

Opening that black box, we find, for the randomized experimental control group design, a single dummy variable only, contrasting the experimental group with numbers 1 with the control group with numbers 0. This is a poor and crippled assessment from the stance of a psychometrician when we consider the treatment being a comprehensive intervention or a whole treatment package or program. What about maintaining treatment differences over time? What about dosage differences? What about treatment integrity and fidelity? What about delivering the treatment as intended? It is another irony or paradox that so much is invested in measuring the dependent variables but forgotten for the independent variables in experiments. What insights result if we look at the independent variable in a typical experimental design from a psychometric stance? What is its reliability? Wittmann (1988), in a multivariate reliability theory, proposed a solution and equations, but we have found no application of that concept so far. Reliability is defined as true variance divided by observed variance. True variance is the systematic variance between groups, and the observed total variance is variance between groups plus variance within groups. Looking at the treatment/control dummy (Figure 10.4), we immediately see that the pooled variance within groups is 0. Thus, an experimenter implicitly assumes that the reliability of the independent variable is always 1! But this is wishful thinking, because of compliance, implementation, John Henry effects (compensatory rivalry), and dosage problems, among many others. We can anticipate that there must be variance within groups, but how large is that variance? Good experimental planning asks for manipulation checks. Unfortunately, these manipulation checks test whether there is any difference between the experimental and the control group only. Often, chi-squares are used for that purpose. With a significant chi-square, we know that the manipulation was successful, but we know little about reliability, except that it is different from zero. To find how much an effect size is attenuated, we must compute that coefficient. In some examples discussed later, we found that reliability was chronically low. Lack of power to detect an effect when it is there is the inevitable consequence. According to Cronbach (1957, 1975), this is another consequence of the two disciplines of scientific psychology. He thought more about the conceptual problems, but the two disciplines also had developed their own favorite tools and failed to synthesize them. Cohen's (1968) seminal paper also took a long time until it was finally brought into data analysis. This caused most graduate programs to teach only ANOVA, which in turn caused the next generation of researchers to learn little about multiple regression/correlation, the general linear model, and how it can be used to analyze almost every design. Those who learn both methods risk wasting a great portion of their time.

The principles of symmetry related to Brunswik's lens model cannot be assessed either verbally or visually alone, but require a mathematical numerical equation, thanks to an elegant solution given by Tucker (1964). Here is the original form of that equation.

$$r_{PR,CR} = G_{PR,CR}R_{PR} \cdot R_{CR} + C_{PR,CR}\sqrt{(1 - R_{PR}^2)(1 - R_{CR}^2)} \tag{1}$$

The observed predictor–criterion correlation is explained by several parameters. The first part is related to a linear model and the second part to a model

194   WITTMANN AND KLUMB

that contains nonlinear aspects and random error. R_{PR} and R_{CR} are linear models of the predictor and criterion, respectively; they have to be computed by regressing a higher level construct on its lower level indicators. $G_{PR,CR}$ is the correlation between these two linear models. The terms $(1 - R_{PR}^2)$ and $(1 - R_{CR}^2)$ contain variance not accounted for by the linear model; thus, they map all systematic nonlinear variance and error. Parameter $C_{PR, CR}$ is the correlation between the nonlinear models of both sides in the sense of orthogonal polynomials, where the linear models already have been partialed. In developing Equation 1, Tucker gave a helping hand to those analyzing problems in human judgment and decision making, but his equation has much more generality, and we consider it as the most important equation psychology has developed thus far. From psychometric theory, we know that no measures are perfectly reliable and correlation coefficients may vary because of selection effects and sampling error, so we simply augmented these concepts into Tucker's lens model equation. Equation 2 shows this augmented equation for the relationship between the ETR box and the CR box, because our focus here is on how we can fool ourselves with experiments.

$$r_{\text{ETR,CR}}^{\text{observed}} = S_l \sqrt{r_{\text{tt}}^{\text{ETR}(l)} \cdot r_{\text{tt}}^{\text{CR}(l)}} \ G_{\text{ETR}(l),\text{CR}(l)}^{\text{true}} \cdot R_{\text{ETR}(l)} \cdot R_{\text{CR}(l)} + \tag{2}$$
$$S^{\text{n}} \sqrt{r_{\text{tt}}^{\text{ETR}(n)} \cdot r_{\text{tt}}^{\text{CR}(n)}} \ C_{\text{ETR}(n),\text{CR}(n)}^{\text{true}} \cdot R^{\text{ETR}(n)} \cdot R_{\text{CR}(n)} + e$$

The additional parameters are as follows: The terms $r_{\text{tt}}^{\text{ETR}(l)}$ and $r_{\text{tt}}^{\text{CR}(l)}$ are the classical psychometric reliabilities of the linear models of the operationalization of the experimental treatment and the criterion, respectively. The terms $r_{\text{tt}}^{\text{ETR}(n)}$ and $r_{\text{tt}}^{\text{CR}(n)}$ are the psychometric reliabilities of the nonlinear models, and e stands for error. S_l and S_n mean linear and nonlinear models denoting selection effects. Dawes and Corrigan (1974) demonstrated the robust beauty of linear models in psychology and the social sciences, so we simplify Equation 2 by dropping the nonlinear term. Parameter S is equal to 1 only when the sample standard deviation is equal to the population standard deviation; when SD_{sample} is smaller than SD_{pop}, S is smaller than 1; and when SD_{sample} is larger than SD_{pop}, S turns out to be larger than 1. S is only a placeholder to denote the selection problems that have been known since Thorndike (1949). Hunter and Schmidt (1990) gave the following equation:

$$r_{\text{sample}} = u \ r_{\text{pop}} \sqrt{(u^2 - 1) \ r_{\text{pop}}^r + 1}, \text{ where} \tag{3}$$
$$u = SD_{\text{sample}} / SD_{\text{pop}}. \tag{4}$$

To demonstrate how large S gets under selection, we have constructed a nomogram for a rough calculation of these effects (Figure 10.5).

The abscissa shows u and the ordinate r_{sample}; for r_{pop}, we have chosen small (.10), medium (.30), and large (.50) effect sizes (Cohen, 1992). Restriction of range occurs when $u < 1$ and enhancement of range when $u > 1$. For small effect sizes in the population, there is a linear relationship: The larger the effect size, the more nonlinear the effect of u is. When the standard deviation in the sample is only half of the standard deviation in the population (i.e., $u = .50$), with a large effect size, we get only a sample effect size = .28, and S would

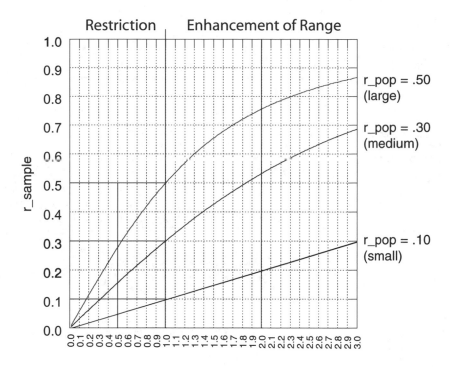

Figure 10.5. Nomogram for selection effects: parameter S.

be .28/.50 = .56. If $u = 2.0$, then the sample effect size is roughly .76. S is then .76/.50 = 1.52; it tells us how much we overestimate the effect in the population. To underscore the importance of the modified Tucker lens-model equation, it is shown again in its linear parts as Figure 10.6.

The true effect size in the population is surrounded by parameters that either attenuate or augment it. There are six dangers of underestimating a true effect and only two dangers of overestimating it. Therefore, the odds of underestimation are higher than those of overestimation! This is an important lesson and gives an idea about how much psychology has fooled itself in regard to its research results. The observed effect sizes are used as a decision aid to evaluate the impact and worth of psychological strategies and interventions. Fortunately, we now have meta-analysis for these summative evaluation purposes. Glass (1983), Hunter and Schmidt (1990), and Rosenthal (Rosenthal, Rosnow, & Rubin, 2000), among many others, have contributed to popularizing meta-analysis. Glass synthesized experiments in psychotherapy, Hunter and Schmidt started synthesizing validity coefficients in personnel selection research and termed their approach "validity generalization," and Rosenthal synthesized the p values from significance testing. All these approaches are now under a common framework. (See Rosenthal et al., 2000.) The d and r families of effect sizes can easily be transformed into one another. The effect size r can be transformed into Cohen's d as

$$d = r / \text{sqrt } (pq(1 - r^2)), \tag{5}$$

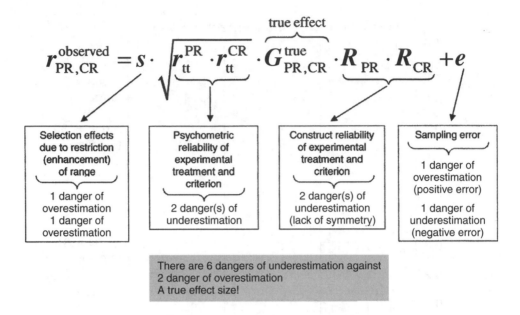

$$r_{PR,CR}^{observed} = s \cdot \sqrt{r_{tt}^{PR} \cdot r_{tt}^{CR} \cdot \overbrace{G_{PR,CR}^{true}}^{\text{true effect}} \cdot R_{PR} \cdot R_{CR}} + e$$

Selection effects due to restriction (enhancement) of range	Psychometric reliability of experimental treatment and criterion	Construct reliability of experimental treatment and criterion	Sampling error
1 danger of overestimation 1 danger of overestimation	2 danger(s) of underestimation	2 danger(s) of underestimation (lack of symmetry)	1 danger of overestimation (positive error) 1 danger of underestimation (negative error)

There are 6 dangers of underestimation against 2 danger of overestimation
A true effect size!

Figure 10.6. The Brunswik lens equation for relating experimental treatment (ETR) to criteria (CR).

where p and q are the proportion of participants in the experimental and control group, respectively. For $p = q = .50$, where we have the same number of participants randomized to both groups, we get the simplification $d = 2r/\sqrt{1 - r^2}$. Inserting Equation 3 into Equation 5, we would learn how much d is attenuated or augmented by the research artifacts discussed earlier.

For the experimental approach, we must reflect on what the possible distribution of the independent variable is. Is it normally distributed, rectangular, or something else? Causes do not have a distribution; they differ only in dosage level or strength. In asking what the right dosage is, we know that dosages too high are often lethal or could be a waste of effort. Lipsey (1990, 1993) discussed the independent variable and the role of theory. He distinguished five different types of dose and response relationships, which differ by the onset process of an effect as a function of dosage. The first is a step function mapping a sharp and maximal onset, the second and third nonlinear functions mapping effects for strong or weak doses, the fourth and fifth U-shaped and inverted-U functions. These theoretical considerations are important in realizing the MAXMINCON principles recommended by Kerlinger (1973), which state that one should maximize (MAX) the effect between groups but minimize (MIN) the variance within and control (CON) for unwanted systematic variance. The experimental and control group must differ in the dosage level, and the split by which we map our treatment dummy must correspond to that level at which we assume that an onset of the response occurs. For such unitary causes, we need a lot of theoretical knowledge about where to make the split. In most program evaluation, whole treatment packages are the interventions, and we can assume that several causes should be at work. Whatever the dose–response functions of the unitary causes are, the composite-cause distributions are probably normal again, so few people will receive a low and few a high composite dose, and we again can hope to profit from the robust beauty of a linear model assuming a linear relationship between response (most often also a normally distributed composite) and composite dosage. Now the question of where to make the split in complying with the MAX principle brings us back to the problems of enhancement of range mentioned earlier. The popular strategy of using extreme groups from both tails of the composite cause brings more power into the design but gives no answer to whether we can generalize such an effect. Nevertheless, once we know parameter S, we can correct the effect we find in such designs after we implement the program to the full population and can guess whether such an effect would be worth the investment. Restriction-of-range problems have their mirror in thinking about how much the psychology students used in our experiments represent the full population. Cohen (1983) warned us about the cost of dichotomization of a normally distributed variable. Assuming a normally distributed composite, he demonstrated a proportional loss of .80 once we make the split at the median; splits farther away from the median result in a still more dramatic reduction of effect size and the inevitable loss of power.

The main point of all these considerations is that psychology is under the permanent threat of underestimating the effects of all types of its interventions and strategies it has developed thus far. Cohen was much depressed finding that the power of the research design to detect medium effect sizes had declined from .48 (Cohen, 1962, 1977) to .25 when Sedlmeier and Gigerenzer (1989) reported their second look at research results.

Meta-Analysis and the Brunswik Lens Model Equation

Hunter and Schmidt (1990) used the parameters of Figure 10.6 to investigate how far the variability in the parameters around the true effect can explain the variability of observed effect sizes. They proposed the 75% rule, meaning that when 75% of the variance of observed effect sizes can be explained by these artifacts, the overall effect can be generalized and there is no need for looking additionally at moderators that can explain the true effect variability. They used this rule mainly for personnel selection research, which is represented by the relationship between the PR and the CR boxes in the five-data-box conceptualization. Their conclusion was that in this area the 75% rule is given, and so far, one can generalize the validity coefficients of the tests used. Consequently, there is no need to validate them anew in each selection situation! Smith, Glass, and Miller (1980) also investigated whether selected aspects of research quality are correlated with effect sizes resulting from the experimental designs used in psychotherapy research. They found no substantial correlations. Wittmann and Matt (1986) looked at German-speaking psychotherapy research only and used a more extended rating scheme of quality according to internal, statistical conclusion, external, and construct validity (Cook & Campbell, 1979); they also distinguished the construct validity of causes and effects and differences in external validity (e.g., do the intentions to generalize correspond to the design used?). This Northwestern rating scheme unraveled substantial correlations with effect sizes. When only the variables used by Smith et al. (1980) were analyzed, there were no substantial correlations, thus replicating their results even in German-speaking psychotherapy research, but this also meant that the extended rating of quality made a difference (Wittmann, 1985, 1987b). Behavioral interventions had higher effect sizes compared with psychodynamic ones. The main reason for that was the use of assessment instruments in the CR box. The former better tailored these instruments to what is treated and what is tested, more behavioral checklists and instruments thought to be sensitive to change in the first place, whereas the latter more often used broad dispositional personality scales based on trait theory and trimmed to stability aspects of behavior. Therefore, the psychodynamics fell more than others did into the asymmetry trap visualized in Figure 10.3c. A lead indicator was whether the design was designed a priori as a follow-up study, taking a larger slice of the time–situation coordinate of the CR box. Those who did design it that way had a better hypothesis about the stability of effects and their generalizability over time, used multimethod and multivariate assessments, and focused more on specific aspects of personality and specific subgroups. One can speculate that when a follow-up design with extended postmeasures over time is used, the researchers would already have accumulated more knowledge about causal effects, making them confident that the intervention works. Otherwise they would not have invested the extra resources these designs require.

With regard to the importance of design validity, we found significant correlations for all four Northwestern standards, but the construct and external validity were relatively more important than internal and statistical conclusion validity. This sheds an interesting spotlight on Cronbach's stance discussed earlier.

To test the Brunswik symmetry principles, we built an index mapping symmetry between the causes and effects in terms of external and construct validity, with low scores indicating high symmetry and high scores indicating high asymmetry. Figure. 10.7 shows effect-size box plots as a function of asymmetry, and the overall distribution bolsters our hypothesis.

Secondary Analysis of Three Selected Research Studies

Encouraged by the promises of the Brunswik symmetry framework, we took a second look at three different single-research studies. The first is a longitudinal study of Fahrenberg, Myrtek, Kulick, and Frommelt (1977) sampling behavioral observations over 8 weeks, which we used as an attempt to validate Eysenck's personality theory (Wittmann, 1987a). The second is a program evaluation study by Lösel, Köferl, and Weber (1987) about the training effects of prison officers (Lösel & Wittmann, 1989). The third is a comprehensive quasi-experimental study by Klumb (1995) to test the validity of a questionnaire related to Donald Broadbent's memory-based theory of cognitive failures and lapses.

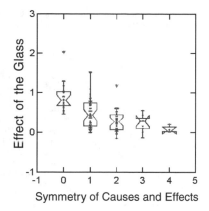

Figure 10.7. German psychotherapy effects as a function of symmetry. 107 effects from Wittman and Matt (1986) and the extension by Spinner (1991). Low scores represent high symmetry.

The Promise of Longitudinal Designs for Personality Traits (Fahrenberg et al., 1977)

Fahrenberg's lab at the University of Freiburg, Germany, is most well known for its focus on psychophysiology. Fahrenberg also developed the most-used German-speaking personality inventory, the *Freiburger Persönlichkeits-inventar* (FPI). The FPI (Fahrenberg, Hampel, & Selg, 2001), among other dimensions, also measures Eysenck's extraversion and emotional lability (neu-roticism) factors. In the study, we assessed 20 students over 8 weeks. At the beginning, the students took the FPI, and over the 2-month period they kept daily diaries with many behavioral observations and self-ratings. Two times per week, they visited the lab, where they took psychophysiological assessments and were rated by the researchers. In the secondary analysis, we scanned Eysenck's research and literature about what he claimed to be indicators of extraversion and neuroticism. We found eight indicators for extraversion and seven indicators for emotional lability in Fahrenberg et al.'s study. From a theoretical stance, we assumed that traits are dispositional constructs. A dispo-sition is a tendency to act in a specific situation (here, a day) in the direction of the dispositional construct. We do not expect that the postulated behavior will show up consistently in each situation, but in the long run those high on the trait should show the behavior or feeling more often than those with low scores on the construct. This postulates higher Brunswik symmetry of traits with aggregated criteria over time. Brunswik symmetry in this case is nothing more than the principle of correspondence in target, context, action, and time proposed by Fishbein and Ajzen (1975) in attitude research. They proposed to distinguish among single acts, repeated single acts, and multiple acts in a relatively specific situation or time frame and repeated multiple-act criteria (RMAC), which aggregate functionally equivalent behaviors and feelings

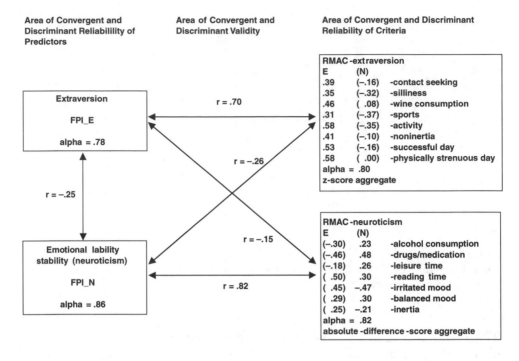

Area of Convergent and Discriminant Reliabilility of Predictors

Area of Convergent and Discriminant Validity

Area of Convergent and Discriminant Reliability of Criteria

Extraversion

FPI_E

alpha = .78

r = .70

r = −.26

r = −.25

Emotional lability stability (neuroticism)

FPI_N

alpha = .86

r = −.15

r = .82

RMAC -extraversion
E	(N)	
.39	(−.16)	-contact seeking
.35	(−.32)	-silliness
.46	(.08)	-wine consumption
.31	(−.37)	-sports
.58	(−.35)	-activity
.41	(−.10)	-noninertia
.53	(−.16)	-successful day
.58	(.00)	-physically strenuous day

alpha = .80
z-score aggregate

RMAC -neuroticism
E	(N)	
(−.30)	.23	-alcohol consumption
(−.46)	.48	-drugs/medication
(−.18)	.26	-leisure time
(.50)	.30	-reading time
(.45)	−.47	-irritated mood
(.29)	.30	-balanced mood
(.25)	−.21	-inertia

alpha = .82
absolute -difference -score aggregate

Figure 10.8. Testing Eysenck's Extraversion–Neuroticism theory in the Brunswik symmetry framework. Time series data of 20 students assessed over 8 weeks (from Fahrenberg et al., 1977). FPI = the German-speaking personality inventory *Freiburger Persönlichkeitsinventar*. RMAC = repeatedly measured multiple-act criteria.

(RMAC) over many situations or periods. For the extraversion RMAC, we could aggregate over 60 days. The RMAC for emotional lability was constructed by means of absolute difference scores. For these indicators, we first computed mean level for each half-week and then an absolute difference score per week, which then was aggregated over all 8 weeks. The reason was dictated by the meaning of the construct: Lability should show up as variability, and the absolute difference scores are an attempt to assess the ups and downs over a longer time. Figure 10.8 shows the results.

Applying Campbell and Fiske's (1959) principles of convergent and discriminant validity yields impressive results. Eysenck's theory postulates extraversion and neuroticism to be independent. The low correlation in this sample is not significant; in addition, the discriminant validity coefficients are insignificant and the convergent validity coefficients are impressively high, much higher than what Mischel (1968) had coined as a personality coefficient. Almost perfect Brunswik symmetry would result with the reliability estimates for correction for attenuation. Although we are aware of the limitations of a sample size of 20 and the dangers of generalization to the whole populations of either students or all persons, the generalizability over time is impressive. The results also hint at a possible solution of the Epstein–Mischel debate. Personality traits might be very good predictors for aggregated multiple-act criteria but not so good for a specific single act. However, we still have to wait for answers to what brings the same amount of predictive validity for situation-specific behavior; that is, what are the decisive situational characteristics, despite the massive restructuring of the majority of psychological departments in the world favoring social psychology? The study had neither an ETR nor an NTR box, but we can nevertheless speculate what must be done once we think about changing these traits. Because of the multifaceted criteria and the predictive success, we can assume that Eysenck's factors are multifaceted as well. So, to change them, we need a corresponding symmetrical intervention, which can only be a multi-faceted treatment package. We saw that variability in the use of alcohol, drugs, and medication plays a role. It was not the mean level in these parameters but their ups and downs, so what triggers their onset? How should we deal with relapse prevention? How can we stabilize mood variability? Should we use medication or cognitive–behavioral interventions? How can we deal with the variability in leisure time? What are the right treatments to better balance social activity with retreat? An experienced clinician should get many hints on how to package a comprehensive composite treatment to change these traits, given that subjects regard them as a problem.

Training Prison Officers With Psychological Interventions (Lösel et al., 1987)

Prison officers are the people who have the highest amount of contact with prisoners. Therefore, training and supplying them with helpful skills should be a promising strategy to empower them as change agents. Behavior therapy and Rogerian types of intervention have a lot to offer for changing behavior, emotions, feeling, and interpersonal skills. Four trainers with a behavioral therapy background and four trainers with a Rogerian background were used. They were partially randomized and matched to train and educate 11 or 12 prison officers in each group. The groups were compared with each other and with an untrained control group. The program-centered training (PCT) groups followed the tradition of behavioral learning theory, whereas the group-centered training (GCT) groups followed the tradition of T-group laboratories. As criterion measures, theory-derived outcome variables were chosen to map effects, which can be best expected on the basis of what each intervention trains. Attitudes toward using psychological knowledge in prison and reactions in specific test situations emphasizing behavioral competencies and communicative sensitivity were used as criterion variables. The first two are closer related to what was taught in the PCT groups, and communicative sensitivity is closer to what was taught in the GCT groups. The training took 1 week, all training sessions were videotaped, and the posttests were given 5 month after training. Data analysis showed no significant differences between the PCT and GCT groups on the first criterion. The effect size was $r = .11$, $t(92) = 1.08$. In

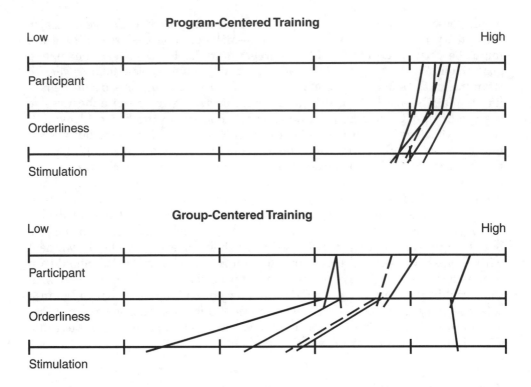

Figure 10.9. Behavior of group trainers as perceived in single courses (plain lines) and on the average (dashed lines).

the second criterion, the effect size was $r = .06$, $t(91) = 0.53$, *ns,* and neither was significantly different from the control group. For the third one, most relevant for the GCT group, there was a significant difference from the control group but no significant difference from the PCT group. Effect size here was again $r = .11$, $t(91) = 1.09$. The summative evaluation would have ended as another example of no-difference research or an additional study to bolster Rossi's (1978) iron law of program evaluation had we not taken a closer look at treatment integrity. All videotaped training sessions were process evaluated by time-sample analysis. As indicators of integrity and intensity, three dimensions assessing trainer behavior from the video time samples were rated and aggregated over all time samples according to participant orientation, orderliness, and stimulation, following Ryans (1960). The results for the eight courses are shown in Figure 10.9.

As can be seen, the PCT group is rated more homogeneous and with higher average intensity on all three dimensions. Within the GCT group, one course is an outlier and seems to be a most intensive PCT course despite this psychologist being hired as a GCT trainer. Additional information about amount of speech and emotional qualities also confirmed that this trainer was closer to PCT than to GCT. Applying our equation for treatment reliability, we found coefficients of .38 for participant orientation, .48 for orderliness, .33 for stimulation, and

.38 for the total scores over all three dimensions. Obviously, realizing Kerlinger's (1973) MAX principle was not successfully established; treatment homogeneity within groups was lacking. As Figure 10.9 hints, the main reason was the GCT trainer, who behaved as a PCT trainer. Regrouping his sessions to PCT and recalculating the treatment reliability brought coefficients of .80 for participant orientation, .87 for orderliness, .79 for stimulation, and .82 for the total score. The improvement is substantial, but does it pay off in higher effect sizes? Regrouping all participants trained by the GCT outlier under PCT substantially affects the result — and, most importantly, in the correct theory-derived direction. Attitude toward improving behavior via psychological knowledge and reactions in test situations showed effect sizes of $r = .26$, $t(92) = 2.58$, $p < .02$, and $r = .21$, $t(91) = 2.00$, $p < .05$, favoring PCT over GCT. Communicative sensitivity favored GCT, with an effect size of $r = .30$, $t(90) = 2.95$, $p < .01$. In an area in which nothing seemed to work, we now have effect sizes at least of medium size and in the right direction postulated a priori by program theory. What a difference for summative conclusions!

Testing Broadbent's Theory of Cognitive Control (Klumb, 1995)

The naturalistic approach to cognitive processes has been criticized by some researchers (e.g., Banaji & Crowder, 1989; Rabbitt, 1990) and has been defended by others (e.g., Ceci & Bronfenbrenner, 1991; Reason, 1991). In our view, it is not a question of accepting or rejecting an approach as a whole but of pointing out concrete problems and, when possible, adding some ideas toward their solution. As a case in point, let us look at Broadbent's theory of cognitive control. This theory has been investigated on the basis of different methods, one of which is the Cognitive Failures Questionnaire (CFQ; e.g., Broadbent, Cooper, FitzGerald, & Parkes, 1982). This inventory assesses the subjective frequencies of a wide range of everyday failures of action, memory, and perception that are assumed to have a common basis: an inefficient and inflexible style of attentional resource management.

In an attempt to validate a German version of the CFQ within the domains of everyday performance that are determined by the content universe of its items, Klumb (1995) designed a quasi-experiment. She selected three settings—libraries, dry cleaners, and a lost-property office—in which everyday mental slips and lapses could be observed with particular frequency and their authors could be questioned. The CFQ score of those clients was determined on the basis of the individuals who returned books late, tried to pick up their cleaned clothes without a ticket, or were looking for an object they had lost, respectively. These individuals constituted the experimental groups. Individuals who did not show the behavior in question at the same times and locations were assigned randomly to the control groups. In the lost-property office, these were people who reported to be present on behalf of somebody else. As a manipulation check, individuals within experimental and control groups were asked to indicate how often each of the three target failures (i.e., returning books late, forgetting dry-cleaner's tickets, and losing objects) had happened to them in the last 6 months. Table 10.1 shows the results.

Table 10.1. Distribution of Answers to the Control Questions for Experimental and Control Groups in the Respective Settings

	Hardly ever	Quite rarely	Occasionally	Quite often	Very often
Library groups					
Experimental	1	9	9	12	13
	2.3%	20.5%	20.5%	27.3%	29.5%
Control	19	19	13	6	1
	32.8%	32.8%	22.4%	10.3%	1.7%
Dry-cleaning groups					
Experimental	0	4	4	4	2
		28.6%	28.6%	28.6%	14.3%
Control	15	7	0	0	1
	65.2%	30.4%			4.3%
Lost-property office groups					
Experimental	1	15	0	2	0
	5.6%	83.3%		11.1%	
Control	8	8	1	1	0
		44.4%	44.4%	5.6%	

The manipulation checks in the library and the dry cleaners yielded significant chi-squares, whereas the one in the lost-property office did not. This yielded an overall manipulation that was still significant. Because the manipulation check was significant, the overall correlation between the treatment dummies and the CFQ scores was computed and turned out to be $r_{pb} = .18$, which is highly significant with a sample size of 176! Is that a convincing demonstration of the validity of Broadbent's CFQ? Probably not. Many will echo Walter Mischel's (1968) synthesis that explaining the meager proportion of 3% to 4% of the behavioral variance dispositional variables cannot successfully predict human behavior. What about the reliability of the treatment dummy? Reliability in the library group is .30, in the dry cleaners .46, and in the lost-property office .07. The true correlation between CFQ and behavior is dramatically attenuated. This lack of reliability resulted in a severe loss of power. What about correcting for attenuation or for effects of dichotomizing the continuous variable of failure intensity?

We could use the full information of all continuous ratings and aggregate this information over all three situations, resulting in a treatment intensity variable called MACT_3. Another possibility would be to believe what people said. Those who told us that such a failure happened to them only quite rarely or hardly ever, although they had forgotten their ticket in the specific situation, were reclassified to the control group; that is, they were assigned a score of 0 in the treatment dummy. Those who agreed that such a failure happened to them more often than occasionally, although not having forgotten their ticket in that specific situation, were reclassified to the experimental group (dummy score of 1). This recoded dummy is called CONDNEW. Now we can compute

Table 10.2. Testing Broadbent's Theory of Cognitive Failures With Different
Variants of Treatment Operationalization

	CFQSCORE E	COND	CONDNEW	CONDSUM	MACT_3
CFQSCORE	1.000				
COND	0.181	1.000			
CONDNEW	0.372	0.542	1.000		
CONDSUM	0.488	0.318	0.667	1.000	
MACT_3	0.542	0.413	0.612	0.794	1.000

Note. Pearson correlation matrix with original treatment dummy COND, reclassified dummy
   CONDNEW; CONDSUM is an aggregate over the three condition dummies and MACT_3 is
   the sum over all original ratings of intensity of cognitive failures in the three situations.
   Number of observations: 176.

the correlations of these modified treatment variables with the CFQ scores.
They are displayed in Table 10.2.

Note that the resulting validity coefficients have climbed from the original
.18 to .54 with MACT_3! The variance explained by CFQ is greater than 25%
compared with the earlier meager 3% to 4%. What about the credibility and
fate of Broadbent's theory? This evaluation is left to you. To be sure, the whole
investigation was a quasi-experiment rather than a true experiment. This fact
notwithstanding, we were able to demonstrate how we can fool ourselves (and
others) in testing theories by not taking into account the reliability of our
treatments!

Five-Data-Box Conceptualization and Symmetry: Some Further Promises for Explanation

The synthesis of the Northwestern school of thought with Cronbach's approach,
the symmetry principles of the lens model, and a bit of thought about the
treatment variables from a psychometricians stance gives some possible explanations for still other problems psychology has faced. Using Cohen's favorite
visualization tools—Venn diagrams—allows us to demonstrate how much more
power we can bring into designs with that synthesis of both schools (Figure
10.10).

When randomization was successful, the ETR-box variables correlated
with neither the NTR-box nor the PR-box variables. This is the major advantage
of getting unbiased estimates of the causal effects of the treatment by using
the Northwestern path. Yet using variables from all three boxes promises to
bring a maximum of power into the design. Selection into treatment is visualized with the overlap of the PR with the NTR box within the CR-box variance.
Yet these selection effects can be modeled according to the knowledge about
time order.

We have seen in the previous examples that treatment reliability often
is very low. This being the case, we can explain another disappointment in
psychological and educational research. Cronbach and Snow (1977) looked

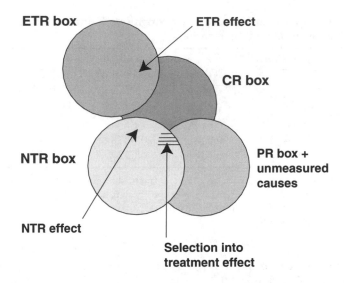

Figure 10.10. Different effects using the five-data-box conceptualization. ETR box = experimental treatment box; CR box = criterion box; PR box = predictor box; NTR box = nonexperimental treatment box.

for aptitude-by-treatment interactions (ATIs), but the overall results of ATI research ended with the depressing summary of Cronbach that interactions were hardly replicable and do not at all generalize. Yet if treatment integrity and therefore its reliability are low, then the reliability of the interaction terms of the partialed product is also low. Aptitude reliability most often is good, but multiplying a variable of poor reliability with one of good reliability still results in an interaction term of mediocre reliability. So should we wonder that interactions did not generalize?[1]

A third promise is a spotlight on the quantitative–qualitative debates. Clinicians often are disappointed that effects they believe they see in their daily practice do not show up after quantification and extensive program evaluation. One can understand that quantification becomes the scapegoat as a consequence. (At the American Evaluation Association now, qualitative interest groups outperform the quantitative ones by a factor of 3 to 4.) The clinicians often check their cases, contrasting them with some matched healthy ones. Although this can be good practice, not being aware of the massive enhancement of range that comes with using such extreme group designs, these individuals easily fell into the trap of overestimating effect sizes. Assume in the context of discovery that they are qualitatively assessing a normally distributed z-score ($SD = 1$) composite cause and have five cases that are 3 standard deviations above the mean. Suppose they contrast them with five cases 3 standard deviations below the mean. Then their sample standard deviation in z scores is larger than 3, so the quotient u (Figure 10.5) is also greater than 3. The

---

[1]Werner Wittmann discussed possibilities for reanalysis with the late Dick Snow at Stanford University but owing to his untimely death, it could not be realized.

nomogram tells us what disappointments result once a representative sample is available. What seems to be a medium-sized (.30) effect goes down to a small one, or what was thought to be a large effect (almost .70) changes to a medium-sized one, which, because of the lack of power, might not even be significant.

Finally, a fourth effect is that we might look in the wrong direction when prediction is less than perfect. The case in Figure 10.3b hints at this; we might have already more information than we need for prediction. It is not that something is missing with regard to the criterion. Our predictor contains reliable systematic, but unwanted, variance, which attenuates validity in the same way as random error does. Theory-derived suppressor principles help here and in Figure 10.3d. The appropriate data analysis is set correlation, with its possibilities of partialing unwanted variance (Cohen et al., 2003).

Summary and Conclusions

The synthesis of the Northwestern school of thought concerning basic and applied research with ideas and challenges from its critics paid off, as demonstrated with examples from different areas of research. Similar successes resulted in large-scale evaluation projects in the German health and rehabilitation system (Wittmann, Nübling, & Schmidt, 2002), as well as research about the relationships among working memory, intelligence, knowledge, and complex problem-solving performance in complex computer-based business games (Wittmann & Suess, 1999) not reported here. The key concepts in all reported examples had been the application of symmetry principles in relating predictors, causes, and effects. Of special additional importance was incorporating psychometric principles into the experimental treatment to improve its measurement and to shed light into the black box. Investing more in the assessment of criteria and taking a larger slice out of human behavior over longer periods helped as well. We are reminded that time-series designs are the strongest quasi-experimental ones in terms of internal validity. Tools coined as ambulatory assessment have been developed to better assess behavior, feelings, emotions, and performance in real-life field settings. Fahrenberg and Myrtek (1996, 2001) contributed to their development and described the potential and promises. We are confident that assessment, measurement, theory testing, and construct validation will reach new horizons by integrating these tools into our research designs.

Epilogue and a Personal Note

It is a great pleasure to have Lee Sechrest, the "Method Man," with his rigorous Northwestern roots and background, as a role model. His ideas about measurement and hints at neglected problems of treatment strength and integrity stimulated our own thinking. We have been impressed by the breadth and the sheer number of areas in which he did research and consultation. We tried to follow his footsteps in psychotherapy, clinical psychology, personality, health, program evaluation, and evaluation research but could hardly keep pace. We are grateful for more than a decade of exchanging ideas, as well as students and coworkers. We enjoyed his regular visits to Germany and the many symposia at international conferences he helped organize. We are grateful for the time he shared with us and especially for his invitations to the famous EGAD (Evaluation Group for the Analysis of Data) dinners at these meetings.

References

American Journal of Evaluation. (2003). Historical records. *American Journal of Evaluation, 24*, 261–288.

Banaji, M. R., & Crowder, R. G. (1989). The bankruptcy of everyday memory. *American Psychologist, 44*, 1185–1193.

Boruch, R. F., & Gomez, H. (1977). Sensitivity, bias, and theory in impact evaluations. *Professional Psychology, 8*, 411–434.

Broadbent, D. E., Cooper, P. F., FitzGerald, P., & Parkes, K. R. (1982). The Cognitive Failures Questionnaire (CFQ) and its correlates. *British Journal of Clinical Psychology, 21*, 1–16.

Brunswik, E. (1955). Representative design and probabilistic theory in functional psychology. *Psychological Review, 62*, 236–242.

Campbell, D. T., & Fiske, D. W. (1959). Convergent and discriminant validation by the multitrait–multimethod matrix. *Psychological Bulletin, 56*, 81–105.

Campbell, D. T., & Stanley, J. C. (1966). *Experimental and quasi-experimental designs for research.* Chicago: Rand McNally.

Cattell, R. B. (1988). The data box: Its ordering of total resources in terms of possible relational systems. In J. R. Nesselroade & R. B. Cattell (Eds.), *Handbook of multivariate experimental psychology* (2nd ed., pp. 69–130). New York: Plenum Press.

Ceci, S. J., & Bronfenbrenner, U. (1991). On the demise of everyday memory: "The rumors of my death are much exaggerated" (Mark Twain). *American Psychologist, 46*, 27–31.

Cohen, J. (1962). The statistical power of abnormal-social psychological research: A review. *Journal of Abnormal and Social Psychology, 65*, 145–153.

Cohen, J. (1968). Multiple regression as a general data-analytic system. *Psychological Bulletin, 70*, 426–443.

Cohen, J. (1977). *Statistical power analysis for the behavioral sciences* (Rev. ed.). New York: Academic Press.

Cohen, J. (1983). The cost of dichotomization. *Applied Psychological Measurement, 7*, 249–253.

Cohen, J. (1992). A power primer. *Psychological Bulletin, 112*, 155–159.

Cohen, J., & Cohen, P. (1975). *Applied multiple regression/correlation analysis for the behavioral sciences.* Hillsdale, NJ: Erlbaum.

Cohen, J., Cohen, P., West, S. G., & Aiken, L. S. (2003). *Applied multiple regression/correlation analysis for the behavioral sciences* (3rd ed.). London: Erlbaum.

Cook, T. D. (1993). A quasi-sampling theory of the generalization of causal relationships. In L. Sechrest & A. G. Scott (Eds.), *New directions for program evaluation: Understanding causes and generalizing about them* (Vol. 57, pp. 39–82). San Francisco: Jossey-Bass.

Cook, T. D. (2002). Randomized experiments in educational policy research: A critical examination of the reasons the educational evaluation community has offered for not doing them. *Educational Evaluation and Policy Analysis, 24*, 175–199.

Cook, T. D., & Campbell, D. T. (1979). *Quasi-experimentation: Design and analysis issues for field settings.* Boston: Houghton-Mifflin.

Cronbach, L. J. (1957). The two disciplines of scientific psychology. *American Psychologist, 12*, 671–684.

Cronbach, L. J. (1975). Beyond the two disciplines of scientific psychology. *American Psychologist, 30*, 116–127.

Cronbach, L. J. (1982). *Designing evaluations of educational and social programs.* San Francisco: Jossey-Bass.

Cronbach, L. J., Ambron, S., Dornbusch, S., Hess, R., Hornik, R., Phillips, D., et al. (1980). *Toward reform of program evaluation*. San Francisco: Jossey-Bass.

Cronbach, L. J., & Snow, R. E. (1977). *Aptitudes and instructional methods: A handbook for research on interactions*. New York: Irvington.

Dawes, R. M., & Corrigan, B. (1974). Linear models in decision making. *Psychological Bulletin, 81*, 95–106.

Epstein, S. (1980). The stability of behavior: II. Implications for psychological research. *American Psychologist, 35*, 790–806.

Epstein, S. (1983). Aggregation and beyond: Some basic issues on the prediction of behavior. *Journal of Personality, 51*, 360–392.

Epstein, S., & O'Brien, E. J. (1985). The person–situation debate in historical and current perspective. *Psychological Bulletin, 98*, 513–537.

Fahrenberg, J., Hampel, R., & Selg, H. (2001). *Freiburger Persönlichkeitsinventar FPI-R* [Freiburger Personality Inventory] (7th ed.). Göttingen, Germany: Hogrefe.

Fahrenberg, J., & Myrtek, M. (Eds.). (1996). *Ambulatory assessment: Computer-assisted psychological and psychophysiological methods in monitoring and field studies*. Göttingen, Germany: Hogrefe & Huber.

Fahrenberg, J., & Myrtek, M. (Eds.). (2001). *Progress in ambulatory assessment: Computer-assisted psychological and psychophysiological methods in monitoring and field studies*. Seattle, WA: Hogrefe & Huber.

Fahrenberg, J., Myrtek, M., Kulick, B., & Frommelt, P. (1977). Eine psychophysiologische zeitreihenstudie an 20 studenten über 8 wochen [A psychophysiological longitudinal study of 20 students over 8 weeks]. *Archiv für Psychologie, 129*, 242–264.

Fishbein, M., & Ajzen, I. (1975). *Belief, attitude, intention, and behavior: An introduction to theory and research*. Reading, MA: Addison-Wesley.

Glass, G. V. (1983). Evaluation methods synthesized: Review of L. J. Cronbach designing evaluations of educational and social programs. *Contemporary Psychology, 28*, 501–503.

Hammond, K. R. (Ed.). (1966). *The psychology of Egon Brunswik*. New York: Holt, Rinehart & Winston.

Hammond, K. R. (1996). *Human judgment and social policy: Irreducible uncertainty, inevitable error, unavoidable injustice*. New York: Oxford University Press.

Hammond, K. R., & Stewart, T. R. (Eds.). (2001). *The essential Brunswik: Beginnings, explications, applications*. New York: Oxford University Press.

Hilgard, E. R. (1955). Discussion of probabilistic functionalism. *Psychological Review, 62*, 226–228.

Hunter, J. E., & Schmidt, F. L. (1990). *Methods of meta-analysis: Correcting error and bias in research findings*. Newbury Park, CA: Sage.

Kerlinger, F. N. (1973). *Foundations of behavioral research*. London: Holt, Rinehart & Winston.

Klumb, P. L. (1995). Cognitive failures and performance differences: Validation studies of a German version of the Cognitive Failures Questionnaire. *Ergonomics, 38*, 1456–1467.

Lipsey, M. W. (1990). *Design sensitivity: Statistical power for experimental research*. Newbury Park, CA: Sage.

Lipsey, M. W. (1993). Theory as method: Small theories of treatments. In L. Sechrest & A. G. Scott (Eds.), *New directions for program evaluation: Understanding causes and generalizing about them* (Vol. 57, pp. 5–38). San Francisco: Jossey-Bass.

Lösel, F., Köferl, P., & Weber, F. (1987). *Meta-Evaluation der Sozialtherapie* [Meta-evaluation of social therapy]. Stuttgart, Germany: Enke.

Lösel, F., & Wittmann, W.W. (1989). The relationship of treatment integrity and intensity to outcome criteria. In R. F. Conner & M. Hendricks (Eds.), *New directions for program evaluation: Vol. 42. International innovations in evaluation methodology* (pp. 97–107). San Francisco: Jossey-Bass.

Matt, G. E. (2003). Will it work in Münster? Meta-analysis and the empirical generalization of causal relationships. In R. Schulze, H. Holling, & D. Böhning (Eds.), *Meta-analysis: New developments and applications in medical and social sciences* (pp. 113–139). Göttingen, Germany: Hogrefe & Huber.

Mischel, W. (1968). *Personality and assessment*. New York: Wiley.

Mischel, W., & Peake, P. K. (1982). Beyond déjà vu in the search for cross-situational consistency. *Psychological Review, 89*, 730–755.

Rabbitt, P. (1990). Age, IQ, and awareness, and recall of errors. *Ergonomics, 33*, 1291–1305.

Reason, J. (1991). Self-report questionnaires in cognitive psychology: Have they delivered the goods? In A. Baddeley & L. Weiskrantz (Eds.), *Attention: Selection, awareness and control* (pp. 406–423). Oxford, England: Oxford University Press.

Rosenthal, R., Rosnow, R. L., & Rubin, D. B. (2000). *Contrasts and effect sizes in behavioral research: A correlational approach.* Cambridge, England: Cambridge University Press.

Rossi, P. H. (1978). Issues in the evaluation of human services delivery. *Evaluation Quarterly, 2*, 573–599.

Ryans, D. G. (1960). *Characteristics of teachers.* Washington, DC: American Council on Education.

Sechrest, L. (1986). Modes and methods of personality research. *Journal of Personality, 54*, 318–331.

Sechrest, L., West, S. G., Phillips, M. A., Redner, R., & Yeaton, W. H. (1979). Some neglected problems in evaluation research: Strength and integrity of treatments. In L. Sechrest (Ed.), *Evaluation studies review annual* (Vol. 4, pp. 15–38). Beverly Hills, CA: Sage.

Sechrest, L., Schwartz, R. D., Webb, E. J., & Campbell, D. T. (1999). *Unobtrusive measures.* Newbury Park, CA: Sage.

Sechrest, L., & Yeaton, W. H. (1981). Assessing the effectiveness of social programs: Methodological and conceptual issues. *New Directions for Program Evaluation, 9*, 41–56.

Sechrest, L., & Yeaton, W. H. (1982). Magnitudes of experimental effects in social sciences research. *Evaluation Review, 6*, 579–600.

Sedlmeier, P., & Gigerenzer, G. (1989). Do studies of statistical power have an effect on the power of studies? *Psychological Bulletin, 105*, 309–316.

Shadish, W. R., Cook, T. D., & Campbell, D. T. (2002). *Experimental and quasi-experimental designs for generalized inference.* Boston: Houghton Mifflin.

Smith, M., Glass, G. V., & Miller, T. I. (1980). *The benefits of psychotherapy.* Baltimore: Johns Hopkins University Press.

Spinner, M. (1991). *Replikation der Meta-Analyse deutschsprachiger Psychotherapieeffektforschung der Jahre 1971–1982 unter Integration unberücksichtigter und neuerer Arbeiten der Jahre 1982–1988* [Replication of the meta-analysis of German-speaking psychotherapy effect size research 1971–1982 considering new research from 1982 to 1988]. Unpublished master's thesis, University of Freiburg, Germany.

Suchman, E. A. (1967). *Evaluative research: Principle and practice in public service and social action programs.* New York: Russell Sage Foundation.

Thorndike, R. L. (1949). *Personnel selection: Test and measurement techniques.* New York: Wiley.

Tucker, L. R. (1964). A suggested alternative formulation in the developments by Hursch, Hammond & Hursch; and by Hammond, Hursch & Todd. *Psychological Review, 71*, 528–530.

Wittmann, W. W. (1985). *Evaluationsforschung: Aufgaben, Probleme und Anwendungen* [Evaluation research: Tasks, problems and applications]. Berlin, Germany: Springer-Verlag.

Wittmann, W. W. (1987a). Grundlagen erfolgreicher forschung in der psychologie [Foundations of successful research in psychology]. *Diagnostica, 33*, 209–226.

Wittmann, W. W. (1987b). Meta-analysis of German psychotherapy outcome studies: The importance of research quality. In W. Huber (Ed.), *Progress in psychotherapy research* (pp. 770–787). Louvain-la-Neuve, Belgium: Presses Universitaires de Louvain.

Wittmann, W. W. (1988). Multivariate reliability theory: Principles of symmetry and successful validation strategies. In J. R. Nesselroade & R. B. Cattell (Eds.), *Handbook of multivariate experimental psychology* (2nd ed., pp. 505–560). New York: Plenum Press.

Wittmann, W. W. (2002). Brunswik-Symmetrie: Ein Schlüsselkonzept für erfolgreiche psychologische Forschung [Brunswik symmetry: A key concept for successful psychological research]. In M. Myrtek (Ed.), *Die Person im biologischen und sozialen Kontext* [The person in a biological and social context] (pp. 163–186). Göttingen, Germany: Hogrefe.

Wittmann, W. W., & Matt, G. E. (1986). Meta-Analyse als Integration von Forschungsarbeiten am Beispiel deutschsprachiger Arbeiten zur Effektivität von Psychotherapie [Meta-analysis as an integration of research exemplified for German studies on the effect of psychotherapy]. *Psychologische Rundschau, 37*, 20–40.

Wittmann, W. W., & Suess, H.-M. (1999). Investigating the paths between working memory, intelligence, knowledge, and complex problem-solving performances via Brunswik-Symmetry.

In P. L. Ackerman, P. C. Kyllonen, & R. D. Roberts (Eds.), *Learning and individual differences. Process, trait, and content determinants* (pp. 77–108). Washington, DC: American Psychological Association.

Wittmann, W. W., & Walach, H. (2002). Evaluating complementary medicine: Lessons to be learned from evaluation research. In G. Lewith, W. B. Jonas, & H. Walach (Eds.), *Clinical research in complementary theories, problems and solutions* (pp. 98–108). London: Churchill Livingston.

Wittmann, W. W., Nübling, R., & Schmidt, J. (2002). Evaluationsforschung und programmevaluation im gesundheitswesen [Evaluation research and program evaluation in health care]. *Zeitschrift für Evaluation, 1*, 39–60.

Wright, S. (1921). Correlation and causation. *Journal of Agricultural Research, 10*, 557–585.

Yeaton, W. H., & Sechrest, L. (1981). Critical dimensions in the choice and maintenance of successful treatments: Strength, integrity, and effectiveness. *Journal of Consulting and Clinical Psychology, 49*, 156–167.

Zee, A. (1989). *Fearful symmetry. The search for beauty in modern physics*. New York: MacMillan.

11

Improving Prediction From Clinical Assessment: The Roles of Measurement, Psychometric Theory, and Decision Theory

Timothy R. Stickle and Carl F. Weems

It is striking to reread the writing of Lee Sechrest on clinical assessment from the 1960s and to realize how little progress has been made in developing useful assessment instruments and procedures since that time. Although one of us (Timothy Stickle) has written with Sechrest on these issues as recently as 5 or 6 years ago and reached many of the same conclusions as he reached long ago, I did not recall, or perhaps failed to appreciate at the time of writing, that a great deal of what we recently published amounts to a summary of many important matters that Sechrest has been trying to get the field of psychology to attend to for at least 40 years. For example, there seems to be a lack of clarity about why we do clinical assessment in the first place. In general, we want to make predictions about behavior—for example, how individuals will behave, what treatment has the greatest likelihood of success, and so forth— and we wish to have some sort of efficiency in our observation. A formalized assessment with structured procedures may sometimes be more efficient than clinical observation over time, and it is very likely to be more efficient than tailing someone to observe their behavior across time and situations (not to mention the ethical problems associated with tailing!). Unfortunately, much clinical assessment conducted by psychologists appears to lack clear goals and offers little practical utility.

The emphasis of this chapter is a discussion of clinical assessment as if its primary purpose is prediction of behavior in a situation or situations. Nonetheless, it is worth mentioning that much of what is typically attained from our assessment tools and procedures is more accurately termed enlightenment.

Some of the material presented here is also presented in Weems and Stickle (2005).

That is, we are often generally "enlightened" by the results of clinical assessments but have limited ability to predict specific behaviors across circumstances. For example, we might say that a youth is perceived to be at the 85th percentile in aggression by her teachers and parents based on responses to behavior checklists. This is probably generally useful information, but it may not help us make specific predictions about her behavior. We might extend our statements a bit more and note that the child tends to be particularly aggressive with same-sex peers. We might add further that she tends to respond more aggressively under stress, but we may (or most certainly will) have difficulty specifying a "cut-point" of the level of stress required to induce aggression. So we are "enlightened" as to a general tendency but can only weakly predict specific behaviors except in the extreme (i.e., when the level of stress is great and the behavior comes as no surprise to anyone acquainted with the individual). In those cases, unfortunately, clinical assessment may not help us improve on predictions that can be made simply on the basis of having nonsystematic observations from parents and teachers. A greater challenge, and one that would be of greater help to clinicians, clients, and families, is predicting specific behaviors in specific contexts from assessment data, rather than relying on less efficient, though reliable, extremes. What has been termed enlightenment here is also sometimes termed an unbounded prediction. That is, we know that the individual has particular tendencies, but we do not really know when he or she is likely to express them (Sechrest, 1968).

It should be noted that recent studies uphold these observations. Evidence is nearly absent in supporting the use of clinical assessment to predict behavior as it relates to treatment response and treatment outcome (see, e.g., Wood, Garb, Lilienfeld, & Nezworski, 2002). Although a handful of studies suggest that providing clients with feedback based on test scores may decrease psychological distress (Finn, 1996; Finn & Tonsager, 1992; Wood et al., 2002), it remains to be demonstrated that individuals are able to distinguish genuine feedback from bogus feedback (e.g., Sundberg, 1955). It is therefore unclear whether classic Barnum effects (response to general and vague "results") can be distinguished from true and more specific responses (Hayes, Nelson, & Jarrett, 1987; Wood et al., 2002).

We conduct clinical assessment for a few other primary purposes that are also related to prediction. Two of these purposes include the revealing of "cryptic" conditions and quantitative tagging (Sechrest, 1968). We are not going to discuss cryptic conditions in any detail. Suffice it to say that although clinical psychology has shown great interest in uncovering so-called cryptic conditions through projective tests and other approaches, there is almost no evidence after 80 years of research that such approaches improve on more direct methods—for example, asking people directly and observing their behavior—except in rare circumstances. (For a review and scholarly discussion, see, e.g., Lilienfeld, Wood, & Garb, 2000.)

Quantitative tags place a value or estimate on dispositions or conditions—for example, the percentile ranking of the previously mentioned youths. We might say, as another example, that a cumulative grade point average is a tag assigned in making decisions about graduate admissions. Such a tag may be considered along with others such as Graduate Record Exam (or GRE) scores and additional information. In clinical assessment, however, quantitative tags can typically be used only to rule in or rule out hypotheses about dispositions. In other words, a quantitative tag provides an estimate of relative standing on some attribute or range of behaviors but is unlikely to be useful beyond generating hypotheses about specific behavioral sets that can be ruled in or out as probable (or not) under particular circumstances or with a particular frequency.

From a variety of surveys about assessment and its use, most psychologists seem to agree that after a few sessions, they have sufficient information from observations of clients to eliminate the need for a formal assessment (Sechrest, Stickle, & Stewart, 1998). There are some exceptions, such as when questions of IQ versus learning disabilities might be at issue with children or adolescents, or when brief, structured observations of parent–child interactions might prove more informative and efficient than typical clinical interviews. Generally, however, formal clinical assessment does not seem to be efficient. A notable illustration of this lack is the large-scale trial of treatment matching for alcohol-related problems called Project MATCH (Project MATCH Research Group, 1997). This well-funded trial attempted to improve on outcomes for alcohol treatment by matching clients to treatments based on assessments of characteristics of those clients thought to enhance response to particular treatments. Unfortunately, little effect was observed, and the treatments appeared to perform about equally, regardless of matching. (See Nathan, 1998.) Our ability to assign particular treatments to particular individuals, with very few exceptions (e.g., Shoham, Bootzin, Rohrbaugh, & Urry, 1996), has a poor history. We simply do not seem to understand the mechanisms well enough, or to be able to measure them with enough validity, to differentially predict who will respond to which treatments ahead of time.

There are several reasons we fail to achieve greater utility from our assessments. The following discussion focuses on measurement and psychometrics, particularly on the validity of assessment measures and procedures. Then, more briefly, some discussion is devoted to the potential gain from an increased use of decision-making theory and techniques with psychological assessment results.

Uses of Assessment

As noted earlier, enlightenment about a person might result from assessment procedures. That is, we might know something general about his or her dispositions, tendencies, and so forth. Unfortunately, that will allow us only to make general statements, and the statements will not be bounded by time or circumstances.

For clinical assessment tools to have value, the measures and procedures used must have incremental validity, the concept Sechrest (1963) formally introduced to the field more than 40 years ago. That is, the assessment has to give us information over and above what we have or could obtain in a cost- and time-efficient manner by other means. If, for example, an interview with a client provides all the necessary information, there is little need to then administer the Minnesota Multiphasic Personality Inventory, an IQ test, or other expensive and time-consuming assessments. Moreover, even if a formal measure or procedure potentially adds something to our understanding of the individual or family, it must do so in a valid fashion; that is, it ought to help us make better predictions. Additional discussion of incremental validity and its relation to construct validity is pursued in the next section.

What Is Validity, Really?

Despite the impression one might gain from the literature, it is only apparently a simple task to validate a measure (Sechrest, 1968). One can pick virtually any peer-reviewed psychology journal of any quality and likely find an article with a statement to the effect that such-and-such a measure is validated or well validated, with little or no reference to the facets to which validity is meant to apply—that is, without reference to what circumstances, persons, traits, other measures, other criteria, and so forth. Moreover, unless the study is a formal validity study, there is scarcely ever any mention of what a measure does not do, that is, its discriminant validity. Typically, what is said is something to the effect that Measure A correlates significantly with Measure B (and perhaps also with Measure C or some set of unspecified measures), and therefore is valid. As a field, we seem to forget that there is no such thing as *the* validity of a test.

An exhaustive recitation of types of validity is beyond the scope of this chapter and likely to be unnecessary for readers of this volume. It is, however, worth mentioning a couple of key points in this area. The relative or incremental validity notion is by now nearly ubiquitous in the literature. Recently published studies that examine incremental validity do so mostly in terms of whether significant variance is accounted for in regression equations, rather than looking at estimates of utility in any more pragmatic metrics, such as time or cost of administration, interpretation, and so forth. Examining whether particular measures account for significant variance is a good base level of examining incremental validity; indeed, that should be an absolute minimum. However, a higher standard for incremental validity of measures is probably in order for clinical assessment. What ought to be required is some demonstration of not only whether there is convergence with other measures of a construct and discrimination from other constructs and measures but also whether the information we derive is at all worthwhile. In other words, it ought to be demonstrated that its value in information justifies the time and cost of administration. Moreover, the measure must provide such information over and above measures that provide similar information in less time or for less cost.

It is worth noting that the idea of construct validity in psychology has largely been trivialized in practice (Sechrest et al., 1998). As originally put forth by Cronbach and Meehl (1955), construct validity required that measures and tests be incorporated into an elaborated theoretical structure, which they termed the *nomological net*. The extensive (and daunting) requirements for embedding measures in theory have been mostly ignored in clinical assessment (and in other areas of psychology as well), thus missing opportunities to capitalize on the provocative and rich implications for better understanding of psychological constructs afforded by Cronbach and Meehl's ideas.

Perhaps the lack of attention to the depth of requirements for construct validity results in part from the fact that, until recently, with modern software and increasing use of confirmatory factor analysis and other structural modeling techniques, the procedures for establishing construct validity have been either unclear, too difficult, or both. In particular, it appears that efforts at establishing construct validity suffer from the same shortcomings as those at establishing incremental validity; these efforts generally fail to distinguish between necessary and sufficient conditions for such inferences and, therefore, stop at establishing some necessary condition without proceeding to the multiple conditions needed to establish sufficient conditions for these inferences. Construct validity, it should be said, exists when everything fits together, not when we have some small bit of evidence of a significant result in a particular direction, or when we obtain or fail to obtain a significant correlation coefficient, and so forth.

Improvements in this area can be made in a number of ways. It does not seem possible to precisely articulate all the conditions for construct validity. It is possible, though, to imagine a number of necessary conditions that together might amount to sufficient conditions. First, the usual approach of establishing some sort of convergent validity is clearly necessary. Second, after Campbell and Fiske (1959), it must be clear that measures distinguish among other, similar or related constructs and therefore can demonstrate discriminant validity. For example, there are numerous measures used in research and clinical practice for which it is not at all clear that what they measure is distinguishable from more general conditions that are related to the condition thought to be assessed by the particular measure (e.g., Reitman, Currier, & Stickle, 2002). These statements are not meant to suggest that the measures are necessarily poor measures. Rather, it is the standards by which measures are evaluated as established or valid that are weak. Many of the measures may, in fact, be excellent. We simply have no way of knowing for sure unless we subject them to more rigorous testing. It is not clear, then, that necessary conditions for construct validity do exist for many of our measures, despite measures being named for the constructs they are thought to measure. Additionally, both convergent and discriminant validity should be established not only concurrently but over time. If the nature of a construct changes over time, then the requirements for measuring it need to be responsive to this aspect. For example, factor invariance across different ages and across time should hold if the disposition is a trait, and should not hold if it is changeable. An observed lack of stability in traits and conditions may be due to changes in the individuals or changes in the way clinicians rate those individuals over time (see Garb, 1998), which reduces construct validity through unreliability.

We offer a specific example later in the chapter, but first we want to comment on the relationship between construct validity and incremental validity. The notion that the simple demonstration of a statistically significant relationship establishes either of these is a bane to our literature. Although such weak evidence is a necessary condition, sufficient evidence for incremental validity of measures, in our view, requires that a given measure be tied to something beyond a significance test. We propose that the concept of a nomological net needs to be used, so that its elaborated structure can provide the context for what, for example, significant variance is being added to. That is, an assessment should make some kind of relative contribution to better measurement of that structure. A known nomological net, which by definition provides the basis for making predictions, can provide the context for demonstrating the value of such assessment measures. That is, it can improve prediction to some degree, which results in greater utility.

Assessment of Child Anxiety: Casting a Nomological Net

A current study that is in progress serves as an example of an attempt to establish construct and incremental validity of assessments in the manner we suggest. The emphasis of this chapter being methodology, an abbreviated summary of our thinking on theoretical matters of the nomological net is summarized. An expanded review and discussion is provided elsewhere (Weems & Stickle, 2005).

   Estimates of the stability and validity of diagnoses of childhood anxiety vary widely. Reports range from 4% to 80% of anxiety disorders diagnosed in childhood that are stable over time (e.g., Keller et al., 1992; Last, Perrin, Hersen, & Kazdin, 1996; March, Leonard, & Swedo, 1995; Newman et al., 1996; see also Silverman & Ginsburg, 1998, for a review). Findings reported in the literature may show such wide variability for several reasons (e.g., the type of disorder, the informant, the sample, the length of the follow-up period). It is interesting, however, that studies of child anxiety have shown wide disparity in stability even for the same disorder across similar time frames. For example, Last et al. (1996) found that about 14% of children with social phobia retained this diagnosis after 3 to 4 years, and Newman et al. (1996) reported that 79% of their participants with social phobia retained the diagnosis 3 to 10 years later. Such inconsistencies in the literature suggest that there are problems with construct validity, that the diagnostic classification system does not measure the "disorder" well in childhood (i.e., there are developmental differences in symptom expression), or that other troubling methodological weaknesses, such as poor diagnostic instruments and reliance on single informants, may affect the extent to which anxiety disorders appear to be stable over time.

Contributing Factors: Descriptive Psychopathology Versus Etiological Mechanisms

The *Diagnostic and Statistical Manual of Mental Disorders* (4th ed.; *DSM–IV*; American Psychiatric Association, 1994) is a notable accomplishment in scientific taxonomy; however, in it, the disorders are grouped primarily on the basis of shared symptomatology. Additionally, the *DSM–IV* diagnoses of childhood disorders are primarily descriptive, emphasizing observed or reported symptoms rather than underlying causal mechanisms (Widiger & Trull, 1993). A major contributing factor to lowered diagnostic validity may result from the failure to adequately use data on etiological mechanisms for forming categories (e.g., Clark, Watson, & Reynolds, 1995; Meehl, 1977; Meehl & Golden, 1982). Both research data and theory suggest that classification at least partly based on etiological mechanisms is likely to improve on validity and stability of groupings, better explain observed heterogeneity, and decrease comorbidity of disorders that share many symptoms (e.g., Andreason & Carpenter, 1993; Clark & Watson, 1991).

The majority of youths who display disordered levels of anxiety do so as a result of a complex interaction among numerous causal mechanisms, including individual risk factors (e.g., behavioral inhibition), problems in their immediate psychosocial context (e.g., parental psychopathology), and problems in their broader psychosocial context (e.g., exposure to violence). Additionally, these causal mechanisms typically operate in a multiplicative fashion rather than in a simple additive fashion. For example, a behaviorally inhibited child with high anxiety sensitivity may develop acute anxiety symptoms if exposed to traumatic stress. Such a child probably has other contributing factors related to family and neighborhood, and his or her vulnerability to developing an anxiety disorder is the product of the interaction between the parent and child, the child and the neighborhood, the parent and the neighborhood, and probably other factors as well (Stickle & Frick, 2002; Weems & Stickle, 2005). Thus, assessment of childhood anxiety and estimates of its stability and long-term outcomes are likely to be inconsistent if they focus mostly on particular risk factors or subsets of symptoms and ignore others that may be contributing to the development or maintenance of the child's long-term outcomes.

Although a focus on risk factors and etiological mechanisms may improve estimates of stability and long-term outcomes, the mechanisms that lead to anxiety disorders often differ across individuals or subgroups of youths who exhibit anxiety. In each case, multiple interacting causal factors contribute to outcomes. The most important causal factors and how they interact to place a child at risk for anxiety disorders may differ across individuals or subgroups (i.e., equifinality). Moreover, individuals with elevations on the same risk factors often do not develop anxiety disorders (i.e., multifinality). Such individual differences in etiology suggest an approach to assessment that does not rely solely on etiological mechanisms. The concepts of equifinality and multifinality serve to underscore the fact that the development of psychopathological conditions, such as anxiety disorders, is complex, not simple, and thus reliance solely on etiological factors would limit a classification system because particular etiological factors may not necessarily lead to or be a problem for every child.

The clinical assessment of anxiety disorders should show increased utility by better assessing the numerous factors, or a nomological net, related to their development and maintenance. We argue here and elsewhere (Weems & Stickle, 2005) that improvement requires assessment of the signs and symptoms (diagnostic criteria) in concert with the underlying mechanisms of the disorder process, as well as a critical examination of the methods used to assess both symptoms and mechanisms. Such an approach, summarized later in this chapter, can help to pinpoint strengths and weaknesses in both the diagnostic criteria and assessment processes and procedures.

A Nomological Net

Anxiety has been broadly conceptualized as a complex response system involving affective, behavioral, physiological, and cognitive components (e.g., Barlow, 1988; Lang, 1977; Marks, 1969). Worry, for example, has been defined as one of the cognitive components of anxiety in that it can be viewed as a normative cognitive response system that prepares the individual to anticipate future danger (e.g., Barlow, 1988; Borkovec, Shadick, & Hopkins, 1991; Mathews, 1990; Weems, Silverman, & La Greca, 2000). Fear, in contrast, has been viewed as a part of the biological response system that prepares the individual for escape (Mathews, 1990). Anxiety disorders are thought to be associated with quantitative or qualitative deviations from the normative mechanisms of the anxiety response system (Barlow, 1988; Vasey & Dadds, 2001). Constructs such as hyperarousal, negative affectivity, intense worry, intense fear, avoidance, withdrawal, trait anxiety, anxiety sensitivity, and cognitive distortions are thought to be some of the specific mechanisms of the anxiety disorder process in youths (Epkins, 1996; Gencoz, Gencoz, & Joiner, 2000; Joiner & Lonigan, 2000; Kendall, 1994; Ollendick, 2000; Silverman et al., 1999; Vasey & Dadds, 2001; Weems, Berman, Silverman, & Saavedra, 2001; Weems, Hammond-Laurence, Silverman, & Ginsburg, 1998; Weems et al., 2000; Weems, Silverman, Saavedra, Pina, & Lumpkin, 1999). That is, deviations from the experience of normal levels of these constructs are associated with anxiety disorders and anxiety-related impairment.

Figure 11.1 presents a general schematic of possible relations between anxiety disorder mechanisms and anxiety disorder diagnoses concurrently and over time. Specifically, the hypothesized underlying mechanisms may be responsible for the disorder or may simply be epiphenomena of anxiety disorders. In other words, anxiety disorders may directly give rise to the deviations in the hypothesized mechanisms. Understanding these interrelations has implications for understanding assessment of anxiety disorders in terms of the construct validity of the classification scheme. Assessing both the symptoms of anxiety disorders and the mechanisms would allow examination of the relative and combined ability of symptoms and mechanisms to predict functional outcomes (e.g., academic, social).

For example, does the diagnosis of generalized anxiety disorder predict poor functional outcomes better than do elevations on measures of specific mechanisms of the disorder, such as hyperarousal, intense worry, or trait anxiety? Additionally, does combining the diagnosis with the mechanisms improve prediction? The answers to such questions again can provide evidence of whether the diagnostic criteria are tapping important core features of the disorder process in childhood, as well as of the extent to which measures of mechanisms improve the construct validity of anxiety and, potentially, provide utility estimates related to the incremental validity not only of symptoms and mechanisms generally but also of each of a wide variety of specific measures used to assess the various dimensions of anxiety.

A nomological understanding of childhood anxiety disorders is not primarily descriptive or etiological. The mechanisms in Figure 11.1 potentially form

Time 1   Time 2

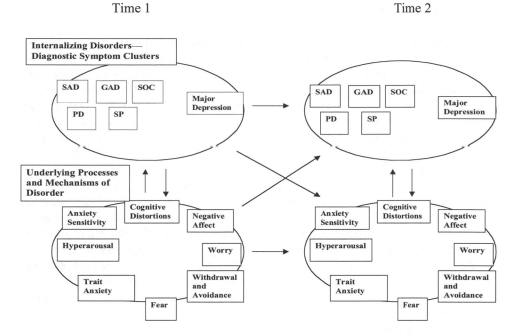

Figure 11.1. A proposed nomological net for childhood anxiety disorders. SAD = symptoms of separation anxiety disorder; GAD = symptoms of generalized anxiety disorder; SOC = symptoms of social anxiety disorder; PD = symptoms of panic disorder; SP = symptoms of specific phobia.

the theoretical structure discussed by Cronbach and Meehl (1955) in their proposed desiderata for construct validation. The theoretical structure or nomo-logical net of anxiety disorders is composed of numerous domains. We consider the two major subdivisions of these domains as (a) the signs and symptoms of anxiety disorders (e.g., *DSM–IV* descriptive diagnostic criteria) and (b) the mechanisms of anxiety disorders (e.g., physiological responses, affect, behavior, and cognitive processes). Moreover, the associations between hypothesized mechanisms that compose the theoretical structure and diagnostic criteria may take various forms. That is, they may have discriminative, predictive, or convergent associations. In the words of Shadish, Cook, and Campbell (2002, p. 69), "The measurement and the construct are two sides of the same construct validity coin."

Although there is likely to be some overlap in the two domains of symptoms and mechanisms, we suggest that detailed assessment of both domains is in keeping with the notion of a nomological net and is a promis-ing avenue for improved measurement of anxiety-related problems. Improved measurement can advance construct validity. An advance in validity will necessarily lead to improved clarification of stability and outcomes over time.

Targets for Improvement

Another factor contributing to lack of clarity about stability and outcomes in research on childhood anxiety disorders may be low correlation among different informants and different methods of assessment. Meta-analysis indicates that the average agreement among youths, parents, teachers, and clinicians is about .25 (Achenbach, McConaughy, & Howell, 1987). It is unclear to what degree low informant reliability results from situational differences in behaviors (Achenbach et al., 1987), method variance (Stickle & Blechman, 2002), inadequate assessment procedures (Sechrest et al., 1998), or poor construct validity (Sechrest, Davis, Stickle, & McKnight, 2000; Sechrest et al., 1998).

An adequate nomological net must operationalize childhood anxiety in several ways both within and across studies (Shadish et al., 2002); that is, minimally, it must use multiple measures. In practical terms, this means both a clearer definition and an explication of the prototypical elements of anxiety (e.g., anxiety sensitivity, hyperarousal), more specific observations about the relationships among these elements (Shadish et al., 2002), a better understanding of the influence of the source of information (e.g., parent, child, clinician), and clearer discrimination between the construct of anxiety and other important and associated conditions (e.g., depression).

A clearer understanding of the correspondence among the diagnostic criteria for anxiety disorders and its underlying mechanisms would be an advance in the construct validity of childhood anxiety disorders. That is, it would constitute a delineation of the critical prototypical elements of anxiety. To increase construct validity, one must clarify optimal measurement strategies of the prototypical elements, be they diagnostic criteria, underlying mechanisms, or both.

One target for improved measurement strategies is to attend to the problem of method variance, which is especially problematic in the assessment of childhood disorders. *Method variance* refers to variability in scores on a trait measure (e.g., anxiety) resulting from something other than the trait (Campbell & Fiske, 1959; Sechrest et al., 2000). Research detailing the characteristics of individual measures and an accounting of how measures of anxiety relate to each other is necessary to establish clarity about the relationships among the different elements of anxiety, the extent to which various elements are stable, and how these elements are associated both with initial impairment and with functional status over time.

In addition to examining the convergent and predictive validity of diagnostic instruments, two other areas can improve assessments of childhood anxiety disorders. We argue that one of them is examining the degree to which increased utilization of information about underlying mechanisms improves validity estimates. Additionally, examining the degree to which the use of multiple informants and multiple modalities (observation, interview, psychophysiology, and self-report) further improves the validity of childhood anxiety disorder assessments appears equally important.

The coverage of specifics of the nomological net is necessarily abbreviated in this chapter. We believe our proposed model, currently being examined empirically, has promise in integrating thinking and research on childhood anxiety. One might reasonably argue that there is an implicit nomological net across the numerous researchers in the area who investigate risk factors and other aspects of the model we discuss. In our view, progress in psychology is much improved by integrating such efforts into a coherent theory and model (e.g., Meehl, 1978). It is our view that models ought to be articulated, tested, and refined or disconfirmed. This chapter, an additional paper with elaboration on the extant research (Weems & Stickle, 2005), and ongoing research are our effort to initiate that progress.

How Using Knowledge From Decision Theory Can Improve Clinical Assessment

Assessment and diagnosis of psychological problems and disorders can be improved by drawing on information used in decision theory and diagnostics in other disciplines. Existing methods to improve the accuracy and utility of decisions are currently underused in psychological assessment. In the simplest case of a binary (e.g., disordered vs. ordered decision), there are four alternatives, two correct and two incorrect. True-positive and true-negative results are correct decisions, and false-positive and false-negative results are incorrect decisions. Figure 11.2a visually presents the diagnostic process in such a case. For this hypothetical example, the task is to distinguish youths who are impaired by anxiety (disordered) from those who are not, and the evidence is provided by multiple measures from multiple sources indicating the number of impairing symptoms from 0 to 8. The two curves in the figure show the probability that a given number of symptoms will occur in conjunction with the diagnostic alternatives (disordered vs. not disordered; Swets, Dawes, & Monahan, 2000). The distributions show symptoms ranging from 0 to 6 for the nonimpaired or nondisordered population, and from 2 to 8 for the disordered population. The two distributions overlap between 2 and 6. Uncertainty about whether any particular individual with between 2 and 6 symptoms is disordered or not is introduced because values in that range are reported on both disordered and nondisordered youths.

The probability distributions of the evidence for diagnosis show that each value on the evidence continuum has a frequency equal to the height of the curve for that group (Swets et al., 2000). Therefore, if a diagnosis is made when a youth exhibits 5 or more symptoms, then we can know the frequency that this is correct by the sections indicated as P(TP), the probability of a true-positive result, and P(FP), the probability of a false-positive result. These two probabilities are equal to the area under the curve and should be considered as joint probabilities rather than as independent ones. That is, knowing whether one is "right" involves a consideration of that joint probability. When the threshold for diagnosis is varied, as in Figure 11.2b, the frequencies of each alternative change (and rather dramatically in this hypothetical example). If we required 6 symptoms for diagnosis, we would eliminate virtually all false positives. However, we would fail to correctly diagnose a large proportion of impaired youths (a high rate of false-negative results).

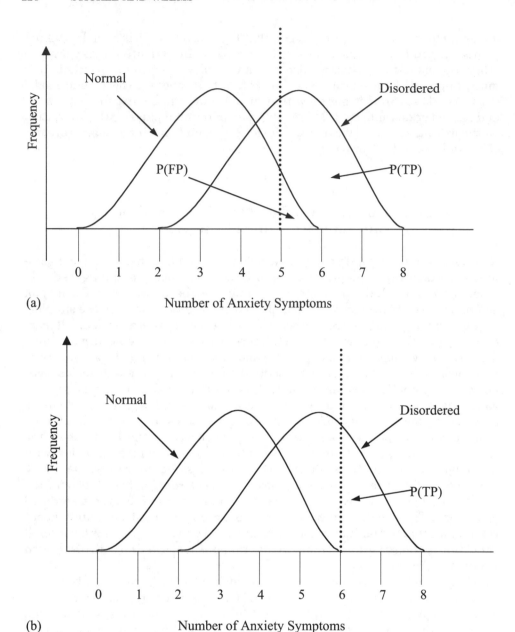

Figure 11.2. (a) Visual representation of diagnostic process in two populations. (b) Visual representation of diagnostic process with no false-positive results. P(TP) = probability of a true positive decision; P(FP) = probability of a false positive decision. The dotted line indicates the decision or cut-point between diagnoses of disorder and nondisorder. From "Psychological Science Can Improve Diagnostic Decisions," by J. A. Swets, R. M. Dawes, and J. Monahan, 2000, *Psychological Science in the Public Interest, 1*, pp. 1–26. © Copyright 2000 by Blackwell. Adapted with permission of the author and publisher.

A decision whether to diagnose in a particular case is influenced by many factors beyond the number of symptoms, including the clinician's judgment about the evidence and the presence or absence of signs and symptoms. (See Garb, 1998, for a review and scholarly discussion.) Statistical prediction rules (SPRs) incorporate probability distributions as noted earlier from combined sources of information and can be used to reduce uncertainty about correct decisions by creating distributions with less overlap. SPRs can also incorporate information to optimize the balance between the various costs of over- or under-diagnosing given a particular application and the consequences of a given decision. In a simple example, for screening purposes, setting a diagnostic threshold at a lower level can be useful when additional information is used to conduct a more refined screening. Alternatively, when an intervention is invasive, costly, or risky, a diagnostic threshold might be set at a somewhat higher level to increase the certainty of a positive diagnosis.

More important, SPRs can be used to set a decision point (e.g., an optimal number of symptoms for diagnosis) to maximize the various considerations of diagnosis, cost, risk, and so forth. In other words, SPRs can maximize the benefit and utility of the diagnostic decision. We provide only a brief conceptual overview of the statistical procedure here. Interested readers can refer to Swets (1996) and Swets, Dawes, and Monahan (2000) for detailed presentations.

There is a set of variations of the well-known receiver operating characteristic (ROC) curve technique. ROC approaches to diagnostic decision making can be used to achieve an optimal balance between objective and subjective information, and to increase both the accuracy and the utility of the diagnostic decision process. SPRs can be derived from ROC analysis, which provides an estimate of the probability of a true-positive diagnosis. Such information can be used alone to make a diagnosis (actuarial decisions) and has been widely demonstrated to outperform clinical judgment about diagnosis (e.g., Dawes, Faust, & Meehl, 1989, 1993; Meehl, 1954). Swets et al. (2000) proposed combining objective and subjective evidence into a single SPR, either to be used as a stand-alone diagnostic decision or to be provided to the clinician who makes the final judgment.

Their proposed approach holds a great deal of promise and is based on balancing information from ROC curves. As noted in Figures 11.2a and 11.2b, the probabilities of making correct or incorrect diagnostic decisions vary with the symptom cutoff (or other threshold). Consideration of that joint probability is necessary to increase accuracy. (If the threshold is raised to decrease the false-positive rate, there is a proportional decrease in the true-positive rate.) An SPR for a particular disorder or condition (e.g., anxiety) is set by selecting variables that discriminate between individuals classified as disordered and individuals classified as nondisordered. This is typically done by using some sort of criterion to determine a diagnosis. In the instance of childhood anxiety, a test of our proposed model will be whether adding measures of the variables we have termed mechanisms increases the accuracy and utility of the information provided by measures of symptoms. Variables are added to a prediction formula to the point of diminishing returns. Determination of the value of any variable or set of variables can be done only over time and numerous trials and by incorporating the relevant cost and time required to gather the information. In short, an SPR provides information about the worth of variables for diagnosis. The utility of that diagnosis also depends, then, on treatment alternatives and their time and cost data.

Part of the promise of a nomological net approach combined with SPRs is the possibility of creating sets of SPRs to assign differential treatments. Assuming a set of effective treatment alternatives with differing mechanisms of action (mediators and moderators), SPRs can be used to combine the relevant information on client characteristics related to the treatment mechanisms of action. With an understanding of the mechanisms of action of treatment (an area still needing considerable work to become viable; e.g., Kazdin, chap. 5, this volume), the utility of assessments can be greatly improved through SPRs. The implementation of SPRs to increase accuracy clearly still requires refinement to make it more pragmatic for use in both research and clinical settings. Nevertheless, it ought to be explored as a core technology for a scientifically oriented practice of psychology.

There are several key points in the application of decision theory to clinical assessment. It should be said that the quality of a prediction based on such an approach relies on the quality of information available to use for diagnosis. To improve the quality of evidence and increase the accuracy of prediction from assessments, we need to take the idea of a nomological net and construct validity seriously. We cannot realistically hope to improve the value of psychological assessment if we do not do a better job elaborating and measuring constructs. Should we make progress in improving the accuracy of decisions, then we can realistically assess the utility of those decisions.

For example, if we are surer about what we are measuring, we can apply this knowledge to how those states, processes, and symptoms should be related to behavior in particular contexts. One prime example is that such assessments may provide a much better idea of mediating mechanisms for treatment targets. To expand a bit on child anxiety mechanisms as an example, if measurement of those mechanisms improves our understanding of the stability of anxiety problems, we can then move to applying our understanding of how those mechanisms affect youths, and they might reasonably be targeted as mechanisms of change in treatments for anxiety.

As we noted earlier, increased utility requires some information about the relative value of intervention alternatives. Again, understanding the nomological net and which features, mechanisms, or symptoms are most impairing for different individuals can help to optimize decisions about treatments, enhance the accuracy of predictions, and increase the value of psychological assessment. For example, an examination of relative cost considerations for alternative treatments or dispositions that might result from assessment results is necessary to balance the relative costs (financial, psychological, opportunity, etc.) of over- or underpredicting impaired status.

To improve prediction—that is, the accuracy and utility of assessments— we should first limit our scope to bounded predictions, using a test or measure to make an inference about a person, couple, or family that is limited in time, situation, or range of behavior (Sechrest, 1968). If such bounded predictions are emphasized more and assessment for enlightenment is emphasized less, a net gain in the utility and credibility of psychological assessment should result. Such an approach enforces a more modest approach to predicting human behavior and is in keeping with the level of prediction about behavior supported by psychological science. Additional improvements to typical approaches can be made by making the use of multitrait, multimethod, multimodality assessments routine and by extending our standards to take construct validity seriously.

Conclusion

Understanding the value of any particular assessment procedure or measure requires that we know what it does in relation to other available measures and procedures. To make sense of that incremental value, it is necessary to do more than simply demonstrate statistically significant variance accounted for in regression analysis. A nomological net ought to be provided as the context for evidence that adding measures to assessment protocols contributes significantly to something of value. We have argued, as Shadish et al. (2002) have noted, that measurement and construct validity are completely dependent on each other. When we begin to look more closely at the validity of our constructs, measures, and assessments, we can begin to improve the accuracy and utility of prediction from psychological assessment.

Although much work remains to conceptualize and measure better constructs, there are numerous opportunities for improvement. Making use of existing tools such as ROC analysis can help optimize aspects of the decision. The extent to which the suggestions in this chapter have practical utility is unknown, but they are worth exploring and can hardly do worse than current approaches.

Epilogue

Lee Sechrest is one of psychology's great minds. Most of how I (Timothy Stickle) think about science and psychology is influenced by having been his student. Upon learning that Sechrest was my dissertation advisor (my dissertation was on a topic in child psychopathology), people often remarked something to the effect, "but I thought he was a measurement person." The truth is that Sechrest has never let traditional content or disciplinary boundaries inhibit his interest in topics or limit his creativity in thinking about problems. Although current demands and contingencies in academic psychology tend to push one to focus on increasingly specialized areas, Sechrest's work, thinking, and writing reflect the fact that he focused on science and psychology broadly, without undue attention to pressures to do otherwise. I do not know to what extent he felt pressure to specialize more; I know only that he has influenced me and many other students to think creatively and to do work that we believe is interesting and important.

I have attempted to write a piece illustrating how Lee Sechrest's ideas and thinking have influenced, and continue to influence, my work in one area of interest. If some notion of his unique way of seeing outside of conventional limits to envision a better, more useful, and important role for psychology comes through, I am indebted to him. Come to think of it, I am indebted to him regardless of whether I have managed to get this across to readers of this volume.

References

Achenbach, T. M., McConaughy, S. H., & Howell, C. T. (1987). Child/adolescent behavioral and emotional problems: Implications of cross-informant correlations for situational specificity. *Psychological Bulletin, 101,* 213–232.

American Psychiatric Association. (1994). *Diagnostic and statistical manual of mental disorders* (4th ed.). Washington, DC: Author.

Andreason, N. C., & Carpenter, W. T. (1993). Diagnosis and classification of schizophrenia. *Schizophrenia Bulletin, 19,*199–214.

Barlow, D. H. (1988). *Anxiety and its disorders: The nature and treatment of anxiety and panic.* New York: Guilford Press.

Borkovec, T. D., Shadick, R., & Hopkins, M. (1991). The nature of normal worry and pathological worry. In R. M. Rapee & D. H. Barlow (Eds.), *Chronic anxiety: Generalized anxiety disorder and mixed anxiety–depression* (pp. 29–51). New York: Guilford Press.

Campbell, D. T., & Fiske, D. W. (1959). Convergent and discriminant validation by the multitrait–multimethod matrix. *Psychological Bulletin, 56,* 81–105.

Clark, L. A., & Watson, D. (1991). Tripartite model of anxiety and depression: Psychometric evidence and taxonomic implications. *Journal of Abnormal Psychology, 100,* 316–336

Clark, L. A., Watson, D., & Reynolds, S. (1995). Diagnosis and classification of psychopathology: Challenges to the current system and future directions. *Annual Review of Psychology, 46,* 121–153.

Cronbach, L. J., & Meehl, P. E. (1955). Construct validity in psychological tests. *Psychological Bulletin, 52,* 281–302.

Dawes, R. M., Faust, D., & Meehl, P. E. (1989). Clinical versus actuarial judgment. *Science, 243,* 1668–1674.

Dawes, R. M., Faust, D., & Meehl, P. E. (1993). Statistical prediction versus clinical prediction: Improving what works. In G. Keren & C. Lewis (Eds.), *A handbook for data analysis in the behavioral sciences: Methodological issues* (pp. 351–367). Hillsdale, NJ: Erlbaum.

Epkins, C. C. (1996). Cognitive specificity and affective confounding in social anxiety and dysphoria in children. *Journal of Psychopathology and Behavioral Assessment, 18,* 83–101.

Finn, S. E. (1996). *Manual for using the MMPI-2 as a therapeutic intervention.* Minneapolis: University of Minnesota Press.

Finn, S. E., & Tonsager, M. E. (1992). Therapeutic effects of providing MMPI–2 test feedback to college students awaiting therapy. *Psychological Assessment, 4,* 278–287.

Garb, H. N. (1998). *Studying the clinician: Judgment research and psychological assessment.* Washington, DC: American Psychological Association.

Gencoz, F., Gencoz, T., & Joiner, T. E., Jr. (2000). Physiological hyperarousal as a specific correlate of symptoms of anxiety among young psychiatric inpatients. *Social Behavior and Personality, 28,* 409–412.

Hayes, S. C., Nelson, R. O., & Jarrett, R. B. (1987). The treatment utility of assessment: A functional approach to evaluating assessment quality. *American Psychologist, 42,* 963–974.

Joiner, T. E., Jr., & Lonigan, C. J. (2000). Tripartite model of depression and anxiety in youth psychiatric inpatients: Relations with diagnostic status and future symptoms. *Journal of Clinical Child Psychology, 29,* 372–382.

Keller, M. B., Lavori, P. W., Wunder, J., Beardslee, W. R., Schwartz, C. E., & Roth, J. (1992). Chronic course of anxiety disorders in children and adolescents. *Journal of the American Academy of Child and Adolescent Psychiatry, 31,* 595–599.

Kendall, P. C. (1994). Treating anxiety disorders in children: Results of a randomized clinical trial. *Journal of Consulting and Clinical Psychology, 62,* 200–210.

Lang, P. J. (1977). Imagery in therapy: An information processing analysis of fear. *Behavior Therapy, 8,* 862–886.

Last, C. G., Perrin, S., Hersen, M., & Kazdin, A. E. (1996). A prospective study of childhood anxiety disorders. *Journal of the American Academy of Child and Adolescent Psychiatry, 35,* 1502–1510.

Lilienfeld, S. O., Wood, J. M., & Garb, H. N. (2000). The scientific status of projective techniques. *Psychological Science in the Public Interest, 1,* 27–66.

March, J. S., Leonard, H. L., & Swedo, S. E. (1995). Obsessive–compulsive disorder. In J. S. March (Ed.), *Anxiety disorders in children and adolescents* (pp. 251–275). New York: Guilford Press.

Marks, I. M. (1969). *Fears and phobias.* New York: Academic Press.

Mathews, A. (1990). Why worry? The cognitive function of anxiety. *Behaviour Research and Therapy, 28,* 455–468.

Meehl, P. E. (1954). *Clinical versus statistical prediction: A theoretical analysis and a review of the evidence.* Minneapolis: University of Minnesota Press.

Meehl, P. E. (1977). Specific etiology and other forms of strong influence: Some quantitative meanings. *The Journal of Medicine and Philosophy, 2*(1), 33–53.

Meehl, P. E. (1978). Theoretical risks and tabular asterisks: Sir Karl, Sir Ronald, and the slow progress of soft psychology. *Journal of Consulting and Clinical Psychology, 46,* 806–834.

Meehl, P. E., & Golden, R. R. (1982). Taxometric methods. In P. C. Kendall & J. N. Butcher (Eds.), *Handbook of research methods in clinical psychology* (pp. 127–181). New York: Wiley.

Nathan, P. E. (1997, September 22). Would a pill placebo have redeemed project MATCH? *Prevention & Treatment, 1,* np. Retrieved October 14, 2005, from http://www.journals.apa.org/prevention/volume1/97_c3-97_a1.html

Newman, D. L., Moffitt, T. E., Caspi, A., Magdol, L., Silva, P. A., & Stanton, W. R. (1996). Psychiatric disorder in a birth cohort of young adults: Prevalence, comorbidity, clinical significance, and new case incidence from ages 11–21. *Journal of Consulting and Clinical Psychology, 64,* 552–562.

Ollendick, T. H. (2000). Sexually abused children: A commentary. *Behaviour Change, 17*(1), 48–50.

Project Match Research Group. (1997). Matching alcoholism treatments to client heterogeneity: Project MATCH posttreatment drinking outcomes. *Journal of Studies on Alcohol. 58*(1), 7–29.

Reitman, D. R., Currier, R. O., & Stickle, T. R. (2002). A critical evaluation of the PSI/SF in a Head Start population. *Journal of Clinical Child and Adolescent Psychology, 31,* 384–392.

Sechrest, L. B. (1963). Incremental validity: A recommendation. *Educational and Psychological Measurement, 23,* 153–158.

Sechrest, L. B. (1968). Testing, measuring, and assessing people. In E. F. Borgatta & W. W. Lambert (Eds.), *Handbook of personality theory and research* (pp. 529–625). Chicago: Rand McNally.

Sechrest, L. B., Davis, M., Stickle, T. R., & McKnight, P. (2000). Understanding method variance. In L. Bickman (Ed.), *Research design: Vol. 2. David Campbell's legacy* (pp. 63–87). Thousand Oaks, CA: Sage.

Sechrest, L. B, Stickle, T. R., & Stewart, M. (1998). The role of clinical psychology. In A. Bellack & M. Hersen (Series Eds.) & C. R. Reynolds (Vol. Ed.), *Comprehensive clinical psychology: Vol. 4. Assessment* (pp. 1–32). New York: Elsevier.

Shadish, W. R., Cook, T. D., & Campbell, D. T. (2002). *Experimental and quasi-experimental designs for generalized causal inference.* Boston: Houghton Mifflin.

Shoham, V., Bootzin, R. R., Rohrbaugh, M. J., & Urry, H. (1996). Paradoxical versus relaxation treatment for insomnia: The moderating role of reactance. *Sleep Research, 24a,* 365.

Silverman, W. K., & Ginsburg, G. S. (1998). Anxiety disorders. In T. H. Ollendick & M. Hersen (Eds.), *Handbook of child psychopathology* (3rd ed.). New York: Plenum Press.

Silverman, W. K., Kurtines, W. M., Ginsburg, G. S., Weems, C. F., Lumpkin, P. W., & Carmichael, D. H. (1999). Treating anxiety disorders in children with group cognitive–behavioral therapy: A randomized clinical trial. *Journal of Consulting and Clinical Psychology, 67,* 995–1003.

Stickle, T. R., & Blechman, E. (2002). Aggression and fire: Antisocial behavior in firesetting and non-firesetting juvenile offenders. *Journal of Psychopathology and Behavioral Assessment, 24,* 177–193.

Stickle, T. R., & Frick, P. J. (2002). Developmental pathways to severe antisocial and aggressive behavior: Implications for interventions for youth with callous–unemotional traits. *Expert Review of Neurotherapeutics, 2,* 511–522.

Sundberg, N. D. (1995). The acceptability of "fake" versus "bona fide" personality test interpretations. *Journal of Abnormal and Social Psychology, 50,* 145–147.

Swets, J. A. (1996). *Signal detection theory and ROC analysis in psychology and diagnostics: Collected papers.* Mahwah, NJ: Erlbaum.

Swets, J. A., Dawes, R. M., & Monahan, J. (2000). Psychological science can improve diagnostic decisions. *Psychological Science in the Public Interest, 1,* 1–26.

Vasey, M. W., & Dadds, M. R. (Eds.). (2001). *The developmental psychopathology of anxiety.* London: Oxford University Press.

Weems, C. F., Berman, S. L., Silverman, W. K., & Saavedra, L. S. (2001). Cognitive errors in youth with anxiety disorders: The linkages between negative cognitive errors and anxious symptoms. *Cognitive Therapy and Research, 25,* 559–575.

Weems, C. F., Hammond-Laurence, K., Silverman, W. K., & Ginsburg, G. S. (1998). Testing the utility of the anxiety sensitivity construct in children and adolescents referred for anxiety disorders. *Journal of Clinical Child Psychology, 27,* 69–77.

Weems, C. F., Silverman, W. K., & La Greca, A. M. (2000). What do youth referred for anxiety problems worry about? Worry and its relation to anxiety and anxiety disorders in children and adolescents. *Journal of Abnormal Child Psychology, 28,* 63–72.

Weems, C. F., Silverman, W. K., Saavedra, L. S., Pina, A. A., & Lumpkin, P. W. (1999). The discrimination of children's phobias using the Revised Fear Survey Schedule for Children. *Journal of Child Psychology and Psychiatry and Allied Disciplines, 35,* 941–952.

Weems, C. F., & Stickle, T. R. (2005). Anxiety disorders in childhood: Casting a nomological net. *Clinical Child and Family Psychology Review, 8,* 107–134.

Widiger, T. A., & Trull, T. J. (1993). Borderline and narcissistic personality disorders. In P. B. Sutker & H. E. Adams (Eds.), *Comprehensive handbook of psychopathology* (2nd ed., pp. 371–394). New York: Plenum Press.

Wood, J. M., Garb, H. N., Lilienfeld, S. O., & Nezworski, M. T. (2002). Clinical assessment of personality. *Annual Review of Psychology, 53,* 519–543.

Part IV

Methodology Mentoring

12 _____

Rear End Validity: A Caution

Bradley H. Smith

One of the unique contributions of this chapter is to give one of the faceless enemies of progress in the behavioral sciences a name. *Rear end validity* is the habit of relying on tradition or accepted practice, rather than sound scientific thinking, to guide procedural decisions in the behavioral sciences. One of the great opponents of rear end validity has been Lee Sechrest. This chapter features some of his informal teachings, namely, "Lee's Laws." I also cite some of the major themes in Sechrest's corpus of writings that should curb the tendency toward rear end validity. Before selectively reviewing Sechrest's formal and informal teaching, I begin with an overview of the classic methodological terms generated during the mid-1950s to the mid-1960s. This overview helps to explain the title of the chapter and the need to continue to develop useful validity terms.

Classic Validity Concepts

The title of this chapter is modeled after Sechrest's (1963) classic "Incremental Validity: A Recommendation," a paper written during a decade that produced an unsurpassed proliferation of classic methodological writings. Most of the meaningful and enduring methodological terms used today were named and described during that fateful decade. For example, Cronbach and Meehl (1955) described the concept of construct validity. Meehl and Rosen (1955) operationalized the crucial concepts of specificity, sensitivity, and efficiency of cutting scores. Campbell and Fiske (1959) explained the utility of the multimethod–multitrait matrix and added the crucial construct validity considerations of trait-method units, convergent validity, and discriminant validity. Campbell and Stanley (1963) elaborated on the concept of quasi-experimentation and defined the terms *internal validity* and *external validity*.

The classic methodological concepts listed earlier in the chapter are so widely accepted as critically important to understanding measurement and research that failing to recognize and correctly describe these terms should be grounds for failing doctoral qualifying exams in the social sciences. However, it is important to realize that the classic validity terms are only a partial list of the myriad important validity considerations pertinent to good research and applied practice. Moreover, it may be appropriate to label destructive practices in behavioral science. Thus, I am taking this opportunity to propose that rear end validity should be added to the methodological lexicon.

Rear End Validity

The working definition of rear end validity in this chapter is "justifying a procedural decision on the sole basis that someone did that same thing previously." It is not rear end validity if there is a strong theoretical or scientific justification for making the procedural decision. Replication is essential to the social sciences. However, only thoughtful replication leads to true progress. Mindless repetition of what has been done before may not only stagnate progress but also perpetuate harmful procedures that either do not fit with a changing social ecology or were never that good to begin with.

An example of rear end validity is adding a measure to a battery simply because someone else used that measure previously. Another example is mindlessly using a two-tailed alpha value of .05 simply because so many others in the social sciences use this cutoff. Perhaps the most heinous type of rear end validity is consciously deciding to use a method that the scientist believes is less appropriate than some alternatives simply because using the inferior method might be more familiar to grant reviewers or journal editors.

Rear end validity has the potential to dampen creativity, fragment science, and inappropriately perpetuate the status quo. These issues are discussed in detail later in this chapter. For present purposes, I reiterate that rear end validity is intended to be a pejorative term. The goal of the chapter is to encourage researchers and service providers to consider to what extent their procedural decisions have been tainted by rear end validity. The cure for rear end validity is thoughtful private and public debate. Sechrest's writings and teachings provide excellent guidance for this debate. To stimulate the debate, the next section reviews some of Lee Sechrest's informal teaching, known to his students as "Lee's Laws." Later sections bring to light some of his writings that are highly pertinent to the issue of rear end validity, especially the issues of incremental validity and translational research.

Lee's Laws

In the early 1990s, an ad hoc subcommittee of the Evaluation Group for the Analysis of Data (EGAD) selected four of Lee Sechrest's frequently expressed guiding principles and dubbed them "Lee's Laws." We created a poster with a picture of Sechrest presiding over his laws. This poster has been on display in the headquarters of EGAD at the University of Arizona for more than a decade. Consequently, Sechrest's recent students and visitors to EGAD should recognize Lee's Laws, which are as follows:

1. Everything eventually turns up.
2. More is better than less.
3. There is rarely such a thing as a true catastrophe.
4. There is nothing in the scientific method that requires doing something stupid.

There are many more memorable sayings in Sechrest's repertoire. I presented several of these pithy statements in my talk at his Festschrift in Tucson in the spring of 2003. However, by unanimous decision of the reconvened ad hoc subcommittee at the Festschrift, only the originally selected laws are published in this volume honoring Sechrest's career. Each law is discussed briefly in the following sections and will reemerge frequently in the discussion of how to fight rear end validity.

Everything Eventually Turns Up

The first law, *everything eventually turns up*, can be interpreted in a number of ways. On a personal level, this law helps to explain Sechrest's filing system, which appears to be random piles of papers strewn throughout EGAD. The scientific potential in Lee's first law is what he calls the helix model of learning. This model of learning is based on the idea that each time a thoughtful person revisits an issue there is some increased understanding of the issue. Rear end validity is thoughtless repetition that does not advance understanding.

According to the helix model, someone new to a concept may be confused at first exposure and, with repeated exposure, may reach a more enlightened level of confusion. Real persistence may eventually result in breakthroughs in understanding. This typically happens with the statistical training of psychology graduate students. Students often unknowingly miss major points in undergraduate statistics, realize that they are missing major points in graduate statistics, and may reach some basic understanding of a specific set of statistical techniques when they analyze their own data during the later years of graduate school. Students who repeatedly publicly discuss statistics make advances. Those who stay away from discussion of statistics or meekly accept what others say about statistics suffer stagnation or deterioration of statistical understanding.

More Is Better Than Less

At a personal level, the second law, *more is better than less*, describes Sechrest's renowned generosity. As graduate students, we originally thought this law applied to food and wine. Sechrest and his wife, Carol, are notoriously hospitable and often lavishly entertain students and colleagues. They set a good example for treating students well and celebrating individual and group accomplishments. Examples include holding annual dinners at four-star restaurants for all members of EGAD, picking up the tab after inviting large groups of students and colleagues to dine at restaurants at conferences, and hosting meals for students at their home, such as the legendary peanut butter soup.

The implications of more is better than less for the social sciences, especially applied behavioral science, is that we must constantly strive to be better. Many psychotherapists breathed a sigh of relief when M. L. Smith, Glass, and Miller (1980) published their quantitative review and concluded that, in general, the therapies reviewed had a positive effect in the .3 to .5 range. These findings have been replicated in subsequent studies (e.g., Lipsey & Wilson, 1993). Many have accepted these reviews as proof that psychotherapy works. Sechrest does not, and one reason is that it violates the principle of more is better than less.

Sechrest is quick to point out that an effect size of .3 to .5 is in the small-to-moderate range. This means that many individuals are not being helped by the intervention. For example, using the binomial effect size calculation (Rosenthal, 1983) with an effect size of .3 means that approximately 35% of the sample does not benefit from the treatment. With an effect size of .5, about 25% of the sample does not improve. In addition to the fact that psychotherapy does not work for 25% to 35% of people seeking help, there is growing concern that some commonly used treatments may cause harm (Dishion & Kavanagh, 2003). Thus, Sechrest's principle of more is better than less suggests that a profession should not be content if its interventions fail to help a sizable minority of clients and may even harm some individuals.

Even if the psychotherapy industry accepts effect sizes in the .3 to .5 range as evidence that psychotherapy works, Sechrest reminds us that effect sizes are meaningful only if the metric of the measures used in the studies is meaningful (Sechrest, McKnight, & McKnight, 1996). For a true understanding of therapeutic change, there needs to be calibration between the measures used in the study and meaningful functioning in everyday life. A study may achieve a mean improvement of 10 points on a depression measure with a standard deviation of 20 points, resulting in an effect size of .5. However, unless that 10-point change is calibrated with something meaningful, the putative improvement is just statistical nonsense. However, if a 10-point change results in a substantial change in functioning, such as a big change in the likelihood of going to work, then the effect size might be taken as evidence of effectiveness. Unfortunately, such calibration is rare, and therefore, the impact of interventions in the behavioral sciences tends to be very poorly understood in terms of its effect on people's lives.

As Sechrest has repeatedly reminded us, our ignorance of the real impact of interventions in the behavioral sciences is unacceptable. The principle of more is better than less should be a rallying cry for improvements in the amount and quality of research related to the impact of psychotherapy and other interventions. When guided by the logic of incremental validity, the principle of more is better than less has the potential to stimulate work that results in substantial improvements in understanding measures and intervention outcomes. For example, new interventions should be required to be better than old interventions, or new measures should explain more variance than old measures.

True Catastrophes Are Rare

Lee's third law, *there is rarely such a thing as a true catastrophe*, reflects his optimism. Because he has so often cautioned us to temper our expectations, such as enumerating some of the likely limitations of prevention (Sechrest, 1993) and measurement (Sechrest, 1985), some might be surprised to hear Lee's students describe him as an optimist. However, to borrow a quote from Ron Gallimore in the *APA Monitor* article on Sechrest's Festschrift (Benson, 2003, p. 45):

> What I learned from Lee in grad school was what many others have as well: How to maintain an optimistic vision of the future of psychology and yet remain a hard-eyed skeptic about the quality of the methods and data underlying it.

Sechrest's optimism can be explained in part by self-agency theory. Specifically, he has high outcome expectations of the potential of behavioral science to improve people's lives. He also has high efficacy expectations that methodological advances will lead to better behavioral science. This configuration of high outcome and high efficacy expectations leads to dogged persistence and a low likelihood of being deterred by setbacks (Bandura, 1997).

Sechrest may appear to have a low opinion of contemporary clinical psychology as it is usually practiced, but this is because he has high expectations for psychology and he measures esteem as a ratio of accomplishment over expectation. Thus, his admonitions and critiques should be viewed as something akin to guidance to a young musician with exceptional potential but who needs to do a lot of work to become a world-renowned concert pianist.

Another consideration regarding Lee's Law that there is rarely such thing as a true catastrophe is based on his life experiences. Sechrest lived through the Great Depression, served as a staff sergeant in the Korean War, and studied some very serious issues. His first two publications were on aircrew combat effectiveness in the Korean War. He studied mental health and living conditions in the Philippines. These experiences, plus some other significant life events, have exposed him to serious suffering, if not outright danger. Thus, he is not an "ivory tower" psychologist. Indeed, he is a hard-eyed realist who is a strong proponent of mundane realism in research. For example, he scoffs at studies of so-called stress when the putative stressor is something trivial like subtracting serial sevens starting at 100. Real stress can be found in combat or dealing with the mentally ill in the Philippines.

Unfortunately, rear end validity often steers stress researchers to study weak laboratory manipulations of stress, which is probably qualitatively different from real-life stress. A noteworthy exception is some of Asch's (1955) experiments in which "equipment problems" were presented to deceive research participants into believing that they were at risk of physical harm. However, given a choice between studying experiments in mundane realism such as Asch's and studying real-life high-stress situations, such as football placekickers as they attempt to kick a game-deciding field goal or extra point, I believe Sechrest would advise us to study the latter. Indeed, he might suggest that it would be better to study something more important than football, because losing a football game is hardly a true catastrophe.

Stupidity Is Not Required

Lee's fourth law, *there is nothing in the scientific method that requires doing something stupid*, has widespread applicability that covers a wide range of issues from measurement to the philosophy of science. Basic issues include the habitual use of outdated or unverified, but unquestioned, laboratory standards. For example, for decades, scientists have used an incorrect standard for the speed of sound (Grossman, 2003). An example in the social sciences is the widespread use of measures that are lacking validity data or even have a preponderance of negative validity evidence, such as the Rorschach test (Wood, Nezworksi, Lilienfeld, & Garb, 2003). Sechrest's several publications challenging the credibility of projective tests were some of his first major assaults on the rear end validity in the social sciences (e.g., Sechrest & Wallace, 1963). Unfortunately, some of these tests, most notably the Draw-a-Person and Rorschach, continue to be some of the most widely used in clinical psychology.

The proponents of projective testing and their intellectual cousins who resist the dissemination of empirically supported treatments often reject attempts to standardize or otherwise rigorously operationalize their procedures by saying that using the scientific method will necessarily harm their interventions (Hawley & Weisz, 2002). For example, some claim that following a treatment manual will lead to a rigid, robotlike delivery of services that will undermine empathy, rapport, and the ability to match therapy to the idiosyncratic needs of the client. Although it may be true that overly rigid adherence to a treatment manual may lead to worse outcomes (Dishion & Kavanagh, 2003), this is not a problem inherent in using treatment manuals. Rather, it is a problem with a particular treatment manual. If that manual does not work, it should not be used. To do otherwise would be stupid.

Those who resist the dissemination of empirically validated treatments often overgeneralize the implications of studies such as Dishion and Kavanagh (2003) to suggest that the findings regarding a particular treatment apply to all standardized treatments. This type of thinking reflects ignorance of the wide array of treatment manuals and the distinction between assessing adherence and assessing competence (Wampold, Davis, & Good, 1990). Adherence is akin to reliability, and competence is akin to validity. Unfortunately, adherence is much easier to measure than competence. Thus, in psychometric terms, many manuals promote reliability but do not attend to validity.

Some treatment manuals are simply books presenting ideas about what should be done in therapy and are relatively nonspecific in their direction to therapists (Waltz, Addis, Koerner, & Jacobson, 1993). At the other extreme are highly scripted protocols, with some rare instances in which every word is written down and recited by the therapist. It remains to be seen where on the continuum of structure manuals work best.

A common complaint about highly structured manuals is that they threaten to take the therapist out of therapy. According to these critics, by being constrained by a manual, some therapists may come across as wooden, or otherwise severely lacking in rapport-building skills and therefore disengaged from the client. I suggest that this argument is specious because even the most highly structured manuals, including those rare ones with scripts, allow for considerable expression of the therapist's engagement and rapport-building skills. To illustrate this point, consider the results of giving a script to an accomplished actor versus someone who does not consider himself or herself to be a thespian. The excellent actor will bring out nuances and passion in the script despite being told what to say word for word. In contrast, the untrained actor will deliver a much less convincing performance. Given that most manuals are not even remotely close to being as structured as a play or other script, I submit that there is plenty of room for the expression of nonspecific therapist skills even in highly structured manuals. Indeed, implicit in most manuals is the idea that the therapist will use appropriate empathy and rapport skills. To do otherwise would be stupid.

Another commonly expressed concern about manuals is that they interfere with clinical judgment. A common clinical practice—or more likely, clinical aspiration—is to attempt to modify treatments in an attempt to match them to the needs of the client. Some have suggested that studying and understanding the interactions between client characteristics and interventions, sometimes called aptitude-by-treatment interactions, or ATIs, will lead to significantly larger effect sizes. In our paper on the topic, Sechrest and I provide a litany of reasons that ATI studies probably will not work (B. Smith & Sechrest, 1991). Indeed, we identified a paradox such that implementing the methodological improvements necessary for ATI research will result in finding more robust main effects rather than finding a myriad of useful ATIs. I believe our cautious comments on ATIs have been partially vindicated by a dearth of successful ATI studies, including the failure of one of the largest ATI studies, Project MATCH (Project MATCH Research Group, 1997), to find the proposed panoply of ATIs.

Given that our perspective on ATIs is correct, the phenomenon of using clinical judgment to individualize therapy should be avoided. Clinical judgment has repeatedly been shown to be inferior to actuarial sources (Sechrest, Gallimore, & Hersch, 1967) and, more recently, worse than some manuals (Wilson, 1996). Therefore, if manuals constrain the use of therapist judgment to modify treatments, that may be a very beneficial consequence of using a manual.

Some Examples of Rear End Validity

Lee's Laws should provide some useful guidance for improving scientific practices and, in some cases, personal quality of life. This section juxtaposes Lee's Laws with common practices in psychology that exemplify rear end validity. These examples of rear end validity are drawn from four sources: measurement batteries, clinical habits, disciplines of scientific psychology, and training in research methods and statistics. This list of sources of bad habits is designed to provide a heuristic for thinking about rear end validity. It may be worthwhile in some future paper to provide a detailed taxonomy of rear end validity;

however, presenting an exhaustive listing of types and subtypes of rear end validity is beyond the scope of this chapter. For present purposes, I present some examples that contrast with major themes in Sechrest's writing and teaching. These examples are at best a partial taxonomy but may be the first steps in developing a detailed taxonomy that will facilitate recognition of rear end validity and promote efforts to eradicate this methodological problem from modern science.

Malignant Growth Within Measurement Batteries

An unfortunate phenomenon in research in behavioral science is to thoughtlessly add redundant measures to the list of variables in a study. For example, some studies of depression include multiple measures such as the Beck Depression Inventory and Hamilton Depression Inventory. Indeed, some studies also add other self-report measures of depression, such as structured interviews. It seems that these multiple measures are added out of fear of missing some important aspect of depression. However, if the measures are so poorly understood that is it not clear what each of the different measures adds to the battery, then the additional measures may cause more harm than good. One of the major negative consequences is when confusion arises if different results are found for different dependent variables and there is no clear understanding of the different implications of the various measures in the battery (Cohen, 1990).

The malignant growth in measurement batteries is not limited to dependent measures. Many researchers reflexively include a host of predictor variables that have no well-articulated reason for inclusion, such as a large array of demographic variables. Such variables may be important to describe the sample and help to judge external validity. However, if there is no clear reason to include them in analyses, they can detract from studying more theoretically relevant variables. One consequence is that redundant or irrelevant predictor variables in a regression equation weaken statistical power by unnecessarily using degrees of freedom and diminishing the efficiency of estimation of parameter estimates (Cohen, 1990). Thus, carelessly including measures can often obscure understanding. Nevertheless, it is all too common to pile on measures simply because they have been used before or in a thoughtless shotgun approach to measurement that may hit the target but can also cause a lot of collateral damage to understanding.

An antidote to malignant growth in measurement batteries is proper application of Sechrest's concept of incremental validity. Once a key measure is selected, it is incumbent on any additional measures to make a statistically (Sechrest, 1963) and conceptually significant (Sechrest et al., 1996) contribution to understanding to the construct of interest. Those measures which fail the test for incremental validity should be eliminated. This practice will simplify analyses and focus the research question.

Unfortunately, rear end validity often acts as a counter to the proper application of incremental validity. Colleagues may complain that a set of variables trimmed by an incremental validity analysis is too narrow or biased.

This has some potent consequences. Journal reviewers and editors may slow or prevent publication because their favorite measures were not included in the manuscript, even if there is a good justification for the parsimonious set of measures in the paper. Applicants for funding often obsequiously add measures developed by or frequently used by members of grant review panels. Grant reviewers often reinforce this behavior by commenting that their pet measures were not included in the battery or by penalizing applications with a highly focused and well-justified set of measures that happens to exclude a reviewer's habitually used measure.

Some of the most egregious examples of malignant growth in measurement batteries are found in collaborative, multisite studies, such as the Collaborative Study of Depression, Project MATCH, and the Multimodal Study of Attention-Deficit/Hyperactivity Disorder. The studies put an awesome response burden on research participants who were provided monetary compensation for the time required to complete the measures. This threatens the external validity of studies. Furthermore, the lengthy and redundant measurement batteries threaten the internal and construct validity of studies by increasing the risk of reactivity to measures.

Cohen (1990) summarized the goal of incremental validity with the term "less is more." This phrase may seem to contradict Lee's second law that more is better than less. Yet the apparent conflict can be reconciled by the knowledge that both Cohen and Sechrest are advocating greater focus on and understanding of constructs. The concept of less is more refers to having fewer extraneous measures and less construct-irrelevant variance (Messick, 1995). The concept of more is better than less refers to better understanding of the ecological validity and practical meaning understanding of the measure, thus increasing construct-relevant variance. From this perspective, the only way to justify deliberately including multiple redundant measures is in a deliberate effort to promote construct validity, such as using a multitrait–multimethod matrix to study construct validity (Campbell & Fiske, 1959).

Clinical Habits

The practice of medicine and applied behavioral science has developed a distinctive culture with a set of habits and expectations that, although they may do some good, may also cause problems. A pertinent example is the habit in clinical psychology of seeing clients once a week for an hour at a clinic. This practice is reified in appointment books and treatment manuals throughout the country. Unfortunately, there are two major problems with this clinical habit. First, it reflects poor understanding of the variable dose of treatment required across the range of presenting problems (B. Smith & Sechrest, 1991). In many cases, such as that of a juvenile delinquent who is about to be placed outside of the home, once-a-week therapy will be too low of a dose (Henggeler, Schoenwald, Borduin, Rowland, & Cunningham, 1998). Sometimes therapists recognize this need by offering more frequent appointments during periods of crisis. However, the default position once the crisis is over is to return to once a week. This probably leads to habitual underserving of some clients primarily because of the rear end validity of once-a-week appointments.

A second major problem with the habitual use of once-a-week therapy appointments in a clinic is that this mode of service delivery creates significant barriers to treatment for many potential clients. There is a growing body of research on the benefits of breaking the once-a-week clinical habit. This includes the creative use of phone contacts and, perhaps most powerfully, appropriate contact out of the office (Snell-Johns, Mendez, & Smith, 2004). For example, several treatment research groups have found major benefits in engagement and retention in therapy, with subsequent better outcomes, from phone contacts prior to the first therapy appointment. Another promising approach is multisystemic therapy (MST) using a family preservation model (Henggeler et al., 1998). This approach includes having mobile therapists provide treatment in homes, schools, and other relevant community settings. Compared with typical once-a-week therapy, MST has achieved dramatically better results with a much broader range of clients.

Unfortunately, rear end validity threatens the dissemination of treatments such as MST. Many therapists dismiss such an approach because it does not match their typical service delivery mode. The use of MST requires a substantial reduction in caseloads, with many more hours a week per case than is the habit. Also, MST requires a 24-hour-a-day, 7-day-a-week, on-call service. Another issue is billing. Many reimbursement sources do not pay for school or home visits, which may be the bulk of MST contacts. Thus, breaking the habit of once-a-week clinic therapy requires quite a bit of novel behavior on the part of therapists and their supervisors. Moreover, the successful use of MST may require considerable guidance beyond the typical norm for supervision of therapists, as well as atypical negotiations with third-party payers. Dissemination studies with MST provided by therapists in community settings have achieved disappointing results (Henggeler, Melton, Brondino, Scherer, & Hanley, 1997), presumably because of lack of fidelity to the treatment model (or barriers presented by rear end validity).

Breaking many of the habits of applied behavioral science may be necessary to make real progress in improving therapy. A consistent finding in meta-analytic reviews of the clinical research literature is that psychosocial treatments delivered in research settings outperform treatments delivered in community settings (Shadish et al., 1993; Weisz, Weiss, Alicke, & Klotz, 1987). This is a disturbing finding which suggests that the previously mentioned weak to moderate-sized effects of therapy may be overestimates of the effects of therapy as it is typically delivered. I submit that much of the difference is due to rear end validity on the part of researchers and community providers. Researchers habitually overemphasize internal validity. Community providers are constrained by habits and limitations on resources that limit their adoption of novel, effective approaches. Thus, rear end validity in the form of an unthinking use of standard approaches to clinical research and practice is a major barrier to innovation and improved effectiveness in the delivery of applied behavioral interventions.

Two Disciplines of Scientific Psychology

In his presidential address to the American Psychological Association in 1957, Lee Cronbach identified two paradigms within psychology—experimental and correlational—with separate traditions of methods, thought, and affiliation. Cronbach regarded the two disciplines of psychology as a serious problem that threatened to fragment scientific resources and diminish the potential of psychology (Cronbach, 1957). He accused the profession of making narrow-minded decisions because of narrow training and overly specialized methods and thinking. Because these practices were habitual rather than thoughtful, they constituted rear end validity.

In a follow-up to his presidential address, Cronbach reported little progress (Cronbach, 1975). It seemed then, and is probably true today, that psychology is caught in the grips of disciplinary ethnocentrism (Campbell, 1969). This form of rear end validity narrows the focus of research through a variety of mechanisms. One mechanism is a proliferation of research journals and professional organizations that focus on specific topics. These journals and professional affiliations cause linguistic drift and development of jargon that limit the sharing of ideas with psychologists outside of the focus area. Another mechanism is when administrative and external funding sources nurture research at the center of a narrow focus area and fail to reward, or even punish, creative research that bridges gaps between focus areas. The consequence has been a proliferation of islands of knowledge, with major gaps between areas that were fortunate enough to become the center of disciplinary attention.

A concrete example of the effects of disciplinary ethnocentrism is that clinical psychologists rarely cite the work of experimental psychologists and vice versa. Presumably, cognitive therapy should benefit from advances in cognitive science. Unfortunately, such citations are exceedingly rare because clinical and experimental researchers are in the habit of benignly, and sometimes maliciously, neglecting each other.

A plausible antidote to the disciplinary ethnocentrism rampant in modern-day psychology is translational research. One of the seminal works in translational research was Dollard and Miller's (1950) book titled *Personality and Psychotherapy: An Analysis of Terms of Learning, Thinking, and Culture.* This book was translational in the sense of providing a dictionary for translating ideas shared by learning theory and psychodynamic therapy. However, Goldstein, Heller, and Sechrest's (1966) book, *Psychotherapy and the Psychology of Behavior Change,* took translational research one step farther. According to Goldstein et al. (1966), translational research is using findings from basic behavioral science to guide therapeutic practice, and testing hypotheses from psychotherapy in basic science studies. Thus, Dollard and Miller's work is semantically oriented, but Goldstein et al.'s is action oriented, as they call for making a change in how clinical and experimental psychologists select hypotheses for investigation. From the perspective of Goldstein et al., clinical science is viewed as a fertile ground for hypotheses for experimental psychologists. Likewise, findings from experimental science are regarded as good prospects for clinical trials.

A sign that there has been little progress in translational research was some of the comments on the paper I published with Lee Sechrest titled "Psychotherapy Is the Practice of Psychology" (Sechrest, Babcock, & Smith, 1993). One comment was that we seemed to contradict ourselves by calling for multidisciplinary work but used the term *psychology* in the title. This comment reflects disciplinary ethnocentrism in which psychology is regarded as a formal discipline. In contrast, Sechrest has been proposing since 1966 that psychology is a topic area and psychologists should be topical experts rather than agents of an arbitrarily defined scientific guild.

Unfortunately, as mentioned earlier, Sechrest has been disappointed by the predominance of the guild mentality in psychology. He has described the Goldstein et al. book as his most important, but probably most underappreciated, contribution (Benson, 2003). On a positive note, the National Institutes of Health has several initiatives to encourage translational research. Unfortunately, translational research is largely unexplored territory that needs to develop novel hypotheses, unfamiliar collaborations, unique funding mechanisms, and supportive peer-reviewed publication outlets. These challenges are highly vulnerable to rear end validity, and it will take a bold, thoughtful, and persistent effort to engage in translational research.

Methodological Decision Trees

An unfortunate practice in research method training is using decision trees or charts to select a single statistical method or research design for a particular set of variables. Such an approach sends the meta-message that there are right and wrong methods, and if you use the right method there may be some automaticity of inference. A more enlightened approach is recognizing the limitations of various research designs or statistical methods and using a collection of complementary procedures to compensate for weaknesses and limitations of other approaches. We have called this approach *methodological pluralism* (Sechrest et al., 1993), and others have called it *critical multiplism* (Shadish, 1993).

A statistical example of methodological pluralism is using exploratory data analysis, especially graphical display of data, in conjunction with multiple regression and correlation. (See Cohen, 1990.) A methodological example of this approach is using quantitative measures in a controlled study combined with focus groups and other qualitative data to judge the impact and mechanism of action or an intervention.

To limit the analysis of data to one single statistical method or to limit measurement to either qualitative or quantitative methods violates Lee's fourth law, because such narrow-mindedness would be stupid. Nevertheless, some have argued that we must abandon certain methods because of their gross limitations or flawed history of implementation (Sechrest et al., 1993). This approach, which might be called methodological singularism or procedural tunnel vision, is the methodological equivalent to extreme fundamentalist religion, which posits that there is only one truth and one way to knowing or establishing the truth. Although philosophers of science tell us that reliance on the scientific method requires an act of faith (Kimble, 1989), these philosophers have also shown that the dogma of a particular scientific paradigm puts constraints on understanding and may inhibit the development of new knowledge.

Two-Tailed, Null Hypothesis Tests With Alpha of .05

The most pervasive, egregious example of rear end validity in the social sciences is the reflexive, uncritical imposition of the two-tailed null hypothesis test with alpha set at 05. The debate between the proponents of null hypothesis testing (Wainer, 1999) and its detractors (Cohen, 1994) is very enlightening and should be required reading for all students of psychology. For present purposes, I grudgingly concede that there is a place for null hypothesis testing in the behavioral sciences. However, there is no justification for blanket application of the two-tailed test with an alpha of .05.

Very few hypotheses in the behavioral sciences are truly two tailed. To posit such a hypothesis, the researcher is implicitly stating that he or she has no idea in what direction the experiment will work. This is rarely stated explicitly. To make such a statement would be either embarrassing or dishonest. Most researchers know enough about their hypotheses that they can state a direction. If they can state a direction, they should use a one-tailed test. This intellectual honesty is rewarded by increased statistical power, which is often deficient in much social science research (Cohen, 1992). Moreover, one-tailed hypotheses have better hypothesis validity (Wampold et al., 1990), because more specific hypotheses are more falsifiable. If researchers cannot state a directional hypothesis, they should be humble and admit that their study is a fishing expedition.

As is the case with two-tailed tests, rigid reliance on an alpha of .05 is unacceptable to the thoughtful scientist. As convincingly stated by Paul Meehl on several occasions, an inflexible decision rule should not be advocated for any decision making in psychology (e.g., Meehl, 1978, 1992; Meehl & Rosen, 1955). Rigid reliance on an alpha of .05 fails to consider the unique needs of study in terms of statistical power and the costs of either Type I or Type II errors. It would be a terrible shame to miss finding an effective treatment or detecting a dangerous side effect because of a Type II error. It would be a costly and demoralizing mistake to widely implement a new educational intervention because of a Type I error.

It might be better to have a more liberal alpha when looking for something very important, thus avoiding Type II errors. However, researchers often make the mistake of mindlessly lowering statistical power by picking a more stringent alpha to avoid Type I errors, typically through slavish adherence to Bonferroni corrections. In most cases, it is better to control for Type I errors through replication. Replication creates a very stringent alpha because the probability of Type I error across two studies is the product of the alpha levels of the two individual studies (e.g., $.05 \times .05 = .0025$.). Thus, replication should be the standard before the widespread implementation of a new intervention. Unfortunately, rear end validity has some of our colleagues paying too much attention to alpha levels and too little attention to statistical power. It is incumbent on journal editors and faculty to eradicate this habit from the behavioral sciences.

Conclusion

Most scientists should be vaguely aware of the concept of rear end validity, but they do not have a good lexicon for communicating about this serious threat to progress in the behavioral sciences. The working definition of rear end validity in this chapter is "justifying a procedural decision on the sole basis that someone did that same thing previously." Such complacent, sloppy decision making is the antithesis of the writings and teachings of Lee Sechrest. Among other things, rear end validity subsumes the worst effects of dominant research paradigms (Chamberlin, 1965). Likewise, rear end validity perpetuates disciplinary ethnocentrism and the related intellectual and administrative practices that lead to major gaps in scientific understanding (Campbell, 1969). Worst of all, because excellence is often novel and unusual, rear end validity perpetuates mediocrity. As often stated by Lee Sechrest, "Mediocrity is so easily achieved it is hardly worth planning for." It is hoped that better recognition of rear end validity and greater attention to Sechrest's ideas will help to set the standard in behavioral sciences well above the mediocre mark.

References

Asch, S. E. (1955, November). Opinions and social pressure. *Scientific American, 193,* 31–35.

Bandura, A. (1997). *Self-efficacy: The exercise of control.* New York: Freeman.

Benson, E. (2003, July/August). Method man. *Monitor on Psychology, 34,* 44–45.

Campbell, D. T. (1969). Ethnocentrism of disciplines and the fish-scale model of omniscience. In M. Sherif & C. W. Sherif (Eds.), *Interdisciplinary relationships in the social sciences* (pp. 328–348). Chicago: Aldine.

Campbell, D. T., & Fiske, D. W. (1959). Convergent and discriminant validation by the multitrait–multimethod matrix. *Psychological Bulletin, 56,* 81–105.

Campbell, D. T., & Stanley, J. C. (1963). Experimental and quasi-experimental designs for research on teaching. In N. Gage (Ed.), *Handbook of research on teaching* (p. 171). Chicago: Rand McNally.

Chamberlin, T. C. (1965). The method of multiple working hypotheses. *Science, 148,* 754–759.

Cohen, J. (1990). Things I have learned (so far). *American Psychologist, 45,* 1304–1312.

Cohen, J. (1992). A power primer. *Psychological Bulletin, 112,* 155–159.

Cohen, J. (1994). The earth is round ($p < .05$). *American Psychologist, 49,* 997–1003.

Cronbach, L. J. (1957). The two disciplines of scientific psychology. *American Psychologist, 12,* 671–684.

Cronbach, L. J. (1975). Beyond the two disciplines of scientific psychology. *American Psychologist, 30,* 116–127.

Cronbach, L., & Meehl, P. (1955). Construct validity in psychological tests. *Psychological Bulletin, 52,* 281–302.

Dishion, T. D., & Kavanagh, K. (2003). *Intervening in adolescent problem behavior: A family-centered approach.* New York: Guilford Press.

Dollard, J., & Miller, N. (1950). *Personality and psychotherapy: An analysis in terms of learning, thinking, and culture.* New York: McGraw-Hill.

Goldstein, A. P., Heller, K., & Sechrest, L. B. (1966). *Psychotherapy and the psychology of behavior change.* New York: Wiley.

Grossman, K. (2003). *How were the speed of sound and speed of light determined and measured?* Retrieved August 1, 2003, from http://www.boulder.nist.gov/timefreq/general/pdf/1882.pdf

Hawley, K. M., & Weisz, J. R. (2002). Increasing the relevance of evidence-based treatment review to practitioners and consumers. *Clinical Psychology: Science and Practice, 9*, 225–230.

Henggeler, S. W., Melton, G. B., Brondino, M. J., Scherer, D. G., & Hanley, J. H. (1997). Multisystemic therapy with violent and chronic juvenile offenders and their families: The role of treatment fidelity in successful dissemination. *Journal of Consulting and Clinical Psychology, 65*, 821–833.

Henggeler, S. W., Schoenwald, S. K., Borduin, C. M., Rowland, M. D., & Cunningham, P. B. (1998). *Multisystemic treatment of antisocial behavior in children and adolescents.* New York: Guilford Press.

Kimble, G. A. (1989). Psychology from the standpoint of a generalist. *American Psychologist, 44*, 491–499.

Lipsey, M. W., & Wilson, D. B. (1993). The efficacy of psychological, educational, and behavioral treatment: Confirmation from meta-analysis. *American Psychologist, 48*, 1181–1209.

Meehl, P. E. (1978). Theoretical risks and tabular asterisks: Sir Karl, Sir Ronald, and the slow progress of soft psychology. *Journal of Consulting and Clinical Psychology, 40*, 806–834.

Meehl, P. E. (1992). Factors and taxa, traits, and types, differences of degree and differences in kind. *Journal of Personality, 60*, 117–174.

Meehl, P. E., & Rosen, A. (1955). Antecedent probability and the efficiency of psychometric signs, patterns, and cutting scores. *Psychological Bulletin, 52*, 194–216.

Messick, S. (1995). Validity of psychological assessment: Validation of inferences from persons' responses and performances as scientific inquiry into score meaning. *American Psychologist, 50*, 741–749.

Project MATCH Research Group. (1997). Matching alcoholism treatments to client heterogeneity. *Journal of Studies on Alcohol, 58*, 7–30.

Rosenthal, R. (1983). Assessing the statistical and social importance of the effects of psychotherapy. *Journal of Consulting and Clinical Psychology, 51*, 4–13.

Sechrest, L. B. (1963). Incremental validity: A recommendation. *Educational and Psychological Measurement, 23*, 153–158.

Sechrest, L. B. (1985). Social science and social policy: Will our numbers ever be good enough? In L. Shotland & M. Mark (Eds.), *Social science and social policy* (pp. 63–95). Beverly Hills, CA: Sage.

Sechrest, L. B. (1993). Preventing problems in prevention research. *American Journal of Community Psychology, 21*, 665–672.

Sechrest, L. B., Babcock, J., & Smith, B. (1993). An invitation to methodological pluralism. *Evaluation Practice, 14*, 227–235.

Sechrest, L. B., Gallimore, R., & Hersch, P. (1967). Feedback and accuracy of clinical prediction. *Journal of Consulting Psychology, 31*, 1–11.

Sechrest, L. B., McKnight, P., & McKnight, K. (1996). Calibration of measures for psychotherapy outcome studies. *American Psychologist, 51*, 1065–1071.

Sechrest, L. B., & Wallace, J. (1963). Figure drawing and naturally occurring events: Elimination of the expansive euphoria hypothesis. *Journal of Educational Psychology, 55*, 32–44.

Shadish, W. R. (1993). Critical multiplism: A research strategy and its attendant tactics. *New Directions for Program Evaluation, 60*, 13–57.

Shadish, W. R., Montgomery, L. M., Wilson, P., Wilson, M. R., Bright, I., & Okwumabua, T. (1993). Effects of family and marital psychotherapies: A meta-analysis. *Journal of Consulting and Clinical Psychology, 61*, 992–1002.

Smith, B., & Sechrest, L. B. (1991). Treatment of Aptitude × Treatment interactions. *Journal of Consulting and Clinical Psychology, 59*, 233–244.

Smith, M. L., Glass, G. V., & Miller, T. I. (1980). *The benefits of psychotherapy.* Baltimore: John Hopkins University Press.

Snell-Johns, J., Mendez, J., & Smith, B. (2004). Evidence-based solutions for overcoming access barriers, decreasing attrition, and promoting change with under-served families. *Journal of Family Psychology, 18*, 19–35.

Wainer, H. (1999). One cheer for null hypothesis significance testing. *Psychological Methods, 4*, 212–213.

Waltz, J., Addis, M. E., Koerner, K., & Jacobson, N. S. (1993). Testing the integrity of a psychotherapy protocol: Assessment of adherence and competence. *Journal of Consulting and Clinical Psychology, 61*, 620–630.

Wampold, B. E., Davis, B., & Good, R. H. I. (1990). Hypothesis validity of clinical research. *Journal of Consulting and Clinical Psychology, 58*, 360–367.

Weisz, J. R., Weiss, B., Alicke, M. D., & Klotz, M. L. (1987). Effectiveness of psychotherapy with children and adolescents: A meta-analysis for clinicians. *Journal of Consulting and Clinical Psychology, 55*, 542–549.

Wilson, G. T. (1996). Manual-based treatments: The clinical application of research findings. *Behavioral Research and Therapy, 34*, 295–314.

Wood, J. M., Nezworksi, M. T., Lilienfeld, S. O., & Garb, H. N. (2003). *What's wrong with the Rorschach? Science confronts the controversial inkblot test.* San Francisco: Jossey-Bass.

13

The Nature of Scientific Legacy: The Case of Lee Sechrest

Patrick E. McKnight, Katherine M. McKnight, and A. J. Figueredo

It is often the case that important figures in the history of science leave not one, but two legacies. The first legacy is the body of work that they directly contributed. This includes the ideas that they personally originated, the discoveries that they made, and the theories to which their names are directly and inextricably tied. The second legacy is the influence these important figures had on others, most notably the students they personally mentored. This influence may extend as far as the sociology of their field, helping to shape the way that research is conducted. A notable example of a dual legacy in the field of theoretical physics is Niels Bohr, who made direct contributions to our understanding of atomic structure. In addition to these direct contributions, he served as the central organizing figure in the Copenhagen School that helped to shape the emerging quantum physics. Although Bohr's model of the atom has been superseded over time by more sophisticated models, his pervasive influence in his field helped to create and direct the quantum theory revolution that redefined modern physics for the remainder of the 20th century (Heisenberg, 1971). Louis Leakey had a similar influence on the field of palaeoanthropology, by not only making major personal contributions to our understanding of human prehistory but also mentoring and shaping the careers of many of the most important figures in primatology, such as Jane Goodall, Dianne Fossey, and Birute Galdikas (Morell, 1996).

Bohr and Leakey serve as useful models of scientists whose contributions have made a significant impact on the field. From their examples, we are able to derive a set of factors that appear to be critical to the evolution of a scientific legacy. First, it appears that a scientific legacy is generated by direct contributions to one's own scientific field via ideas, theory generation, discoveries, and so on. We call this the *direct* impact. A scientific legacy also appears to be the result of having an impact on the field through others, via written work, mentoring, and so on. We call this the *indirect* impact. A dual legacy is the combination of both a direct and an indirect impact, and it is not likely that the latter can occur without the former. That is, a scientist is not likely to have

249

a strong indirect impact on a field if he or she is not first recognized for his or her direct contributions. A direct impact, however, is not related or impeded by the lack of an indirect impact. We emphasize the notion of a dual legacy because it is likely that those who have dual legacies are those who impart the greatest impact in science, or any field for that matter. With rare exception, most scientists make little to no impact directly, and it is therefore important to recognize and attend to the indirect impact. Because few scientists ever make a substantial direct contribution and not every person who makes a noteworthy contribution is capable of interacting, mentoring, or even supporting the work of others, the indirect contribution is the most critical factor in judging a person's dual legacy potential. Of course, the absence of any direct contributions might weigh heavily on the indirect contributions. When these two elements are present, a person has the ability to leave a strong and lasting scientific legacy.

Another notable feature of a scientific legacy is that the scientist's contribution may not be correct at any point in time. What may pass as a contribution at some level may offer itself more heuristically to the field by being incorrect as much as any other contribution may offer for its validity. For example, Seligman's (Seligman & Csikszentmihalyi, 2000) latest push toward "positive psychology" may be incorrect and largely held by contemporary researchers as vitally flawed; however, this research program's heuristic value is likely to be substantial. Many psychological scientists are likely to defend their own thinking about contemporary problems in light of positive psychology, and challenges to their theories might lead to stronger theories. Also, as science progresses, a scientist's contribution might be superseded by new information. Regardless of the information gain, the scientist who made an original contribution will remain an important figure in his or her field because of the impact the scientist had at the time and the opportunity that contribution created for others to expand on ideas and extend the field.

The Scientific Legacy as a Framework for Progress

A scientific legacy has historical as well as scientific implications. Historically, a scientific legacy informs current and future scientists of the roots from which current scientific knowledge has grown. Isaac Newton attributed his contributions to science partly to his having "stood on the shoulders of giants." Those giants were other physicists, mathematicians, and astronomers whose legacies provided the data and insights that led Newton to his great contributions (Hawking, 2002). Thus, scientific legacies serve as a history of ideas from which we can learn how scientific knowledge evolved into its current form.

An accounting of the evolution of scientific ideas can influence the progress of science as well. A legacy provides a framework that guides future scientific development. Bohr's work stimulated an entirely new approach to thinking about dynamic systems, whereas Leakey guided the future of paleontology by focusing on the possible relationships between the no longer directly observable behavior of fossil human ancestors and the directly observable behavior of the surviving great apes. Both of these scientists promoted an idea, perspective, or methodology, and others learned from the results of their application. Simonton (1988) described the unique process of scientific discovery and progress, noting that an individual's scientific contributions need not be correct, but those contributions must foster further inquiry and assist others in advancing the field of inquiry. This is the indirect impact that contributes to a scientist's legacy.

Simonton (1988) referred to the scientific process as the *chance configuration* theory of science—an evolutionary-based theory in which scientific gains are made by chance only when the discoverer is adequately knowledgeable about the relevant content and unrestricted by the current theoretical perspectives. These gains are more likely to occur when an individual scientist is very productive. That is, the more work a scientist produces, the more likely he or she is to chance upon a significant contribution to his or her field. In order for this chance occurrence to result in a significant contribution, the scientist must first recognize it as important and then persuade others. Thus, according to the chance configuration theory of science, a scientist must be innovative, prolific, and persuasive to leave a lasting legacy.

Lee Sechrest's Legacy

We have thus far identified some key factors in the determination of a scientific legacy: innovation, productivity, and persuasiveness, as well as having a direct and indirect impact on one's field. In the field of psychology, Lee Sechrest is an example of a person who has and continues to build a scientific legacy. He has had both a direct and an indirect effect on his field, and an examination of those effects might illuminate some of the characteristics that are desired of a scientist who wishes to leave a legacy.

Lee Sechrest's direct contributions to all areas of scientific inquiry, such as measurement, methodology, and policy, are well noted in the social science literature. We highlight a few notable contributions. In the early part of his career, he actively collaborated with other eminent methodologists to develop the seminal work on unobtrusive measures (Webb, Cambpell, Schwartz, & Sechrest, 1966), promoting an alternative method for obtaining information whereby the object of study is unaware that he or she is being observed. Later, as noted by other contributors to this Festschrift, he turned his attention to a completely different subject, namely, the scientific basis of behavior change (Goldstein, Heller, & Sechrest, 1966). Additionally, he has contributed to methodological perspectives such as incremental validity (Sechrest, 1963), calibration (Sechrest, McKnight, & McKnight, 1996), and effect size estimation (Sechrest & Yeaton, 1981). His methodological contributions span the domains of psychological assessment (e.g., Sechrest, 1963), social and personality psychology (e.g., Sechrest, 1976), school psychology (e.g., Sechrest, 1964), cross-cultural psychology (e.g., Sechrest, 1977), clinical psychology (e.g., Sechrest & Olbrisch, 1977), health care (e.g., Sechrest & Cohen, 1979), criminality (e.g., Sechrest & Olsen, 1971), and even fringe areas of psychology, such as astrologers as marriage counselors (Sechrest & Bryan, 1968). There are few disciplines within psychology in which he has not made some contribution, and a perusal of his voluminous curriculum vitae serves as a reliable and valid unobtrusive measure of his productivity.

Moreover, across this broad range of topics, Sechrest has made numerous methodological contributions in the areas of design, measurement, and statistics. For example, in the field of clinical psychology, he has promoted the notion of calibrating measures to observable, understandable phenomena to comprehend the practical meaning of a score on a particular psychological measure. (See Sechrest et al., 1996.) For example, we might calibrate scores on a depression inventory into lost hours in productivity at work, reduction in smiles or laughing, and so on. Building on the work of others (see Wolfe, 1978), Sechrest recognized the importance of an idea that had not yet been promoted in as persuasive and accessible a manner. He made the idea accessible through the use of practical and salient examples and by suggesting methods familiar to social scientists (e.g., linear regression) for calibrating measures. According to the Science Citations Index (an unobtrusive measure of one's influence on other scientists), his work on calibration has been cited in a wide range of fields, including social work, health care, program evaluation, substance abuse, career assessment, clinical psychology, developmental psychology, behavioral therapy, and social skills training, to name but a few. This range attests to Sechrest's ability to persuade others of the significance of an idea. He continues to persuade other scientists through mentoring, workshops, conferences, and other scientific meetings.

Although Sechrest has contributed directly to social science, he also maintains the second part of the dual legacy—a strong indirect contribution to science. He has worked and published with no fewer than 150 others. Of those collaborators, most were students. As a measure of his indirect effect on science, his work in many of the areas in which he directly contributed is now supported by those students, who continue to make their own direct contributions. Their subsequent contributions are often related to the content of their collaborations with him or, at a minimum, influenced by their work with him. For example, Sechrest's original work on unobtrusive measures gained momentum by his collaboration with others, some of whom continue to publish papers on unobtrusive measures in different content areas, such as psychotherapy outcomes research (e.g., Patterson & Sechrest, 1983). At this very Festschrift, former student Elizabeth Midlarsky presented her work on unobtrusive measures of altruism. (See Midlarsky, Fagin Jones, & Nemeroff, chap. 2, this volume.) Citations of his work include the importance of unobtrusive measures in the assessment of pain, depression, staff behaviors, and couples' interactions during couples therapy. These citations further reflect his indirect contributions to science.

As scientists, we are compelled not only to pay tribute to scientific legacies, as with a Festschrift, but also to understand how other scientists might replicate such an accomplishment. By identifying some of the elements present in Sechrest's direct and indirect contributions to social science, we might gain some insight into the process. For example, many scientists who make a strong direct impact on their field do so by communicating their ideas in a clear, insightful, and accessible manner.[1] Sechrest crafted most of his contributions in a manner that allowed almost any reader within and even outside the area of psychology to comprehend them. Moreover, the accessibility of his direct contributions has led to the application of several of his ideas to fields well beyond the scope of his intentions. For example, he coined the term *incremental validity* in 1963. It has since become a familiar concept in subdisciplines within psychology (e.g., personality, psychometrics, industrial/organizational), as well as fields outside psychology, for example, management (Howard, 1974), management information systems (Webster & Martocchio, 1992), accounting (Ashton, 1975), and sociology (Wiatrowski, Griswold, & Roberts, 1981), among others. Few scientists can claim such universal accessibility of their contributions. This clarity and accessibility are two criteria we posit to be important to the degree of influence of one's direct and indirect contributions to science.

Another related feature we believe is relevant to Sechrest's legacy is pragmatism. His pragmatism reflects a utilitarian attitude toward science. That is, he concerns himself with the utility of the knowledge to be produced rather than the content itself. Although a particular study domain might be in vogue or politically correct at a given time, he will not favor the pursuit of such a program if it does not appear to be targeting a useful question or producing useful information. Instead, he asks the difficult, but ultimate, question of scientific endeavors: "So what?" That is, what useful information is this study or research program likely to yield? This has often earned him the reputation as an iconoclast[2] and the ire of many a social scientist.

Sechrest's pragmatism and utilitarian stance extend to his assessment of the tools of science. This includes study design, measurement, and statistical analyses. His attitude has led him to some rather unpopular views among fellow methodologists. With respect to statistical procedures, for example, Sechrest often questions common statistical conventions that appear to be hindering more than enlightening scientific progress and the accumulation of knowledge. He remains skeptical, for example, about an intense focus on decreasing standard errors of estimates, cutoff values for fit indices, and concerns about p values, when it is clear that scientists have not taken care to design a methodologically sound study design. His direct scientific contributions in the areas of effect size estimation, incremental validity, interpreting no-difference findings, the analysis of change by using longitudinal data, and a host of other areas reflect his concern with the appropriate, principled use of the tools of science as a key means by which to improve scientific progress. He does not advocate the use of these tools solely on the basis of rules or convention. Instead, he focuses on their utility in terms of the knowledge they produce. Much of his focus is on the application of these tools in psychotherapy outcomes research and program evaluation, and how to best use them to decrease uncertainty regarding a particular phenomenon of interest.

---

[1] One notable exception to this point is Albert Einstein, whose primary contribution could be read and understood by no more than two people at the time of its publication!

[2] At a colloquium series several years ago in which Sechrest introduced the invited speaker, Robyn Dawes, as an iconoclast, Dawes cheerfully responded by noting that "it takes one to know one!"

Sechrest's approach to questioning and testing the merits of different scientific tools often includes collaborating with students and colleagues in a theoretically driven and largely empirical manner. He works on the assumption that empirically driven work without the guidance of theory (e.g., "data mining") leads to little progress and that theoretical work without empirical support is likewise doomed. The marriage of theory and application is the hallmark of most of his work and interest. Many of the publications and scientific conference presentations by Sechrest and his collaborators from EGAD (Evaluation Group for Analysis of Data) at the University of Arizona focus on testing the utility of some of the research tools available to scientists. For example, Walsh, Katz, and Sechrest (2002) discussed the pitfalls of using proxy variables such as race and ethnicity when trying to determine the effect of cultural factors on adaptation to illness. Instead, they advocated methods that directly measure those factors and assess their effects. Hill and Sechrest (2000) quantitatively assessed the utility of propensity scores in quasi-experiments via meta-analysis, and Morales and Sechrest (2000) demonstrated a principled approach to combining data. EGAD conference presentations inspired by Sechrest's interests empirically address a wide variety of methodological concerns, such as different methods for handling missing data, the misuse of composite variables, the influence of measurement reliability on effect size, the effect of missing data on growth curve estimation, and the utility of random assignment. Sechrest advocates not only the questioning of conventional methodological approaches but also the empirical assessment of the utility of these approaches whenever possible. We elaborate on a few more examples of his influence in the next section.

Further examination of his collaborations is instructive regarding the qualities of a scientific legacy. As many of the Festschrift participants can attest, Sechrest is generous with his time and energy and often includes people in a collaborative effort, even if they are unprepared to fully grasp the content at hand. Generosity is reflected in his willingness to work with anyone who requests his input, in his tradition of giving his students the opportunity to write with him and publish as first author, and in his willingness to share career-shaping opportunities. For example, he invited one student to oversee a project for which he was hired to assess educational reform in California, resulting in that student's career-changing interest in education policy. Involving students and colleagues in large-scale program development and evaluation has led to a number of rewarding contributions and career trajectories for several of his collaborators. He offers international travel to his students to present papers at scientific conferences in places such as Germany, Singapore, Greece, and Australia. These international meetings serve to spread the influence of his ideas directly by exposing others to them and indirectly by building collegial relationships with his international colleagues.

Sechrest's generosity extends to freely sharing his ideas. A colleague once apologized for "taking" an idea and not sufficiently acknowledging his contribution, to which Sechrest replied that it was no great offense and that he would be in a great deal of trouble if all he had was that one idea. This generosity and unpossessive nature carry throughout his academic and professional life. He expends great effort working with students and colleagues to help them become better scientists and thinkers. These characteristics of pragmatism, skepticism, generosity, and selflessness may be important features that define those who leave noteworthy legacies.

The Evaluation Group for Analysis of Data

Many of Lee Sechrest's indirect contributions to science are the result of an environment he created in which he encouraged students and colleagues to pursue their interests with an exploratory, nonjudgmental attitude. The main venue for this generative environment is the Evaluation Group for Analysis of Data (EGAD), of which Sechrest was the founding member. An analysis of the EGAD environment might also provide insight into the key elements of a remarkable scientific legacy.

EGAD has met weekly now for just over 15 years and has regularly brought together students and faculty from a variety of disciplines with a shared interest in research methodology, measurement, and data analysis. Although Lee Sechrest has had multiple indirect effects through his various activities at both the national and the international level, some of which are the subjects of other chapters in this Festschrift, his principal impact at the local level has been in serving for these many years as "Emperor for Life" of EGAD. As a result, EGAD has become a recognizable entity with a characteristic style at various national and international venues.

Although the EGAD influence was a constant and pervasive one for those most directly involved, this environmental background was punctuated by the yearly EGAD ritual of preparing panel presentations for the annual meeting of the American Evaluation Association and, in recent years, various international organizations, such as the European Association for Psychological Assessment, the International Society for the Study of Individual Differences, and the Australasian Evaluation Society. What Sechrest encouraged in his students and collaborators was a playful and experimental attitude toward research methodology in general and methods of measurement in particular. Every year, EGAD members assemble in collaborative groups and collect or generate data sets that could be subjected to a variety of analytical methods for comparison. Several years in a row, we prepared panel presentations on complementary theories of measurement, in which we subjected the same data to analytical procedures from several different theories of measurement and compared and contrasted the results across methods. These complementary—or perhaps supplementary—theories of measurement included classical test theory, generalizability theory, item response theory, scale construction, confirmatory factor modeling, multitrait–multimethod modeling, and more. The approach was always to see if these procedures produced common or unique results and, more importantly, altered our understanding of the data structure. After these efforts, we would produce and deliver didactic presentations that helped enlighten fellow methodologists and substantive researchers regarding what each alternative theory and procedure had to offer. Because we had no previous commitment to any single set of methods—courtesy of Sechrest's model of an open (yet critical) attitude—we presented these results in an evenhanded way rather than advocating for any particular approach to measurement, as is often done by enthusiasts of some new technique. Instead, we emphasized the complementary and mutually reinforcing nature of the various measurement theories available within our methodological armamentarium, impartially weighing both the merits and limitations of each. In addition, we would explore any possible effects that different strategies for measurement might have on other important methodological issues, such as handling missing data and working with small data sets. In recent years, we have also been exploring the complex relationships between latent and emergent variables (or cause-and-effect indicators; see Bollen & Lennox, 1991) and the similarities and differences in the principles involved in their construct validation.

Aside from the aforementioned measurement examples, the EGAD environment is, perhaps, best explained by presenting several more examples of the work that has come from our years of collaboration. As described previously, there exists a social milieu in EGAD that may be best summarized by the following adjectives: multidisciplinary, cooperative, noncomplacent, skeptical, empirical, and theory driven. We, as EGAD members, follow a simple credo: Question what is not questioned. Our questioning is then followed by a routine of analyses that provides us either support for what has eluded questioning or evidence to contraindicate that which goes unquestioned. Almost all of our work is empirical and quantitative in nature, but most of our efforts are strongly driven by theory. This abstract explanation cannot portray the workings of EGAD, so we will provide several examples of the EGAD "way" in action.

Example 1: Calibration

Following Sechrest's insistence that the numbers generated by social science instruments offer little to no meaning, several EGAD members pursued the idea of calibrating measures. Although the idea was not revolutionary, the insistence that researchers actively pursue calibrating measures to equate outcomes, compare measures, and estimate important or noticeable differences in one single research program was novel. Our efforts to explain (Sechrest et al., 1996) and illustrate (McKnight, 1997) calibration have drawn interest and may prove useful if for no other reason but to stimulate other researchers' interests in measurement.

Example 2: Missing Data

All researchers at some point suffer from the uncertainty of how to handle missing data. Our own uncertainty drove us to study the effects of techniques for handling missing data. We simulated different missing-data deletion procedures with a "real" (i.e., not simulated) data set and then applied several imputation, deletion, and modeling procedures to see if the procedures could (a) reproduce the full data-set values, (b) provide sufficiently different results, and (c) help us understand some general guidelines for handling missing data. In addition to simply applying these procedures, we perturbed the data by varying reliability and sample size. These efforts led to a journal article (Figueredo, McKnight, McKnight, & Sidani, 2000) as well as a book (McKnight, McKnight, Sidani, & Figueredo, in press) detailing the results of years of work on the missing-data problem. Sechrest's pragmatic and utilitarian ideals guided the development of both the simulations and the manuscripts that followed.

Example 3: Confirmatory Versus Exploratory Factor Analysis

Many data analysts argue over the respective merits of confirmatory versus exploratory procedures. In no other area of data analysis are these arguments more pervasive than in factor analysis. We aimed to understand the differential information or the incremental validity between confirmatory factor analysis (CFA) and exploratory factor analysis (EFA) approaches to data analysis. Reflecting Sechrest's pragmatism, we used his data set of grocery store box measurements (i.e., height, width, and depth) and formed composite variables from the original length measures. His intention was to collect data for variables that are familiar to everyone, free of psychology content. Thus, composites of tall, narrow, and shallow dimensions could be recognized as cereal boxes, whereas those which were short, wide, and deep were of the type that contained, for example, tea bags. The composite variables were then altered by adding random error to each in an effort to mimic the less reliable social science instruments. Following the work of Overall (1964), we sought to check the relative utility of CFA and EFA in uncovering the original height, width, and depth measures. To our amazement, neither procedure gave us much insight into the original measures; however, EFA provided a few hypotheses that led us to conclude that what might appear simple may be far more complex in data analysis (McKnight & Stickle, 2005). These simulations, therefore, provided us the opportunity to challenge our own biases and adopt a more evenhanded view of the utility of each procedure.

Example 4: Proxy Variables

Another measurement issue that Sechrest has focused on is the use of variables that serve as proxies for the more interesting and theoretically relevant underlying constructs. His insistence that researchers measure directly what is theoretically relevant has stimulated inquiry into the utility of proxy variables in research and the problem with relying on those variables in social science (Walsh et al., 2002). Sechrest and his colleagues looked at the effects of race and ethnocultural factors as proxy variables and as "unpacked" variables to show that the proxy variables tended to mask theoretically relevant variance and therefore adversely affected the statistical results.

Example 5: Method Variance

One of the more intellectually challenging topics discussed in EGAD is the concept of method variance. Owing our allegiance to Campbell and Fiske's (1959) notion of method variance from their seminal paper on the multitrait–

multimethod (MTMM) matrix, we sought to uncover what is meant by method variance. Several EGAD members (e.g., Davis, 2002; Figueredo, Ferketich, & Knapp, 1991) have looked closely at MTMM analyses and have been uncomfortable about explaining an independent effect of method variance. Through our discussions and simulations, we arrived at a tentative conclusion that pure method effects cannot exist, but rather, those effects may be correlated errors or residuals owing to a method-by-trait interaction. Analytic results, theoretical perspectives, and scientific conjecture have driven us to this conclusion. Obviously, there is more work to be done, but this line of research illustrates the developmental process of most of our EGAD initiates guided by his influence.

The intellectual atmosphere created and actively fostered by Lee Sechrest thus prevented the ossification, at least within our own group, of any official dogma regarding the "one true way" to approach any given problem in measurement and contributed instead to an iconoclastic and somewhat irreverent attitude that served the more pragmatic requirements of data analysis. The emphasis was instead on critical thinking, perpetual questioning, and active experimentation with many available methods or approaches. According to our philosophy, which is largely influenced by Sechrest's pragmatism, all methods were evaluated for their incremental validity and for their capacity to alter our uncertainty. Rather than convince ourselves with either logical arguments or abstract mathematical demonstrations, we applied the targeted method to either empirical or simulated data and compared and contrasted the results with those that could be obtained using alternative procedures. This approach did not produce any radically new theories of measurement, but instead helped to train and enlighten us in the application of each new approach and the nature of its unique contribution to our total "bag of tricks."

All of these descriptions of the type of work done in EGAD provide a very pale reflection of the actual experience of participating in the group. For those who have been part of it, there are rich memories of passionate discussions and disputations held in an open and collegial atmosphere among friends, whether in the EGAD seminar room during our regular meetings on Thursday afternoons, in picturesque centuries-old German beer halls, in restaurants overlooking the Acropolis in Athens, riding kamikaze taxis in Naples, or sailing on a moonlit night over the Mediterranean Sea on our way to an international conference. There were also many humorous moments, including a famous "laughing complaint" from a cognitive psychology seminar down the hall in which participants were skeptical of the mirth they heard emanating from a research methodology group. And through it all, there has been the spirit of loyalty and camaraderie shared by people inspired by a sense of shared and lofty goals. These are also an inexpressible, but intrinsic, part of the legacy of Lee Sechrest. Although we cannot be sure just what kind of similar activity might go on at other institutions where research in the methodology of measurement is pursued, we cannot help but get the impression from the books and articles produced elsewhere that this characteristic EGAD style is relatively unique. We attribute that unique atmosphere to Sechrest's direct and indirect influences and thank him for this great gift.

References

Ashton, R. H. (1975). User prediction models in accounting: An alternative use. *The Accounting Review, 50,* 710–722.

Bollen, K. A., & Lennox, R. (1991). Conventional wisdom on measurement: A structural equation perspective. *Psychological Bulletin, 110,* 305–314.

Campbell, D. T., & Fiske, D. W. (1959). Convergent and discriminant validation by multitrait–multimethod matrix. *Psychological Bulletin, 56,* 81–105.

Davis, M. F. (2002). Method variance in the social sciences (Doctoral dissertation, University of Arizona, 2002). *Dissertation Abstracts International, 62,* 4265.

Figueredo, A. J., Ferketich, S. L., & Knapp, T. R. (1991). Focus on psychometrics: More on MTMM: The role of confirmatory factor analysis. *Research in Nursing & Health, 14,* 387–391.

Figueredo, A. J., McKnight, P. E., McKnight, K. M., & Sidani, S. (2000). Multivariate modeling of missing data within and across assessment waves. *Addiction, 95*(Suppl. 3), 361.

Goldstein, A. P., Heller, K., & Sechrest, L. B. (1966). *Psychotherapy and the psychology of behavior change.* New York: Wiley.

Hawking, S. S. (Ed.). (2002). *On the shoulders of giants: The great works of physics and astronomy.* Philadelphia: Running Press.

Heisenberg, W. (1971). *Physics and beyond: Encounters and conversations.* New York: Allen & Unwin.

Hill, R., & Sechrest, L. B. (2000). The use of propensity scores in quasi-experiments: A meta-analysis [Abstract]. *International Journal of Psychology, 35,* 224.

Howard, A. (1974). An assessment of assessment centers. *Academy of Management Journal, 17,* 115–134.

McKnight, P. E. (1997). Calibration of psychological measures: An illustration of three quantitative methods (Doctoral dissertation, University of Arizona, 1997). *Dissertation Abstracts International, 58,* 4460.

McKnight, P. E., McKnight, K., Sidani, S., & Figueredo, A. J. (in press). *The researcher's practical guide to missing data.* New York: Guilford Press.

McKnight, P. E., & Stickle, T. (2005). *Confounded indicators and operations in factor analysis.* Manuscript in preparation.

Morales, A., & Sechrest, L. B. (2000). Rules and principles for combining data [Abstract]. *International Journal of Psychology, 34,* 286.

Morell, V. (1996). *Ancestral passions: The Leakey family and the quest for humankind's beginnings.* New York: Touchstone.

Overall, J. E. (1964). Note on the scientific status of factors. *Psychological Bulletin, 61,* 270–276.

Patterson, D. R., & Sechrest, L. B. (1983). Non-reactive measures in psychotherapy outcome research. *Clinical Psychological Review, 3,* 391–416.

Sechrest, L. B. (1963). Incremental validity: A recommendation. *Educational and Psychological Measurement, 23,* 153–158.

Sechrest, L. B. (1964). Studies of classroom atmosphere. *Psychology in the Schools, 1,* 103–118.

Sechrest, L. B. (1976). Personality. *Annual Review of Psychology, 27,* 1–27.

Sechrest, L. B. (1977). On the dearth of theory in cross-cultural psychology: There is madness in our method. In Y. H. Poortinga (Ed.), *Basic problems in cross-cultural psychology* (pp. 73–82). Amsterdam: Swets & Zeitlinger.

Sechrest, L. B., & Bryan, J. H. (1968). Astrologers as useful marriage counselors. *Trans-action, 6,* 34–36.

Sechrest, L. B., & Cohen, R. Y. (1979). Evaluating outcomes in health care. In G. C. Stone, F. Cohen, & N. E. Adler (Eds.), *Health psychology* (pp. 369–394). San Francisco: Jossey-Bass.

Sechrest, L. B., McKnight, P. E., & McKnight, K. M. (1996). Calibration of measures for psychotherapy outcome studies. *American Psychologist, 51,* 1065–1071.

Sechrest, L. B., & Olbrisch, M. E. (1977). Special considerations in conducting evaluations of encounter groups. *Professional Psychology, 8,* 516–525.

Sechrest, L. B., & Olsen, K. (1971). Graffiti in four types of institutions of higher education. *Journal of Sex Research, 7,* 62–71.

Sechrest, L. B., & Yeaton, W. (1981). Meaningful measures of effect. *Journal of Consulting and Clinical Psychology, 49,* 766–767.

Seligman, M. E. P., & Csikszentmihalyi, M. (2000). Positive psychology: An introduction. *American Psychologist, 55,* 5–14.

Simonton, D. K. (1988). *Scientific genius: A psychology of science.* Cambridge, England: Cambridge University Press.

Walsh, M. E., Katz, M. A., & Sechrest, L. B. (2002). Unpacking cultural factors in adaptation to Type 2 diabetes mellitus. *Medical Care, 40*(Suppl.), I-129–I-139.

Webb, E., Campbell, D. T., Schwartz, R. D., & Sechrest, L. B. (1966) *Unobtrusive measures: A survey of nonreactive research in social science.* Chicago: Rand McNally.

Webster, J., & Martocchio, J. J. (1992). Microcomputer playfulness: Development of a measure with workplace implications (in theory and research). *MIS Quarterly, 16,* 201–226.

Wiatrowski, M. D., Griswold, D. B., & Roberts, M. K. (1981). Social control theory and delinquency. *American Sociological Review, 46,* 525–541.

Wolfe, M. (1978). Social validity: The case for subjective measurement, or how applied behavior analysis is finding its heart. *Journal of Applied Behavior Analysis, 11,* 203–214.

Epilogue

Robert F. Boruch

Lee Sechrest is an alarmingly productive scientist. Throughout his career, he has managed to refresh the way we look at problems and to turn some problems inside out so that we could learn more. His 1956 doctoral dissertation illustrates the perspective, "Patients' Interpretations of Their Psychotherapists," rather than vice versa, to make the point.

Many of Sechrest's contributions lie squarely in the psychological therapeutic arena. Yet many do not. His taste for interesting issues transcends the artificial boundaries of an academic discipline or a professional practice. Certainly, his work on unobtrusive measures does so, inasmuch as it is, at least, a research agenda for measurement, program evaluation, sociology, and the management and planning of museums and zoos.

Sechrest has probably authored or coauthored more papers for the *Journal of Educational Psychology* and related periodicals than many educational psychologists. His works appear in journals and proceedings of conferences on epidemiology (factor analysis), public policy and law (psychology and inferences about policy), management education, criminology (rehabilitation), medicine, program evaluation (health), diabetes, heart transplants, and statistics.

Our colleague's contributions are not bounded by geography. His research on in-country mental disorder appears in the *Philippine Sociological Review, Asian Studies,* and other places. His sensitivity to cultural aspects of measurement and classification in mental illness observation is reflected in various papers in the *Journal of Cross-Cultural Psychology* and the *Journal of Forensic Psychology*, among others. Sechrest has not been silent about the state of theory in cross-cultural psychology; one of his paper's subtitles is "There Is Madness to Our Method." Even when he is silent, which is not for long, we can hear the gears whirring—for example, in Colombia for the Calí trials on cultural enrichment for children in the barrios, and in other countries to which he has dedicated his efforts.

Sechrest is no slouch about studying important problems in interesting target populations. Recall his work with Lisa Shusterman on nurses' attitudes about hospital deaths, his research on the nature and practice of surpluses and sharing of goods among prisoners, psychopathic hyperventilators, and homosexuals in the Philippines, and many more.

Sechrest evidently objects to seeing good research go unused, and he favors discovering ways to see that it is exploited sensibly. Witness his portfolio of work on the use and misuse of effect size estimates, which has found its way into the literature on meta-analysis and into contemporary editorial review processes for research journals. Witness his important efforts with Everett Rogers, Tom Backer, and others to construct state-of-the-art publications on when, how, and why the dissemination and use of information occur in the health sector. In this, Sechrest had the benefit of serving time with the utilization research mob at the University of Michigan, communing with kindred spirits such as James Fairweather and Louis Tornatzky, and teaching us about the work products.

Many of us, or at least one of us, relish his talent for creating titles or subtitles that could drive an entire research agenda. Among these are "Dogma or Data: Bragging Rights" (*American Psychologist*), "The Past Future of Clinical Psychology" (*Journal of Consulting and Clinical Psychology*), and "Shall We, Then, All Hang Separately?" (*The Clinical Psychologist*). Cleverness at titling ideas does count. Yet so do intellectual freshness and substance, and Sechrest continues to give us these.

Some readers know that Sechrest is offbeat. This is partly on account of his work with Marilyn Pflederer on children's responses to musical stimuli in the 1960s. The pun (mine), poor as it was, is also a testimony to Sechrest's sense of humor—his relish in discovering the absurd (as in the Rorschach tests).

Our colleague Lee Sechrest is polymathic with a sense of humor. He is a *rara avis*. Bless you, Lee Sechrest, for your virtues on the occasion of this Festschrift in your honor.

Bibliography of Lee B. Sechrest

Academic Positions

Pennsylvania State University, assistant professor, 1956–58
Northwestern University, assistant professor to professor, 1958–1973
Florida State University, professor, 1973–1980
University of Michigan, director of the Center for Research on the Utilization of Scientific Knowledge and professor of Medical Care Organization and of Psychology, 1980–1984
University of Arizona, head, Department of Psychology 1984–1989; professor 1984–2002; professor emeritus, 2003–present

Bibliography

1952

Hemphill, J. K., & Sechrest, L. B. (1952). A comparison of three criteria of aircrew effectiveness in combat over Korea. *Journal of Applied Psychology, 36*, 323–327.

1954

Hemphill, J. K., & Sechrest, L. B. (1954). Motivational variables in the assuming of combat obligations. *Journal of Consulting Psychology, 18*, 113–118.

1956

Sechrest, L. B. (1956). *Patients' interpretations of their psychotherapists*. Unpublished doctoral dissertation, Ohio State University.

1959

Snyder, R., & Sechrest, L. B. (1959). An experimental study of directive group therapy with defective delinquents. *American Journal of Mental Deficiency, 63*, 117–123.

1961

Barger, P., & Sechrest, L. B. (1961). Convergent and discriminant validity of four Holtzman Inkblot Test variables. *Journal of Psychological Studies, 12*, 227–236.

Kieferle, D., & Sechrest, L. B. (1961). Effects of alterations in personal constructs. *Journal of Psychological Studies, 12*, 173–178.

Sechrest, L. B. (1961). Psychopathology, Ltd. [Review of the book *Clinical psychopathology*]. *Contemporary Psychology, 6*, 69–70.

Sechrest, L. B., & Barger, B. (1961). Verbal participation and perceived benefit from group psychotherapy. *International Journal of Group Psychotherapy, 11*, 49–59.

Sechrest, L. B., & Jackson, D. N. (1961). Social intelligence and accuracy of interpersonal predictions. *Journal of Personality, 29*, 167–182.

Shore, E., & Sechrest, L. B. (1961). Concept attainment as a function of number of positive instances presented. *Journal of Educational Psychology, 52*, 303–307.

Wallace, J., & Sechrest, L. B. (1961). Relative difficulty of conjunctive and disjunctive concepts. *Journal of Psychological Studies, 12*, 97–104.

1962

Jackson, M., & Sechrest, L. B. (1962). Early recollections in four neurotic diagnostic categories. *Journal of Individual Psychology, 18*, 52–56.

Lawton, M., & Sechrest, L. B. (1962). Figure drawing of boys from father-present and father-absent homes. *Journal of Clinical Psychology, 18*, 304–305.

Sechrest, L. B. (1962). Clinical psychology: Potluck. [Review of the book *Progress in clinical psychology*]. *Contemporary Psychology, 7*, 96–97.

Sechrest, L. B. (1962). The motivation in school of young children: Some interview data. *Journal of Experimental Education, 30*, 327–335.

Sechrest, L. B. (1962). Stimulus equivalents of the psychotherapist. *Journal of Consulting Psychology, 18*, 172–176.

Sechrest, L. B., & Jackson, D. N. (1962). The generality of deviant response tendencies. *Journal of Consulting Psychology, 26*, 395–401.

Sechrest, L. B., & Strowig, R. W. (1962). Teaching machines and the individual learner. *Educational Theory, 12*, 157–169.

Sechrest, L. B., & Tutko, T. (1962). Conceptual performance and personality variables. *Journal of Consulting Psychology, 26*, 481.

Wallace, J., & Sechrest, L. B. (1962). Assimilation and utilization of information in concept attainment under varying conditions of information presentation. *Journal of Educational Psychology, 53*, 157–164.

1963

Sechrest, L. B. (1963). George A. Kelly: The psychology of personal constructs. In R. Heine & J. Wepman (Eds.), *Theories of personality* (pp. 206–233). Chicago: Aldine.

Sechrest, L. B. (1963). Implicit reinforcement of responses. *Journal of Educational Psychology, 54*, 197–201.

Sechrest, L. B. (1963). Incremental validity: A recommendation. *Educational and Psychological Measurement, 23*, 153–158.

Sechrest, L. B. (1963). Pick a number [Review of the books *Social indicators* and *On the accuracy of economic observations*]. *Contemporary Psychology, 13*, 238–239.

Sechrest, L. B. (1963). Symptoms of mental disorder in the Philippines. *Philippine Sociological Review, 11*, 189–206.

Sechrest, L. B., & Jackson, D. N. (1963). Deviant response tendencies: Their measurement and interpretation. *Educational and Psychological Measurement, 23*, 33–45.

Straits, B., & Sechrest, L. B. (1963). Further support of some findings concerning the psychological characteristics of smokers and nonsmokers. *Journal of Consulting Psychology, 27*, 279.

Sechrest, L. B., & Wallace, J. (1963). Figure drawings and naturally occurring events: Elimination of the expansive euphoria hypothesis. *Journal of Educational Psychology, 55*, 32–44.

Sechrest, L. B., & Wallace, J. (1963). The frequency hypothesis and content analysis of projective tests. *Journal of Consulting Psychology, 27*, 387–393.

Williams, T., & Sechrest, L. B. (1963). The ascribed usability of personal constructs as a function of their generality. *Journal of Psychological Studies, 14*, 75–81.

Zelin, M., & Sechrest, L. B. (1963). The validity of the "mother" and "father" cards of the Rorschach. *Journal of Projective Techniques, 27*, 114–121.

1964

Sechrest, L. B. (1964). Mental disorder in the Philippines. *University of the Philippines Research Digest, 3*, 5–9.

Sechrest, L. B. (1964). School psychology in Japan. *Psychology in the Schools, 1*, 385–387.

Sechrest, L. B. (1964). Studies of classroom atmosphere. *Psychology in the Schools, 1*, 103–118.

1965

Kumler, M., Glickman, S., & Sechrest, L. B. (1965). Conscious perseveration and persistence of autonomic activity: A replication. *Journal of Psychology, 61*, 77–80.

Sechrest, L. B. (1965). Vicarious reinforcement in children at two age levels. *Journal of Educational Psychology, 56*, 100–106.

Sechrest, L. B., & Kaas, J. (1965). Concept difficulty as a function of stimulus similarity. *Journal of Educational Psychology, 56*, 327–333.

1966

Goldstein, A. P., Heller, K., & Sechrest, L. B. (1966). *Psychotherapy and the psychology of behavior change.* New York: Wiley.

Webb, E., Campbell, D. T., Schwartz, R. D., & Sechrest, L. B. (1966). *Unobtrusive measures: A survey of nonreactive research in social science.* Chicago: Rand McNally.

1967

Sechrest, L. B. (1967). Culture, law, and psychiatry. *Psychiatric Spectator, IV*(9), 9–11.

Sechrest, L. B. (1967, September). Mental restoration: A world challenge. *The Rotarian*, 23–25.

Sechrest, L. B. (1967). Naturalistic assessment of social attitudes. *Human Development, 10*, 199–211.

Sechrest, L. B., Gallimore, R., & Hersch, P. (1967). Feedback and accuracy of clinical prediction. *Journal of Consulting Psychology, 31*, 1–11.

Sechrest, L. B., & Wallace, J. (1967). *Psychology and human problems.* Columbus, OH: Merrill.

1968

Johnson, S., & Sechrest, L. B. (1968). Comparison of desensitization and progressive relaxation in treating test anxiety. *Journal of Consulting and Clinical Psychology, 36*, 280–286.

Pflederer, M., & Sechrest, L. B. (1968). Conservation in musical experience. *Psychology in the Schools, 5,* 99–105.

Pflederer, M., & Sechrest, L. B. (1968). Conservation-type responses of children to musical stimuli. *Council for Research in Music Education Bulletin, 13,* 19–36.

Sechrest, L. B. (1968). Exercise as an operant response in retarded children. *Journal of Special Education, 2,* 311–317.

Sechrest, L. B. (1968). Personal constructs and personal characteristics. *Journal of Individual Psychology, 24,* 162–166.

Sechrest, L. B. (1968). Testing, measuring, and assessing people. In E. Borgatta & W. Lambert (Eds.), *Handbook of personality theory and research* (pp. 529–625). Chicago: Rand McNally.

Sechrest, L. B., & Bryan, J. H. (1968). Astrologers as useful marriage counselors. *Transaction, 6,* 34–36.

Sechrest, L. B., Flores, L., & Arellano, L. (1968). Language and social interaction in a bilingual culture. *Journal of Social Psychology, 76,* 155–162.

1969

Sechrest, L. B. (1969). Nonreactive assessment of attitudes. In E. P. Willems (Ed.), *Naturalistic viewpoints in psychological research* (pp. 147–161). New York: Holt, Rinehart & Winston.

Sechrest, L. B. (1969). Philippine culture, stress, and psychopathology. In W. Caudill & T. Y. Lin (Eds.), *Mental health research in Asia and the Pacific* (pp. 306–334). Honolulu, HI: East-West Center Press.

Sechrest, L. B., & Flores, L. (1969). Homosexuality in the Philippines and the United States: The handwriting on the wall. *Journal of Social Psychology, 74,* 3–12.

Sechrest, L. B., & Flores, L. (1969). Sibling position of Philippine psychiatric patients. *Journal of Social Psychology, 77,* 135–137.

1970

Koppell, M., & Sechrest, L. B. (1970). A multitrait–multimethod matrix for sense of humor. *Educational and Psychological Measurement, 30,* 77–85.

Mathis, B. C., & Cotton, J. (1970). *Psychological foundations of education: Learning and teaching.* New York: Academic Press.

Patterson, M., & Sechrest, L. B. (1970). Interpersonal distance and impression formation. *Journal of Personality, 38,* 161–166.

Sechrest, L. B. (1970). Conceptions and management of cases of mental disorder in some Negro Oriental barrios. *Philippine Sociological Review, 18,* 1–17.

Sechrest, L. B. (1970). Experiments in the field. In R. Naroll & R. Cohen (Eds.), *Handbook of method in cultural anthropology* (pp. 196–209). New York: Doubleday.

Zimmerman, M., & Sechrest, L. B. (1970). Brief focused instruction and musical concepts. *Journal of Research in Musical Education, 18,* 25–36.

1971

Sechrest, L. B. (1971). Anthropsychology [Review of the book *Socialization: The approach from social anthropology*]. *Contemporary Psychology, 16,* 665–666.

Sechrest, L. B. (1971). Situational sampling and contrived situations in assessment of behavior. *Pakistan Journal of Psychology, 4,* 3–19.

Sechrest, L. B. (1971). Unobtrusive measures in selection and evaluation. In H. B. Haley, A. G. D'Costa, & A. M. Schafer (Eds.), *Personality measurement in medical education* (pp. 147–169). Washington, DC: Association of American Medical Colleges.

Sechrest, L. B., & Flores, L. (1971). The occurrence of a nervous mannerism in two cultures. *Asian Studies, 9*, 55–63.

Sechrest, L. B., & Olsen, K. (1971). Graffiti in four types of institutions of higher education. *Journal of Sex Research, 7*, 62–71.

1972

Duncan, C. P., Melton, A., & Sechrest, L. B. (Eds.). (1972). *Human memory: Festschrift for Benton J. Underwood.* New York: Appleton-Century-Crofts.

Sechrest, L. B. (1972). Psychology and educational testing [Review of the book *Psychological and educational testing*]. *Journal of Educational Measurement, 9*, 3.

Sechrest, L. B. (1972). [Review of the book *Learning mechanism in smoking*]. *American Journal of Psychiatry, 129*, 247–248.

Sechrest, L. B., Fay, T. L., & Zaidi, S. M. H. (1972). Problems of translation in cross-cultural research. *Journal of Cross-Cultural Psychology, 3*, 41–56.

1973

Sechrest, L. B. (1973). Another dubious cookbook [Review of the book *Cross-national research: Social psychological methods and problems*]. *Contemporary Psychology, 18*, 433–434.

Sechrest, L. B. (1973). Cultural differences in mental illness: Their implications for legal policy and decision making. *Journal of Forensic Psychology, 5*, 14–24.

Sechrest, L. B. (1973). Use of innocuous and noninterventional measures in evaluation. In B. Worthen & J. Sanders (Eds.), *Educational evaluation* (pp. 289–297). Worthington, OH: C. A. Jones.

Sechrest, L. B., Fay, T. L., & Zaidi, S. M. H. (1973). Attitudes toward mental disorder among college students in the United States, Pakistan, and the Philippines. *Journal of Cross-Cultural Psychology, 4*, 342–359.

Sechrest, L. B., & Wallace, J. (1973). *The nature and study of psychology.* Itasca, IL: Peacock.

Shusterman, L. B., & Sechrest, L. (1973). Attitudes of registered nurses toward death in a general hospital. *Psychiatry in Medicine, 4*, 416–425.

1974

Guthrie, G., & Sechrest, L. B. (1974). Psychology of, by, and for Filipinos. In *Philippine studies: Geography, archaeology, psychology and literature* (Special Report No. 10, pp. 44–70). DeKalb: Northern Illinois University, Center for Southeast Asian Studies.

Haring, O., Middlekauf, G., & Sechrest, L. B. (1974). An internal auditing system for improving the quality of medical care. *Journal of the American Medical Women's Association, 29*, 178–187.

Sechrest, L. B., & Flores, L. (1974). Surplus and sharing in a prison sample. *Journal of Social Psychology, 94*, 33–44.

1975

Sechrest, L. B. (1975). Another look at unobtrusive measures: An alternative to what? In W. Sinaiko & L. Broedling (Eds.), *Perspectives on attitude assessment: Surveys and their alternatives* (pp. 103–116). Washington, DC: Smithsonian Institution.

Sechrest, L. B. (1975). Research appreciation [Review of the book *Reading statistics and research*]. *Contemporary Psychology, 20*, 958–959.

Sechrest, L. B. (1975). Research contributions of practicing clinical psychologists. *Professional Psychology, 6*, 413–419.

Sechrest, L. B., & Bootzin, R. (1975). Preliminary evaluation of participation by psychologists in encounter groups. *Professional Psychology, 6*, 59–69.

1976

Clark, R. D., III, & Sechrest, L. B. (1976). The mandate phenomenon. *Journal of Personality and Social Psychology, 34*, 1057–1061.

Sechrest, L. B. (1976). On the need for experimentation in cross-cultural research. *Annals of the New York Academy of Sciences, 285*, 104–118.

Sechrest, L. B. (1976). Personality. *Annual Review of Psychology, 27*, 1–27.

Sechrest, L. B. (1976). Personality theory and identity advocacy. *Personality and Social Psychology Bulletin, 2*, 230–233.

Sechrest, L. B. (1976). The psychologist as program evaluator. In P. Wood (Ed.), *Career opportunities for psychologists: Expanding and emerging areas* (pp. 251–258). Washington, DC: American Psychological Association.

Sechrest, L. B. (1976). [Review of the book *Handbook on evaluation research*, Vols. 1 & 2]. *American Journal of Psychiatry, 133*, 1218.

Sechrest, L. B., & Cohen, L. (1976). The APA evaluation of teaching of psychology. *Teaching of Psychology, 3*, 130–134.

1977

Sechrest, L. B., (1977). Administrative functions and research requirements. In L. B. Sechrest (Ed.), *Emergency medical services: Research methodology* (DHEW Publication. No. PHS 78-3195, pp. 3–5). Washington, DC: U.S. Government Printing Office.

Sechrest, L. B. (Ed.). (1977). *Emergency medical services: Research methodology* (DHEW Publication No. PHS 78-3195). Washington, DC: U.S. Government Printing Office.

Sechrest, L. B. (1977). Evaluation results and decision-making: The need for program evaluation. In L. B. Sechrest (Ed.), *Emergency medical services: Research methodology* (DHEW Publication No. PHS 78-3195, pp. 16–23). Washington, DC: U.S. Government Printing Office.

Sechrest, L. B. (1977). Experimental design and causal inference. In L. B. Sechrest (Ed.), *Emergency medical services: Research methodology* (DHEW Publication No. PHS 78-3195, pp. 33–44). Washington, DC: U.S. Government Printing Office.

Sechrest, L. B. (1977). On the dearth of theory in cross-cultural psychology: There is madness in our method. In Y. H. Poortinga (Ed.), *Basic problems in cross-cultural psychology* (pp. 73–82). Amsterdam: Swets & Zeitlinger.

Sechrest, L. B. (1977). Personal construct theory. In R. Corsini (Ed.), *Current personality theories* (pp. 203–242). Itasca, IL: Peacock.

Sechrest, L. B. (1977). Unobtrusive measures. In B. Wolman (Ed.), *International encyclopedia of psychiatry, psychoanalysis, psychology, and neurology* (Vol. 11, pp. 341–344). New York: Aesculapius.

Sechrest, L. B., & Olbrisch, M. E. (1977). Special considerations in conducting evaluations of encounter groups. *Professional Psychology, 8*, 516–525.

Sechrest, L. B., & Sukstorf, S. (1977). Parental visitation of the institutionalized retarded. *Journal of Applied Social Psychology, 7*, 286–294.

1978

Pacht, A., Bent, R., Cook, T. D., Klebanoff, L. B., Rodgers, D. A., Sechrest, L. B., et al. (1978). Continuing evaluation and accountability controls for a national health insurance program. *American Psychologist, 33*, 305–313.

1979

Bent, R., Claiborn, W., Rosenberg, A., Shueman, S., Stricker, G., Sechrest, L. B., et al. (1979). A system of peer review for outpatient psychological services. *Journal Supplement Abstract Service: Catalog of Selected Documents in Psychology, 9,* 89 (Ms. No. 1969).

Sechrest, L. B. (1979). A passion for theory [Review of the book *New perspectives in personal construct theory*]. *Contemporary Psychology, 24,* 19–20.

Sechrest, L. B. (1979). Becoming a health psychologist: Educating health psychologists in traditional graduate training programs. *Professional Psychology, 10,* 489–595.

Sechrest, L. B. (Ed.). (1979). *New directions in the methodology of behavioral science: No. 1 Unobtrusive measures today.* San Francisco: Jossey-Bass.

Sechrest, L. B., & Cohen., R. Y. (1979). Evaluating outcomes in health care. In G. C. Stone, F. Cohen, & N. E. Adler (Eds.), *Health psychology* (pp. 369–394). San Francisco: Jossey-Bass.

Sechrest, L. B., & Peterson, F., Jr. (1979). Use of observers to measure EMT performance. In *Emergency medical services research methodology: Workshop 2. NCHSR Research Proceedings* (DHEW Publication No. PHS 79-3225-2, pp. 19–24). Washington, DC: U.S. Government Printing Office.

Sechrest, L. B., & Phillips, M. (1979). Unobtrusive measures: An overview. In L. B. Sechrest (Ed.), *New directions in methodology for behavior science: No. 1. Unobtrusive measures today* (pp. 1–17). San Francisco: Jossey-Bass.

Sechrest, L. B., & Redner, R. (1979). Strength and integrity of treatments in evaluation studies. How well does it work? In *Review of criminal justice evaluation, 1978: Part II. Review of evaluation results—Corrections* (pp. 19–62). Washington, DC: National Criminal Justice Reference Service.

Sechrest, L. B., West, S. G., Phillips, M., Redner, R., & Yeaton, W. (Eds.). (1979). *Evaluation studies review annual* (Vol. IV). Beverly Hills, CA: Sage.

Sechrest, L. B., West, S. G., Phillips, M., Redner, R., & Yeaton, W. H. (1979). Some neglected problems in evaluation research: Strength and integrity of treatments. In L. B. Sechrest, S. G. West, M. Phillips, R. Redner, & W. H. Yeaton (Eds.), *Evaluation studies review annual* (Vol. IV, pp. 15–35). Beverly Hills, CA: Sage.

Sechrest, L. B., White, S., & Brown, E. (Eds.). (1979). *Rehabilitation of criminal offenders: Problems and prospects.* Washington, DC: National Research Council.

1980

Brown, E., & Sechrest, L. B. (1980). Research methods in cross-cultural psychology. In H. Triandis (Ed.), *Handbook of cross-cultural psychology* (Vol. 2, pp. 297–318). Boston: Allyn & Bacon.

Sechrest, L. B. (1980). Evaluation researchers: Training and disciplinary identity. In L. Sechrest (Ed.), *Training in evaluation research* (pp. 1–18). San Francisco: Jossey-Bass.

Sechrest, L. B. (Ed.). (1980). *Training in evaluation research: New directions in evaluation research.* San Francisco: Jossey-Bass.

1981

Martin, S., Sechrest, L. B., & Redner, R. (Eds.). (1981). *New directions in the rehabilitation of criminal offenders.* Washington, DC: National Academy Press.

Sechrest, L. B. (1981). All about grids [Review of the book *A manual for repertory grid technique*]. *Contemporary Psychology, 26,* 89–90.

Sechrest, L. B. (1981). Limitations on the interpretation of effect size measures in evaluative research. In *American Statistical Association 1980 Proceedings of the Section on Survey Research Methods* (pp. 382–385). Washington, DC: American Statistical Association.

Sechrest, L. B. (1981). Moderator observations and closing remarks. In *Symposium on Traffic Safety Effectiveness (Impact) Evaluation Projects* (pp. 9–14, 353–354). Chicago: National Safety Council.

Sechrest, L. B. (1981). Psychology and national health policy [Review of the book *Psychology and national health insurance: A sourcebook*]. *Contemporary Psychology, 26,* 89–90.

Sechrest, L. B. (1981). The standards: A general review [Review of the book *Standards for evaluations of education programs*]. *Evaluation News, 2,* 145–148.

Sechrest, L. B., & Mabe, P. (1981). Translating research findings into policy in emergency medical services. *Health Policy Quarterly, 1,* 57–72.

Sechrest, L. B., & Yeaton, W. (1981). Assessing the effectiveness of social programs: Methodological and conceptual issues. In S. Ball (Ed.), *New directions in evaluation research* (No. 9, pp. 41–56). San Francisco: Jossey-Bass.

Sechrest, L. B., & Yeaton, W. (1981). Critical dimensions in the choice and maintenance of successful treatments: Strength, integrity, and effectiveness. *Journal of Consulting and Clinical Psychology, 49,* 156–167.

Sechrest, L. B., & Yeaton, W. (1981). Empirical bases for estimating effect size. In R. F. Boruch, P. M. Wortman, D. S. Cordray, & Associates (Eds.), *Reanalyzing program valuations: Policies and practices for secondary analysis of social and educational programs* (pp. 212–224). San Francisco: Jossey-Bass.

Sechrest, L. B., & Yeaton, W. (1981). Estimating effect size. In P. M. Wortman (Ed.), *Methods for evaluating health services* (pp. 61–85). Beverly Hills, CA: Sage.

Sechrest, L. B., & Yeaton, W. H. (1981). Estimating magnitudes of experimental effects. *Journal Supplements Abstract Service: Catalog of Selected Documents in Psychology, 11,* 39 (Ms. No. 2355).

Sechrest, L. B., & Yeaton, W. (1981). Meaningful measures of effect. *Journal of Consulting and Clinical Psychology, 49,* 766–767

Webb, E., Campbell, D. T., Schwartz, R. D., Sechrest, L. B., & Grove, J. (1981). *Nonreactive measures in the social sciences* (2nd ed.). Boston: Houghton-Mifflin.

1982

Sechrest, L. B. (1982). Evidence, method, and strategy in evaluation research. In *Proceedings of Second Symposium on Traffic Safety Effectiveness (Impact) Evaluation Projects* (pp. 5–9). Chicago: National Safety Council.

Sechrest, L. B. (1982). Reaction: Program evaluation—The independent and dependent variables. *Counseling Psychology, 10*(4), 73–74.

Sechrest, L. B., Ametrano, D., & Ametrano, I. (1982). Program evaluation. In J. R. McNamara & A. G. Barclay (Eds.), *Critical issues, developments, and trends in professional psychology* (pp. 190–226). New York: Praeger.

Sechrest, L. B., & Hoffman, P. E. (1982). The philosophical underpinnings of peer review. *Professional Psychology, 13,* 4–18.

Sechrest, L. B., & Yeaton, W. (1982). Magnitudes of experimental effect. *Evaluation Review, 6,* 579–599.

Stricker, G., & Sechrest, L. B. (1982). The role of research in criteria construction. *Professional Psychology, 13,* 19–22.

Tornatzky, L., & Solomon, T. (1982). Contributions of social science to innovation and productivity. *American Psychologist, 35,* 737–746.

1983

Huey, S., & Sechrest, L. B. (1983). Hyperventilation syndrome and psychopathology. In *Psychological documents* (Doc. No. 2584). Washington, DC: American Psychological Association.

Patterson, D., & Sechrest, L. B. (1983). Nonreactive measures in psychotherapy outcome research. *Clinical Psychology Review, 3,* 391–416.

Sechrest, L. B. (1983). Personal-constructs theory. In R. J. Corsini & A. J. Marsella (Eds.), *Personality theories, research and assessment* (pp. 229–285). Itasca, IL: Peacock.

Sechrest, L. B. (1983). Some cautions about analyses in complex social research. In *Third Symposium on Traffic Safety Effectiveness (Impact) Evaluation Projects* (pp. 8–13). Washington, DC: U.S. Department of Transportation, National Highway Traffic Safety Administration.

Sechrest, L. B., Ametrano, D., & Ametrano, I. (1983). Evaluation of social programs. In C. E. Walker (Ed.), *The handbook of clinical psychology* (Vol. 1, pp. 129–166). Homewood, IL: Dow Jones-Irwin.

Sechrest, L. B., & Belew, J. (1983). Nonreactive measures of social attitudes. *Applied Social Psychology Annual, 4,* 23–63.

Sechrest, L. B., Mabe, P. A., & Howland, K. (1983). Using observer methods in EMS research. *Emergency Health Services Quarterly, 4,* 51–60.

Sechrest, L. B., & West, S. G. (1983). Measuring the intervention in rehabilitation experiments. *International Annals of Criminology, 21*(1), 11–19.

1984

Sechrest, L. B. (1984). Nonreactive measures of attitude and morale. In *Proceedings of the Second Symposium on Motivation and Morale in the NATO Forces.* Brussels, Belgium: NATO Defense Research Group DS/A/DR 398.

Sechrest, L. B. (1984). Reliability and validity. In A. S. Bellack & M. Hersen (Eds.), *Research methods in clinical psychology* (pp. 24–54). New York: Pergamon Press.

Sechrest, L. B. (1984). [Review of the book *The development and application of social learning theory: Selected papers*]. *Centennial Psychology: Journal of the History of the Behavioral Sciences, 20,* 228–230.

Sechrest, L. B. (1984). Social science: Keep it legal [Review of the book *Solutions to ethical and legal problems in social research: Quantitative studies in social relations*]. *Contemporary Psychology, 29,* 946–947.

1985

Dickman, S., & Sechrest, L. B. (1985). Research on memory and clinical practice. In G. Stricker & R. H. Keisner (Eds.), *From research to clinical practice: The implications of social and developmental research for psychotherapy* (pp. 15–44). New York: Plenum.

Sechrest, L. B. (1985). Evaluating health care. *American Behavioral Scientist, 28,* 527–542.

Sechrest, L. B. (1985). Experiments and demonstrations in health services research. *Medical Care, 23,* 677–695.

Sechrest, L. B. (1985, Spring). It's your quarter: President's message. *The Clinical Psychologist, 38,* 21, 23.

Sechrest, L. B. (1985, Spring). The lithotripter and the monolith: President's message. *The Clinical Psychologist, 38,* 45, 47.

Sechrest, L. B. (1985). Observer studies: Collection of data by remote control. In L. Burstein & H. Freeman (Eds.), *Collecting evaluation data: Problems and solutions* (pp. 49–66). Beverly Hills, CA: Sage.

Sechrest, L. B. (1985, Fall). Shall we, then, all hang separately? President's message. *The Clinical Psychologist, 38,* 73–75.

Sechrest, L. B. (1985). Social science and social policy: Will our numbers ever be good enough? In L. Shotland & M. Mark (Eds.), *Social science and social policy* (pp. 63–95). Beverly Hills, CA: Sage.

Sechrest, L. B. (1985, Winter). Specialization: Who needs it? President's message. *The Clinical Psychologist, 38,* 1–3.

Vinokur, A., Burstein, E., Wortman, P. M., & Sechrest, L. B. (1985). Group decision making by experts: A field study of panels evaluating medical technologies. *Journal of Personality and Social Psychology, 49,* 70–84.

1986

Cohen, L., Sargent, M. M., & Sechrest, L. B. (1986). Use of psychotherapy research by professional psychologists. *American Psychologist, 41*, 198–206.

Sechrest, L. B. (1986). Modes and methods of personality research. *Journal of Personality, 54*, 318–331.

Sechrest, L. B., & Yeaton, W. H. (1986). Use and misuse of no-difference findings in eliminating threats to validity. *Evaluation Review, 10*, 836–852.

1987

Sechrest, L. B. (1987). Approaches to ensuring quality of data and performance: Lessons for science. In D. N. Jackson & J. P. Rushton (Eds.), *Excellence in science: Origins and achievement* (pp. 253–283). Beverly Hills, CA: Sage.

Sechrest, L. B. (1987). Classification for treatment. In D. M. Gottfredson & M. Tonry (Eds.), *Prediction and classification: Criminal justice decision making* (pp. 293–322). Chicago: University of Chicago Press.

Sechrest, L. B. (1987). Critical issues in the development of cross-cultural research methodology. In K. F. Mauer & A. I. Retief (Eds.), *HSRC investigation into research methodology: Psychology in context—Cross-cultural research trends in South Africa* (Research Report Series 4, pp. 37–63). Pretoria, South Africa: Human Sciences Research Council.

Sechrest, L. B. (1987). Post-doctoral training in health policy studies. In G. Stone & J. Matarazzo (Eds.), *Training in health psychology* (pp. 389–402). Chicago: University of Chicago Press.

Sechrest, L. B. (1987). Quality in training: Running around in circles. *The Clinical Psychologist, 40*, 11–13.

Sechrest, L. B. (1987). Reactions to conference: Perspective of health services research scientist—A research agenda for personal health risk assessment methods in health hazard/health risk appraisal. *Health Services Research, 22*, 612–615.

Sechrest, L. B. (1987). Research on quality assurance. *Professional Psychology: Research and Practice, 18*, 113–116.

Sechrest, L. B., & Chatel, D. (1987). Evaluation and accountability in education and training: An overall perspective. In B. Edelstein & E. Berler (Eds.), *Evaluation and accountability in clinical psychology: A national perspective* (pp. 1–37). New York: Plenum.

Sechrest, L. B., & Pitz, D. (1987). Commentary: Measuring the effectiveness of heart transplant programs. *Journal of Chronic Diseases, 40*(Suppl. 1), 155–158.

Sechrest, L. B., & Rosenblatt, A. (1987). Research methods in juvenile delinquency. In H. C. Quay (Ed.), *Handbook of juvenile delinquency* (pp. 417–450). New York: Wiley.

Sechrest, L. B., & Rosenblatt, A. (1987). Research on peer review. In G. Stricker & A. Rodriquez (Eds.), *Quality assurance in mental health services* (pp. 81–101). New York: Plenum Press.

Sechrest, L. B., & Yeaton, W. H. (1987). Assessing factors influencing acceptance of no-difference research. *Evaluation Review, 11*, 131–142.

Sechrest, L. B., & Yeaton, W. (1987). No-difference research. In D. S. Cordray, H. S. Bloom, & R. J. Light (Eds.), *New directions in program evaluation: No. 34. Evaluation practice in review* (pp. 67–82). San Francisco: Jossey-Bass.

1988

Sechrest, L. B., & Scott, A. (1988). The effectiveness of the program evaluation process. In C. S. de Beer (Ed.), *RSA 2000: Vol. 10. Dialogue with the future* (No. 1, pp. 31–40). Pretoria, South Africa: Human Sciences Research Council.

Pion, G., Howard, A., Cordray, D. S., Sechrest, L. B., Molaison, V., Hall, J., et al. (1988). Membership opinions about APA: A recent snapshot. *American Psychologist, 43*, 1029–1044.

Wortman, P., Vinokur, A., & Sechrest, L. B. (1988). Do consensus conferences work? A process evaluation of the NIH Consensus Development Program. *Journal of Health Politics, Policy and Law, 13,* 469–498.

1989

Scott, A., & Sechrest, L. B. (1989). Strength of theory and theory of strength. *Evaluation and Program Planning, 12,* 329–336.

Sechrest, L. D. (1989). A call for multiple methods [Review of the book *Multiple methods in program evaluation*]. *Contemporary Psychology, 34,* 576.

Sechrest, L. B. (1989). A mental health crisis? [Review of the book *The mental health crisis in America*]. *Contemporary Psychology, 34,* 387–388.

Sechrest, L. B. (1989). [Review of the book *Evaluation Studies Review Annual,* Vol. 11.] *Contemporary Psychology, 34,* 356.

Sechrest, L. B. (1989). [Review of the book *The future of mental health services research: Coping with crisis*]. *Contemporary Psychology, 34,* 387–388.

Sechrest, L. B. (1989). Summary comments: Research on worksite interventions. In K. Johnson, J. H. LaRosa, C. J. Scheirer, & J. M. Wolfe (Eds.), *1988 methodological issues in worksite research proceedings* (pp. 113–124). Bethesda, MD: U.S. Department of Health and Human Services.

Sechrest, L. B. (1989). Two thumbs up [Review of the book *Evaluation studies review annual,* Vol. 11]. *Contemporary Psychology, 34,* 356.

1990

Aiken, L., West, S. G., Sechrest, L. B., & Reno, R. (1990). Graduate training in statistics, methodology, and measurement in psychology: A survey of Ph.D. programs in North America. *American Psychologist, 45,* 721–734.

Kaemingk, K., & Sechrest, L. B. (Eds.). (1990). AIDS research and public policy [Special issue]. *Evaluation and Program Planning, 13.*

Kaemingk, K., & Sechrest, L. B. (1990). AIDS research and policy decisions. *Evaluation and Program Planning, 13,* 1–7.

Pion, G., & Sechrest, L. B. (1990). Assessing competencies for delivering services to seriously emotionally disturbed children: The first step in the process. In P. Magrab & P. Wohlford (Eds.), *Improving psychological services for children and adolescents with severe mental disorders: Clinical training in psychology* (pp. 67–71). Washington, DC: American Psychological Association.

Sechrest, L. B. (1990). A case for separate-but-equal in clinical training. In L. Bickman & H. Ellis (Eds.), *Preparing psychologists for the 21st century: Proceedings of the National Conference on Graduate Education in Psychology* (pp. 69–75). Hillsdale, NJ: Erlbaum.

Sechrest, L. B. (1990). Developing cross-discipline measures of clinical competencies in diagnosis, treatment, and case management. In D. L. Johnson (Ed.), *Service needs of the seriously mentally ill: Training implications for psychologists* (pp. 29–31). Washington, DC: American Psychological Association.

Sechrest, L. B., Freeman, H., & Mulley, A. (Eds.). (1990). *Health services research methodology: A focus on AIDS.* Rockville, MD: National Center for Health Services Research.

Sechrest, L. B., & Hannah, M. (1990). The critical importance of nonexperimental data. In L. Sechrest, J. Bunker, & E. Perrin (Eds.), *Research methodology: Strengthening causal interpretations of nonexperimental research* (pp. 1–7). Rockville, MD: National Center for Health Services Research.

Sechrest, L. B., Perrin, E., & Bunker, J. (Eds.). (1990). *Research methodology: Strengthening causal interpretations of nonexperimental data.* Rockville, MD: National Center for Health Services Research.

1991

Sechrest, L. B. (1991). Prevention in primary care: Several perspectives. In *Primary care research: Theory and methods* (pp. 203–211). Washington, DC: Department of Health and Human Services, Agency for Health Care Policy and Research.

Smith, B. H., & Sechrest, L. B. (1991). The treatment of aptitude–treatment interactions. *Journal of Consulting and Clinical Psychology, 59*, 233–244.

1992

Bootzin, R., Sechrest, L. B., Scott, A., & Hannah, M. (1992). Common methodological problems in health services research proposals. *EGAD Quarterly, 1*, 101–107.

Figueredo, A. J., Hetherington, J., & Sechrest, L. B. (1992). Water under the bridge: A response to Bingham, R. D., Heywood, J. S., and White, S. B., Evaluating schools and teachers based on student performance: Testing an alternative methodology. *Evaluation Review, 16*, 40–62.

Goldberg, L. R., Grenier, J. R., Guion, R. M., Sechrest, L. B., & Wing, H. (1991). *Questionnaires used in the prediction of trustworthiness in pre-employment selection decisions: An APA Task Force report.* Washington, DC: American Psychological Association.

Sechrest, L. B. (1992). Evaluation redux again [Review of the book *Evaluation: A systematic approach*]. *Contemporary Psychology, 37*, 563.

Sechrest, L. B. (1992). The past future of clinical psychology: A reflection on Woodworth. *Journal of Consulting and Clinical Psychology, 60*, 18–23.

Sechrest, L. B. (1992). Roots: Back to our first generations. *Evaluation Practice, 13*, 1–7.

Sechrest, L. B. (1992, Fall). Effective dissemination: A formidable task. *The National AHEC Bulletin, 10*, 8, 13.

Sechrest, L. B., & Scott, A. G. (1992). Theory-driven approaches to cost–benefit analysis: Implications of program theory. In H. Chen & P. H. Rossi (Eds.), *Using theory to improve program and policy evaluations* (pp. 243–257). New York: Greenwood Press.

Simon, L., Sales, B., & Sechrest, L. B. (1992). Licensure of functions. In D. K. Kagehiro & W. S. Laufer (Eds.), *Handbook of psychology and law* (pp. 542–563). New York: Springer-Verlag.

Yeaton, W. H., & Sechrest, L. B. (1992). Critical dimensions in the choice and maintenance of successful treatments: Strength, integrity, and effectiveness. In A. E. Kazdin (Ed.), *Methodological issues and strategies in clinical research* (pp. 137–156). Washington, DC: American Psychological Association.

1993

Babcock, J., Gallagher, S., & Sechrest, L. B. (1993). Evaluation of interdisciplinary rural health training programs. In Bureau of Health Professions, *Interdisciplinary development of health professionals to maximize health provider resources in rural areas* (pp. 55–57). Rockville, MD: Office of Program Development, Health Resources and Services Administration.

Glueckauf, R. L., Bonds, G. R., Sechrest, L. B., & McDonel, E. (Eds.). (1993). *Improving assessment in rehabilitation and health.* Newbury Park, CA: Sage.

Scott, A. G., & Sechrest, L. B. (1993). Survey research and response bias. In *American Statistical Association 1993 Proceedings of the Section on Survey Research Methods* (pp. 238–243). Washington, DC: American Statistical Association.

Sechrest, L. B. (1993). Measurement: From the beginning to what end? In R. L. Glueckauf, L. B. Sechrest, G. R. Bond, & E. C. McDonel (Eds.), *Improving assessment in rehabilitation and health* (pp. 253–273). Newbury Park, CA: Sage.

Sechrest, L. B. (Ed.). (1993). *New directions in program evaluation: No. 60. Evaluation: A pluralistic enterprise.* San Francisco: Jossey-Bass.

Sechrest, L. B. (1993). Preventing problems in prevention research. *American Journal of Community Psychology, 21*, 665–672.

Sechrest, L. B., Babcock, J., & Smith, B. H. (1993). An invitation to methodological pluralism. *Evaluation Practice, 14*, 227–235.

Sechrest, L. B., & Figueredo, A. J. (1993). Program evaluation. *Annual Review of Psychology, 44*, 645–674.

Sechrest, L. B., Kihlstrom, J., & Bootzin, R. (1993). Writing multiple-choice test items. *APS Observer, 6*(1), 11–12, 22–23.

Sechrest, L. B., & Maller, S. (1993). Methodology. In D. Mostofsky & Y. Loyning (Eds.), *The neurobehavioral treatment of epilepsy* (pp. 285–326). Hillsdale, NJ: Erlbaum.

Sechrest, L. B., & Scott, A. G. (1993). Assessing the competencies of clinical psychologists. In P. Wohlford, H. F. Myers, & J. E. Callan (Eds.), *Public–academic linkages for improving psychological services and training* (pp. 185–194). Washington, DC: American Psychological Association.

Sechrest, L. B., & Scott, A. G. (Eds.). (1993). *New directions for program evaluation: No. 57. Understanding causes and generalizing about them.* San Francisco: Jossey-Bass.

1994

Burns, L. R., & Sechrest, L. B. (1994). Key challenges posed by the Clinton health care reform proposal [Review of "U.S. health care in transition: Reforming America's health system analysis, reactions, alternatives"]. *Health Care Management: State of the Art Reviews, 1*, 81–90.

Lane, R. D., Caruso, A. C., Brown, V. L., Axelrod, B., Schwartz, G. E., Sechrest, L. B., & Marcus, F. I. (1994). Effects of non-right-handedness on risk for sudden death associated with coronary artery disease. *American Journal of Cardiology, 74*, 743–747.

Dennis, M. L., Fetterman, D. N., & Sechrest, L. B. (1994). Integrating qualitative and quantitative evaluation methods in substance abuse research. *Evaluation and Program Planning, 17*, 419–427.

Sechrest, L. B. (1994). Program evaluation: Oh, what it seemed to be. *Evaluation Practice, 15*, 359–365.

Sechrest, L. B. (1994). Recipes for psychotherapy. *Journal of Consulting and Clinical Psychology, 65*, 952–954.

Sechrest, L. B., Backer, T. E., & Rogers, E. M. (1994). Effective dissemination of health and clinical information. In L. B. Sechrest, T. E. Backer, E. M. Rogers, T. F. Campbell, & M. L. Grady (Eds.), *Effective dissemination of clinical and health information* (pp. 1–7). Rockville, MD: Agency for Health Care Policy and Research, U.S. Department of Health and Human Services.

Sechrest, L. B., Backer, T. E., & Rogers, E. M. (1994). Synthesis of effective ideas for dissemination. In L. B. Sechrest, T. E. Backer, E. M. Rogers, T. F. Campbell, & M. L. Grady, (Eds.), *Effective dissemination of clinical and health information* (pp. 187–196). Rockville, MD: Agency for Health Care Policy and Research, U.S. Department of Health and Human Services.

Sechrest, L. B., Backer, T. E., Rogers, E. M., Campbell, T. F., & Grady, M. L. (Eds.). (1994). *Effective dissemination of clinical and health information.* Rockville, MD: Agency for Health Care Policy and Research, U.S. Department of Health and Human Services.

Sechrest, L. B., & Sidani, S. (1994). Measurement. In B. Crabtree, W. Miller, R. B. Addison, V. J. Gilchrist, & A. Kuzel (Eds.), *Exploring collaborative research in primary care* (pp. 14–24). Thousand Oaks, CA: Sage.

Sechrest, L. B., & Smith, B. H. (1994). Psychotherapy is the practice of psychology. *Journal of Psychotherapy Integration, 4*, 1–30.

1995

Lane, R. D., Sechrest, L. B., Reidel, R., Brown, V., Kaszniak, A. W., & Schwartz, G. E. (1995). Alexithymia and nonverbal emotion information processing deficits. *Psychosomatic Medicine, 57*, 84.

Sechrest, L. B., & Sidani, S. (1995). Quantitative and qualitative: Is there an alternative? *Evaluation and Program Planning, 18,* 77–87.

1996

Glider, P., Hughes, P., Mullen, R., Coletti, S., Sechrest, L. B., Neri, R., et al. (1996). Two therapeutic communities for substance-abusing women and their children. *NIDA Research Monograph, 166,* 32–51.

Lane, R. D., Sechrest, L. B., Reidel, R., Weldon, V., Kaszniak, A., & Schwartz, G. E. (1996). Impaired verbal and nonverbal emotion recognition in alexithymia. *Psychosomatic Medicine, 58,* 203–210.

Sechrest, L. B. (1996). [Review of the book *Empowerment evaluation: Knowledge and tools for self-assessment and accountability*]. *Environment and Behavior, 29,* 422–426.

Sechrest, L. B., & Bootzin, R. R. (1996). Psychology and inferences about public policy. *Psychology, Public Policy, and Law, 2,* 377–392.

Sechrest, L. B., McKnight, P., & McKnight, K. (1996). On calibrating measures for psychotherapy research. *American Psychologist, 51,* 1065–1071.

Sechrest, L. B., & Sidani, S. (1996). Qualitative methods in evaluation. In E. Rahdert (Ed.), *Methodological issues in evaluation of substance-abuse treatment programs* (pp. 292–309). Rockville, MD: National Institute on Drug Abuse.

Sechrest, L. B., Stewart, M., Stickle, T. R., & Sidani, S. (1996). *Effective and persuasive case studies.* Cambridge, MA: Human Services Research Institute.

Valiente, C., & Sechrest, L. B. (1996). Evaluación de la effectividad de programas de rehabilitación psicosocial [Evaluation of the effectiveness of psychosocial rehabilitation programs]. In J. A. Aldez & C. Vazquez (Eds.), *Esquizofrenia: Fundamentos psicológicos y psiquiátricos de la rehabilitación* [Schizophrenia: Basic psychology and psychiatry of rehabilitation] (pp. 341–373). Madrid, Spain: Siglo Veintiuno de España Editores.

1997

Sechrest, L. B., & Walsh, M. (1997). Dogma or data: Bragging rights. *American Psychologist, 52,* 536–540.

1998

Lane, R. D., Sechrest, L. B., & Riedel, R. (1998). Sociodemographic correlates of alexithymia. *Comprehensive Psychiatry, 39,* 377–385.

Lane, R. D., Shapiro, D. E., Sechrest, L. B., Riedel, R., Kaszniak, A. W., & Schwartz, G. E. (1998). Pervasive emotion recognition deficit common to alexithymia and repression. *Psychosomatic Medicine, 60,* 92.

Martinez, M. E., Marshall, J. R., & Sechrest, L. B. (1998). Factor analysis and the search for objectivity. *American Journal of Epidemiology, 148,* 17–19.

Lane, R., Riedel, R., & Sechrest, L. B. (1998). Sociodemographic correlates of alexithymia. *Comprehensive Psychiatry, 39,* 377–385.

Sechrest, L. B. (1998). A readable reference [Review of *Handbook of personality psychology*]. *American Scientist, 86,* 486–487.

Sechrest, L. B. (1998). Don Campbell and measurement in the social sciences. *American Journal of Evaluation, 19,* 403–406.

Sechrest, L. B. (1998). [Review of the book *Understanding health care outcomes research*]. *International Journal for Quality in Health Care, 10,* 455–456.

Sechrest, L. B., Stickle, T., & Stewart, M. (1998). The role of assessment in clinical psychology. In M. Hersen & A. Bellak (Series Eds.) & C. R. Reynolds (Vol. Ed.), *Comprehensive clinical psychology: Vol. 4. Assessment* (pp. 1–32). Tarrytown, NY: Elsevier Science.

Taylor, C., Schwartz, G. E., Russek, L. G., & Sechrest, L. B. (1998). A matter of life or death: Organizational change in the real world. *Journal of Management Education, 22,* 400–407.

1999

Campbell, D. T., Webb, E., Schwartz, R. D., & Sechrest, L. B. (1999). *Unobtrusive measures* (Rev. ed.). Thousand Oaks, CA: Sage.

Caspi, O., Koffler, K., & Sechrest, L. B. (1999). Use of alternative medicine by women with breast cancer [Letter]. *New England Journal of Medicine, 341,* 1155.

Lane, R. D., Laukes, C., Steptoe, A., Chesney, M., Sechrest, L. B., Marcus, F., et al. (1999). Severe chronic stress often precedes idiopathic ventricular fibrillation (IVF). *Psychosomatic Medicine, 61,* 113–114.

Sechrest, L. B., Stewart, M., & Stickle, T. (1999). *A synthesis of findings concerning CGIAR Case Studies on the Adoption of Technological Innovations.* Rome: United Nations Impact Assessment and Evaluation Group.

Sidani, S., & Sechrest, L. B. (1999). Putting the program theory into operation. *American Journal of Evaluation, 2,* 227–238.

2000

Barrett, L. F., Lane, R., Sechrest, L. B., & Schwartz, G. (2000). Sex differences in emotional awareness. *Personality and Social Psychology Bulletin, 26,* 1027–1035.

Caspi, O., & Sechrest, L. B. (2000). Integrity and research: Introducing the concept of dual blindness—How blind are double blind clinical trials in alternative medicine. *Journal of Alternative and Complementary Medicine: Research on Paradigm, Practice, and Policy, 6,* 479–485.

Figueredo, A. J., Brookes, A., Leff, H. S., & Sechrest, L. B. (2000). A meta-analytic approach to growth curve analysis. *Psychological Reports, 87,* 441–465.

Hill, R., & Sechrest, L. B. (2000). The use of propensity scores in quasi-experiments: A meta-analysis [Abstract]. *International Journal of Psychology, 35,* 224.

Lane, R. D., Allen, J., Schwartz, G., & Sechrest, L. B. (2000). Emotional awareness in men is positively correlated with skin conductance response magnitude during emotional arousal. *Psychosomatic Medicine, 62,* 1402.

Lane, R. D., Sechrest, L. B., Riedel, R., Shapiro, D. E., & Kaszniak, A.W. (2000). Pervasive emotion recognition deficit common to alexithymia and the repressive coping style. *Psychosomatic Medicine, 62,* 492–501.

Morales, A., & Sechrest, L. B. (2000). Rules and principles for combining data [Abstract]. *International Journal of Psychology, 34,* 286.

Sechrest, L. B. (2000). Reliability of performance and tests [Abstract]. *International Journal of Psychology, 35,* 318.

Sechrest, L. B. (2000). The road not taken [Review of the book *The scientific practice of clinical psychology*]. *Contemporary Psychology, 45,* 195–196.

Sechrest, L. B. (2000). Unobtrusive measures. In A. E. Kazdin (Ed.), *Encyclopedia of psychology* (Vol. 8, pp. 142–143). Washington, DC: American Psychological Association.

Sechrest, L. B., Davis, M., Stickle, T., & McKnight, P. (2000). Understanding "method" variance. In L. Bickman (Ed.), *Research design: Donald Campbell's legacy* (pp. 63–87). Thousand Oaks, CA: Sage.

Walsh, M., Smith, R., Morales, A., & Sechrest, L. B. (2000). *Ethnocultural research: A guide to race, ethnicity, and culture for the mental health services researcher.* Cambridge, MA: Human Services Research Institute.

Weldon, V., & Sechrest, L. B. (2000). Nonlinear models in individual growth curve analysis [Abstract]. *International Journal of Psychology, 35,* 301.

2001

Figueredo, A. J., & Sechrest, L. B. (2001). Approaches used in conducting health outcomes and effectiveness research. *Evaluation and Program Planning, 25,* 41–59.

2002

Bissell, K., & Sechrest, L. B. (2002). Applications of growth curve analysis in longitudinal data sets [Abstract]. *International Journal of Psychology, 35,* 302.

Heppner, K., & Sechrest, L. B. (2002). Confirmatory factor analysis of the Children's Health Questionnaire—Parental Form 50. *Quality of Life Research, 11,* 763–772.

Sechrest, L. B., & Coan, J. A. (2002). Preparing psychologists to prescribe. *Journal of Clinical Psychology, 58,* 649–658.

Walsh, M. E., Katz, M. A., & Sechrest, L. B. (2002). Unpacking cultural factors in adaptation to Type 2 diabetes mellitus. *Medical Care, 40*(Suppl.), I-129–I-139.

2003

Caspi, O., Sechrest, L. B., Pitluk, H. C., Marshall, C. L., Bell, I. R., & Nichter, M. (2003). On the definition of complementary, alternative, and integrative medicine: Societal mega-stereotypes vs. the patients' perspectives. *Alternative Therapies and Health, 9*(6), 58–62.

McKnight, K., & Sechrest, L. B. (2003). Program evaluation. In M. Hersen, S. N. Haynes, & E. M. Heiby (Eds.), *Comprehensive handbook of psychological assessment: Vol. 3. Behavioral assessment.* New York: Wiley.

McKnight, P., & Sechrest, L. B. (2003). The use and misuse of the term "experience" in contemporary psychology: A reanalysis of the experience–performance relationship. *Philosophical Psychology, 16,* 431–460.

2004

Davis, M. F., Keagy, J. C., Madden, W. A., Schloss, E. P., Meaney, F. J., Lewis, V., Kline, C., et al. (2004). Understanding medical expenses for children with special health care needs. *Journal of the Arizona–Nevada Academy of Science, 37,* 62–67.

2005

Davis, M. F., Sechrest, L. B., & Shapiro, D. (2005). Measuring progress toward smoking cessation. *Journal of Applied Measurement, 6,* 164–172.

Lane, R. D., Laukes, C., Marcus, F. I., Chesney, M. A., Sechrest, L. B., Gear, K., Fort, C. L., et al. (2005). Psychological stress predicting idiopathic ventricular fibrillation. *Psychosomatic Medicine, 67,* 359–365.

McKnight, K. L., Sechrest, L. B., & McKnight, P. (2005). Psychology, psychologists, and public policy. *Annual Review of Clinical Psychology, 1,* 557–576.

Sechrest, L. B. (2005). Validity of measures is no simple matter. *Health Services Research, 40,* 1584–1604.

Author Index

Numbers in italics refer to listings in the reference sections.

Subject Index

Achieved relative treatment strength, 115–117
Adherence to treatment manual or protocol, 117
and reliability, 238
Adversity, and personal growth, 59–60
Affective reactivity, 70–71, 72
Affect regulation, 66, 67, 71, 72
Agricultural extension system, U.S., 23
Agriculture, education contrasted with, 11
Alcohol consumption
and Alcoholics Anonymous reliance, 59
and coping skills, 56
help-seeking for (stressors and social resources in), 55
Alcoholics Anonymous, 59
Alpha levels, 245
Altruism, 43
and Holocaust rescuers project, 31–32, 33, 34, 35, 36–42
study of with Sechrest, 29
Altruistic Moral Judgment Scale, 39, 40, 41
Altruistic personality, 37
Altruistic Personality project, 33
Altruistic Scale for the Elderly (ASE), 35
American Board of Radiology, 5
American Evaluation Association, xvii, 206, 255
1997 Annual Convention of, 143
American Journal of Evaluation, 185
American Psychological Association (APA), xvi, xvii, 5
Publication Manual of, 163
Task Force on Statistical Inference of, 163
American Psychological Society, 5
American Psychologist, 262
ANCOVA (analysis of covariance), 145, 149, 150, 151, 152, 154, 155
Animal laboratory research, 93–94
ANOVA (analysis of variance), 151, 152–154, 187, 188, 193
Anxiety, 220
child (assessment of), 218–223
APA Monitor, 237
APA Task Force on Statistical Inference, 163
A priori treatment strengths, 109, 110
Aptitude-by-treatment interactions (ATIs), 205–206, 239
Aristotle, 78
Asian Studies, 261
Assessment, 213
ambulatory, 207

of child anxiety, 218–223
and cryptic conditions, 214
decision theory in, 223–227
and incremental validity, 215–216, 216
and mechanisms of change, 96–97
and prediction, 213–214, 226–227
and nomological net, 220
in psychotherapy mechanisms research, 90–91
and quantitative tags, 214–215
and Sechrest, 187, 213
and social context or coping strategies, 57–58
of treatment differentiation, 112
of treatment integrity, 118
utility lacking in, 215
See also Measures and measurement
ATIs (aptitude-by-treatment interactions), 205–206, 239
Attachment relationship, 63
Attrition, and randomized studies, 132–133, 136, 137, 139
Australasian Evaluation Society, 255
Authoritarianism–tolerance, in Holocaust rescuers' project, 39, 40, 41
Autonomy, and Holocaust rescuers' project, 38–39, 40, 41

Backer, Tom, 262
Balanced F Scale, 39
Balancing strata rationale, for propensity score estimation, 152–154
Barnum effects, 214
Basis of cause, vs. cause, 80
Beck, Aaron, 66, 68
Beck, Judith, 68
Beck Depression Inventory, 240
Beck Depression Inventory—II (BDI–II), 68, 69, 70
Beck Institute for Cognitive Therapy and Research, 68, 72
Behavioral interventions
and assessment instruments, 198
in training of prison officers, 201–203
Berlin, Isaiah, xv
Bernays, J., 78
Berra, Yogi, quoted, 161
Bohr, Niels, 249, 250
Box–Cox family of transformation, 170
Brain weight data on mammals, as data analysis example, 168–173

Stress, 65–66
 and cognitive therapy for depression, 66–73
 and coping strategies, 58
 in daily process research on depression, 64–65, 66
 and growth, 59–60
 and Life Stressors and Social Resources Inventory, 49–51
 and Sechrest, 237–238
 transactional model of, 65, 66, 67
Symmotry, 188 180, 207
 Brunswik, 188–197, 199
 and five data-box conceptualization, 205–207

Tailing, 213
Talmud, quoted, 29
Teaching
 changing of difficult, 12–18
 cultural nature of, 15–16
 R & D system for, 13, 18–20, 21–26
  and Japanese system of lesson study, 20–21
 See also Education; Professional development programs
Technology changes, and treatment integrity, 120
"Technology model of psychotherapy research," 117
Theoretical coherence of treatments, 105–106
Theoretical structure. See Nomological net
Theory
 as guide in studying mechanisms, 94–95
 and Sechrest, 254
Therapeutic alliance or relationship
 research on, 98
 and study of mechanisms, 85–86
Therapeutic processes, 83. See also Mechanisms of change
"There Is Madness to Our Method" (Sechrest), 261
Third International Mathematics and Science Study, 15
 and TIMSS Video Study, 15–16, 16, 17, 22
Thorndike, John, 25
Timeline problems, in study of psychotherapy mechanisms, 84, 85, 86, 87, 89, 90, 96
Time-series designs, 207
TIMSS Video Study, 15–16, 16, 17, 22
Titles, Sechrest's creating of, 262
Tornatzky, Louis, 262
Tragic drama, cathartic effect in, 78
Trait–method units, 233
Transactional model, of stress and coping, 65, 66, 67
Transformation, 164
Transitory conditions, 48, 49, 52–54

Translational research, 63–64, 72–73, 82, 243–244
Treatment(s)
 differential, 226
 Sechrest et al. on, 104
Treatment differentiation, 112
Treatment fidelity, 105, 117, 118. See also Treatment integrity
Treatment integrity, 103, 105, 115–118, 121
 and criminal rehabilitation efforts, 77
 factors affecting, 118–121
 lack of, 187
 and mechanisms of change, 95–96
 and reliability, 206
 and treatment strength, 110
 See also Treatment strength and integrity
Treatment manuals, 81, 121, 238–239
 and once-a-week appointments, 241
Treatment reliability, 205–206, 238
Treatment settings, research vs. community, 242
Treatment strength, 103, 104–107, 121
 and cause–effect models, 107–108
  cause–effect congruity model, 107, 108–110
  counterfactual model, 107, 110–113, 114, 116
  dose–response models, 107–108, 113–115, 119–120
 and mechanisms of change, 95
 optimal, 105
 and treatment integrity, 110
Treatment strength and integrity, 103–104
 status of, 121–122
Tucker's lens model equation, 193–194
 modified, 195
Tukey, John, quoted, 161
Tunnel vision, procedural, 244
Two-tailed null hypothesis tests with .05 alpha value, 234, 245

Universities, grants as crucial to, 161
University of Arizona, xvi, 5–6, 254
University of Michigan, 262
Unobtrusive measurement, and Sechrest, xvi, 3, 251, 252, 261
Unobtrusive Methods (Webb, Campbell, Schwartz, and Sechrest), 107
Utilitarian stance. See Pragmatism of Sechrest

Validity, 216–218
 classic concepts of, 233–234
 and competence, 238
 construct, 3, 79, 106, 197, 198, 216–217, 218, 220, 233, 241
 and assessment, 227

About the Editors

Richard R. Bootzin, PhD, is professor of psychology at the University of Arizona. He has authored or edited more than 10 books and 150 articles and chapters. Dr. Bootzin is a fellow of the American Psychological Association and the American Psychological Society. He is a past member of the board of directors of the Sleep Research Society and a current member of the board of directors of the American Psychological Society. Dr. Bootzin is a past president of the Society for a Science of Clinical Psychology and the Academy of Psychological Clinical Science.

Patrick E. McKnight, PhD, is assistant professor in the Department of Psychology at George Mason University, Fairfax, Virginia. In his brief career, he has authored 20 articles; written a book on missing data; acted as a consultant or investigator on over 40 grants; and made more than 80 professional presentations on research methodology, data analysis, and measurement. Dr. McKnight is an active member of the American Evaluation Association, serving as the chair of the quantitative topical interest group for the past 3 years.